Rethinking Special Education for a New Century

• Individualized Education Program • Accountability • Accommodation •

Individuals with Disabilities Education Act

Learning Disabilities

Due Process Hearing • Section 504 • Litigation • Discipline • Inclusion

• Least Restrictive Environment • Free Appropriate Public Education •

Chester E. Finn, Jr., Andrew J. Rotherham, and Charles R. Hokanson, Jr., *Editors*

With a Preface by Madeleine Will

Published by the Thomas B. Fordham Foundation and the Progressive Policy Institute

May 2001

Table of Contents

Moving Forward

Foreword

Chester E. Finn, Jr., Andrew J. Rotherham, and Charles R. Hokanson, Jr.*

A quarter century ago, President Ford signed historic legislation seeking to ensure educational equity for children with disabilities and special needs. This legislation, now known as the Individuals with Disabilities Education Act (IDEA), was a major milestone in the quest to end the chronic exclusion and mis-education of students with exceptional needs. It helped open the door to fairness and access for millions of such youngsters and paved the way to greater educational success for many of them during the past 25 years.

But the law of unintended consequences was also at work during this period, as were Washington's well-known tendencies to over-regulate, over-manage, and make more complex. Even as important reforms began to sweep through regular K-12 education, the IDEA program was becoming set in its ways. Not every change it brought about turned out to be positive, and, although it has surely helped address many education challenges, it has created some, too.

For too long, most politicians, policymakers, and others involved with the IDEA and the special education system that law has helped to construct considered it taboo to discuss these problems and challenges. It seemed at times as if anything less than unadulterated praise for the IDEA was indicative of hostility towards its goals or—worse—towards children with special needs. Thus, the IDEA has come to be viewed as the "third rail" issue of education policy: It's fine to support more spending, maybe even suggest some incremental changes along the program's margin (generally by way of expanding it and closing loopholes), but it has not been okay to probe its basic assumptions and practices, much less criticize them. Well-intentioned people who have attempted to highlight deficiencies, inequities, and problems with special education have been criticized as interlopers with bad motives or political agendas and told to leave such matters to the "stakeholder community." Hence, the federal special education program has been subjected to astonishingly little objective policy analysis—certainly nothing resembling its fair share of scrutiny considering that it now touches about 12 percent of American children and spends $7.4 billion annually at the federal level. Indeed, once state and local funds are added to the federal dollars, experts estimate that $35-$60 billion is spent annually on special education in this country. By some estimates, 40 percent of all new spending on K-12 education over the past 30 years has flowed into special education.

Because it's been so difficult, risky, and unrewarding to probe and ponder the special education program, many aspects have been insulated from the scrutiny that has led to important reforms in other areas of education over the past decade. It's time, we believe, to cut through that insulation and subject this important program to examination—not, let us be clear, because we have any ax to grind or points to score but because millions of needy children depend on this program for their education. The least we can do is attempt to determine whether it's doing a

---

* Dr. Finn is President of and Mr. Hokanson is Finance Director and Research Fellow at the Thomas B. Fordham Foundation. Mr. Rotherham is Director of the 21st Century Schools Project at the Progressive Policy Institute.

good job for them. In this matter, every American is a stakeholder. We all share the responsibility to help ensure that special-needs students receive the high-quality education to which they are entitled.

This volume is a beginning, not an end. It does not hold the solution to every problem that confronts the special education system and neither do the authors or editors. We do believe, however, that the ideas, research, and reporting set forth in these pages provide an excellent starting point for policymakers seeking to rethink special education.

What does rethinking mean? It starts by posing some crucial questions. For example, is the current regulatory/civil rights model the best way to ensure quality education for youngsters with disabilities? Are students being needlessly referred to special education because of other deficiencies in our educational system—for example, because they receive poor reading instruction—rather than because they have extraordinary needs? Is race a factor in special education assignment? Does the program's focus on compliance come at the expense of achievement?

Many more questions follow, and further analysis should follow as well. This set of papers, findings, ideas, and recommendations ought not to end the analytic process. It should merely help to launch it—to stimulate fresh thinking in the policy community, spark further dialogue about how to ensure that youngsters with disabilities succeed in school, and inform the debate when the next IDEA reauthorization cycle begins.

Our goal in assembling this volume is to view special education in general and the IDEA in particular with some distance and objectivity. Several of the following chapters examine general aspects of the program; others are up-close case studies. Practically all of the authors are astute observers and practiced analysts for whom this was a new topic. Special education is relatively new to us, too. This means we may have overlooked some key points and misunderstood others. We invite readers to point out our omissions and misjudgments, all in the interest of continuing a needed conversation about this important program.

Fourteen of this volume's chapters were first presented and discussed at a two-day conference in November 2000, co-sponsored by the Thomas B. Fordham Foundation and the Progressive Policy Institute. Following that discussion, the authors undertook revisions, and the editors did what editors do—hassled the authors, tweaked the words, poked at the ideas, and mulled our own conclusions. The editors' thinking on this subject is contained in the final chapter, which sets forth our conclusions in summary fashion and offers several principles to guide efforts to reform special education.

Our goal is to stimulate further analysis, debate, and discussion prior to the next IDEA reauthorization cycle, which should begin in 2002. We have not looked into every aspect of the program. Important issues await the attention of others; we urge that attention be paid. And we intend to be back with more detailed recommendations after more discussion, analysis, and (hopefully) consensus-building. In the meantime, we earnestly hope that this volume will contribute to a serious debate that goes well beyond how much money is being appropriated and instead asks how well the program is working and what might work better.

That discussion needs to go beyond the false choice that has so often been posed about the education of disabled children. It often seems as if policymakers have only two options: to maintain today's status quo, or return to the dreadful treatment accorded many disabled children before 1975. On National Public Radio recently, a university professor who studies the IDEA gave voice to this view, saying, "when people start complaining [about the IDEA], I say, 'Stop, do you want to go back to the 1960's?'" If we accomplish nothing else with this volume, perhaps we will at least open the eyes of policymakers to the fact that there are many other options worthy of consideration.

The authors and editors are anything but a homogeneous group with regard to political and educational philosophy. We do share, however, a commitment to asking difficult questions, tackling thorny issues, probing for important facts, and voicing truths even when they're uncomfortable. Only through this process can we improve the quality of education that we provide to young Americans.

The editors thank the authors for their intelligence, perspicacity, hard work, and willingness to endure our ministrations. We're grateful as well to those who participated in the November conference, especially those who chaired panels and commented on the draft papers. (A list of the conference's presenters, panel discussants and moderators, and attendees are included at the end of the volume.) We're deeply obliged to our colleagues on the staffs of the Progressive Policy Institute and the Thomas B. Fordham Foundation. And we offer special thanks to Madeleine Will, for many years the senior federal official responsible for special education and a universally respected figure in this field, for her guidance, support, advice, and friendship throughout this endeavor. In addition, we acknowledge and appreciate a generous grant to the Progressive Policy Institute from the Annie E. Casey Foundation that provided financial support for the commissioning of several conference papers, as well as conference- and volume-related expenses. The views expressed in these papers are those of the authors alone, however, and are not necessarily shared by advisors, conferees, funders, or sponsoring institutions.

Through research, publications and articles, and work with policymakers, the 21st Century Schools Project at the Progressive Policy Institute supports initiatives to increase accountability, raise standards, foster equity, and increase choice and innovation in public education. The Project's goals are a natural extension of the mission of the Progressive Policy Institute, which is to define and promote a new progressive politics for the 21st century. The Institute is a project of the Third Way Foundation. For further information, please call 202-547-0001 or visit the Institute's website: www.ppionline.org.

The Thomas B. Fordham Foundation supports research, publications, and action projects in elementary/secondary education reform at the national level and in the Dayton area. Further information can be obtained at the Foundation's website (www.edexcellence.net) or by writing to 1627 K Street, NW, Suite 600, Washington, DC 20006. (The Foundation can also be e-mailed through its website.) This report is available in full on the Foundation's website, and hard copies can be obtained by calling 1-888-TBF-7474 (single copies are free). The Foundation is neither connected with nor sponsored by Fordham University.

Washington, D.C.
May 2001

Preface

*Madeleine Will**

Chester Finn and Charles Hokanson of the Thomas B. Fordham Foundation and Andrew Rotherham of the Progressive Policy Institute have achieved something quite important, and I commend them for it. They have ignited a process of discussion and debate about special education that has the potential for positive and long-lasting results.

Under the auspices of their respective institutions, these three gentlemen have issued a "Call To Examine." They commissioned a set of papers from analysts and journalists, proceeded to organize and hold a conference where these papers were discussed, and now have published fourteen of them in this volume. Moreover, they have undertaken this examination of special education in a collaborative and open manner—seeking the advice and partnership of parents of children with disabilities, educators, and others with expertise in our field.

As the editors have stated in their foreword, this volume is meant to serve as an initial basis for discussion and should be regarded as a request for new and fresh ideas. They encourage students with disabilities and their families and special education professionals to respond to the ideas contained herein. They urge all who have an interest in the way in which special education services are delivered in this country to offer up their own best thinking about strategies for improving the education of students with disabilities.

The collaborative nature of this undertaking notwithstanding, it is important to note that with the publication of this series of essays comes an element of controversy. Make no mistake: *Rethinking Special Education for a New Century* is a thorough critique that is always stimulating, sometimes brilliant, sometimes harsh, and sometimes misguided. After all, these essays were written, as stated in the editors' foreword, mostly by individuals who "are astute observers and practiced analysts for whom this was a new topic." I hasten to add that one could not have expected these authors to have developed the perspective and insight that comes from living with a disability or living with a person who has a disability. Nor could one have expected them to have the perspective and insight that comes from teaching and working within the special education system.

What one will find in the following pages, however, is the sound of the beginning (the first salvo, if you will) of the 2002 IDEA reauthorization. My sincerest hope is that this next reauthorization will occur in the context of an informed, wide-ranging, and civilized debate. My sincerest hope is also that my colleagues and friends in the universe of special education and disability policy will welcome the participation of those outside our universe who seek to understand our vision for students with disabilities and offer to join with us in re-shaping it for the 21st century.

---

* Ms. Will is Vice President of Strategic Planning and Advocacy at Community Options, a Princeton-based nonprofit agency providing employment services and appropriate housing for people with disabilities. She formerly served as Assistant Secretary for the Office of Special Education and Rehabilitation Services in the U.S. Department of Education.

Chapter Highlights

Special Education History and Issues

1. The Evolution of the Federal Role
   Tyce Palmaffy

Only in the past few years has Washington's share of special education funding risen higher than about 12 percent, despite Congress' 1975 promise to pay 40 percent of the incremental costs of educating students with disabilities pursuant to federal mandates. Meanwhile, those mandates—elaborated by Congress, the Education Department, and the federal courts—have steadily raised the financial obligations of states and school districts, and the number of students receiving special education services has soared. Although the Individuals with Disabilities Education Act (IDEA) and its predecessor, the Education for All Handicapped Children Act (EAHCA), have succeeded in extending public education to millions of youngsters who previously had received an inappropriate education—or none at all—complaints about special education are widely voiced by local and state education officials, advocates for the disabled, parents, and teachers. Moreover, policymakers find that federal special education mandates complicate the handling of just about every other education reform.

This chapter traces the history of federal special education policy. During the 1950s and 1960s, civil rights advocates and parents of disabled children formed a powerful force for federal legislation, also scoring victories in the courts. In 1973, Congress passed Section 504 of the Rehabilitation Act, affirming the principle that disabled children should be educated in regular classrooms. Two years later came EAHCA, which expanded the federal special education financial commitment into a sizable program of grants to the states.

Palmaffy introduces key terms and issues, defines what handicapping conditions the IDEA covers, and describes the evolution of the federal courts' answers to two questions: What constitutes an "appropriate" education, and to what lengths must schools go to place disabled students in regular classrooms? The author emphasizes that:

- The courts have clung to a case-by-case approach in determining what an "appropriate" education is;
- The courts have also obliged schools to provide a range of supplementary aids and services in order to mainstream students effectively;
- For the most part, court decisions regarding the services provided to disabled youngsters disregard cost or the impact on nondisabled peers;
- The IDEA's definitions of such categories as specific learning disabilities and behavioral disorders are hazy enough to allow for some striking differences from place to place in how the law is applied; and
- The 1997 IDEA reauthorization sought to fold disabled students into the broader education standards-and-accountability movement but had limited success in accomplishing this.

2. Time to Make Special Education "Special" Again
Wade F. Horn and Douglas Tynan

Although the IDEA has succeeded in opening up educational opportunities for children with disabilities, Drs. Horn and Tynan emphasize that it has also had some unintended negative consequences. These include the creation of incentives to define an ever-increasing percentage of school-aged children as disabled, an enormous redirection of financial resources from regular education to special education, and, perhaps most importantly, the application of an open-ended "accommodation" philosophy to populations better served with prevention or intervention strategies. Although the federal program was initially intended to address the educational needs of the severely disabled, today approximately 90 percent of special education students have lesser disabilities, such as a specific learning disability, speech and language delays, mild mental retardation, or an emotional disorder.

Drs. Horn and Tynan conclude that, for many special education students, the goal should be independence rather than lifetime accommodations. They note that little attention is paid by federal accountability systems to whether students in special education are advancing in core subjects or acquiring the skills necessary for making special services and accommodations no longer necessary. Instead, the focus remains on process rather than results.

Reforming special education so that it is better targeted, more cost-efficient, and more effective in improving educational outcomes for students with disabilities requires three things:

- First, recognition that special education consists of three separate groups of students (children with significant sensory, cognitive, and physical disabilities; children with neurological dysfunction; and children with behavioral problems), each with different educational needs;
- Second, the funding structure for special education must be changed to reward schools for improving the educational outcomes of disabled youngsters, not just identifying and serving them; and
- Third, the IDEA should be recommitted to empowering students to overcome their disabilities by equipping them with coping and compensatory mechanisms, whenever possible, rather than teaching youngsters to expect a lifetime of special accommodations and services.

3. Effectiveness and Accountability (Part 1): The Compliance Model
Patrick J. Wolf and Bryan C. Hassel

Experts estimate that $35-60 billion is spent each year to provide a "special" education to disabled children in the United States. The wide range of cost estimates itself hints at an insufficient level of accountability in these programs, while raising the important question of what society is receiving as a return on its substantial investment in special education services and what accountability systems operate to track and report their progress. In other words, how do we know whether special education is working in the United States? How should we define "working" in this context?

The authors focus primarily on the "compliance model" of accountability that currently governs most special education programs. They conclude that it fails even to ensure widespread compliance with applicable laws and regulations, while generating undesirable outcomes and perverse incentives. They then outline other possible models for improving effectiveness and accountability and assess the strengths and weaknesses of these alternatives.

The mandates contained within the 1997 IDEA amendments, Drs. Wolf and Hassel note, are too vague and allow too many exceptions to represent a true "sea change" from procedural compliance. Indeed, they conclude that the accountability systems being implemented in the wake of IDEA '97 appear flawed in theory, design, and practice. Could there be a better way? The authors explore this question in Chapter 14.

4. The Moral Foundations of Special Education Law
Mark Kelman

In this chapter, Professor Kelman sets forth three controversial propositions that should drive today's and tomorrow's debates over special education.

First, he contends, policymakers must deal with issues of testing accommodation, especially the burgeoning use of extra time by students with learning disabilities. Whatever one's view of testing accommodation, Professor Kelman writes, determinations of what skills are appropriate to test and what can and cannot be justly tested and rewarded are policy issues. Casting them as issues of discrimination—do those with disabilities have the opportunity to succeed on tests?—assumes naively that norms against discrimination mandate equality of group outcome, rather than that inequalities be justified by real distinctions in relevant performance.

Second, policymakers must address the linked issues of discipline and segregation, scrutinizing all claims that non-disabled students face disruption. They must decide how to make vexing trade-offs: Higher levels of integration may well improve the educational experience of disabled children but at some cost to nondisabled children.

Third, policymakers must tackle bona fide issues of scarcity and resource allocation. The IDEA currently gives legal priority to claims by students with learning disabilities to receive incremental resources, over similar claims by students not diagnosed as having disabilities. In a world of limited resources, Kelman argues, it is plainly not enough to say that children with learning disabilities "deserve" more resources; their claims inevitably compete with claims that could be made by other needy youngsters, such as poor achievers, the socioeconomically disadvantaged, and the gifted but understimulated.

The author concludes that we will not make rational policy in this area until we see that many claims often made in debate over special education policy are important education issues but not proper civil rights claims.

5. Special but Unequal: Race and Special Education
Matthew Ladner and Christopher Hammons

It is well known that public schools place a disproportionate percentage of minority students into special education programs and classes. In Virginia, for example, African Americans represent 20 percent of the state's population but 28 percent of its special education students, including

51 percent of those labeled "educable mentally retarded."

Closely analyzing county- and district-level data, Drs. Ladner and Hammons find that:

- There is no correlation between special education enrollment and per-pupil district expenditures;
- The more urban a school district, the lower the percentage of minority students enrolled in special education programs in that district;
- Districts with more white teachers have a greater rate of minority enrollment in special education, especially among African-American students, while enrollment by white students is unaffected by the racial composition of the faculty;
- Districts with high percentages of minority students—regardless of whether they are urban or rural, rich or poor—tend to place fewer of their pupils in special education programs, and conversely, the whiter the school district the more apt are its minority kids to be sent to special education.

Drs. Ladner and Hammons's data indicate that race plays a powerful role in the placement of children in special education. In fact, race impacts special education enrollment rates far more than any other variable. Although there is likely no single overarching explanation that applies to all districts, the fact that the special education process is strongly impacted by race surely gives cause for concern as well as further research.

Special Education in Practice

6. Special Education at Coles Elementary School
Robert Cullen

This chapter profiles a single elementary school in Manassas, Virginia. The author focuses especially on Marge Scheflen's classroom for second- to fifth-graders diagnosed with learning disabilities. In this case study, he describes how her classroom is designed for children deemed to have normal intelligence and abnormal needs and details how this teacher uses "guided reading strategies" to meet the specific needs of each student. He also profiles several youngsters, including a trio of hearing-impaired boys; an autistic, hearing-impaired kindergartner; and a fifth grader with reading and writing difficulties.

Cullen's observations and conclusions include:

- The ratio of students to staff in Mrs. Scheflen's room never exceeded 4:1, suggesting why special education is costly;
- About 18 pupils at the school take Ritalin or other medications intended to improve their ability to focus;
- Eighteen of Coles Elementary's 50 staff members are involved in special education;
- Special education in Prince William County, Virginia, is a classic case of unfunded mandates falling on the shoulders of local taxpayers; and
- The difficult special education eligibility cases are the ones where a child has a learning disability and needs special help, yet his/her scores don't show a required 23-point gap between IQ and achievement.

7. How Special Education Policy Affects Districts
Anna B. Duff

This chapter examines two Michigan school districts with good reputations for compliance with special education laws. The author shows how, in trying to ensure that special-needs children get an education, federal and state government have created a massive procedural maze that frustrates teachers, parents, and administrators alike.

Among her observations and conclusions:

- The law states that, to get special education services, a student must need those services to overcome his or her disabilities, but differences in determining whether students "need" special education services can play a big role in how many students are eventually certified for the program;
- The goals listed on a student's individualized education program (IEP) are supposed to be determined individually, but in fact most follow formulas set forth in statewide guides;
- The focus on inclusion is not only changing the way that "regular education" classrooms work, it is also creating two important pressures on schools districts: the potential for rising costs due to the demand for paraprofessionals, and the potential for conflict with parents concerning the extent of children's "inclusion";
- As courts have expanded the services that districts are required to fund, districts have become very aggressive in seeking out Medicaid payments to cover some special education expenses;
- Increasing litigation of special education claims threatens what little ability school districts have to control costs; yet the same procedures that shield districts from litigation can also act as a ceiling on district efforts to provide a special education; and
- Including students with disabilities in Michigan's testing regime will at the very least provide everyone—parents, students, teachers, and districts—clearer information about what is actually being achieved in special education.

8. *How Federal Special Education Policy Affects Schooling in Virginia*
Frederick M. Hess and Frederick J. Brigham

The authors of this case study examine how federal special education policy impacts public education in Virginia. Between 1995 and 1998, special education consumed 23 to 25 percent of the state's education budget, though disabled youngsters made up 13-14 percent of the state's student population. At the state Department of Education (DOE), federal special education initiatives are handled by a separate group of professionals; nobody is charged with coordinating policy with other parts of the agency. In essence, Virginia runs parallel school systems, one for general education and one for special education, and the current structure ensures that special education policy decisions are mostly made by people removed from actual school practice and from the general K-12 policy process.

Professors Hess and Brigham conclude that special education today is unwieldy, exasperating, and ripe for rethinking. They offer a number of observations, including:

- Special education mandates force educators to abide by open-ended and nebulous directives;

- The monitoring of special education relies upon documentation and paper trails, requiring much time and effort and forcing educators to base program decisions upon procedures rather that determinations of efficiency or effectiveness;
- IEPs intended as flexible instruments of learning have evolved into written records of compliance with formal instruments;
- Protections afforded to special education students in the domain of discipline have made it more difficult to enforce clear and uniform standards in school; and
- As states (like Virginia) have moved toward a standards-based curriculum and a results-based accountability system, the question has arisen of how to track the progress of disabled students and whether they will be treated as part of the reformed education system or (reminiscent of pre-IDEA discrimination) as a separate educational world.

9. The Rising Costs of Special Education in Massachusetts: Causes and Effects
Sheldon Berman, Perry Davis, Ann Koufman-Frederick, and David Urion

Spending on special education is always controversial. The past decade has witnessed rapid increases in both the number and percentage of children assigned to special education. At the same time, it has become more costly to provide them with special education, as special education averages 2.28 times the per-pupil cost of regular education.

The authors explore how special education costs compromise other school investments, creating a vicious cycle in which this program's rising costs result in less money for regular classrooms and fewer resources for struggling students, even as more students receive special education services leading to further increases in the program's costs. Although some people suspect that special education cost and enrollment increases result from school districts failing to contain costs and unnecessarily identifying children as having special needs, this Massachusetts study shows that school districts have done a good job containing costs but are being asked to serve increasing numbers of children with more significant special needs for more costly services.

The authors describe how advances in medical technology are boosting the survival rates of disabled infants and have also enabled other disabled students to attend school. Simultaneously, they argue, state policies and social norms have shifted away from the institutionalization of severely handicapped children, placing responsibility for them on local school districts. A rise in the number of children in poverty and dysfunctional family environments also results in more children with special needs.

In addition, the authors contend that Massachusetts' failure to adequately fund the education of youngsters with severe disabilities is compromising school districts' ability to implement the kinds of instructional improvements intended by the state's recent Education Reform Act. It would be tragic, they conclude, if education reform were declared a failure when, in fact, the Reform Act's experiment was never really tried.

10. Nasty, Brutish...and Often Not Very Short: The Attorney Perspective on Due Process
Kevin J. Lanigan, Rose Marie L. Audette, Alexander E. Dreier, and Maya R. Kobersy

The due process hearing is one of the most visible and unique features of the U.S. system for providing special education. The authors, four lawyers at a major Washington law firm, provide a historical background on the special education due process mandate and detail its statutory and regulatory framework. They observe that special education litigation under the IDEA boils down to two questions: Did the school district comply with procedural safeguards? And did it provide a FAPE? They note the widespread belief among school officials that the IDEA is one-sided, protecting parents and students while burdening schools and districts.

This chapter also provides an inside look at how due process hearings and special education litigation "really" work. The authors tell of delays and tactical posturing and the frustrations of parents seeking accommodations or new placements for their children. The current regime is complex and technical, thus quite difficult for parents to navigate successfully without legal representation or well-trained advocates. Indeed, due process does not lend itself to quick resolution of any dispute, unless both parties genuinely desire such a resolution. Particularly telling is the authors' case study of a 14-year-old mentally retarded girl whose mother unsuccessfully sought, for two years, to have her daughter placed in a full-time residential facility at public expense.

In discussing federal policy reforms, the authors call for better data on post-1997 mediation efforts as well as more research into the costs of due process litigation under the IDEA and possible alternative approaches.

11. Navigating the Special Education Maze: Experiences of Four Families
Siobhan Gorman

This chapter offers case studies of the special education experiences of four very different families and offers insights into larger policy issues.

- The first family is wealthy and has received high quality services for their handicapped son, but the family has had to supplement those services using its own resources, indicating that even a relatively affluent school district struggles to serve a fast growing population of special-needs students;
- A middle-class family in rural North Carolina has struggled to obtain proper services for its learning-disabled son, eventually resorting to emotionally and financially taxing litigation, and finally sending the boy to a private school;
- A District of Columbia family has a seventh-grade foster son who has reached seventh grade without learning to read, in large part because of failings in the regular education classrooms of his troubled urban school system; and
- A lower-middle income family with several adopted children who have "social-emotional" disabilities has found that special education, especially for poor and minority children, has become a catchall for youngsters with all manner of problems.

When special education is used to respond to such divergent needs, the author contends, one-size-fits-all policies intended to protect children from falling through cracks may have the opposite effect. The varied experiences of these families provide a critical real-world counterpoint to the rhetorical generalizations that often surround special education. Gorman's chapter also highlights several important issues that deserve consideration: the influence of income, how schools define disabilities, and how the attitudes of parents and schools impact the services that students receive from special education.

Moving Forward

12. Rethinking Learning Disabilities
G. Reid Lyon, Jack M. Fletcher, Sally E. Shaywitz, Bennett A. Shaywitz, Joseph K. Torgesen, Frank B. Wood, Anne Schulte, and Richard Olson

Despite their high—and rising—incidence, learning disabilities (LD) include the least understood and most debated disabling conditions that affect school-aged children. This chapter's principal authors insist that debates over the definition and classification of LD; the diagnostic criteria and assessment practices used in the identification process; the content, intensity, and duration of instructional practices employed; and the policies and legal requirements that drive the identification and education of those with LD can all be informed by scientific data and recent research. They also contend that sufficient data exist to guide early identification and prevention programs for children at-risk for LD, particularly reading programs that benefit many of these youngsters, and they estimate that sound prevention programs should sharply reduce the numbers of children who are identified as LD and who typically require intensive, long-term special education programs. Indeed, they estimate that the number of children identified as poor readers and served through special education could be reduced by up to 70 percent through early identification and prevention programs. They also argue that, given what is known about LD, it is irresponsible for the federal government to continue policies dictating an inadequate identification process for LD. Instead, the relevant government agencies should develop evidence-based alternatives for identifying LD, specific strategies to implement these alternatives, and a research and policy agenda to ensure that these youngsters are phased into the regular classroom as quickly as possible.

Drs. Lyon and Fletcher and their colleagues also recommend improvements in the definition of LD. They say we should:

- Replace the current exclusionary definition with evidence-based definitions that specify precise characteristics necessary to identify children with LD in reading, mathematics, written expression, and oral language;
- Jettison the IQ-achievement gap as a primary marker for LD;
- Stop excluding from consideration for special education youngsters who are performing poorly due to inadequate instruction, cultural and social factors, and emotional disturbance; and
- Consider a student's response to well-designed and well-implemented early intervention and remediation programs as part of the identification of LD.

13. The Little-Known Case of America's Largest School Choice Program
Daniel McGroarty

The author examines special education as a genre of school choice. He notes that this branch of American public education gives parents more choices, control, and involvement than any other. We learn, for example, that public school districts are paying private school tuitions for approximately 2 percent of the nation's 5.6 million special-needs students, or about 126,000 children, at an estimated annual cost to taxpayers of $2 billion.

Because the degree of choice extended to special-needs students depends in large part on parents' pushiness, it should come as no surprise, McGroarty writes, that in many school districts there is not one special education program but two, separate and unequal. This dual system, keyed to parents' differing levels of savvy and persistence, unlawfully deprives some special-needs students of essential services while providing others with a premium private education at public expense.

McGroarty asks, "Is it possible to remedy the inequities of the *de facto* 'choice' system that exists in special education at present, not by eliminating the degree of parental choice that exists for some families, but by extending greater choice to all parents of special-needs students?" To answer this question, he examines several places where school choice programs now operate. These include Milwaukee, Cleveland, and Florida, which has a remarkable but little-known program to "voucherize" special education. He concludes that school choice might well be a way to serve special-needs students in keeping with the expansive ideal that originally animated the IDEA.

14. Effectiveness and Accountability (Part 2): Alternatives to the Compliance Model
Bryan C. Hassel and Patrick J. Wolf

Continuing their analysis from Chapter 3, the authors consider what alternatives to the "compliance model" might be available to promote outcome-based measures of achievement and real accountability for performance with respect to the education of disabled youngsters. They first examine alternatives to compliance that have arisen outside K-12 education. These include "smart regulation," incentives for performance, and customer choice.

Drs. Hassel and Wolf then develop a broad framework for the application of these approaches within special education. Their framework would make student learning results the central driving force of special education policy, not an overlay on a compliance system. Their proposal is guided by three principles:

- An obsession with educational results rather than inputs and processes;
- A big "toolbox," permitting the selection of multiple strategies so as to provide the incentives and flexibility to enable problems to be solved; and
- Retention of certain needed residual rules, meant to support the overall results-orientation of the system by ensuring that goals are set for student learning, results are measured, and a safety net remains in place.

Noting that the accountability system governing special education is already moving away from a "one-size-fits-all" compliance system, Drs. Hassel and Wolf call on policymakers to accelerate this evolutionary process.

Conclusions and Principles for Reform
Chester E. Finn, Jr., Andrew J. Rotherham, and Charles R. Hokanson, Jr.

The volume's editors argue that the past 25 years' record of accomplishment for disabled youngsters is at best half the story. They also believe that federal special education policy is deeply troubled. The choice confronting today's policymakers, they contend, is not between keeping the program as it is or returning to the unacceptable pre-IDEA education of the disabled, but rather between maintaining the status quo or modernizing the program, building on what is known about both special education and regular education.

In recent years, K-12 education in the United States has undergone a profound shift from access-and-services to results-and-accountability. Special education hasn't kept up. It is also out of sync with profound organizational changes elsewhere in K-12 education and in the world outside.

The editors identify a number of policy failures in need of attention:

- Many youngsters' preventable and remediable conditions are growing into intractable problems;
- Special education suffers from "mission creep" as it keeps growing, causing its goals to become unattainable, its operation impossibly complex and costly, and its purpose cloudy;
- The one-size-fits-all approach has created a legal and policy straitjacket, creating a system that is full of adversarial procedures, rife with litigation, unresponsive to innovation, discouraging to diversity, and hostile to creativity;
- The IDEA creates perverse incentives for educators, schools, and parents alike;
- Special education distorts the priorities and fractures the programmatic coherence of schools and school systems;
- Different rules for disabled children foster a "separate but unequal" system; and
- Special education collides with standards-based education reform, exempting many students (and the educators and schools that serve them) from meeting state or district academic standards, even as such standards are being strengthened for "regular" education.

To address these and other policy failures, the editors urge policymakers to consider six principles for reforming special education:

- Make IDEA standards- and performance-based wherever possible, using Section 504 as the civil rights underpinning of special education;
- Streamline the number of special education categories into a very few groupings;
- Focus on prevention and intervention wherever possible, using research-based practices;
- Encourage flexibility, innovation, and choice, allowing schools to work with students and parents to customize services and placements to meet varying needs, and fostering the integration of special education into the school's larger mission, while giving parents sound options for their children's education;

- Provide adequate funding to ensure the program's success; and
- End double standards wherever possible.

The editors urge policymakers to question the status quo, explore ways to improve education for youngsters, and not shy away from efforts to ensure that all young Americans receive the education they deserve. This process will require openness to criticism and fresh ideas, a willingness to entertain reforms, and a capacity to change.

Chapter 1

The Evolution of the Federal Role

Tyce Palmaffy

As the year 2000 drew to a close, Congress took a substantial step toward fulfilling an old promise: to pay 40 percent of the extra costs of educating students with disabilities. That promise was attached to the landmark 1975 federal law that mandated the provision of a "free appropriate public education" to all disabled students. The original timetable stipulated regular increases until the 40 percent plateau was met by 1982. Yet only in the past few years has the federal share of special education spending risen higher than about 12 percent.

> *Only in the past few years has the federal share of special education spending risen higher than about 12 percent, despite Congress' 1975 promise to pay 40 percent of the extra costs of educating students with disabilities.*

In the meantime, the Department of Education, Congress, and federal courts have steadily increased the financial obligations of states and school districts. For instance, several categories of disabilities, such as autism and attention deficit disorder (ADD), have been added to the list of disabilities covered by the special education law. During the 1980s, Congress also extended special education services to disabled infants and preschoolers. Most recently, the 1999 Supreme Court case of *Cedar Rapids Community School District v. Garret F.*[1] elicited a wave of fear and anger over the exploding costs of special education. School administrators viewed the Court's ruling that a school district must pay for the full-time nursing care of a paralyzed teenager as illustrative of the enormous burdens being placed on their budgets.

[handwritten: ADD is not included under IDEA]

As a result, local administrators, state education officials, and advocates for the disabled have all come to see the federal government as a sort of deadbeat dad, siring legislative offspring and then failing to support them adequately. School personnel and advocates for the disabled usually find themselves on opposing sides, yet the "40 percent" figure has long been a galvanizing issue. Moreover, to a number of congressional Republicans, special education is yet another of the loathed "unfunded mandates" that Washington imposes on the states. Here is a federal education program they believe *should be* fully funded. Add in a few years of budget surpluses, and it's easy to understand why federal grants to the states for special education grew from $2.3 billion in 1996 to $6.3 billion in fiscal 2001, a threefold increase (excluding grants for the preschool and infants and families programs). President Clinton requested a total appropriation under the Individuals with Disabilities Education Act (IDEA) of $6.4 billion in 2001, up from $6 billion in 2000. Congress instead approved $7.4 billion in total spending. Still, it would take another doubling in spending to come near the 40 percent mark.

One cannot escape the issue of cost when dealing with special education. There hasn't been a rigorous accounting of what special education costs nationwide since 1988. That tally put the incremental cost of special education—what is spent over and above the cost to educate a nondisabled student—at $19 billion during the 1985-86 school year.[2] The study also confirmed an earlier study's finding that disabled children cost about twice as much to educate as the nondisabled.[3] The Center for Special Education Finance extrapolated these estimates to the 1995-96 school year and came up with an incremental cost of somewhere between $30.9 billion and $34.8 billion.[4] The expansion of services to children with ADD and attention deficit hyperactivity disorder (ADHD)—there was a 280 percent increase in the "other health impaired" category of disabled children between the 1988-89 and 1997-98 school years—combined with normal inflation and the increasing coverage of younger children has probably pushed the incremental cost near $40 billion.

Yet the IDEA has also been a remarkably successful piece of legislation. Before its enactment in 1975, federal statistics showed that, of the more than 8 million children from birth to age 21 with disabilities, only half were receiving an appropriate education. Another 2.5 million were receiving an inappropriate education, and 1.75 million, usually those with severe disabilities, received no public education whatsoever. Now these students are at least in schools, often with a series of supplementary aides and specialized curricula that allow them to participate along with their nondisabled peers.

> **G. Reid Lyon of the National Institute of Child Health and Human Development has called the "learning disabled" category a "sociological sponge to wipe up the spills of general education."**

Along with special education's growth, however, came a long list of complaints. Some contend that far too many children are being shunted into special education when the real problem is that they haven't been taught very well in the regular classroom. G. Reid Lyon of the National Institute of Child Health and Human Development has called the "learning disabled" category a "sociological sponge to wipe up the spills of general education."[5] Others contend that not enough students are receiving the services to which they're entitled. For instance, some cities—Washington, D.C., is a glaring example—have such heavy backlogs that children go for years without even being evaluated for services, their disabilities weighing them down like clothes in a swimming pool. Moreover, for the children placed in special education, the label itself sometimes acts as an unbearable weight, sticking them with poorly trained teachers and the stigma of diminished expectations.

Policymakers also find special education frustrating because it complicates our handling of just about every other promising education reform. Within the debate over school vouchers, for instance, there is always the lurking concern that private schools will view disabled children much as an HMO might view Vice President Dick Cheney. How can we ensure that private schools won't discriminate against disabled students? In the standards-and-accountability debate, there is the enduring question of whether schools are pushing low-performing students into special education classes in order to exclude them from high-stakes tests. The solution might be to bring special education students into mainstream testing regimes, but might that corrupt information on overall student performance?

Policy in special education is a complicated stew of statutory language, precedent-setting court decisions, and federal regulations. The vague language of the law has left much of the interpretation to the courts, where the definitions and substantive requirements of special education have evolved over time. The law has developed at the hand of Congress as well, most recently—and some say most dramatically—during the 1997 reauthorization of the IDEA. What follows is the story of how the interaction among courts, Congress, schools, and parents has molded special education into its current form.

From the Margin to the Center

During the 1950s and '60s, two distinct movements converged to form a powerful lobby in pursuit of federal legislation to address the education of children with disabilities. On the one hand were civil rights advocates inspired by the Supreme Court's 1954 decision in *Brown v. Board of Education.*[6] They viewed the court's striking down of racial segregation as a clear sign that the public schools' segregation and exclusion of children with disabilities were also unconstitutional. On the other hand were parents—many of them white and middle class—whose children were having trouble in school. They argued that their children's academic difficulties were caused by "learning disabilities" that masked their true intellectual potential. The goal was to define academic failure as primarily a medical problem, one that might be remedied if sufficient resources and extra help were steered toward these "underachieving" children.[7] By 1968, the grassroots lobby for the learning disabled had secured enactment of statutes in 13 states that recognized the existence of learning disabilities and granted funds for their treatment.

> *By 1968, the grassroots lobby for the learning disabled had secured enactment of statutes in 13 states that recognized the existence of learning disabilities and granted funds for their treatment.*

These movements arose against a backdrop of animosity and discrimination toward the disabled. The eugenics movement of the late 19th and early 20th centuries viewed the physically handicapped and mentally retarded as a drag on human progress. Its followers sought to institutionalize and sterilize the disabled in order to keep them from passing on their genes. In the 1926 case *Buck v. Bell*, the U.S. Supreme Court, in the voice of Justice Oliver Wendell Holmes Jr., legitimized the movement's reasoning in ruling that a young girl who had been labeled "backwards" could be sterilized. Justice Holmes wrote, "The principle that sustains compulsory vaccination is broad enough to cover the cutting of the Fallopian tubes.... Three generations of imbeciles are enough."[8]

Educating the disabled was viewed by some as futile, a waste of resources. Laws that required parents to school their children sometimes exempted children with disabilities. In a typical case, *Board of Education of Cleveland Heights v. State ex rel. Goldman*, a child with an IQ below 50 was excluded from a special school in Ohio. In 1934, the court of appeals ruled that "[a]s a matter of common sense it is apparent that a moron of very low type, or an idiot or imbecile who is incapable of absorbing knowledge or making progress in the schools, ought to be excluded."[9] When severely disabled children weren't denied an education altogether, they seldom benefited from whatever education was offered to them—often in segregated settings that rarely amounted to much more than warehousing.[10]

In the wake of the *Brown* decision, many states continued to exclude the disabled from public schools. A North Carolina statute, still on the books as late as 1969, allowed the state to label a child as "uneducable" and made it a crime for parents to challenge the decision.[11] Other states and districts tended to place disabled children in separate schools and classrooms, which was more cost-effective than educating them in regular classrooms. Civil rights advocates, however, argued that schools were underestimating the benefits of placing disabled children in the regular classroom. They pushed for "inclusion," arguing that if we mean to help disabled children become self-sufficient, they need to learn how to live among and interact with their nondisabled peers.

> **PARC and Mills and the principles they elucidated fueled a surge in litigation that resulted in similar decisions in 27 states by 1974. Many states also enacted laws mandating education for the disabled.**

Civil rights advocates scored their first victories in the courts. Fears that schools, in reaction to the *Brown* decision, were now labeling black children as "mentally retarded" in order to exclude them from school was one motivator of a wave of litigation. Two famous cases defined the rights of the disabled and set up a framework for subsequent legislation. In the 1972 case *Pennsylvania Association for Retarded Children (PARC) v. Commonwealth of Pennsylvania,*[12] commonly known as the *PARC* decision, parents of mentally retarded children filed a class-action suit challenging Pennsylvania statutes that barred them from public schools. The suit alleged that the state had violated the 14th Amendment's guarantees of equal protection and due process by arbitrarily excluding children from school without any kind of hearing or legitimate reason for doing so. The resulting consent decree outlined both the state's duty to educate the mentally retarded and a series of rules and procedures meant to protect students' rights.

Another 1972 case, *Mills v. Board of Education of District of Columbia,*[13] involved a broader class of students, including those with behavioral problems, emotional disturbance, and hyperactivity. *Mills* also alleged equal protection and due process violations. Here, however, the District's Board of Education acknowledged its obligation to educate all children but claimed that it did not have the resources to do so. The board's claim of inadequate resources turned out to be no defense. Said the court: "Their failure to fulfill this clear duty to include and retain these children in the public school system, or otherwise provide them with publicly supported education, and their failure to afford them due process hearings and periodical review, cannot be excused by the claim that there are insufficient funds."[14]

PARC and *Mills* established three principles that have guided special education law ever since. One is that the Constitution's guarantees of equal protection and due process prevent schools from excluding students solely on the basis of their disabilities. Another is that parents of disabled children must have a range of opportunities—such as impartial hearings and access to the courts—to challenge a school's decisions regarding their children's educational programs. ③ And, finally, exorbitant costs are no excuse for failure to grant the disabled access to the public education system. *PARC* and *Mills* and the principles they elucidated fueled a surge in litigation that resulted in similar decisions in 27 states by 1974. Many states also enacted laws mandating education for the disabled.

there were t.v. ads telling people to bring their disabled kids to school

The agitations of civil rights advocates pushed Congress to act as well. In 1966, Congress amended the new Elementary and Secondary Education Act to include funds for the education of disabled children and to create the Bureau of Education for the Handicapped within the U.S. Office of Education. A number of grants for disabled children were then consolidated under the Education for the Handicapped Act (EHA) of 1970, the first freestanding statute devoted to students with disabilities. Further amendments in 1974 significantly boosted federal grants for states to help them pay for the rights being secured through lawsuits and required states to detail their plans for achieving the goal of full educational opportunities for disabled children.

> **Prior to enacting the Education for All Handicapped Children Act (EAHCA) in 1975, Congress' most significant action on behalf of disabled children was passage of Section 504 of the Rehabilitation Act of 1973.**

Prior to enacting the Education for All Handicapped Children Act (EAHCA) in 1975, Congress' most significant action on behalf of disabled children was passage of Section 504 of the Rehabilitation Act of 1973.[15] Section 504 was a broad antidiscrimination statute that applied not only to public schools but also to any institution that received federal funds. It read: "No otherwise qualified individual with a disability…shall, solely by reason of his disability, be excluded from participation in, or be denied the benefits of, or be subject to discrimination under any program or activity receiving Federal financial assistance." In granting specific protections to disabled students, Section 504 relied heavily on the *Mills* and *PARC* decisions and affirmed the principle that disabled children should be educated in regular classrooms.

By 1974, most of the legal protections that characterize special education as we know it were in place. Both case law and statutes prohibited the exclusion of disabled students from public school and required schools to make every effort to place disabled children in classrooms with their nondisabled peers. Parents had the right to be notified of, and to challenge, any changes in their disabled child's educational placement. But passing a civil rights law is one matter; enforcing it is another. The Rehabilitation Act gave disabled children certain rights, but not the funds to encourage and help schools to identify, evaluate, and serve all disabled children, or to set up the kinds of due process protections specified by the laws.

A Clear Mandate   *Unfunded Mandate*

Some funds, together with a clearer, more specific mandate, came with passage of the EAHCA in 1975. (Henceforth, this statute will be referred to as the IDEA, its name since 1990.) Congress justified the legislation on two major grounds: as an antidiscrimination measure, and as a long-term investment in the nation's economic health. The goal was to make small educational investments early in a disabled child's life that might lead to him or her becoming a self-sufficient, productive adult who would need fewer social services later on.

The IDEA expanded the EHA's small financial commitment into a multibillion dollar program of grants to the states. The intent was not to pay for all the costs of providing special education to disabled children; it was to help states fulfill their duty to uphold the 14th Amendment's equal-protection guarantee. At the time, Congress promised eventually to pay 40 percent of the incremental cost of special education—those expenses above what schools spend on regular students. The Senate estimated the cost of implementing the law nationwide at $1.9 billion in 1978, while the House estimate was set at $3.8 billion. The funding formula was based on the percentage of children labeled as disabled in a state, with a cap of 12 percent to dissuade states from overlabeling in pursuit of extra funds. The bill, signed by then-President Gerald Ford, enjoyed enormous popularity: The final vote was 375 to 44 in the House, 83 to 10 in the Senate.

> *Section 504 precludes discrimination on the basis of disability, and anyone with a physical or mental impairment which "substantially limits one or more major life activities," including learning, is covered by its protections.*

The IDEA followed a trend, best represented by Medicare and Medicaid, of setting up entitlements that give a certain class of people legally enforceable rights without regard to the costs of exercising them. In the 1970s, writes education scholar Paul Hill, these entitlements sometimes joined with the idea that Congress should leave the interpretation and enforcement of laws to the courts rather than write reams of regulations and set up new bureaucracies. Hill has called the IDEA the "high water mark of resource allocation by court decision."[16]

The IDEA is not technically an "unfunded mandate."[17] By foregoing federal special education funding, states could avoid being subject to the law's requirements. No rational state would comply with the law, write law professors Mark Kelman and Gillian Lester, if federal funds did not cover the costs of compliance. But the IDEA is not disabled children's only line of defense. Section 504, though less targeted at education and less detailed, substantially overlaps with the IDEA's requirements. It precludes discrimination on the basis of disability, and anyone with a physical or mental impairment which "substantially limits one or more major life activities," including learning, is covered by its protections. A state would have to forego *all* federal funds in order to avoid the special education mandates of Section 504. In fact, only one state, New Mexico, didn't immediately apply for federal funds under the IDEA, but by 1984 even New Mexico had complied with the statute.

Though schools must comply with both Section 504 and the IDEA, it is primarily the IDEA that drives policy in special education, with one exception: Students with ADD have sometimes appealed to Section 504 because schools were reluctant to cover them as "other health impaired," emotionally disturbed, or learning disabled under the IDEA. The Office of Civil Rights within the Department of Education handles Section 504 complaints, and its staff seems more willing to identify children with ADD as disabled.[18] In a survey by Professors Kelman and Lester, districts reported widespread fears and uncertainty surrounding the requirements of Section 504, mainly because they seem to cover a broader and less well-defined set of disabilities—anything that "substantially limits" a major life activity. "If a student can describe herself as disabled whenever her ability to perform a 'major life activity' is compromised," write Kelman and Lester, "there is no obvious limit on who can make claims: every weakness can be described as a handicap." Kelman and Lester concluded that school administrators' worries stemmed more from their familiarity with the procedures and rules of the IDEA, and their relative lack of experience with Section 504, than from any legitimate threat of looming Section 504 litigation.[19] (Title II of the Americans with Disabilities Act provides antidiscrimination protections similar to Section 504, but it rarely has been invoked in K-12 education litigation.[20])

What the IDEA Covers

The IDEA mandates that all disabled students be provided a "free appropriate public education" (FAPE) in the "least restrictive environment" (LRE). Each disabled child must have an individualized education program (IEP) that details the range of services to be provided and where a student's education is to take place, with the law expressing a heavy preference for the mainstreaming of disabled children whenever possible. The law also mandates that districts establish procedures for ensuring that parents are involved in the development of each IEP and that they have opportunities to challenge a district's decisions about the range of services it will provide.

> A parent's first line of defense in special education is his or her child's IEP. It is the tool that allows parents to ensure that their disabled children are receiving an "appropriate" education.

The law covers a range of handicapping conditions, including mental retardation, deafness, speech or language impairments, blindness, serious emotional disturbance, physical and health disabilities, and, significantly, "specific learning disabilities." It requires schools to grant children with these conditions whatever special education they require as well as the "related services" they need to attend school and benefit from education. These may include transportation services, assistive listening devices, Braille textbooks, and medical services, "except that such medical services shall be for diagnostic or evaluation purposes only," in the words of the statute.

A parent's first line of defense in special education is his or her child's IEP. It is the tool that allows parents to ensure that their disabled children are receiving an "appropriate" education. The law requires school districts to seek out, identify, and evaluate all children who may be eligible for special education services. Once a potentially disabled child is identified, a team of experts (including the child's teachers) convenes to assess whether he is indeed disabled and, if so, to design a suitable course of treatment. During these meetings, school representatives, the child's teacher, the parents, and any experts called by parents or the school develop the student's IEP, which gives a written diagnosis of the child's problems, a detailed account of the special services he will receive, and a statement of academic objectives and goals. At any point, the child's parents may challenge the district's decisions regarding diagnosis or treatment and suggest alternatives. If the two parties can't reach an agreement, the parents may ask for a hearing in front of an impartial officer. If either party doesn't agree with the hearing's result, it can appeal to the state board of education and, ultimately, to the courts.

That "specific learning disabilities" were included as a handicapping condition under the IDEA represented a major coup for disability advocates. This term covers children who, outside of school, might not be considered disabled. Any discussion of special education must keep the distinction between students with learning disabilities (LD) and physical or severe mental disabilities clear. In the days before Section 504 and the IDEA, children with LD were seldom if ever excluded from school. Their needs rarely rise above having a well-trained teacher who can diagnose and help them cope with their learning difficulties. No one expected that they would eventually account for more than half of all children served under the IDEA and for a third of the nation's spending on special education.

> *The question of why learning disabled children are more deserving of extra help than everyday low achievers is one that LD advocates have never quite answered.*

The IDEA defines learning disabilities as "psychological processing disorders that interfere with one's ability to perform a number of learning tasks." These learning deficits cannot result from physical disabilities, mental retardation, emotional disturbance, or environmental or socioeconomic factors. As Professors Kelman and Lester put it in *Jumping the Queue*, this is a "negative" definition of LD. A learning disability is assumed to be present if we can't find other factors, such as poverty, that would explain low achievement. In practice, the law considers a student to be learning disabled if he exhibits a discrepancy between his intellectual ability, usually measured on an IQ test, and his actual achievement, usually measured by various standardized tests. These students, it is said, are "underachieving," i.e., not achieving at the level predicted by their innate ability. In theory, schools must determine whether this discrepancy is the result of factors other than a specific learning disability, but in practice it is difficult if not impossible to isolate which factor causes a child's inability to measure up to his potential.[21] This has led to frequent criticism that special education services are given to children who are failing in school but who don't suffer from an identifiable learning disability (in other words, their low test scores are predicted by equally low IQ scores or other factors, such as a poor learning environment at home). In fact, evaluations of special education have found that only about 50 percent of students classified as LD actually presented an achievement/aptitude discrepancy.[22] The rest are students who perform poorly relative to their peers but don't score well on aptitude tests either. However, the question of why learning disabled children are more deserving of extra help than everyday low achievers is one that LD advocates have never quite answered.

Questions for the Courts

The history of special education law since 1975 is, essentially, the evolution of the federal courts' answers to two questions: What constitutes an appropriate education, and to what lengths must schools go to place disabled students in regular classrooms? In fact, the law itself has not changed much during the past quarter century. What has expanded is its scope. In the 1980s, Congress approved large increases in funding for the preschool program for children ages 3–5 with disabilities and created a new early intervention program for infants and toddlers. In 1986, Congress gave parents the right to be reimbursed for attorneys' fees if they prevailed in court. The law's name was changed to the Individuals with Disabilities Education Act in 1990 and several new categories of disability, including autism and traumatic brain injury, were added to the list of handicapping conditions. Congress has also lengthened the list of "related services" that schools must provide. Social work services, rehabilitative counseling, and transition from school to work are just a few of the services that have been added since 1975. Advocates claim that fundamental changes were made in 1997—an assertion we examine below—but, otherwise, the statutory language of the IDEA in the year 2000 looks much like that of the EAHCA of 1975.

> **The Court viewed Congress' creation of strict rules and procedures as the vehicle through which parents could ensure that their children were receiving an appropriate education.**

Where the law has changed most is in the courts. The statute's vague language has left many of its terms open to various interpretations, thus inviting litigation. Serious questions were left unanswered, such as: What is an "appropriate" education? Do schools need to provide those services necessary to maximize the potential of disabled children to the degree that the potential of nondisabled children is maximized? Or was the law meant to grant disabled children mere access to the public schools, not the right to any particular level of education? Can evidence that a child is not progressing in school be used as prima facie proof that he is not receiving an appropriate education? Can a district take other students' interests into account when faced with implementing a costly IEP? How much can the interests of disabled and nondisabled children be balanced against one another? Can other students' interests be taken into account when placing a disabled child in the "least restrictive environment," especially when that child is disruptive and interferes with the education of his peers? In essence, to what lengths must schools go to accommodate students with disabilities?

An "Appropriate" Education

The first IDEA case to go before the Supreme Court was *Hendrick Hudson District Board of Education v. Rowley*, in 1982.[23] The fundamental issue was how to define an "appropriate" education. Amy Rowley, a deaf child whose school district had provided speech therapy, tutoring, and a hearing aid to help her cope with her disability, claimed that the district's refusal to provide a full-time sign-language interpreter in first grade constituted a failure to provide an appropriate education. She had been doing well in regular classes but, she claimed, not as well as she would have with an interpreter.

Federal courts at both the district and appellate levels ruled in favor of Rowley. The district court defined an appropriate education as one that gives a student with a disability the chance to achieve at the same level as a student of equal "intellectual caliber" but without a disability.[24] This conformed to earlier decisions that had interpreted the Act to guarantee a level of education that would help a disabled child achieve at the level he would have achieved without the disability.[25]

But the Supreme Court overturned the lower courts, ruling that such a standard involved "impossible measures and comparisons."[26] For one, it would mean determining each student's "intellectual caliber." Also, said the Court, the range of disabilities is so wide that a single standard could never apply to all students. After all, by definition a mentally retarded student has no nondisabled peers of similar "intellectual caliber." Impaired intellectual functioning is a mentally retarded child's disability. The Court substituted a two-part test that focused more on whether the district had followed proper procedures in determining the services it would provide to Amy Rowley. It first asked whether the school had complied with the law's procedural mandates, such as properly evaluating Amy's needs and involving her parents in the development of her IEP. Second, it asked whether Amy's IEP was "reasonably calculated to enable the child to receive educational benefits."[27] If the school met both requirements, then the Court would not overturn its decisions. Because the school district had followed the law's procedural requirements and Amy Rowley was making substantial progress in school, the Court upheld the district's decision to deny her a full-time interpreter.

> *In the end, the courts have clung to a case-by-case approach in determining what an "appropriate" education is.*

In essence, the court deferred to the opinions of local professionals as to what constituted an "appropriate" education. In passing the IDEA, then-Justice William Rehnquist wrote on behalf of the majority, Congress did not extend an "invitation to the courts to substitute their own notions of sound educational policy" for those of school authorities.[28] The Court viewed Congress' creation of strict rules and procedures as the vehicle through which parents could ensure that their children were receiving an appropriate education. If schools followed those requirements in coming to a decision, they were deemed to have adhered to the law.

Disability-rights advocates viewed the *Rowley* decision as a major setback. They had celebrated the IDEA as visionary, transformative legislation that would vastly improve the educational experiences of disabled students. The Court's low standard of "some educational benefit" was not what they had envisioned. The Court, they claimed, had ignored the congressional intent of providing equal educational opportunity to disabled students; its decision was said to be motivated by concern over the costs of providing an education to disabled students. Bonnie Tucker, a disability attorney, wrote, "The obvious rationale for the Court's blatant disregard of congressional intent was its unspoken fear that a contrary result would have opened the floodgates by allowing every seriously handicapped child in the nation to receive full-time individualized educational assistance where needed."[29]

Later courts have used the *Rowley* decision to deny services to disabled students that, while potentially beneficial, were not required by the law. In the 1988 case *Kerkam v. McKenzie*, for example, the D.C. Circuit Court of Appeals wrote, "Proof that loving parents can craft a better program than a state offers does not, alone, entitle them to prevail under the Act."[30] In particular, courts have often relied on *Rowley* to refuse parents' requests for expensive private schooling in lieu of the public school placement offered by the school district, even while acknowledging that the private placement offered a superior educational experience. In *Doe v. Board of Education,* the Sixth Circuit compared the private school placement to a Cadillac, the public school placement to a Chevrolet, and held that the state was "not required to provide a

Cadillac, and that the proposed IEP [was] reasonably calculated to provide educational benefits," and thus satisfied the FAPE requirement.[31]

Because the *Rowley* case involved a student who was making substantial progress from grade-to-grade without extra services—a fact that the Supreme Court emphasized in its decision—plaintiffs have tried to use the *Rowley* holding to request more services when the current level of services has been of limited benefit to the child. This argument has sometimes met with success. In some cases involving severely handicapped students, the courts have declared the *Rowley* standard basically irrelevant to the facts at hand. Other courts have interpreted *Rowley* to mean that, if a child is not progressing from grade-to-grade, more services are required. But one important decision, *E.S. v. Independent School District*, broadly interpreted *Rowley* to hold that an educational program of only marginal benefit was still appropriate.[32] The plaintiff, a dyslexic child entering 7th grade, was reading at a 3.8 grade level and had progressed only .8 grade equivalents after three years of special education. The school district provided her with a program of one-on-one instruction during the summer but when her parents asked the district to continue the program during the year, the district refused, even though she had made substantial summertime progress. The court denied the services to her, holding that she hadn't proved that one-on-one tutoring was necessary for her to benefit from education. It can be argued that such cases actually represent a strong departure from *Rowley*.[33] The *Rowley* court specifically limited its findings to the facts of the case at hand, where Amy Rowley was making substantial progress without the extra services she was requesting.

> *In designing an "appropriate" education, school districts generally may not oppose an otherwise "appropriate" education because it is too costly.*

In the end, the courts have clung to a case-by-case approach in determining what an "appropriate" education is. *Rowley* established the precedent that the law does not require schools to maximize a disabled child's potential, nor even to spend as much on disabled students as on the nondisabled.[34] An "appropriate" education, according to the courts, can range from a plan that delivers almost no educational benefit to one that maximizes a disabled child's potential. *Rowley* held that Congress' intent in passing the IDEA "was more to open the door of public education to handicapped children on appropriate terms than to guarantee any particular level of education once inside."[35] In short, courts respect the decisions of educators regarding an "appropriate" education, so long as they follow the procedural rules in its design.

In designing an "appropriate" education, school districts generally may not oppose an otherwise "appropriate" education because it is too costly. The courts have held, however, that a district may choose one IEP among several appropriate ones because it is less expensive than the others. In *Greer v. Rome City School District*, the court held that the issue of cost may be raised in certain limited conditions. It wrote: "If the cost of educating a handicapped child in a regular classroom is so great that it would significantly impact upon the education of other children in the district, then education in the regular classroom is not appropriate."[36] In *Jumping the Queue*, however, Professors Kelman and Lester argue that these conditions make no sense: only the smallest of districts would be seriously burdened by the costs of even the most expensive IEP.[37]

No courts, they note, have found that a given IEP can be opposed on the grounds that giving all similar students the same IEP would bankrupt the district.

Least Restrictive Environment

At issue in *Greer* was the other bedrock principle of special education law: the "least restrictive environment," or inclusion, mandate. The law requires that disabled children be served in regular classrooms to the "maximum extent possible," a direct reply to the past exclusion of disabled children from public schools. The further away from a regular classroom, the more restrictive the placement is said to be. A disabled student's IEP must document the extent to which disabled students are to be educated in the regular classroom; to pull a disabled pupil out of his regular classroom, the

> *The courts have required schools to consider a range of supplementary aids and services in order to mainstream students effectively.*

school must have a compelling reason. This is a controversial issue because it is often more efficient to serve disabled students in separate, centralized classrooms and schools. It may be more effective as well. For instance, if ten dyslexic students need specialized instruction in reading, it may make more sense to teach them together than to try to serve each one individually in his regular classroom. Schools also attempt to exclude disabled students, especially emotionally disturbed students, because their behavior can make it difficult for teachers to manage their classrooms. They sometimes wind up devoting more time to discipline than to instruction.

The courts have generally placed the burden on schools to justify any segregation of disabled students from regular classrooms. They have required schools to consider a range of supplementary aids and services in order to mainstream students effectively, from training regular classroom teachers in special education techniques to adding specially trained aides to the regular classroom to assist disabled children. In doing so, the courts have held that districts may engage in a series of balancing exercises in which the interests of nondisabled children are weighed against the interests of the disabled. In *Daniel R.R. v. State Board of Education*, the leading precedent in this area, the court stated that one factor in deciding whether a student can be excluded from the regular classroom is the effect of inclusion on his classmates.[38] Daniel was a six-year-old child with Down syndrome who had the communication skills of a two-year-old. The problem was that his presence in a regular classroom put enormous demands on the teacher to the detriment of his classmates.

The court concluded that Daniel's presence was "unfair to the rest of the class. When Daniel is in the pre-Kindergarten classroom, the instructor must devote all or most of her time to Daniel. Yet she has a classroom filled with other, equally deserving students who need her attention." The court held that, "Although regular education instructors must devote extra attention to their handicapped students, we will not require them to do so at the expense of their entire class."[39] The court further ruled that, if it were not appropriate to place a child in the regular classroom, the district then had to ensure that he was mainstreamed with nondisabled peers in academic and extracurricular pursuits to the maximum extent possible.

Although the court ruled against Daniel's request for placement in the regular classroom, it established a general policy in favor of inclusion. It told districts that they had to make serious efforts to place disabled children in the regular classroom, that the courts would not tolerate "mere token gestures" to meet the law's "least restrictive environment" mandate.

In a later case, *Oberti v. Board of Education*, the court ruled in favor of Rafael, a child with Down syndrome, precisely because the district had made little effort to accommodate his disability.[40] The district had placed Rafael in a special education class in a neighboring district after his behavior in a mainstreamed developmental kindergarten classroom proved extremely disruptive. His behavior problems ranged from toilet accidents to touching, hitting, and spitting on other children. But the court, relying on expert testimony that Rafael's behavioral problems would have subsided if he had been given proper supports, ruled that the district had not exhausted its options before excluding Rafael from the regular classroom. His IEP had no plan to address his behavior problems and provided for no communication between his regular and special education teachers.

Oberti was the first case to detail the kinds of supplementary aids and services that districts would have to try before excluding a disabled child from regular classrooms. Potential accommodations suggested by the court included modifying the curriculum to address differences in ability; modifying a disabled child's curriculum to allow him to work on the same assignments as his classmates but at his own pace; parallel instruction, in which a child works independently on one assignment while his classmates work on a different assignment that would not benefit him; special education training for the regular teacher; and special instruction in a "resource room" for part of the day. In *Clyde K. v. Puyallup School District*, the court ruled that a student who had violently attacked two students and assaulted staff members could be placed in a separate school, in part because the district had provided supplementary services and special training for staff.[41]

> **Under the umbrella of the "least restrictive environment" concept, one group of cases has been particularly controversial: those dealing with severely disabled students who need medical care during the school day in order to remain in the regular classroom.**

Under the umbrella of the "least restrictive environment" concept, one group of cases has been particularly controversial: those dealing with severely disabled students who need medical care during the school day in order to remain in the regular classroom. The IDEA says that schools must provide medical services, but only when they are for purposes of diagnosis or evaluation. The Supreme Court first entered this thicket in 1984, in *Irving Independent School District v. Tatro*.[42] Amber Tatro was an 8-year-old born with spina bifida. Her incompletely developed spinal cord caused her to need a procedure called "clean intermittent catheterization," or CIC, every three to four hours to prevent damage to her kidneys. It was a relatively easy procedure that a layperson could be trained in an hour to do, but the district refused to provide this service. Here the Court established what is called a "bright-line test," a clear, easily understood guideline for schools to follow. The Court held that the "medical services" exclusion applied only to services that needed a physician's attention. Therefore, if a student needed the care in order to attend school, and such care could be provided by someone other than a physician, then it fell within the range of services required by the IDEA.

Some later courts departed from *Tatro* in cases where students needed more complicated procedures than CIC. They said that when the number and complexity of services rose, they could become excluded "medical services" even if a physician was not required to perform them.[43] This became known as the "nature of services" standard. Other courts, meanwhile, adhered to the *Tatro* standard, causing tension among circuit courts that the Supreme Court decided to resolve in 1999 in *Cedar Rapids Community School District v. Garret F.*[44] The Cedar Rapids school district insisted that full-time, continuous nursing care fell under the "medical services" exclusion, but the Court, in a 7–2 decision, reaffirmed *Tatro's* bright-line test that any service not needing a physician's supervision was by definition not medical.

> *For the most part, court decisions regarding the services provided and the extent to which students can be removed from the regular classroom must disregard cost or the impact on nondisabled peers.*

The cases in which LRE has been at issue have in some ways expanded the *Rowley* decision. The courts have used the congressional preference for mainstreaming to require a range of supplements and services that may not fit into the Supreme Court's definition of an "appropriate" education yet are necessary to keep a child in the regular classroom.[45] The Supreme Court has yet to take up an LRE case, so the standard has been left to differ from circuit to circuit. For instance, the more conservative Fourth Circuit, based in Richmond, has been less likely to factor in the nonacademic benefits of placing a disabled student in the regular classroom, especially if a district can show that the services offered in a segregated setting are superior.[46] In the 1983 case *Roncker v. Walter*, by contrast, the Sixth Circuit held that, when the segregated environment offers a superior education, the court must inquire as to whether the features that make it superior can be replicated in the regular classroom.[47] The Fifth Circuit's response in *Daniel R.R.* was that this "necessitates too intrusive an inquiry into educational policy choices that Congress deliberately left to state and local school officials."[48]

Despite the inconsistencies, what has emerged in the case law is a broad set of protections for disabled children. For the most part, decisions regarding the services provided and the extent to which disabled students can be removed from the regular classroom must disregard cost or the impact on nondisabled peers. There is a strong presumption that disabled children should be taught alongside their nondisabled peers. Children whose behavior disrupts the classroom or endangers themselves or their peers may be excluded from the regular classroom, but only after the school has tried a range of interventions. Still, it is not true, as is often said, that special education students have a right to an infinite array of educational services.

Legal Actions and IDEA Enforcement

Whatever one thinks of special education's goals and achievements, there is no denying that it is a well-regulated program. As early as 1982, just seven years after the IDEA passed Congress, the RAND Corporation was finding that school-level special education administrators understood the regulations facing them better than the administrators of other federal education programs. Title I administrators, for instance, still understood only the basic principles of the program and often couldn't evaluate the legality of certain arrangements, even though their law was passed a decade before the IDEA.[49]

Because the law gives specific, legally enforceable rights to certain individuals, schools face powerful incentives to provide the necessary services to eligible children. Administrators need to stay abreast of the law or they can find themselves in court. This bottom-up, decentralized form of regulation relies on strong networks of parent groups, who quickly disseminate new legal findings and regulations. The U.S. Department of Education nourishes the regulatory system by funding parent information and assistance centers that provide parents with pro-bono legal representation. In poor areas, such as Baltimore, where parents have been ill-informed of their legal rights, districts have operated for years under the shadow of class-action suits brought on behalf of their disabled students.

Legal actions (and the threat of legal actions) by parents have led to a backlash, both from special education's critics and from advocates for the disabled. School administrators complain about having their professional decisions challenged by parents and having to worry more about administrative hearings than the actual quality of services being given to students. Advocates for the disabled, by contrast, worry about the regulatory burden being placed on parents. In a scathing indictment of federal enforcement efforts that was issued in January 2000, the National Council on Disability wrote, "Enforcement of the law is too often the burden of parents who must invoke formal complaint procedures and request due process hearings to obtain the services and supports to which their children are entitled under law."[50] There is a powerful minority of parents who know their legal rights and aren't afraid to exercise them. But most parents are at a decided disadvantage vis-à-vis school administrators. They don't know their rights, have little experience with the legal system, and tend to respect the decisions of professional educators.

> *The IDEA's definitions of such categories as specific learning disabilities and behavioral disorders are hazy enough to allow for some striking differences in how the law is applied.*

This has led to the criticism that affluent parents are most able to avail themselves of the law's protections. They tend to be well-educated and more forceful and confident in their dealings with school administrators. They also have the means to back up any threats of litigation. They are the most likely to secure private school or full-time residential placements when their children are severely disabled. In short, they are less likely to be bullied around, and more likely to do the bullying.

But the availability of legal action as a recourse is not just a boon to wealthy, pushy parents. In a study of Massachusetts special education directors, Thomas Hehir found that legal decisions tend to reverberate throughout the education system, expanding the services available to all disabled children. To avoid the courts, districts attempt to settle most disputes through negotiation with parents. In the end, few cases actually ever reach a judge. "The threat of a hearing," write Hehir and Sue Gamm, "is an essential element in the relationship between districts and parents because it raises the stakes in disputes over placement."[51] They contend that the IDEA's critics have focused too much on the effects of administrative hearings themselves, ignoring all the hearings that never happen as a result of settlements reached prior to the formal initiation of legal actions.

Still, the law's definitions of such categories as specific learning disabilities and behavioral disorders are hazy enough to allow for some striking differences in how the law is applied. In a mainly anecdotal survey of more than 20 school districts, Professors Kelman and Lester found that the selection of students diagnosed as LD often depended on the characteristics of the district. Wealthy districts tended to ignore the legal definition of LD (as a discrepancy between aptitude and achievement) in favor of serving any low achievers who might benefit from extra help. Low-income districts also tended to ignore the aptitude/achievement discrepancy requirement, mainly because their students presented such low aptitude scores that severe discrepancies were rare. Administrators in low-income schools tended to believe that all their children had special needs, and that they would be served one way or another, whether with special education or compensatory funds. They also tended to use the LD diagnosis more often to deal with behavioral problems, as a mechanism to remove problem children from the classroom. Working-class districts tended to use discrepancy scores most often, in order to keep their special education rolls down.[52]

> *The widespread crackdown on school violence in the mid-1990s further spotlighted the protections afforded to disabled students that, at times, shielded them from discipline.*

The 1997 Reauthorization

Until 1997, each reauthorization of the IDEA was mainly an exercise in expanding the population of eligible children or the range of services to which they were entitled, either by extending coverage to younger ages or by adding named disabilities (such autism, traumatic brain injury, and ADD). Both trends have served to increase dramatically the number of children served. The changes wrought during the 1997 reauthorization, however, were hailed as the most significant since the IDEA's passage.

These changes were in response to several long-standing criticisms of special education. One is the perception that the IDEA's protections for disabled students are undermining efforts to crack down on violence in the schools. Another concern is that special education contributes to the "fragmentation" of schools—in essence, the lack of integration that occurs when several different programs, each with its own funding stream and staff, co-exist within the same school. For example, special and regular education teachers tend to inhabit their own spheres, rarely collaborating. The IDEA contributed to their isolation from one another by prohibiting federally funded special education teachers from teaching nondisabled children. The risk of "leakage"— of funds and services that were designated for special education students also helping nondisabled children—often encouraged schools to segregate disabled students from their peers. This effectively diminishes disabled children's access to the general curriculum. A related worry is that disabled students have been excluded from the effort to hold all students and schools to common standards of achievement, the so-called standards-based reform movement. Finally, Congress tried to address the concern that federal funding formulas encourage overlabeling and segregation of disabled students.

Pressure from parent groups, teacher unions, and organizations representing both school boards and administrators pushed the issue of school discipline to the top of Congress' agenda in the mid-1990s. The widespread crackdown on school violence, best represented by the adoption of "zero tolerance" policies in many districts and by Congress' passage of the Gun Free Schools Act of 1994, further spotlighted the protections afforded to disabled students that, at times, shielded them from discipline. In essence, the courts have held that a student may not be subject to expulsion or long-term suspension if his misbehavior is a "manifestation" of his disability. This is an extension of the law's general prohibition on changing a disabled child's classroom placement without both a recommendation from the student's IEP committee and the parents' consent. The law's "stay put" provision further prevents a district from changing a child's placement while any appeal of its decision is underway. The Supreme Court has held that any suspension of a disabled student for more than 10 days constitutes a change in placement.[53]

Coming on the heels of the 1994 Title I cycle, the 1997 IDEA reauthorization sought to fold disabled students into the broader standards and accountability movement.

A disabled student may be expelled or suspended if his misbehavior is not related to his disability. In practice, however, determining whether a given behavior is a manifestation of a disability, especially in cases of LD and emotional and behavioral disorders, is almost impossible; and neither courts nor regulators have given much guidance. This has led to several high-profile cases where two or more students were involved in the same crime, such as gun possession on school grounds, but at least one student escaped punishment due to his disability, the rationale evidently being that students with learning disabilities or behavioral disorders have diminished capacity to understand the consequences of, or to control, their actions. The issue of discipline also sparked the most serious altercation to date between the federal Department of Education (DOE) and a state over special education. In 1994, in a dispute over a Virginia statute that allowed districts to deny educational services to disabled students who had been expelled from school, the Clinton administration attempted to withhold Virginia's entire $60 million special education grant. The DOE argued that Virginia was still obligated to educate a child who had been expelled from school for reasons unrelated to his disability.

The DOE eventually lost in court, but Congress sealed this loophole during the 1997 reauthorization by requiring districts to provide the educational services laid out in a student's IEP even after he has been expelled. But the reauthorization created an exception to the "stay put" provision: If a student brings a weapon to school or commits a drug offense, or if a hearing officer determines that the student is likely to injure himself or others, the school can immediately place him in an alternative educational setting for up to 45 days. Still, there can be no cessation of the educational services guaranteed by the student's IEP.

In 1997, Congress also attempted to solve the school "fragmentation" problem by aligning federal special education policy with the prevailing standards-based reform movement. By the 1990s, state policymakers had embraced two broad education reform strategies: (1) to establish academic standards and tests to determine how well schools were performing; and (2) to give schools flexibility and control over instructional methods and budgetary issues in exchange for holding them accountable for results. President George W. Bush's catch phrase for this pairing is "authority and accountability." This strategy first seeped into federal policy during the 1994 reauthorization of Title I, the $11 billion compensatory program for low-income students. On the accountability side, the 1994 Title I amendments required all states to create standards regarding what students need to learn from grade to grade and tests to assess whether they are meeting the standards. On the authority side, Title I used to insist that Title I funds flow only to Title I-eligible students, a procedural rule that encouraged schools to pull Title I students out of the regular classroom, thus segregating the students and fragmenting the school. The 1994 reauthorization loosened this restriction by making it easier for schools with high proportions of low-income students to use their Title I funds for schoolwide priorities.

Coming on the heels of the 1994 Title I cycle, the 1997 IDEA reauthorization sought to fold disabled students into the broader standards and accountability movement. It required that IEPs be designed with the goal of giving disabled students access to the general curriculum. States were also to design their standards and assessments with the needs of disabled students in mind. For children whose disabilities prevent them from participating in regular state testing programs, alternative assessments, such as portfolios of student work, must be developed. In 1997, the National Center for Educational Outcomes found that only half the states even had policies regarding the participation of disabled students in statewide assessments.[54] Now federal law requires that states set performance goals for disabled children and include all students in their testing programs. To address the fragmentation problem while maximizing the inclusion of special education students in regular classrooms, Congress eased the rules prohibiting nondisabled students from benefiting incidentally from special education funds. For instance, a special education teacher or aide working in a regular classroom may now teach a reading lesson to a mixed group of disabled and nondisabled children.

> *States must ensure that their funding mechanisms don't encourage overlabeling or the placement of disabled children in more segregated settings.*

To address concerns that federal funding formulas were unintentionally encouraging both the overlabeling and segregation of disabled children, Congress adjusted the IDEA funding formula as well. Most federal special education money is still allocated to states based on the percentage of their population that is deemed to be disabled. But any funds appropriated for state grants in excess of $4.9 billion are now distributed on the basis of a state's total school population and its population in poverty instead of its number of disabled students—a system called census-based funding. The reasoning is that this will not punish states whose special education rolls are shrinking, but it will discourage overidentification. Census-based funding is controversial among advocates for the disabled because it could give schools too little incentive to identify children as disabled; it could encourage underlabeling. Census-based funding also risks failing to account for true differences in the proportion and types of disabled children from one district to another.

> **Hardly anyone seems pleased with the special education system, yet hardly anyone seems clear about how to fix it.**

States, too, must now ensure that their funding mechanisms don't encourage overlabeling or the placement of disabled children in more segregated settings. States often provide higher reimbursements to school districts for more segregated placements under the rationale that these placements are more costly. Moreover, with the state grant appropriation exceeding $4.1 billion, any districts that receive larger awards may reduce local spending somewhat. This relaxes the usual "supplement, not supplant" regulations that govern nearly all federal education programs, and responds to the complaint that special education expenses are overburdening local school districts.

Conclusion

Hardly anyone seems pleased with the special education system, yet hardly anyone seems clear about how to fix it. On the one hand, advocates for the disabled say that too few children are receiving the services to which they are entitled. They claim that either schools are reluctant to provide the services and parents don't know their rights, or that the courts have limited the services to which the disabled are entitled. On the other hand, public education interest groups and many policymakers think of special education as a runaway train of exploding costs and limited accountability. These are sharply divergent views. The former holds, in essence, that there are too few students on the special education rolls. The latter seems to imply that there are too many. And there is strong evidence supporting both sides. On the one hand, class-action lawsuits against urban districts such as Baltimore, New York, Chicago, and Washington, D.C., have uncovered thousands of students who never received the services they were entitled to. On the other hand, the weight of the evidence from federal studies of reading disabilities shows that many children would have avoided remaining on the special education rolls if their problems had been diagnosed and dealt with earlier.

What everyone seems to agree on is the need for the federal government to satisfy its 40 percent promise. But it's not clear that this is a promise worth keeping. In a world of limited funds for education, should the federal government devote more of its resources to educating the disabled than it devotes to educating the poor? At 40 percent of national special education spending, the federal commitment to special education would far exceed its current commitment to the Title I program. Washington has played an important role in ameliorating disparities in wealth among the states; the Title I program is far more targeted to poor areas and children than is spending under the IDEA. We might want the federal government to fully fund both programs, but in the near future they'll continue to compete for resources with one another and with other funding priorities. And it's fair to say, in this case, that the poor don't have much of a lobby, at least compared to the well-organized and powerful coalition of parents and advocates for the disabled. It is important, also, to recall that the IDEA is a civil rights law first, and a grants program second. Before passage of the IDEA, federal courts were already requiring schools to meet their constitutional obligations to serve all disabled students. Spending under the IDEA is intended to help them do so.

Conventional wisdom also seems to hold that special education needs to become more results-oriented. Put aside the troubles inherent in designing a workable and efficient accountability system that is to be applied to a population as diverse in their needs and abilities as disabled students. A more pressing issue is the risk of a further cost explosion when lawmakers call for a higher standard of performance in special education. The broader standards movement has already given ammunition to a wave of litigation claiming that the schools need more resources to meet the higher standards set by legislatures. In the hyper-legalized world of special education, where each child holds a legally enforceable right to a certain standard of education, subtle changes in the law can dramatically change the obligations of school districts. Parents and advocacy groups could use the new focus on results to claim that Congress has now set a standard higher than the "educational benefit" standard the Supreme Court elucidated in *Rowley*. Courts could agree and begin awarding an increasingly expensive set of services to disabled children who aren't meeting the higher standards set by Congress. For almost 20 years courts have used the *Rowley* decision to limit the range of expensive interventions available to disabled students. At a time of great concern over the costs of special education, is *Rowley* a decision policymakers wish to nullify?

[1] 119 S.Ct. 992 (1999).

[2] M.T. Moore, E.W. Strang, M. Schwartz, and M. Braddock, *Patterns in Special Education Service Delivery and Cost* (Washington, DC: Decisions Resources Corporation, December 1988).

[3] See J.S. Kakalik, W.S. Furry, M.A. Thomas, and M.F. Carney, *The Cost of Special Education* (Santa Monica, CA: The Rand Corporation, 1981).

[4] Thomas B. Parrish and Jean Wolman, "Trends and New Developments in Special Education Funding: What the States Report," in *Funding Special Education,* eds. Thomas B. Parrish, Jay G. Chambers, and Cassandra M. Guarino (Thousand Oaks, CA: Corwin Press, 1999), 203-229.

[5] Richard Lee Colvin and Duke Helfand, "Special Education in State Is Failing on Many Fronts," *Los Angeles Times* (December 12, 1999), sec. A, p. 1.

[6] 347 U.S. 483 (1954).

[7] See Gerald Coles, *The Learning Mystique: A Critical Look at "Learning Disabilities"* (New York: Fawcett Columbine, 1987).

[8] 274 U.S. 200 at 207 (1926), as cited in Thomas Hehir and Sue Gamm, "Special Education: From Legalism to Collaboration," in *Law and School Reform,* ed. Jay P. Heubert (New Haven: Yale University Press, 1999), 210.

[9] 47 Ohio Appendix 417, 191 N.E. 914 at 914-15 (1934), as cited in Hehir and Gamm, "Special Education, at 240.

[10] See Rebecca Weber Goldman, Comment, "A Free Appropriate Education in the Least Restrictive Environment: Promises Made, Promises Broken by the Individuals with abilities Education Act," 20 *U. Dayton L. Rev.* 243, 246-47 (1994).

[11] See Mark C. Weber, "The Transformation of the Education of the Handicapped Act: A Study in the Interpretation of Radical Statutes," 24 *U.C. Davis L. Rev.* 350, 356 (1990).

[12] 343 F. Supp. 279 (E.D. Pa. 1972).

[13] 348 F. Supp. 866 (D.D.C. 1972).

[14] Ibid. at 876.

[15] P.L. 93-112 (1973), 29 U.S.C.A. §§ 701-796 (1996).

[16] Paul T. Hill and Doren L. Madey, *Educational Policymaking through the Civil Justice System* (Santa Monica, CA:

The Rand Corporation, 1982).

17 See Mark Kelman and Gillian Lester, *Jumping the Queue: An Inquiry into the Legal Treatment of Students with Learning abilities* (Cambridge, MA: Harvard University Press, 1997), 234 n. 14.

18 Ibid. at 38.

19 Ibid. at 112-15.

20 Jane K. Babin, Comment, "Adequate Special Education: Do California Schools Meet the Test?" 37 *San Diego L. Rev.* 211, 220 (2000).

21 See Kelman and Lester, *Jumping the Queue*, 10.

22 See Kenneth A. Kavale and Steven R. Fortness, "What Definitions of Learning Disability Say and Don't Say," *Journal of Learning abilities*, 33, no. 3 (2000), 239.

23 458 U.S. 176 (1982).

24 483 F. Supp. 528, 534 (S.D.N.Y. 1980).

25 See generally Weber, "The Transformation of the Education of the Handicapped Act."

26 458 U.S. 176, at 198.

27 Ibid. at 207.

28 Ibid. at 206.

29 Bonnie Tucker, "*Board of Education of the Hendrick Hudson Central School district v. Rowley*: Utter Chaos," 12 *Journal of Law & Education* 235, 235 (1983).

30 862 F.2d 884, 886 (D.C. Cir. 1988).

31 9 F.3d 455, at 459-460 (6th Cir. 1993).

32 135 F.3d 566 (8th Cir. 1998).

33 See Babin, "Adequate Special Education," 229.

34 458 U.S. 176, 199-200.

35 Ibid. at 192.

36 950 F.2d 688, at 697 (11th Cir. 1991).

37 Kelman and Lester, *Jumping the Queue*, 56.

38 874 F.2d 1036 (5th Cir. 1989).

39 Ibid. at 1051.

40 995 F.2d 1204 (3rd Cir. 1993).

41 35 F.3d 1396 (9th Cir. 1994).

42 468 U.S. 883 (1984).

43 See, e.g., *Neely v. Rutherford County School*, 68 F.3d 965 (1995), *cert. denied*, 116 S.Ct. 1413 (holding that a child whose breathing tube required regular suctioning was not entitled to full-time nursing services because of the risk and potential liability involved in providing such care); *Detsel v. Board of Education of Auburn Enlarged City School District*, 820 F.2d 587 (1987), *cert. denied*, 108 S.Ct. 495 (holding that a child who required constant respirator assistance was not entitled to full-time nursing services because of the burdensome costs and because it required a health professional with skills beyond those of a school nurse).

44 119 S.Ct. 992 (1999).

45 See generally Weber, "The Transformation of the Education of Handicapped Act."

46 See *Devries v. Fairfax County Sch. Bd.*, 882 F.2d 876 (4th Cir. 1989).

47 700 F.2d 1058 (6th Cir. 1983).

48 874 F.2d. 1036, at 1046 (5th Cir. 1989).

49 Hill and Madey, *Educational Policymaking Through the Civil Justice System*, 20.

50 National Council on Disability, *Back to School on Civil Rights* (Washington, DC: National Council on Disability, 2000).

51 Hehir and Gamm, "Special Education," 215.

52 Kelman and Lester, *Jumping the Queue*, 68-74.

53 See *Honig v. Doe*, 484 U.S. 305 (1988).

54 U.S. Department of Education, *Twenty-first Annual Report to Congress on the Implementation of the Individuals with Disabilities Education Act* (Washington, DC: U.S. Department of Education, 1999), IV-9.

Chapter 2

Time to Make Special Education "Special" Again

Wade F. Horn and Douglas Tynan

Introduction

Prior to the 1950's, the federal government was not routinely involved in the education of children with special needs. A few federal laws had been passed providing direct educational benefits to persons with disabilities, mostly in the form of grants to states for residential asylums for the "deaf and dumb," and "to promote education of the blind." These laws, however, were in the tradition of providing residential arrangements for persons with serious disabilities, services that had existed since colonial times.

Without applicable federal law, how—and even whether—children with disabilities were to be educated within the public schools was left to the discretion of states and their local school districts. Although some public schools undoubtedly provided exceptional services to children with disabilities, others did not. Indeed, as recently as 1973, perhaps as many as one million students were denied enrollment in public schools solely on the basis of their disability.[1]

> **The IDEA has been largely successful in opening up educational opportunities for children with disabilities. Unfortunately, the IDEA also has had some unintended negative consequences.**

This state of affairs changed dramatically in 1975 with passage of the Education of All Handicapped Children Act (EAHCA). Renamed the Individuals with Disabilities Education Act (IDEA) in 1990, this landmark legislation mandated that children with disabilities must receive a "free appropriate public education" (FAPE) in the "least restrictive environment" (LRE). Critical components of the law include requirements for an initial evaluation to determine eligibility for services and accommodations, individual education planning, the provision of individualized services, and procedural safeguards to ensure the active involvement of a child's parents.

The IDEA has been largely successful in opening up educational opportunities for children with disabilities. Unfortunately, the IDEA also has had some unintended negative consequences. These include the creation of incentives to define an ever-increasing percentage of school-aged children as having disabilities, an enormous redirection of financial resources from regular education to special education, and, perhaps most importantly, the application of an accommodation philosophy to populations better served with prevention or intervention strategies.

Background

In the first half of the 20th century, the federal government's involvement in education was minimal. Special education services in particular were limited to providing states with funds to help establish and run residential facilities for persons with serious disabilities.[2] With the passage of the National Defense Education Act (NDEA) of 1958, the federal government began to play a greater role in elementary and secondary education. Congress also began to provide support to universities to train leadership personnel in developing programs for children with mental retardation. In 1963, Congress expanded these efforts to include grants to train teachers and researchers in a wide range of disabilities. With the passage of these two pieces of legislation, the federal government began to encourage, but not require, the inclusion of children with disabilities in the public school setting.[3]

Absent such a federal mandate, no state had yet developed a comprehensive program for all children with disabilities. Although by 1973 some 45 states had passed laws providing for the education of children with disabilities, these were not inclusive, and many children continued to be shut out of American schools. Moreover, although school attendance was required for all children, individual children could be excused from that requirement by being classified as "uneducable" by their local school district. Many states did, in fact, turn children away. Many other children were inappropriately placed. Children who had average academic ability combined with physical handicaps, for example, were often placed in classes for children with mental retardation.

> *In the early 1970s, the federal courts, in response to litigation brought by parents of children with disabilities, began to rule that schools owed students equal protection under the law and could not discriminate against individual students on the basis of disability.*

In the early 1970s, the federal courts, in response to litigation brought by parents of children with disabilities, began to rule that schools owed students equal protection under the law and could not discriminate against individual students on the basis of disability. In the landmark 1971 case of *Pennsylvania Association for Retarded Citizens v. Commonwealth of Pennsylvania*, a group of mentally retarded children had been denied access to school because they had not attained a mental age of five years as required by state law for school entry. The court ruled that school entry could not be denied to these children based upon mental incapacity but did not specify how such children should be educated once in school.

A year later in *Mills v. Board of Education of the District of Columbia*, the court ruled that school districts could not refuse to provide educational services to children with disabilities because of inadequate financial resources. Rather, the court asserted, schools were required to provide an appropriate educational experience for students with disabilities regardless of the costs involved, a legal principle later included in federal special education legislation.[4] As a result of these and other court rulings, pressure was mounting on the Congress to pass legislation clarifying schools' role in the provision of special education services and accommodations for students with disabilities.

In 1973, Congress responded by passing the Rehabilitation Act, which stated, in part, that agencies accepting federal funds, including local schools, could not discriminate on the basis of disability. In essence, this meant that all children, including those with special needs, had a right to attend school. However, neither funding nor a process for monitoring compliance was included in the Act.

Subsequently, in 1975, Congress passed the EAHCA, requiring that all children must receive a free appropriate public education. Now renamed the IDEA, this landmark federal legislation included requirements for individual evaluation, eligibility determination, individual education planning, and the provision of individualized services.

It also authorized the amount of funding the federal government would contribute to special education based upon a percentage of the national average per-pupil expenditure (APPE) for all educational services provided to special education pupils. Specifically, the EAHCA authorized Congress to appropriate a sum equal to 5 percent of APPE in 1977, 10 percent in 1978, 20 percent in 1979, and 40 percent in 1980 and beyond. The actual level of funding appropriated by Congress, however, never exceeded 12.5 percent of the national APPE. Recently, bipartisan support has emerged in Congress to fully fund the IDEA, although the necessary financial resources have not yet been dedicated to accomplish this goal.

As required by the IDEA and its implementing regulations,[5] the special education system is predicated upon first classifying students into one or more federally defined disability categories. Once classified, students are then provided special education services and accommodations.

> **Recently, bipartisan support has emerged in Congress to fully fund the IDEA, although the necessary financial resources have not yet been dedicated to accomplish this goal.**

Either parents or teachers can refer a child for an initial screening. This involves a team comprised of the child's parents, his or her classroom teacher, a school administrator, and an education specialist.

In this initial meeting, available standardized test scores and classroom performance are reviewed. If this screening suggests a significant problem, the team may refer the child for a comprehensive multi-disciplinary evaluation. Such an evaluation typically includes testing by an educator as well as a psychologist, and may also involve evaluations by specialists in speech and language, occupational therapy, and physical therapy. At a follow-up team meeting, reports from the various specialists are reviewed to determine whether the child meets the classification criteria in any of the 13 mandated special education categories.[6] If so, an individualized education program, or IEP, is developed reflecting, at least in theory, each child's unique educational needs.

Those children who do not meet the district's criteria for eligibility do not have to receive special education services or accommodations, even though they were initially referred because of school difficulty. As a result of this process, two distinct classes of students experiencing academic difficulty emerge: those classified as disabled who receive special education assistance, and those not classified who do not.

Between states there are differing systems for carrying out the federal mandate to identify, classify, and provide services for children with disabilities. Within states, and between school systems, there exists enormous variability regarding which students are found to be eligible for special education services. Generally, in wealthier suburban districts where parents have ready access to attorneys, advocates, and outside specialists, most referred children do qualify and receive services. However, in inner cities or rural areas where parents have less access to advocates, children with disabilities are more likely to be refused special education services.

stats

> **Approximately 90 percent of special education students have been classified as having relatively mild disabilities, such as a specific learning disability, speech and language delays, mild mental retardation, or an emotional disorder.**

During the eligibility determination process, parents may elect to procure and pay for an independent evaluation which the school must consider, or the parent may appeal to a hearing officer for the school to pay for a second evaluation. Parents may also appeal and request a different set of services or accommodations than the one offered by the school. This is quite different from the usual process that occurs when the parent of a child in a regular education program makes a service request.[7]

Currently, more than 10 percent of all school children in grades K-12 are in the special education system. Of these, approximately 90 percent have been classified as having relatively mild disabilities, such as a specific learning disability, speech and language delays, mild mental retardation, or an emotional disorder. Students in these categories are typically identified after they have attended school for some period of time in a standard classroom. The remaining 10 percent of children in special education fall into categories reflecting a greater severity of disability, such as moderate to severe mental retardation, early infantile autism, sensory handicaps such as blindness or deafness, and severe physical and health impairments. Children with these latter disabilities typically are identified in infancy or during the preschool years and frequently require specialized assistance or nursing care in order to attend school.

Problems with the Current System

Although no one argues with the importance of providing a free appropriate public education for children with disabilities and few dispute the good it has done for so many disabled children, several problems have arisen since the passage of this landmark federal statute. These problems include an extraordinary growth in the percentage of children receiving special education; rapidly expanding costs of providing special education, often at the expense of regular education; and the application of an accommodation strategy to populations better served with a prevention or intervention model.

Table 1: Number & Percentage of Children Served Under the IDEA, Part B, Ages 3-21

School Year	Total No. of Children Served	Percentage Change in No. Served From Previous Year	Percentage of Children Served Under the IDEA, Part B *
1976-77	3,708,601	**	**
1977-78	3,777,286	1.8	**
1978-79	3,919,073	3.8	**
1979-80	4,036,219	3.0	5.7
1980-81	4,177,689	3.5	5.9
1981-82	4,233,282	1.3	6.0
1982-83	4,298,327	1.5	6.2
1983-84	4,341,399	1.0	6.3
1984-85	4,363,031	0.5	6.4
1985-86	4,370,244	0.2	6.4
1986-87	4,421,601	1.2	6.5
1987-88	4,485,702	1.4	6.6
1988-89	4,568,063	1.8	6.8
1989-90	4,675,619	2.4	6.9
1990-91	4,807,441	2.8	7.0
1991-92	4,986,043	3.7	7.2
1992-93	5,155,950	3.4	7.4
1993-94	5,373,077	4.2	7.66
1994-95	5,430,223	3.5	7.7
1995-96	5,627,544	3.6	7.83
1996-97	5,787,893	2.8	7.96
1997-98	5,972,341	3.2	8.11
1998-99	6,114,803	2.3	8.3
1999-2000	6,125,833	0.2	8.2

Percentage Change in Total No. of Children Served	
1980-81 to 1989-90	11.9
1990-91 to 1999-2000	27.4
1976-77 to 1999-2000	65.0

Sources: U.S. Department of Education, Office of Special Education Programs (OSEP), *21st Annual Report to Congress on the Implementation of the Individuals with Disabilities Education Act* (Washington, DC: U.S. Department of Education, 1999), Tables AA1 (1995-99) and 1.3 (1995); also earlier reports and updated tables.

* Calculated based on data from U.S. Census Bureau, Current Population Reports, P25-1095, *Statistical Abstract of the United States: 1999*, Table 14. Percentages to two decimal places are official figures taken from the OSEP's *Annual Reports to Congress*.

Growth in Special Education

In 1999-2000, 6.1 million children ages 3-21 years were found eligible for special education services and accommodations, up from 3.7 million in 1976-77— an increase of 65 percent. (See Table 1.) The increasing number of children in special education is a function not only of the increase in overall student population, but also of growth in the proportion of students determined to need special education. Specifically, 12.8 percent of the student population in grades K-12 were receiving special education services and accommodations in 1997-1998, compared to 8.3 percent of the student population in 1976-77.[8]

There are several reasons why both the number and percentage of children identified as qualifying for special education under the IDEA have grown so rapidly over the past several decades. First, since passage of the EAHCA, both Congress and the U.S. Department of Education have responded to pressure from advocacy groups by expanding the definition of students eligible for special education. For example, children ages three to five are now eligible for services under the IDEA, as are children with autism and traumatic brain injuries. Furthermore, autism, once defined as a rare disorder affecting about 6 per 10,000 children, is now considered more common and children with mild autism, known as Asperger Disorder, are thought to number between 25 and 50 per 10,000 children.[9]

> *In contrast to an extraordinary 233 percent growth since 1976-77 in the number of children diagnosed with SLDs, the number of children served in all other disability categories combined increased only 13 percent during the same time period.*

Even more significantly, in 1991 the U.S. Department of Education issued a "policy clarification" indicating that children diagnosed with attention deficit disorder (ADD) and attention deficit hyperactivity disorder (ADHD) may be eligible for special education services and accommodations under both the "other health impaired" category of the IDEA and Section 504 of the Rehabilitation Act. On March 12, 1999, the U.S. Department of Education codified this policy clarification into law when it published regulations which, among other things, revised the definition of the "other health impaired" disability category by adding both ADD and ADHD as qualifying conditions. Given the extraordinary increase in the number of children diagnosed in recent years as having ADD or ADHD,[10] the inclusion of these two diagnoses under "other health impaired" virtually assures continued growth in the number of students served through special education into the foreseeable future.

Second, the number of children identified under a single category—"specific learning disability" or SLD—has increased exponentially over time. As shown in Table 2, 796,000 children in special education in 1976-77, or 22 percent of the total special education population, were identified as evidencing a specific learning disability. By 1997-98, that number had grown to 2,726,000, or 46 percent of the total number of students in special education. Indeed, in contrast to an extraordinary 233 percent growth since 1976-77 in the number of children diagnosed with SLDs, the number of children served in all other disability categories combined increased only 13 percent during the same time period.

Table 2: Children Ages 0 to 21 Years Old Served in Federally Supported Programs for the Disabled, by Type of Disability.

Disability Category (#s in thousands)	1976-77 Number Served	1976-77 Percent Served	1980-81 Number Served	1980-81 Percent Served	1985-86 Number Served	1985-86 Percent Served	1990-91 Number Served	1990-91 Percent Served	1995-96 Number Served	1995-96 Percent Served	1997-98 Number Served	1997-98 Percent Served
1. Specific Learning Disability	796	21.6%	1,462	35.3%	1,862	43.1%	2,130	44.7%	2,579	44.7%	2,726	46.2%
2. Speech or Language Impairments	1,302	35.3%	1,168	28.2%	1,125	26.1%	985	20.7%	1,022	18.3%	1,059	17.9%
3. Mental Retardation	959	26.0%	829	20.0%	660	15.3%	534	11.2%	570	10.2%	589	10.0%
4. Serious Emotional Disturbance	283	7.7%	346	8.4%	375	8.7%	390	8.2%	438	7.9%	453	7.7%
5. Hearing Impairments	87	2.4%	79	1.9%	66	1.5%	58	1.2%	67	1.2%	69	1.2%
6. Orthopedic Impairments	87	2.4%	58	1.4%	57	1.3%	49	1.0%	63	1.1%	67	1.1%
7. Other Health Impairments	141	3.8%	98	2.4%	57	1.3%	55	1.2%	133	2.4%	190	3.2%
8. Visual Impairments	38	1.0%	31	0.7%	27	0.6%	23	0.5%	25	0.4%	25	0.4%
9. Multiple Disabilities	n/a	n/a	68	1.6%	86	2.0%	96	2.0%	93	1.7%	106	1.8%
10. Deafness-Blindness	n/a	n/a	3	0.1%	2	<0.05%	1	0.0%	1	<0.05%	1	<0.05%
11. Autism and Other	n/a	n/a	n/a	n/a	n/a	n/a	n/a	n/a	39	0.7%	54	0.9%
12. Preschool Disabled	n/a	n/a	n/a	n/a	n/a	n/a	441	9.3%	544	9.8%	564	9.6%
TOTALS	3,692		4,142		4,317		4,761		5,573		5,904	

Sources: U.S. Department of Education, Office of Special Education and Rehabilitative Services, *Annual Report to Congress on the Implementation of the Individuals with Disabilities Education Act* (Washington, DC: U.S. Department of Education, various years); National Center for Education Statistics, *Digest of Education Statistics, 1999,* Table 53 (Washington, DC: U.S. Department of Education, 2000); and unpublished tabulations.

Unfortunately, the SLD category is rife with controversy. In the 1975 law, SLD was defined as "a disorder in one or more of the basic psychological processes involved in understanding or in using language, spoken or written, which may manifest itself in an imperfect ability to listen, think, speak, read, write, spell, or do mathematical calculations," manifesting in a "severe discrepancy" between a student's achievement in one or more subject areas and his or her intelligence, as usually measured by an IQ test. This federal definition notwithstanding, there are no universally accepted validated tests or diagnostic criteria to determine the presence or absence of learning disabilities, nor is there a clear line of demarcation between students who have milder forms of SLDs and those who do not have SLDs.[11]

According to many experts, the lack of a clear definition of and objective diagnostic criteria for SLD makes it possible to diagnose almost any low- or under-achieving child as SLD. Indeed, Dr. James Ysseldyke, director of the National Center on Educational Outcomes at the University of Minnesota, asserts that over 80 percent of all school children in the United States could qualify as SLD under one definition or another.[12]

A third reason for the extraordinary growth in special education is the suspicion that some school districts place non-disabled but low-achieving students into special education classes in order to obtain state and federal funds that are available only after a child is identified as disabled under the IDEA. Although it is unlikely that children without any learning difficulties are being placed in special education, not every low-achieving child is also disabled. However, when services are provided to low-achieving but non-disabled students in regular education, local school districts cannot claim reimbursement for the cost of these services even if they are exactly the same as services provided to students with disabilities. This funding structure provides enormous financial incentives for local school districts to over-identify low-achieving but non-disabled students as needing special education.[13]

The incentive to over-identify low-achieving children as disabled may be especially powerful in schools serving low-income populations. In cases where a child is under-achieving at school because of economic disadvantage, compensatory educational programs are supposed to be funded through Title I of the Elementary and Secondary Education Act (ESEA), not through the IDEA.[14] Indeed, economic disadvantage as a reason for under- or low-achievement is an explicit exclusionary criterion under the IDEA. However, because IDEA funds do not substitute for funding under Title I, students in low-income school districts who are also identified as disabled are effectively "double counted"—once for purposes of drawing down funds under Title I and a second time for purposes of reimbursement for special education services under the IDEA. In essence, low-income, low-achieving students can be "two-fers" when it comes to maximizing the procurement of federal and state funds. (See Box 1.)

> **The incentive to over-identify low-achieving children as disabled may be especially powerful in schools serving low-income populations.**

A fourth reason for the growth in special education may be recent education reform efforts aimed at holding schools more accountable for student outcomes. Until recently, students identified as receiving services under special education were not generally required to participate in statewide assessments.[15] Given that merit raises, promotions, and bonuses for both principals and teachers often ride on the results of statewide exams, the temptation exists for local school districts to raise their scores artificially by excluding the participation of low-achieving, special education students in statewide assessments. Although the 1997 amendments to the IDEA were intended to prohibit this practice, three states that recently enjoyed large gains on national reading tests (Kentucky, Louisiana, and South Carolina) also evidenced large increases in the percentage of special education students excluded from taking the tests.[16]

A final reason for the growth in the number of children in special education comes from a surprising source: parents themselves. Not long ago, being in special education carried with it a certain amount of social stigma. Today, due in large part to the success of disability advocacy groups, there is much less stigma attached to special education. Indeed, what special education brings with it today is the possibility of such attractive accommodations and special programs as the assistance of a personal tutor, a lap-top computer, extra or even unlimited time on classroom tests and college entrance exams, a personal note taker, and immunity from severe discipline when the student violates behavior codes because of his or her disability.

The fact that being found eligible for special education brings with it entitlement to an array of often expensive services and accommodations may help explain why nearly one in three high school students is officially designated as disabled in affluent Greenwich, Connecticut.[17] It may also explain why clinicians in affluent communities frequently report an upsurge in parental requests for diagnostic evaluations, especially for SLDs and ADD, of high school juniors—just as high school students are preparing to take college entrance exams such as the SAT and ACT. Indeed, while children from families with more than $100,000 in annual income account for just 13 percent of the SAT test-taking population, they make up 27 percent of those who receive special accommodations when taking the SAT.[18]

In addition, an entire industry of professionals and paraprofessionals has arisen dedicated to identifying learning disabilities and assisting parents in obtaining mandated services. Educators and psychologists who provide private testing, attorneys who specialize in special education law, and parent advocates who help families negotiate the maze of special education services all thrive in affluent communities and are frequently the most forceful advocates for special education placement and accommodations.

Box 1: The Low-IQ, Low-Achieving Student

Most regular and special education administrators recognize that one type of child is inadequately served by both systems: the child with a low IQ score, but not low enough to qualify him as mentally retarded. By the sixth grade, these children are often two to three years behind their peers academically and cannot keep up with the more complex work of middle and high school. However, they do not meet the criteria for a learning disability classification, which requires that there be a significant discrepancy between achievement and intellectual ability, because both their IQ and achievement scores are low.

With luck, these students are passed on until they can be admitted to a high school-level vocational education program, where they often thrive for the first time in their academic careers. Some schools bend the classification rules and label these children as learning disabled or mentally retarded and, in doing so, create a reasonably successful program for them by combining traditional special education services with vocational training. Others are not so lucky. After repeated school failure and perhaps several grade retentions, they often choose to drop out of school as soon as it is legally permissible.

Source: W. Douglas Tynan and Roberta Latsha, "Minutes from Quarterly Joint Meeting on Coordination of Services of Central Susquehanna Special Educators and the Department of Pediatrics, Geisinger Medical Center, Danville, PA" (November, 1999).

Increasing Costs of Special Education

A second, and related, unintended consequence of the IDEA is the skyrocketing cost of special education, often at the expense of regular education. (See Table 3.) According to the National School Boards Association, the per-pupil cost of special education is 2.1 times the cost of regular education. Considering that the average per-pupil expenditure in the United States is about $6,200, the average cost for students in special education is $6,200 x 2.1, or approximately $13,000 annually.[19] Hence, the average excess cost of special education (the amount spent over and above the $6,200 spent in regular education) is about $6,800 per

Table 3: IDEA, Part B, Section 611 Grants to States Program: Funds Appropriated (1977-2000)

Appropriation Year	IDEA, Part B Section 611 Grants to States	Per Child Allocation
1977	$251,770,000	$71
1978	566,030,000	156
1979	804,000,000	215
1980	874,500,000	227
1981	874,500,000	219
1982	931,008,000	230
1983	1,017,900,000	248
1984	1,068,875,000	258
1985	1,135,145,000	272
1986	1,163,282,000	279
1987	1,338,000,000	316
1988	1,431,737,000	332
1989	1,475,449,000	336
1990	1,542,610,000	343
1991	1,854,186,000	400
1992	1,976,095,000	410
1993	2,052,728,000	411
1994	2,149,686,000	413
1995	2,322,915,000	418
1996	2,323,837,000	413
1997	3,790,213,633	535
1998	4,293,796,632	544
1999	4,310,700,000	545
2000	4,989,000,000	624

Sources: U.S. Department of Education, Office of Special Education Programs, *Twentieth Annual Report to Congress on the Implementation of the Individuals with Disabilities Education Act* (Washington, DC: U.S. Department of Education, 1998), Table III-2, p. III-43, and updated data; also information from Data Analysis Systems (DANS) and the Office of the Under Secretary, U.S. Department of Education.

pupil. Because the IDEA covers 6.1 million children ages 3-21 years, the total cost of special education for these children is $79.3 billion, which is $41.5 billion more than the cost of regular education for this group of children.

Under the IDEA, the federal government is supposed to pay 40 percent of the costs of special education. In reality, federal funding has never exceeded 12.5 percent of the costs of special education.[20] Today, Washington provides well over $5 billion in total funding to local school districts, or about 12 percent of the costs of special education. On average, states pay 56 percent of the costs, with a range of 11 percent to 95 percent.[21] The remaining 32 percent is paid for by local school districts. Thus, the IDEA is perhaps the largest unfunded federal mandate for education ever placed on state and local government.

Making matters worse, because special education, unlike regular education, is a federal mandate, schools can be sued for not providing services that parents think their child deserves once he or she is identified as in need of special education. This has led some school districts to spend extraordinary sums on special education placements, services, and accommodations in order to avoid even more costly lawsuits.[22]

Indeed, special education is now the largest categorical program in public schools. The District of Columbia, for example, spends almost a third of its total education budget on the 10 percent of its students who are in special education.[23] Overall, the Economic Policy Institute estimates that each year special education absorbs 38 cents of every new tax dollar raised for the public schools.[24]

> **For many in special education the goal can—and should—be independence rather than a lifetime dependence on special accommodations, often at taxpayers' expense.**

A particularly expensive result of qualifying a child for special education is the possibility that, in doing so, a public school may be obligating itself to pay for all or part of a child's private school tuition. In fact, public school districts today pay for the private school tuition of more than 100,000 special education students at an estimated cost of $2 billion annually and part of the cost of private school for an additional 66,000 special education students.[25] An extreme example of this is the case of one southern California school district that reportedly pays for a severely brain-injured boy to attend a specialized school in Massachusetts, flying his parents and sister out for regular visits, at a total annual cost of $254,000.[26]

The problem with escalating costs is that they may lead to a weakening of public support for special education. As ever-increasing numbers of children are determined eligible for ever more expensive special education placements, services, and accommodations, there may be a gradual erosion in the public's confidence in the entire special education system. Indeed, a recent Phi Delta Kappa/Gallup poll found that 65 percent of parents say that the extra attention paid by instructors and classroom assistants to disabled students comes at the expense of their own children.[27]

Training for a Lifetime of Entitlement

A third major problem with special education today is the application of an accommodation model to low- and under-achieving students who may benefit more from prevention, intervention, and compensatory strategies. When initially passed in 1975, the EAHCA was largely intended to ensure that students with significant physical and sensory disabilities were not denied a free appropriate public education. For these students, the appropriate intervention was, and remains, the provision of special accommodations such as access ramps for those using wheelchairs, books written in Braille for the blind, and sign language interpreters for the deaf to make public education accessible. There was no expectation that special education would, by itself, ameliorate the physical or sensory handicap, thereby making these special accommodations no longer necessary. It would be ludicrous, for example, to argue that a goal of special education ought to be to make deaf students hear or blind students see.

There are, however, certain subgroups of students with disabilities for which it is reasonable to expect that special education will help them overcome or compensate for their handicapping condition so that they no longer need special services or accommodations. Special education should, for example, work to ameliorate emotional and behavior disorders, so that students with these disorders no longer need alternative placements. Similarly, when working with students with SLDs, ADD, and ADHD, the goal should be to help these children learn self-directed compensatory strategies so that they can succeed without the aid of special services or accommodations. In other words, for many in special education the goal can—and should—be independence rather than a lifetime dependence on special accommodations, often at taxpayers' expense.

> *Little attention is paid by federal accountability systems to whether students in special education are advancing in core subjects or acquiring the skills necessary for making special education and accommodations no longer necessary.*

Unfortunately, special education has largely failed to help most special education students achieve such independence. Instead, most children determined to be in need of special education under the IDEA can expect to receive special education services and accommodations until they leave school. In fact, according to data collected in 1993 by the Department of Education from 16 states, only 1 to 12 percent of special education students over the age of 14 years are declassified each year.[28] Other developments, such as accommodations provided under the Americans with Disabilities Act, surely reinforce the tendency toward permanent accommodations for disabilities, even those that can be remediated.

A focus on process not outcomes. Contributing further to this problem is the fact that accountability within federal and state systems focuses on due process requirements and fiscal management rather than educational outcomes. Hence, local schools are told they are "doing it right" if they provide appropriate eligibility assessments, hold timely IEP meetings, provide parents with appropriate procedural safeguards, and draw down funds appropriately. Little attention is paid by federal accountability systems to whether students in special education are advancing in core subjects or acquiring the skills necessary for making special education and accommodations no longer necessary.

There is even a question as to whether many of the accommodations typically provided to special education students are doing what proponents advocate. For an accommodation to be useful, it should demonstrate "differential advantage" for special education students. That is, the accommodation, whether it be giving extended time to complete a test, allowing students to have the instructions and test questions read aloud to them, or providing large print or Braille forms of the test, should improve the scores of students with disabilities above and beyond improvements that students without disabilities might achieve if they were provided with the same accommodation.

We know, for example, that the use of large print does give a differential advantage to students with vision impairment. That is, if students with vision impairment and those without take the same large-print test, scores are comparable. If they take a standard small-print test, those with vision impairment do worse. The purpose of providing an accommodation is not simply to raise test scores, but to level the playing field so that students with and without disabilities have an equal opportunity to demonstrate their skills and knowledge.

Unfortunately, some accommodations routinely provided to special education students have not demonstrated such differential advantage. Take, for example, the provision of extra time to take tests. According to research by Lynn Fuchs and her colleagues at Vanderbilt University, giving more time on conventional math and reading tests does not help grade-school students with learning disabilities any more than it does non-learning disabled students, although it may provide a differential advantage on more complicated math tests that require extensive reading and writing.[29] Moreover, although studies by the College Board have found that providing extended time on the SATs increases the scores of students with learning disabilities by an average of 45 points on verbal and 38 points on math, no studies have yet been done to determine whether giving more time on the SATs satisfies the requirement for differential advantage.[30]

> **What the provision of special accommodations does seem to accomplish is teaching students in special education that they are entitled to operate under a different set of rules than everyone else.**

Another way to determine whether an accommodation is appropriate is to examine its effects on the test's predictive validity: for example, the extent to which an accommodation enhances or reduces the ability of the test either to predict an outcome or to measure the underlying ability it was designed to measure. One danger in providing accommodations to special education students is that in so doing the test may no longer validly assess the ability or skill it was designed to measure or predict the outcome it was designed to predict.[31] This seems to be the case for at least some accommodations routinely provided to special education students. Research has generally found, for example, that giving students with learning disabilities extra time on the SAT tends to predict greater college success than these students actually achieve.[32]

Two sets of rules. What the provision of special accommodations does seem to accomplish is teaching students in special education that they are entitled to operate under a different set of rules than everyone else. Nowhere is this more evident than in how school disciplinary rules are differentially applied to students in special education compared to those in regular education.

According to the "stay put" provisions of the IDEA, once placement in special education has begun it can only be changed by a child's IEP committee. If the student's parents do not consent to a change in placement and request a hearing, the student must "stay put" in the current placement until the hearing process is concluded. Suspensions that last longer than 10 days (or have the cumulative impact of more than 10 days) and expulsions are both considered changes in placement and hence are prohibited under the "stay put" provisions of the IDEA.

There are two exceptions to this. First, disciplinary sanctions of 10 days or less are not considered a change in placement and consequently are not subject to this restriction (although if the current suspension combined with earlier suspensions would total over 10 days, the student could not be suspended). Second, a school can propose disciplinary sanctions greater than 10 days or expulsions if it believes the misbehavior is not related to the disability. If, however, the parent disagrees and requests a hearing, the student must "stay put" in his or her current placement until the hearing is held.

The "stay put" provision can lead to a situation in which two students, one in regular education and the other in special education, both bring weapons or an illegal substance to school, yet only the student in regular education is suspended or expelled. It is true that a special education student can be suspended or expelled for weapons or drug violations if the behavior is unrelated to his or her disability. But it is very difficult to argue that such behavior is unrelated to a student's disability if, for example, that student was diagnosed with an emotional or behavioral disorder.

> *Many students with disabilities who have grown used to special accommodations in primary and secondary schools are confronted with a harsher reality when they enter college or the workforce.*

This situation is not merely hypothetical. Several years ago, a group of six Fairfax County, Virginia, students brought a .357 magnum handgun onto school property. Five of the students were expelled. The sixth was not. The reason? He was classified as "learning disabled" with a specific weakness in "written language skills." The special education student later bragged to teachers and students at the school that he was immune from expulsion.[33]

Unfortunately, this is not an isolated episode. In another case, also in Fairfax County, five gang members used a meat hook to assault another student. Only three of the perpetrators were expelled. The other two were special education students. When Virginia Governor George Allen tried to challenge the wisdom of using federal law to protect violent special education students, the Clinton administration threatened to pull millions of dollars in federal education dollars from the state.[34]

Due to these and other examples of problems arising from the "stay put" provision, in 1997 Congress passed amendments to the IDEA giving schools a little more latitude in disciplining violent special education students. For example, in situations involving a "substantial likelihood" of injury, a hearing officer may unilaterally place a student involved with weapons or drugs in an alternative educational setting. For this to occur, however, the school must show that it made reasonable efforts to minimize the risk of harm in the current placement, "including the use of supplementary aids and services." Furthermore, if the recommendation is expulsion, the IEP team must conduct a review to determine whether the misconduct was a manifestation of the child's disability. If so, no expulsion.

These qualifications continue to ensure that special education students will be treated differently in cases of serious violations of school rules compared to regular education students. Indeed, in April 1999, the National School Boards Association urged federal lawmakers to make further amendments to the IDEA to provide greater flexibility to suspend, expel, or reassign students whose misconduct jeopardizes safety or unreasonably disrupts classroom learning.[35]

Losing sight of the "end game." The end result of special education's focus on process rather than outcome, accommodations rather than prevention and intervention, and exceptions to disciplinary codes rather than uniform enforcement is encouragement for special education students to see their disability as rationale for a lifetime entitlement to special accommodations. Unfortunately, this expectation brings its own negative consequences. For example, although it is true that many colleges offer accommodations to students with disabilities under Section 504 of the Rehabilitation Act, the extensive supports of special education required under the IDEA generally do not apply to colleges and universities. Consequently, many students with disabilities who have grown used to special accommodations in primary and secondary schools are confronted with a harsher reality when they enter college or the workforce.

Take, for example, the case of *Bartlett v. New York Board of Law Examiners*. In this case, Marilyn Bartlett, a former special education student who had failed the New York bar exam several times, argued that she was entitled to unlimited time to take the bar exam because her reading disorder qualified her for special accommodations under the Americans with Disabilities Act. The U.S. Second Court of Appeals ruled that she was not entitled to unlimited time to take the bar exam because, as evidenced by the fact that her standardized reading test scores were in the average range, she had successfully compensated for her reading disability.[36]

What this and other cases illustrate (see Boxes 2 and 3) is that special education has largely lost sight of the appropriate "end game." Special education laws were originally intended to integrate children with special needs into the mainstream of American life. Today, however, special education in far too many instances serves to separate, not integrate, through the use of special rules and procedures not available to non-disabled students. In these instances, special education has ceased to see its mission as teaching compensatory and coping skills so that students are empowered to participate fully in the mainstream of American society, and instead it seems focused on encouraging a sense of lifetime entitlement to special accommodations.

As Robert Sternberg, IBM Professor of Education at Yale, has pointed out, we could decide to offer special accommodations throughout the student's life, but are we prepared to have professional note-takers for judges, attorneys, or physicians?[37] With the number of persons believed to have learning disabilities approaching 20 percent of the population, can society afford this canopy of protective services and accommodations? Even more importantly, by accommodating their weaknesses, we are ignoring their areas of intellectual strengths. As such, special education is training these students to work in fields that will be difficult for them rather than allowing them to discover the areas in which they may have special competence.

Box 2: Nicholas P. v. Andover Academy

A particularly illustrative example of the way special education encourages dependence, rather than independence, is the case of Nicholas P. and the Phillips Academy in Andover, Massachusetts. Nicholas had scored 1410 on the SAT and was a National Merit Scholarship finalist, both accomplished without any special accommodations during testings. But because Nicholas had been in therapy and on medication for ADHD since he was five, the school provided him with extra time on some tests and opted him out of its third-year foreign language course, among other special accommodations.

When Nicholas began to fail at school, Phillips Academy told him to remove his stereo, telephone, and computer games from his dorm room. Nicholas refused, and his grades continued to decline. When the faculty voted 168-2 to require him to withdraw from school, he sued. His attorneys argued in a federal district court that the fact that he has ADHD made it not only unfair, but also illegal, for Andover to flunk him out. The school defended itself in court papers asserting, "Allowing students to pick and choose only the portions of a syllabus he finds interesting enough to read, and hand in written assignments (or not) when it suits him, would fundamentally alter, not to mention lower, the Academy's stringent academic requirements."

U.S. District Judge Edward F. Harrington, who heard the case, eventually ruled that Nicholas' problem was not ADHD, but laziness. His ruling blamed "a willful lack of effort on [Panagopoulos'] part, invariably excused by a parent who indulged his lack of discipline and who failed to support the school in its efforts to assist him to do his work."

Source: "Americans with Bad Attitudes Act," The American Enterprise (May/June 1999): 10-11.

Ultimately, then, the true victims are the students themselves. By teaching special education students that there are two standards—one for them and one for everyone else—they are being encouraged to rely upon special accommodations rather than being challenged to achieve at high levels. In so doing, we run the risk of failing to integrate those with special needs into the mainstream of American life, as we shunt them off into a different room in which different rules apply and standards are forever lowered.

Recommendations for Reform

Reforming special education so that it is better targeted, more cost-efficient, and more effective in improving the educational outcomes of students with disabilities requires three things. First, policymakers should recognize that special education, as currently comprised, is really made up of three distinct subpopulations of students, each with very different educational needs. Second, change the funding structure for special education so that it rewards schools for improving the educational outcomes of students with disabilities and not just for identifying and serving them. Third, re-commit special education to helping students overcome their disabilities and to teaching coping and compensatory mechanisms,

Box 3: Elizabeth Guckenberger, et al. v. Boston University

This case also tested the limits of the special accommodations that colleges and universities are required to make in response to demands from students with disabilities. This case involved a class action suit brought against Boston University (BU) by a group of students identified as having ADHD, ADD, and various learning disabilities. The group made three claims against BU. First, the University was establishing unreasonable criteria by which students would qualify as disabled. Second, BU failed to provide reasonable procedures for reviewing student requests for accommodations. Third, BU prohibited across the board course substitutions in the area of foreign languages and mathematics (for students claiming disabilities in those areas).

Prior to 1995, BU was considered to be a leader in providing services to students with learning disabilities. For example, in brochures distributed to high schools, BU advertised the availability of such services as note-taking assistance and extended time on examinations. Course substitutions were also routinely allowed for mathematics and foreign language so that a course on the "Anthropology of Money" could be substituted for a mathematics course, or a foreign culture course could be substituted for a foreign language class. As a result, the number of entering students self-identified with learning disabilities rose from 42 in 1990 to 429 in 1995.

Following an internal review of these policies in 1995, Jon Westling, then provost of the university, changed the criteria for disability to include current evaluations (less than three years old) by a doctoral-level specialist (previously a letter from any therapist would suffice). Westling also implemented a review of all supporting materials and announced that course substitutions would no longer be available to students with disabilities. These announcements caused great upheaval within the student body and resulted in several staff resignations in the Learning Disability Program. Guckenberger, a law student with a well-documented reading disability who had been provided the note-taking, test-taking, and reduced semester credit-hour accommodations throughout her years at BU and who did graduate, nevertheless sued the University because of the emotional problems caused by this upheaval in the Learning Disability Program.

The court's ruling focused on three main points. First, the court ruled that whereas a master's-level evaluator could diagnose learning disabilities, BU could require that a doctoral-level provider make a diagnosis of ADD or ADHD. Second, it was unfair to require students like Guckenberger to go through policy changes after school entry without advance warning. Third, federal law does not require a university to modify its degree requirements by permitting course substitutions.

Although the University did have to pay some modest sums to the students involved, the message from the court was clear that, even though accommodations necessary to complete course work, such as note-taking services, could be required, course work and scholarship requirements for a degree did not have to be altered. In essence, the court limited the amount of special accommodations that colleges and universities are required to make in response to the requests of students with disabilities.

Sources: Robert J. Sternberg and Elena L. Grigorenko, *Our Labeled Children* (Reading, MA: Perseus Books, 1999); see also a series of articles on *Guckenberger v. Boston University* in the *Journal of Learning Disabilities* 32 (July/August 1999): 286-361.

whenever possible, rather than teaching such students to expect a lifetime of special accommodations and services.

Disentangling Special Education Sub-populations

The first step in special education reform is to recognize that the system currently serves three very distinct populations: (1) those with significant developmental disabilities and sensory and physical handicaps; (2) those with milder forms of neurological conditions, such as learning disabilities and ADD; and (3) those with conduct or behavioral problems.

Children with significant sensory, cognitive, and physical disabilities. The first group is comprised of students with a significant need for special education services and accommodations. This is the group for whom the original law was passed. These are children born with birth defects, serious sensory or physical disabilities, and significant cognitive delays. In the vast majority of such cases, these children will have been identified as disabled during infancy and preschool years, frequently by health-care professionals or early childhood education specialists, and they will already have begun receiving intervention services before they enter elementary school. For these children, there is no need for an elaborate identification process within the schools. Long before they enter kindergarten, we know who they are, and, to a large extent, we know their medical, rehabilitation, and educational needs.

> *Within a system of classification designed to define the educational needs of children rather than merely provide a diagnosis of disabilities, emphasis would be placed on monitoring the progress for each child in a realistic fashion.*

The key to educating these students is to fund adequately appropriate accommodations (for instance, interpreters for the deaf, curb cuts for those in wheelchairs, books written in Braille for the blind, and so forth), while including them to the maximum extent possible in the education mainstream. To a very large extent, this is what special education currently provides these students. Nevertheless, certain changes can—and should—be made to enable special education to more effectively and efficiently serve these students.

Although these students currently are placed in several different categories under the IDEA, and often are labeled "multi-handicapped," the official categories generally are not associated with different types of school placements. It is not unusual, for example, for a special education classroom at the elementary school level to include children categorized as autistic, speech and language delayed, and mentally retarded, all with the same teacher and classroom curriculum. Given the similarity in actual placement for these students, it would be more efficient to include them in one category, simply as children with significant special needs, rather than going through the current costly and time-consuming diagnostic and categorization process.[38]

Once a child is identified as having significant special needs, emphasis would then be placed on developing a functional curriculum for that child, including inclusion in the education mainstream to the maximum extent possible. Subcategories designed to help identify specific needs and for tracking purposes would be used as descriptors of each child's needs, rather than as a quasi-diagnostic tool. Thus, a child born blind and deaf and thought to be mentally retarded would be classified as a child with significant special needs, with the subcategories of blindness, deafness, and mental retardation. In this way, children with milder versions of a particular disorder (for example, mild autism or Asperger Disorder) who can function quite well in a standard classroom with minimal levels of assistance are not confused with those having a more severe form of the same disorder who may need high levels of service.

Within a system of classification designed to define the educational needs of children rather than merely provide a diagnosis of disabilities, emphasis would be placed on monitoring the progress of each child in a realistic fashion. A functional analysis of each child's needs would be completed, and realistic, achievable, and measurable goals would be set forth in each child's IEP. Given that many children with significant special needs will require special services and accommodations even into adulthood, the focus of special education curricula for these students would be the development of skills necessary for daily living and vocational training.[39] Schools would be held accountable for failures to progress in targeted areas of the curriculum. Thus, for example, in the case of an autistic child who cannot communicate and fails to improve after a year in school, that lack of progress would be a signal for the school to change the curriculum approach or an opportunity for the parents to change schools.

> **Some early reading specialists assert that reading disabilities are the result not so much of neurological dysfunction as of how most schools currently teach reading.**

A renewed emphasis on skill development may also affect where children receive their education. The 1997 amendments to the IDEA emphasized inclusion. Although this is often helpful, it should not be done at the expense of the child's overall progress. Thus, a deaf student in a small town that has difficulty hiring staff who are expert in sign language may be more appropriately served by attending a residential school for deaf children for at least some period of time during which the student can become fluent in sign language. In many handicapping conditions, particularly disabilities affecting language development, there is a sensitive period for the development of specific skills, a window of opportunity for skill development that should not be missed. Many children with significant disabilities would benefit from intensive work for one or two years in a separate program, followed by more intensive efforts toward inclusion.[40]

Although comprising fewer than ten percent of all children in the special education system and less than one percent of all children in school,[41] students with significant developmental disabilities and sensory and physical handicapping conditions do have very special needs and are more expensive to educate. Indeed, it is these children who 30 years ago were largely excluded from the public schools. The right of these students to have access to a free appropriate public education must be maintained under any change to the current structure of special education services and accommodations.

Children with neurological dysfunction. The second, and by far the largest, group of students currently in special education is comprised of those with mild forms of neurological dysfunction, such as mild mental retardation, learning disabilities, and ADD. The first question that needs to be addressed concerning this subgroup of special education students, especially given the emphasis under the 1997 IDEA amendments for inclusion of these students in the regular classroom, is what is so "special" about the special education they receive?

In many cases, the answer is not much, except for the fact that they are classified differently from their peers. In terms of the educational strategies most likely to enhance their educational outcomes, the majority of research finds that those strategies most effective with this group of students are the same strategies that are helpful to most students in regular education. This includes approaches such as frequent individualized monitoring and feedback, and intensive direct instruction. What this group of special education students needs is not so much different interventions but good teaching, albeit perhaps with greater consistency, intensity, and slower pacing than other students require.[42]

> *We should re-construct regular education so as to maintain students with relatively mild disabilities more effectively in the regular classroom.*

Thus, rather than perpetuating the myth that students with relatively mild disabilities are receiving a different kind of instruction compared to non-disabled students, we should re-construct regular education so as to maintain these students more effectively in the regular classroom. Indeed, Robert Sternberg and Elena Grigorenko of the Yale Child Study Center, as well as G. Reid Lyon of the National Institutes of Health, assert that reading disabilities, the most common form of learning disability, are the result not so much of neurological dysfunction as of how most schools currently teach reading. If all schools were to teach phonological awareness, sound-symbol relationships, and reading comprehension, and did so effectively and early, most reading problems could be avoided, say these early reading specialists. For those relatively few children who develop reading problems despite this approach, the regular education teacher could implement in-class interventions, perhaps with the assistance of a reading specialist. In this way, reading problems would come to be perceived as a regular education function, rather than being referred to special education programs.[43]

This approach is in marked contrast to the current system which emphasizes identification rather than intervention and has curiously little involvement by the classroom teacher. If, for example, a child is falling behind in reading, under the current system a referral is made for testing his or her reading level and establishing an estimate of his or her IQ. A psychologist and a reading specialist typically do this evaluation, not the teacher who teaches the child each day. From the start, the process is largely disengaged from what goes on in the classroom.

An alternative model would involve a functional analysis of reading done by the teacher, perhaps with the help of a psychologist and reading specialist. Instead of being concerned with documenting an IQ-achievement discrepancy score, time would be spent analyzing the particular reading problem. By reviewing actual classroom reading samples, supplemented by some additional testing materials, factors involved in the reading process such as motivation, phonemic processing, vocabulary level, reading rate, and the ability to self-correct errors could be assessed in far less time and with far less expense than the current system of formal educational and IQ testing.[44]

Under this model, the classroom teacher would remain responsible for the child's progress and would work along with reading specialists to construct in-classroom interventions to enhance the child's reading ability. If, for example, a child was found to have a poor reading vocabulary, an intervention would be designed to increase his or her vocabulary, with an assessment to be done six weeks later to determine the child's progress toward an expanded reading vocabulary. The emphasis in this model would be on helping the child develop, through active precision teaching, the skills and coping mechanisms necessary to achieve at higher levels in school. Progress would be gauged by regular academic outcome standards with the goal of empowering the student, not simply accommodating his or her disability.[45]

A similar approach could be used for children with ADD and ADHD. In a recently published large-scale treatment study of students with ADHD,[46] the best outcomes were found for those children who received a combination of relatively low doses of medication, a classroom behavior modification program, and behavioral family therapy to help parents better manage their child's home behavior. Rather than being taught to rely on medication to manage their symptoms, the children in the combination treatment were systematically taught, both at home and in school, the skills necessary to maintain behavioral control even in the absence of medication. These results suggest that students with ADD and ADHD would benefit more if schools would structure their environments more clearly, with obvious rules and boundaries and clear consequences for good and bad behavior, rather than relying on medication alone to enhance educational outcomes.

> *Effective treatment of behavioral disorders involves making these individuals strictly accountable for their behavior, insisting on compliance with requests and helping them learn to cope calmly with stressful situations.*

In such a revised setting, accommodations would be reviewed to make sure they are designed either to help the child develop compensatory skills or to allow the child to perform at a higher level. Thus, if we start by writing down homework assignments for a child who has difficulty remembering to write them himself, an appropriate education plan would include eventually having the child write down assignments himself. The goal of the curriculum, then, would be to teach compensatory skills, not an expectation for endless accommodations.

Children with behavioral problems. The third major sub-group of students currently receiving special education services and accommodations is comprised of those with conduct or behavioral problems. Students with these types of disorders, when seen in the mental health system, are usually diagnosed as having either oppositional defiant disorder or conduct disorder, characterized by refusals to comply with requests, emotional overreaction to stressful situations, and failure to take responsibility for their own actions.

Effective treatment of these disorders involves making these individuals strictly accountable for their behavior, insisting on compliance with requests and helping them learn to cope calmly with stressful situations.[47] Unfortunately, once these students are identified as in need of special education, many of the accommodations routinely provided them—and most especially a lowered standard of acceptable behavior—actually work to undermine these desirable goals. This sets up these students for later failure as they frequently come to expect the same kinds of accommodations outside the school as well. Unfortunately for these students, systems external to the school, such as the criminal justice system and the job market, are far less accommodating to disruptive and non-compliant behavior.

An alternative approach would be to develop school- and system-wide interventions designed to reduce these problems overall, rather than classifying and then segregating individual students. For example, in a series of interventions carried out by the May Institute in New England, considerable improvement in behavior and reduction in behavior-related referrals for special education were achieved efficiently and economically. In one city, a school-wide program to reinforce compliance with rules resulted in a 40 percent drop in detentions. In a second, the need for special education placements was reduced almost three-fold after implementation of a positive reinforcement program for rules compliance at a cost of less than $10 per year per child. A third school-wide intervention resulted in a 30 percent reduction in disciplinary referrals to the principal after a program incorporating positive reinforcement for compliance plus close monitoring of behavior was implemented at a cost of only $30 per elementary school student.[48]

> *In constructing a voucher program for special education, it must be recognized that students with disabilities usually are more expensive to educate than students without special needs.*

For those students who persist in defying rules despite such interventions, it is questionable whether they should be included within the framework of special education at all. It is a fine line between a psychiatric disorder that can be treated and criminal behavior that should be adjudicated, and the distinction is even more difficult in the high school years.

Reforming Special Education Funding

Currently, schools draw down special education funds based on the number of students identified as having a qualifying disability under the IDEA. As noted earlier, this creates an incentive to identify low-achieving students. If the current system resulted in substantial improvements in educational outcomes for these students, there would be no necessity for reform. But evidence is mixed at best as to whether student performance is enhanced once they are placed in special education.[49]

One reform being advocated by some is a move to census-based funding for special education. Under such a scheme, funding for special education would be based not on the number of children identified as in need of special education, but on total student enrollment. Census-based funding has the advantage of providing schools with the flexibility to set up schoolwide interventions. (Although the 1997 amendments to the IDEA allowed some movement in this direction, identification and classification remain the focus of the system.) Critics, however, worry that census-based funding provides schools with little incentive to provide the more expensive accommodations and services needed by the severely disabled and that it does not necessarily result in better outcomes for students with disabilities.

Moreover, census-based funding does not take into account real differences that may exist across school districts in the percentage of students with severe disabilities requiring intensive special education services. This can happen, for example, when parents of children with severe disabilities move into a school district with greater proximity to a specialized medical facility, resulting in an over-representation of such students in that school district. Or a quirk of fate can cause an over-representation of students with severe disabilities in some school districts. For example, a small Pennsylvania school district of only 400 K-12 students includes a pair of severely autistic twins and a child with a severe head injury. Under census-based funding, such districts would be unfairly penalized financially.

One approach to deal with the issue of low-frequency, high-need children would be to have schools identify that relatively small group of children who have severe special needs, then let state governments help fund local programs for this population. Another approach would be to attach funding to students identified as in need of special education through the use of vouchers. Parents could use the voucher to pay for both the evaluation process and the specialized educational experience of their choice. This could be done either within, or independent of, a broader school voucher program.

Special education seems to have lost sight of the appropriate end game.

In constructing a voucher program for special education, it must be recognized that students with disabilities usually are more expensive to educate than students without special needs. Too often, voucher advocates have assumed that every student, regardless of educational needs, would receive vouchers of equivalent value. Without taking into account the fact that students with disabilities frequently cost more to educate successfully, students with disabilities might be placed at a disadvantage relative to other students participating in a voucher program. The obvious solution is to tag the value of special education vouchers to the average estimated cost of teaching a student with a specified disability.

The use of vouchers also would help reduce the current adversarial nature of special education. By providing parents with choice at the outset, for example, there would be no need for an extensive appeals process. If a child were failing in regular education and an assessment needed to determine why, the parent would have the choice of having the evaluation done at school or by an independent expert who accepted vouchers. Parents could then seek schools that are most effective at teaching students with their child's particular type of disability. Market pressure would be placed on education programs to produce positive results since parents could always move their child to a different program or provider the following year.

Parents should also be allowed to use special education vouchers to pay for the costs of vocational education programs, one of the more successful education interventions for high school students with disabilities. According to the National Longitudinal Transition Study of Special Education Students, students with mild disabilities who took a concentration of vocational courses were 40 percent more likely to be competitively employed after high school than their peers who did not take a concentration of vocational courses, and they earned an average of $6,247 more annually. Those who took only survey courses in vocational interests still earned nearly $4,000 more per year.[50] Yet vocational education is an under-utilized intervention for many students in special education today.[51]

In addition to vouchers for individual students, federal and state special education grants to schools should be made contingent upon educational improvements by the subgroup of special education students with neurological dysfunctions as measured by independent tests. This contrasts sharply with current accountability mechanisms which are focused on process (for example, was an IEP developed, and were parents informed of their due process rights?), not outcomes (for example, did the child's academic skills improve?).

> *Federal legislation ensuring that no student be left behind is an important principle. It is now time to ensure that this principle actually translates into better outcomes for students with special needs.*

Absent a voucher system, one possibility for holding schools more accountable for outcomes is to base funding on the number of students who achieve the goals set forth in their IEPs. This, however, may simply result in the "dumbing down" of students' IEPs by setting very low educational goals. An alternative would be to use the current statewide assessment tests and differentiate the scores of students in regular education from the scores of students in special education. Under the assumption that the purpose of special education is to improve the academic performance of these students, schools would be held accountable for measurable gains over time in the special education population relative to those in regular education.

Empowerment, not Entitlement

Disaggregating the needs of the three major sub-populations currently in special education together with reform of the funding mechanism would go a long way toward improving the educational experience of students with disabilities. Both of these reforms, however, would ultimately prove inadequate if, at the same time, special education did not also reorient itself toward helping students compensate more effectively for their disabilities so that they can be better integrated into the mainstream of American life.

As discussed earlier, special education seems to have lost sight of the appropriate end game. Rather than viewing its mission as helping students with disabilities overcome, or at least effectively compensate for, their disabilities, special education has become a training ground for a sense of entitlement to a lifetime of accommodations. Unfortunately, students grown accustomed to special accommodations during schooling often find themselves at a distinct disadvantage later in life when employers are less likely—or able—to provide them with similar accommodations in the workplace.

We are not arguing that every disability is remediable, nor that every handicapping condition can be successfully compensated for. Rather, we argue that special education has over-generalized an accommodation model appropriate for students with severe physical, sensory, and cognitive disabilities to include students with behavioral disorders and milder forms of neurological dysfunction.

> *A major overhaul of special education is needed to ensure that the original goal of offering an appropriate education to all children is reached.*

Instead, students with mild forms of neurological dysfunction, such as learning disabilities and ADD, should be taught how to effectively cope with their learning difficulties rather than demanding special accommodations. Doing so will require better differentiation between effective accommodations and lowered standards. For example, although taking a tape recorder to class to assist in note-taking is an appropriate coping mechanism, demanding the substitution of a course in "The Anthropology of Money" for a mathematics course is not.

Even more importantly, schools should cease classifying students with conduct problems under the IDEA. What these students need is to learn better self-control. The key to teaching self-control is not lowering behavioral standards, but developing clear and consistent rules, reinforcing positive behavior, providing immediate consequences for rule infractions, and the teaching of cognitive strategies for coping with high-stress situations. Indeed, in our desire to be compassionate with this population of students, we are inadvertently doing harm by teaching them that they are, in important ways, exempt from consequences that other students face when they misbehave. Moreover, as Abigail Thernstrom has argued elsewhere,[52] court decisions that multiply students' rights and restrict the ability of schools to exercise disciplinary powers have resulted in increasing disorder in the schools—limiting the ability of both disabled and non-disabled students to benefit from their educational experience.

Conclusion

Special education today is costly and, even worse, ineffective. The elaborate eligibility and classification systems set up in response to well-meaning federal legislation have not translated into improved outcomes for most students with special needs. Indeed, despite elaborately developed individual programs, over 90 percent of children in special education receive similar services.[53] Moreover, by focusing on weaknesses and accommodations, we have given these children unreasonable expectations of how the larger community will respond to their academic weaknesses. As a result, many special education students have a rude awakening in store for them when they arrive at college or enter the job market.

A major overhaul of special education is needed to ensure that the original goal of offering an appropriate education to all children is reached while at the same time ensuring that as many students as possible are integrated into the mainstream of American life. To accomplish this, we must first recognize that special education, as currently constructed, really serves three distinct groups of students: those with significant physical, sensory, and cognitive handicaps; those with milder forms of neurological dysfunction, such as SLD and ADD; and those with behavioral disorders.

A transformed special education system would continue to provide appropriate accommodations and special services to the first group designed, at least in part, to help integrate them as much as possible into regular education. For the second group of students, regular and special education would re-focus its efforts both to prevent academic problems through more effective instructional strategies and to teach compensatory skills so that, in the long run, these students are no longer in need of special accommodations or services. The third group, students with behavioral disorders, would be excluded from special education per se, and instead benefit from system-wide programs focusing on clear rules, positive reinforcement for appropriate behavior, and effective limit setting, all designed to prevent conduct problems in the first place. School choice, preferably in the form of vouchers, would ensure that parental preferences are respected.

A reformed education system would take into account the differing needs of important subgroups of special education students; empower parents, not lawyers; and encourage the development of coping and compensatory strategies, not a lifetime of disability. Federal legislation ensuring that no student be left behind is an important principle. It is now time to ensure that this principle actually translates into better outcomes for students with special needs. In short, it is time to make special education "special" once again.

---

1 U.S. Congress, Committee on Education and Labor, Select Subcommittee on Education, *Hearings*, 93rd Congress, 1st Session (1973).

2 See Public Law 34-5 (February 16, 1857), "An Act to Establish the Columbian Institute for the Deaf and Dumb"; and Public Law 45-186 (March 3, 1879), "An Act to Promote the Education of the Blind."

3 Public Law 85-804 (September 1958), "National Defense Education Act"; Public Law 85-926 (September 6, 1958), "An Act to Encourage the Expansion of Teaching in the Education of Mentally Retarded Children Through Grants to Institutions of Higher Learning and to State Educational Agencies."

4 See Edwin W. Martin, Reed Martin, and Donna L. Terman, "The Legislative and Litigation History of Special Education," *The Future of Children* 6 (Spring 1996): 25-39.

5 Procedural safeguards for the IDEA are delineated in the U.S. Code of Federal Regulations, Title 34, Subtitle B, Chapter III, Part 300.

6 The 13 mandated special education categories are autism, deafness and blindness, developmental delay, emotional disturbance, hearing impairment, mental retardation, multiple disabilities, orthopedic impairment, other health impairment, specific learning disability, speech or language impairment, traumatic brain injury, and visual impairment.

7 See Daniel J. Reschly, "Identification and Assessment of Students with Disabilities," *The Future of Children* 6 (Spring 1996): 40-53.

8 See U.S. Department of Education, Office of Special Education and Rehabilitative Services, *Annual Report to Congress on the Implementation of The Individuals with Disabilities Education Act*, (Washington, DC: U.S. Department of Education, various years); National Center for Education Statistics, Common Core of Data Survey, *Digest of Education Statistics, 1999* (Washington, DC: U.S. Department of Education, 2000), table 53; and unpublished tabulations.

9 See Ami Klin and Fred Volkmar, "Asperger's Syndrome," in *Handbook of Autism and Pervasive Developmental Disabilities*, 2d ed., eds. Donald Cohen and Fred Volkmar (New York: John Wiley & Sons, 1997), 54-80.

10 Between 1990 and 1993, the annual number of outpatient pediatric visits for ADHD increased from 1.7 million to 4.2 million. Moreover, production of methylphenidate, the most common pharmacological intervention for both ADD and ADHD, more than quadrupled during this same time period.

11 Of particular concern is the difficulty distinguishing SLDs in reading, the most frequent form of which is often referred to as dyslexia, from low achievement in reading. Indeed, the National Institute of Child Health and Human Development consensus report on the subject concluded after reviewing all the relevant research on the

---

topic that it is impossible to clearly differentiate an SLD in reading from low achievement. Instead, these researchers concluded, "dyslexic children simply represent the lower portion of the continuum of reading capabilities." Cited in Daniel J. Reschly, "Identification and Assessment of Students with Disabilities," 45.

[12] Cited in Robert Worth, "The Scandal of Special Education," *Washington Monthly* (June 1999): 34-38.

[13] In a March 19, 1995, interview with *The Sunday Star-Ledger*, then-New Jersey Education Commissioner Leo Klagholz was quoted as saying, "We spend the money every year, but we have no way of knowing whether the money we spend is actually going for the education of disabled children." Klagholz concluded, "I'm not sure school officials actually sit around and say they can increase state aid by increasing the number of classified children. But the incentive is there and, sometimes, close calls can be justified on the grounds of the good they believe they are doing by increasing a district's resources." Robert T. Brown, "Klagholz Fears Schools Inflate Special Ed Need," *The Sunday Star-Ledger*, 19 March 1995.

[14] Under the 1997 amendments to the IDEA, schools are now allowed to use special education funds to explore programs that are non-categorical, are coordinated with other federal and state funded programs within the school, and are part of an educational "whole" (Part B funds). However, schools still get special education funds based on the number of children identified as eligible under the IDEA. What the 1997 amendments allow is greater flexibility in *spending* the money. So, for example, if a school defines a resource classroom for reading as one that has fewer than ten students and there are six children identified as in need of special education, the school can include four additional children in that resource classroom who are poor readers but not identified as in need of special education under the IDEA. The school doesn't receive any additional funds for the latter four students, however.

[15] A study conducted by the National Assessment of Educational Progress (NAEP), U.S. Department of Education, found that schools routinely tried to exclude low-achieving students from standardized exams by, for example, sending them on field trips, telling them to stay home, or simply encouraging them not to participate in the tests. Of the 27 states that routinely tracked how many students with disabilities participated in statewide assessments, only about half tested special education students.

[16] See Andrea Tortora, "Omitting Special Ed Kids May Have Aided Scores," *The Cincinnati Enquirer*, March 12, 1999.

[17] See Walter Olsen, "Under the ADA, We May All Be Disabled," *Wall Street Journal*, May 17, 1999, sect. A, p. 27.

[18] See Michael Cardman, "SAT Accommodations Soar for Wealthy, White Males," *Education Daily* 33, no. 10 (2000): 4.

[19] See "Special Education: Honoring the Federal Commitment," as posted on the National School Boards Association website: <<www.nsba.org/advocacy/issueupdates/idea.htm>>.

[20] See Donna L. Terman, Mary B. Larner, Carol S. Stevenson, and Richard E. Behrman, "Special Education for Students with Disabilities: Analysis and Recommendations," *The Future of Children* 6 (Spring 1996): 12.

[21] See Thomas B. Parrish and Jay G. Chambers, "Financing Special Education," *The Future of Children* 6 (Spring 1996): 121-138. Note these percentages are for 1987-88, the last year that states were required to report special education expenditures to the U.S. Department of Education. The last independent national special education cost study was based on 1985-86 data.

[22] In Montgomery County, Maryland, for example, the school system's legal fees increased 240 percent between 1990 and 1995.

[23] See Robert Worth, "The Scandal of Special Education," *Washington Monthly* (June 1999): 34-38.

[24] See Richard Rothstein and Karen Hawley Miles, *Where's the Money Gone? Changes in the Level and Composition of Education Spending* (Washington, DC: Economic Policy Institute, 1995).

[25] In New Jersey, fully five percent of special education students attended private schools at taxpayers' expense during the 1994-95 school year, with an additional seven percent having part of their private school costs paid for by the public school system. In Washington, D.C., private placements account for over a third of the District's $167 million special education budget, even though less than one-sixth of the District's special education students attend private schools.

[26] See Worth, "The Scandal of Public Education."

[27] Cited in Jonathan Fox, "Sending Public School Students to Private Schools," *Policy Review* (January/February 1999): 25-29.

[28] See U.S. Department of Education, Office of Special Education Programs, *Implementation of the Individuals with Disabilities Education Act: Seventeenth Annual Report to Congress* (Washington, DC: U.S. Department of Education, 1995), p. A-159, table AD1.

[29] See ibid.; see also Lynn S. Fuchs, Susan B. Eaton, Carol Hamlett, and Kathy Karns, "Supplementing Teacher Judgements of Test Accommodations with Objective Data Sources," *School Psychology Review* (in press); and Lynn S. Fuchs, Douglas Fuchs, Susan B. Eaton, and Carol Hamlett, "Reading Test Accommodations for Students with Learning Disabilities: Using the Dynamic Assessment of Test Accommodations (DATA) to Supplement Teacher Judgements" (Peabody College of Vanderbilt University, unpublished manuscript).

[30] See Wayne J. Camara, Tina Copeland, and Brian Rothschild, *Effects of Extended Time on the SAT I: Reasoning Test Core Growth for Students with Learning Disabilities*, College Board Report No. 98-7 (New York: College Board, 1998).

[31] See Beth Azar, "Fairness a Challenge When Developing Special-Needs Tests," *APA Monitor* (December 1999): 31.

[32] See Camara, Copeland, and Rothschild, *Effects of Extended Time on the SAT I*, 1; see also W. Willingham, M. Ragosta, R.E. Bennett, H. Braun, D.A. Rock, and D.E. Powers, *Testing Handicapped People*, (Boston, MA: Allyn & Bacon, 1988).

[33] See Kenneth Smith, "Disabled Educators," *The Washington Times* (May 6, 1999), sect. A, p. 19.

[34] See ibid.

[35] Personal communication, 59th Annual Conference and Exposition, National School Boards Association, Alexandria, VA.

[36] See Eli J. Lake, "Appeals Court to Revisit Key Learning Disorder Ruling," *Education Daily* 32, no. 122 (1999): 4.

[37] See Robert J. Sternberg and E. L. Grigorenko, *Our Labeled Children* (Reading, MA: Perseus Books, 1999).

[38] For further discussion, see Mark Wolery and James Schuster, "Instructional Methods with Students Who Have Significant Disabilities," *Journal of Special Education* 31 (1997): 61-79.

[39] For further discussion, see Diane M. Browder, Timothy Minarovic, and Edward Grasso, *Functional Approaches to Low Incidence Populations: Functional and Noncategorical Identification and Intervention in Special Education* (Des Moines, IA: Iowa Department of Education, 1998).

[40] See H. Goldstein and E. Hockeberger. "Significant Progress in Child Language Intervention: An 11-Year Retrospective," *Research in Developmental Disabilities* 12 (1991): 401-424.

[41] See Browder, Minarovic, and Grasso, *Functional Approaches to Low Incidence Populations*.

[42] See Terman, Larner, Stevenson, and Behrman, "Special Education for Students with Disabilities: Analysis and Recommendations," 4-24.

[43] For further discussion, see G. Lyon Reid and Vinita Chhabra, "The Current State of Science and the Future of Specific Reading Disability," *Mental Retardation and Developmental Disabilities Research Review* 2 (1996): 2-9; and Sternberg and Grigorenko, *Our Labeled Children*.

[44] See Sternberg and Grigorenko, *Our Labeled Children*.

[45] See ibid.

[46] See Peter Jensen and the MTA Cooperative Group, "A 14-Month Randomized Clinical Trial of Treatment Strategies for Attention-Deficit/Hyperactivity Disorder," *Archives of General Psychiatry* 56 (1999): 1073-1086.

[47] See Alan E. Kazdin, *Treatment of Antisocial Behavior in Children and Adolescents* (Homewood, IL: Dorsey Press, 1985).

[48] See Dennis Russo and Robert Putnam, *Implementing Effective Behavioral Strategies in Schools and School Systems* (paper presented at the 31st Annual Convention of the Association for the Advancement of Behavior Therapy, November 12, 1999, in Toronto, Ontario).

[49] For further discussion of the effectiveness of special education, see Mark Kelman and Gillian Lester, *Jumping the Queue: An Inquiry into the Legal Treatment of Students with Learning Disabilities* (Cambridge, MA: Harvard University Press, 1998); and Edwin W. Martin, "Learning Disabilities and Public Policy" in *Better Understanding Learning Disabilities: New Views from Research and Their Implications for Education and Public Policy*, eds. G. Reid Lyon, D.B. Gray, John F. Kavanaugh, and Norman A. Krasnegor (Baltimore, MD: Paul H. Brookes, 1993): 325-342; and M.C. Wang and E.T. Baker, "Mainstreaming Programs: Design Features and Effects," *Journal of Special Education* 19 (1986): 503-526.

[50] See Mary M. Wagner and Jose Blackorby, "Transitions from High School to Work or College: How Special Education Students Fare," *The Future of Children* 6 (Spring 1996): 103-120.

[51] See Lose Blackorby, "Participation in Vocational Education by Students with Disabilities," in *The Secondary School Programs of Students with Disabilities: A Report for the National Longitudinal Transition Study of Special Education Students*, ed. Mary M. Wagner (Menlo Park, CA: SRI International, 1993), 51-548.

[52] See Abigail Thernstrom, "Courting Disorder in the Schools," *The Public Interest* 136 (Summer 1999): 18-34.

[53] See S. Epps and G. Tindal, "The Effectiveness of Differential Programming in Serving Students with Mild Handicaps," *Handbook of Special Education: Research and Practice,* vol. 1 (Oxford: Pergamon Press, 1987), 213-248; Reschly, "Identification and Assessment of Students with Disabilities," 40-53; and M.C. Wang, M.C. Reynolds, and H.J. Walberg, eds., *Implementation of the Individuals with Disabilities Education Act: Seventeenth Annual Report to Congress* (Washington, D.C.: U.S. Department of Education, Office of Special Education Programs, 1995).

Chapter 3

Effectiveness and Accountability (Part 1): The Compliance Model

Patrick J. Wolf and Bryan C. Hassel*

A recent article in *The Washington Post* revealed some alarming features of the special education program in our nation's capital. Special-needs students languish in inappropriate school settings for years before the District of Columbia's public school system conducts an initial assessment of their disabilities and assigns them to a special program or school that

> **How do we know whether special education is working in the United States, and how do—and should—we define "working" in this context?**

might promote their educational progress. It is unclear how or even whether "progress" is defined for special education students in the D.C. system. Administrators confessed to *Post* reporter Justin Blum that they "do not know how many special education students graduated (from high school) last year." Although an elaborate reporting system is in place, one that requires special education teachers and administrators to complete reams of paperwork, Blum reported that "there are serious errors at nearly every step of the process and...missing documents and unreturned phone calls hinder efforts to correct them." The D.C. Office of Special Education even advises people to ignore graduation rates reported in previous years because they are totally unreliable.[1]

Experts estimate that $35-60 billion is spent each year to provide a "special" education to disabled children in the United States. The wide range of cost estimates itself hints at an insufficient level of accountability in these programs, while also provoking the important question of what society is receiving as a return on its substantial investment in special education. In this chapter, we address critical questions regarding what standards of effectiveness are used to evaluate the progress of children receiving special education services and what accountability systems operate to track and report their progress. In other words, how do we know whether special education is working in the United States, and how do—and should—we define "working" in this context?

The chapter focuses primarily on the "compliance model" of accountability that currently governs most special education programs. Compliance accountability is a form of monitoring

---

* The authors acknowledge the helpful comments of Chester E. Finn, Jr., Charles R. Hokanson, Jr., Stephanie Jackson, and Marci Kanstoroom on previous drafts of this chapter. Juanita Riano provided excellent and timely research assistance. We own any remaining shortcomings.

and oversight that stresses *documentation* of various *processes* and *activities*, including initial assessment, pupil assignment, reassessment, reassignment, and the use of education funds.

Within a compliance model, effectiveness tends to be defined in terms of whether or not procedural regulations were satisfied, the proper steps taken, and the right paperwork processed correctly and on time. The compliance view of accountability is deeply entrenched in the history, theory, and practice of government involvement in special education in the United States despite recent efforts to "reinvent" special education by focusing more on educational results. Ironically, the compliance model fails even to ensure widespread compliance with federal and state laws and regulations, while generating unexpected, undesirable outcomes and perverse incentives.

> *Ironically, the compliance model fails even to ensure widespread compliance with federal and state laws and regulations, while generating unexpected, undesirable outcomes and perverse incentives.*

Having laid bare the nature of the current compliance model for accountability and effectiveness in special education, we proceed in Chapter 14 to describe possible alternative models and assess their strengths and weaknesses. We think that it is possible and desirable to define success more appropriately for children with special educational needs, and to design monitoring systems that accurately reveal useful information about how well we are serving these vulnerable youngsters.

Definitions

Many important special education terms are defined in other chapters. Here we focus on clarifying what is meant by effectiveness, accountability, and the compliance model. "Effectiveness" is a measure of goal achievement. An effective program achieves the goals that have been set in advance for it. The goals themselves may be focused on resources (for example, inputs), processes and activities (services), results (outcomes), or the social consequences of the results (as impacts).[2] Impacts and outcomes are generally considered to be superior to services and input as effectiveness criteria, because they focus on what a program or agency actually accomplishes, not merely what it expends or what it does.

"Accountability" is advanced when individuals and organizations are held responsible for the operation and effectiveness of programs and institutions under their control. Thus, achieving accountability requires that accurate performance information be collected and reported in some public venue. Accountability systems in the government sector seek to enable a clear and accurate "accounting" of what has been accomplished through the use of public funds and the operation of public programs. They also serve as a means for holding public officials and private contractors "accountable" for the lack of accomplishments or the misuse or abuse of public funds and programs.

Up to this point, the compliance model has dominated effectiveness and accountability considerations and activity in special education. According to this model, effectiveness is largely defined in terms of the prescribed expenditure of resources and the execution of correct processes and activities that are mandated by special education laws and regulations. A major assumption of the compliance model is that the correct operation of the special education "process" implies actual "progress" for special-needs students—meaning that greater inputs and services generate desirable outcomes and favorable impacts. To ensure accountability, the compliance model requires that every step of the special education process be thoroughly documented. Other major assumptions are that the issuance of regulations and documentation of compliance with those regulations (1) ensure that public funds and programs are not being misused and (2) provide a complete and accurate public record of what is being accomplished regarding the education of students with special needs. As we will see, the compliance model is being challenged by contemporary special education reforms, and an examination of how it operates in states, communities, and schools strongly suggests that such a challenge is overdue. But first we will examine more carefully the theory undergirding the compliance model.

Effectiveness and Accountability in Theory

The compliance model of accountability in special education is intended to solve the "agency problem" that is inherent in policy implementations which rely upon delegation of authority.[3]

> **To ensure accountability, the compliance model requires that every step of the special education process be thoroughly documented.**

Principal-agent theory, as applied to policy implementation and oversight, holds that the formulators and overseers of policy are "principals" who delegate the task of actual implementation of policy to subordinates, or "agents." Principals and their agents are assumed to have more or less diverse, even divergent preferences and goals for policy implementation. At the extreme, some rational-choice theorists contend that agents will tend to "shirk" the implementation work, "subvert" the policy goals of their principals in order to further the agents' own purposes, and even "steal" whatever program resources they can.[4] To solve this "agency problem," the designers and overseers of policy need to operate an accountability system that will mitigate the supposed tendency of subordinates to shirk, subvert, and steal. The "agency problem" is essentially an accountability problem. Because the operators who actually deliver services to people might not do so in the "proper" way if left to their own devices, we must design a system to compel their proper behavior or force them to account for improper behavior.

According to economist William Ouchi, there are three general ways by which organizations can address the agency problem. They can be organized as a bureaucracy, a market, or a clan.[5] Bureaucracies, including most government organizations, use administrative hierarchies of supervision to address the agency problem. Organizations that rely on market forces to diffuse the agency problem include many entrepreneurial businesses. Organizations that take the form of clans to address the agency problem include families, sports teams, and many nonprofit agencies.

Table 1 describes the basic components of accountability systems employed by the three general types of organizations. We will modify Ouchi's terminology slightly by referring to his bureaucracy model as a *compliance* model, his market model as a *competition* model, and his

Table 1. General Models for Addressing the Agency Problem

Model	Theme	Focus of Effectiveness	Ex Ante Accountability	Ex Post Accountability	Rewards	Sanctions
Bureaucracy (Compliance)	Heavy Hand	Activities (Processes)	Rules and Regulations, Certification	Paperwork, Audits, Hearings	Continued Funding, Jurisdiction	Written Warnings, No Promotion, Decertification
Market (Competition)	Hidden Hand	Outcomes (Results)	None	Consumer Choice	Increased Revenue, Increased Salary, Continued Operation	Loss of Revenue, Bankruptcy
Clan (Community)	Helping Hand	Varied	Values and Norms	Reputation	Praise, Role Enhancement	Scolding, Role Reduction, Banishment

clan model as a *community* model of accountability.

The compliance model traditionally focuses on organizational activities or processes.[6] What tends to be most important under the compliance model is what people do, how much they do, and how they do it. At the front end, the compliance model prescribes the formulation of elaborate rules and explicit regulations to guide the behavior of agents. It relies upon a heavy hand to shape and enforce behavior. Compliance accountability systems often require some form of credentialing (such as teacher certification) before an agent is allowed even to operate within the system.

After operations have begun, the *compliance* model calls for accountability checks that generally involve documentation of organizational activities and workflows that can later be audited by overseers. Agents that are judged to have operated according to the rules and procedures set by the principal tend to be rewarded with continued responsibility for their programs. Where organizational paperwork reveals a lack of compliance on the part of an agent, however, the agent may be issued a warning, denied promotion, or even decertified. For example, a military officer who fails to comply with the regulations of his service may first receive a "letter of reprimand." If the officer receives several such reprimands, he may be passed over for promotion to a higher rank. If noncompliance worsens, the officer may be involuntarily discharged from the service.

> **The competition model relies upon consumer choice to enforce accountability.**

The *competition* model of accountability provides a sharp contrast to the compliance model. Its focus of effectiveness usually is on outcomes or results, not activities and processes. Generally, correct procedures are not specified in advance. This model relies upon the hidden hand of market incentives to shape behavior. The goal is to achieve the "bottom line" in whatever way you can.

The *competition* model relies upon consumer choice to enforce accountability. If consumers like what the agency is doing, and have reason to believe that its positive performance will continue, they will support it. If they are disappointed with the services provided by the organization and other options are available to them, they will take their business elsewhere. James Q. Wilson has referred to this system of accountability as permitting "clients to vote with their feet."[7]

Government agencies employing the competition model may construe the idea of "consumer" in one of two ways. One approach regards the ultimate beneficiaries of the government service as consumers and gives them the power to vote with their feet in selecting the provider of the service. In the education arena, for example, policymakers can give families the ability to use a "voucher" to pay tuition so that their children can attend a preferred school. In this variant of the competition model, agents are held accountable in that, if they fail to convince beneficiaries to "buy" their services, they go out of business. The other variant regards government agencies as consumers who buy products from other governmental units or outside contractors. In education, for example, a state education agency might select a certain educational assessment company (in lieu of a competitor company) to provide the instruments for the agency's testing regime.

Agents that achieve positive outcomes under a *competition* model of accountability are rewarded with bonuses or increased revenue and the ability to stay in business. Conversely, agents that fail to achieve positive outcomes (or whose customers vote against them with their feet) will be denied salary bonuses, docked pay, and, if the agent falls well short of the performance goal, possibly fired. Organizations that fail to achieve their outcome targets may lose revenue, forfeit the contract with the principal, and, as a result, risk bankruptcy. Market models of accountability are non-directive at the front end; however, the rewards and sanctions under such a system can be dramatic at the tail end of operations.[8]

> *Agents that achieve positive outcomes under a competition model of accountability are rewarded with bonuses or increased revenue and the ability to stay in business.*

Performance measurement is not unique to the *competition* model of accountability. Organizations that are structured as bureaucracies (or even clans) often can and sometimes do measure their performance. Performance measurement is more common in systems of competition, however, because managers who face market rewards and sanctions value information about how well their programs and employees are doing. Because they do not want customers to go elsewhere, managers and organizations that face high stakes competition regularly assess performance in order to nip problems in the bud and identify productive programs and employees in which to invest additional resources.

The third type of accountability system is the *community* model. Organizations that function as communities view effectiveness as context-dependent. They will focus on impacts and outcomes if what they are doing is amenable to those effectiveness criteria; however, they will pay close attention to services and processes if more results-oriented effectiveness measures would be inappropriate. John Dilulio illustrates this point in his portrayal of the Federal Bureau of Prisons (BOP) as a clan or community-type organization.[9] If a jailbreak or riot has occurred, BOP personnel will do whatever it takes to catch the fugitive or quell the disturbance, consistent with preserving the safety of innocent people. Such an approach represents a results emphasis. However, during the daily operations of BOP facilities, staff members focus on the standard operating procedures and rule-based behaviors that their principals have specified for them. Such an approach represents a process emphasis.

Clan-like organizations can make quick adjustments in how they operate and what they emphasize because they rely upon values, norms, and relationships, not hierarchy or regulations, to guide members' behavior. This model employs a helping hand to shape behavior. Several scholars have pointed out that Catholic schools tend to have a strong sense of community because their administrators and teachers usually share a set of educational, personal, and spiritual values that shape the environment of the school and the behavior of those in it.[10] Such norms and values often include concern for the welfare of every student, emphasis on the importance of cooperation, a focus on mastering basic skills, and insistence on maintaining a clean and orderly school. School leaders are confident that staff members share their values and that they therefore need not prescribe what teachers do in classrooms. Because of shared values, principals can be assured that teachers will take appropriate actions when confronted with various situations. As Dilulio notes, such "strong culture" organizations address the principal-agent problem by relying upon operators who are "principled agents."[11]

> *Agencies can be distinguished from one another based on whether their outcomes can be reliably measured and unequivocally ascribed to agency actions and policies.*

With principled agents delivering services to the organization's clients, community-based agencies often do not overly concern themselves with ex *post* accountability instruments. Their leaders instead tend to rely on their own constant readings of whether the community is thriving and, if not, what might be done to improve its condition. Operators and clients who have performed particularly well in the view of the leader might receive praise during a community gathering or have their roles within the organization enhanced in some way. Operators and clients who have performed poorly in the view of the leader might receive a private admonition, role reduction, or, in extreme cases, banishment from the community.

Each of these three models of accountability has certain theoretical advantages. The *compliance* model ought to be more reliable and consistent than the *competition* or *community* models, because its rules of behavior are clearly specified in advance and adherence to those rules is monitored. With the compliance model, agents and clients know up front what they must do and how they can expect to be treated. By contrast, the *competition* model has virtues of flexibility and adaptability. Agents can use whatever appropriate and creative means they think will advance the organization's goals. Moreover, market-based organizations receive clear feedback from customer decisions and comments regarding what is and is not working, and they can adjust accordingly. Because *community* models of organizing rely upon personal allegiance to norms and values instead of rules and supervision or customer information to ensure accountability, they tend to be the most efficient means for addressing the agency problem. However, an important limitation of the *community* model, with its heavy reliance on the culture of the organization, is that it tends to succeed only within the confines of individual agencies. A principal that needs to control the behavior of agents in different organizations, sectors, and levels of government, as in special education, would find it difficult to do so using culture alone.

Choosing an Accountability Model for Special Education

Which type of accountability system would be best for special education? The eminent political scientist James Q. Wilson has developed a typology of government organizations that provides us with guidance regarding this important question.[12] According to Wilson, agencies can be distinguished from one another based on whether their outcomes can be reliably measured and unequivocally ascribed to agency actions and policies. They also differ based on whether a clear technology or single method of operating applies to the agency's mission. Agencies with measurable results and clear ways of doing things are considered to be *production* agencies, according to Wilson. Because they are so favorably situated, production agencies can employ any of the three accountability models successfully. Agencies with unmeasurable outcomes but clear technologies are called *procedural* agencies. Because what is to be done is clearer than what is achieved, the compliance model of accountability is generally used for procedural agencies. Bureaucracies with measurable outcomes but various viable technologies are considered to be *craft* agencies. The competition model of accountability is best suited to craft agencies because of its emphasis on results, such as consumer choices, that can be measured. Finally, agencies with neither measurable results nor single ways of doing things are called

> **The variety and demands posed by special-needs children seem certain to frustrate attempts to specify in advance precisely what special education must consist of, as opposed to what it should accomplish.**

coping agencies. Because their missions involve uncertainty regarding both process and result, the community model is the best system for promoting effectiveness and accountability in these agencies.

Where does special education fit into this typology? Schools themselves are properly treated as craft agencies, according to Wilson. There is little agreement as to precisely how teachers should conduct the process of educating their students; however, standardized tests and other assessments do offer the ability to measure student achievement, at least regarding the skills and topics covered by the exams. Thus, regular education would appear to lend itself to accountability systems based on performance measurement that are typically part of the market model. However, special education is different. It is difficult to measure accurately the educational achievement of certain students with special needs. As such, at least some special education students and programs may reasonably be considered coping projects. For them, the community model of accountability may be most appropriate.

Clearly, special education is not a procedural or production mission. The education landscape is littered with pedagogical approaches and reforms that were billed as trustworthy technologies for helping all students to learn.[13] Even less certainty surrounds approaches to teaching students with special needs. Fierce battles continue over whether deaf students should be taught orally or using American Sign Language, and whether non-English-speaking students should be immersed in English or receive the bulk of their instruction in their native tongue.[14] Many educators and policymakers have behaved as if a single sure technology exists for all special education situations, but in reality the variety and intensity of demands posed by special-needs children seem certain to frustrate attempts to specify in advance precisely what special education must consist of, as opposed to what it should accomplish.

The example of a private educational center for emotionally disturbed students illustrates these challenges. At the time of our visit, the center enrolled 53 students in grades 1-12, with an average class size of four students.[15] Nearly half of the staff were professional counselors. The intensive psychological therapy and small class sizes that characterized the program came at an annual cost of $36,000 per student, which was borne by the local county school system for all of the children in the school.[16]

This organization closely fits the "clan" model. Effectiveness is defined in various ways, depending on context. Effectiveness measures include a student's level of participation in the activities of therapy sessions and behavior in class, as well as the outcomes of learning coping skills and transitioning from the program back to a regular school. Nearly half of the students sent to the school make sufficient progress in their therapy and education programs to transfer to a "less restrictive" school environment. School administrators refer to such outcomes as "transitioning out" of the school under "favorable" or "successful" circumstances.[17] A small number of students—typically one or two but sometimes none in a given year—remain in the school through 12th grade and thus formally graduate from the high school component of the center.[18] The students who neither transition out of the center successfully nor graduate from its high school leave the school "unsuccessfully" by quitting the program prematurely. The center's failure rate of about 50 percent is considered very low, given the propensity of emotionally disturbed students to quit special education programs and school itself.[19]

> Measuring results that can be appropriately attributed to special education interventions can be challenging.

Although students are tested each year in accordance with state guidelines, the test results are primarily used for diagnostic purposes. The teachers advocate customized testing of their students "in their best medium" and at the time of day when a given student tends to be most balanced emotionally. They claim that, for some severely emotionally disturbed students, getting them to remain in their chair for an entire class (a process measure) might be the most appropriate measure of progress.[20] The teachers who work with emotionally disturbed students every day at this school consider their job to be primarily a coping mission.

The environment and operation of the school are shaped by a set of values that produces a strong and distinct culture. The values include openness, informality, trust, personal responsibility, and flexibility. These values, and the academic activities that take place at the school, are all oriented toward addressing the emotional problems that are the source of each student's disability. As the director stated, "The learning that takes place in the classroom is therapy."[21] Students refer to teachers, counselors, and administrators by their first names to prevent them from being intimidated by the intensity of the classroom and counseling sessions that comprise each school day. Students are encouraged to take ownership of the school; pictures of each student adorn the hallway, and student leaders are given the authority to assign maintenance tasks to other students and ensure that the tasks are completed properly. A high school student was selected to provide us with a tour of the school, unchaperoned. The teachers are extraordinarily flexible and accommodating; they readily greeted us as we were ushered into classrooms, primarily while classes were in session. Most of the classes consisted of small group projects or individual tutorials. The junior high and high school students serve as mentors for the elementary school students. On the morning that we visited, the regular high school English classes were replaced by a student-led poetry "slam."

> **Particularly in the area of special education, accountability systems tend to combine elements of more than one model.**

Even this "clan-like" school is required to participate in many compliance-oriented oversight activities. The school must maintain its accreditation in order to receive referrals from various public school jurisdictions in the area. Staff members participate in the development, implementation, and annual review of progress toward the goals of individualized education programs (IEPs). Administrators must complete a blizzard of paperwork in order to justify their operations and be reimbursed by the county for their services. The efficacy of this exercise in documentation is questionable, however. As the director told us:

> The amount of paper we generate for accountability purposes to the county and state is enormous.... But I don't know if it's effective because I have no idea...what they're using it for, you know what I mean? ...I present them with a [budget] packet that is an inch thick every year.... I don't know...who does what to it all. And I always wonder, 'Is this being used?'[22]

Finally, the school is subject to market accountability. Although its student body is the result of referrals from various public schools in the region, many of the referrals are based on parental demands (backed by legal counsel) that the child be assigned to this particular school. Moreover, the county may refer emotionally disturbed students to any of more than 100 public and private school programs in the area. The director told us, "Every year I worry if we'll have enough kids to pay the staff. And always it works out.... Our middle school is full, basically. The high school is about full, and I've got a lot of referrals coming in. And the elementary school is—basically, it will be full. Every year it sort of works out, and you try the best you can and continue."[23] The positive reputation and high success rate of the center are important reasons why it has been allowed to continue to teach and counsel emotionally disturbed students.

A teacher we interviewed at the center described a particularly innovative aspect of the program. Every Thursday is a work day at the school. The students are organized into landscaping and maintenance work crews, with student supervisors elected by the community of staff and students. That way, said the teacher, "the students learn to work with each other and for each other and over each other."[24] The students are paid by the center for their work, with their pay grade determined by regular evaluations of their work by peers and center staff, "so they are very much held accountable for their ability to be part of their team and get the job done."[25] On "work day," the students are organized into a bureaucracy, motivated by market incentives, and evaluated by the fellow members of their clan.

This private, nonprofit school for special-needs students exemplifies the conclusions of this chapter. First, we see that measuring results that can be appropriately attributed to special education interventions can be challenging. At the extreme, the standardized outcome measures central to performance-based accountability may be either impossible to obtain or inappropriate measures of achievement. Second, particularly in the area of special education, accountability systems tend to combine elements of more than one model. Real-world examples of pure compliance, competition, or community models of oversight and accountability are rare. What distinguishes one system from another is whether its central tendency is oriented toward compliance, competition, or community. Third, compliance aspects of the special education oversight system are designed and implemented in ways that may not contribute to, and actually may undermine, accountability. In the following sections we explore further the imprecise, poorly targeted, hybrid nature of past and present systems used to hold people accountable for effectiveness in special education.

> *A compliance regulatory system has dominated the oversight of special education programs since responsibility for such programs became increasingly federalized in the 1960s.*

The Emergence of the Compliance Model in Special Education

A compliance regulatory system has dominated the oversight of special education programs since responsibility for such programs became increasingly federalized in the 1960s. This reliance on compliance regulation may have resulted from a desire to guarantee positive outcomes, organizational culture, the fear of litigation, or all of these.

Children with special educational needs rightly evoke sympathy. Policymakers and implementers may be especially motivated to seek a guarantee that all such students receive appropriate educational interventions, and that no special-needs student is neglected. Thus, they might be tempted by the heavy hand of compliance oversight and the apparent (but not always real) guarantees of universal and appropriate service that it promises. This can occur in spite of the fact that the definition of "appropriate" will vary significantly by type and severity of disability and even change over time (due to advances in research, technology and pedagogy).

Government organizations have a propensity for the process regulation that is central to compliance oversight.[26] As Max Weber explained, formalization generates clarity, standardization, and reliability that can make the job of the bureaucrat more manageable.[27] Some researchers have argued that public education in America suffers from a culture that is particularly quick to formalize and bureaucratize.[28] Because the compliance model's forms of process regulation admit less ambiguity and tolerate less variety, they can also provide protection against litigation. Civil rights tend to be defined in terms of procedures, such as "equal access" and "due process." Thus, when special education is wrapped in the language of rights, policy implementers may seek procedural regulations of the compliance model as protection against legal claims of impropriety. This tendency may be particularly strong in special education, as children with special needs are legally guaranteed an "appropriate education" in "the least restrictive environment." Because disputes over the operational definitions of these ambiguous terms tend to be settled by the courts (see Chapter 10), implementers seek legal protection by engaging in compliance-model process regulation.

A brief history of special education policy reveals how all three forces—sympathy, organizational culture, and fear of litigation—appear to have played a role in making compliance-style oversight central to the special education accountability system. Prior to the 1950s, states, localities, and community organizations provided most of the educational services for children with disabilities with no federal funding or oversight, under conditions that were variable, uneven, often unequal, and frequently separate.[29] Advocates for people with disabilities drew upon the example of *Brown v. Board of Education of Topeka* and the civil rights movement for inspiration and direction in seeking similar access and equity for children with special needs.[30] The first federal laws concerning the education of special-needs students were the Education of Mentally Retarded Children Act of 1958 and the Elementary and Secondary Education Act of 1965. Both measures provided funding meant to improve the quality of special education; however, neither law contained meaningful accountability mechanisms.

The first federal special education laws with oversight teeth were Section 504 of the Rehabilitation Act of 1973 and the Education for All Handicapped Children Act of 1975 (EAHCA). The former required states and localities to ensure that disabled children be granted access to education programs and facilities. The latter mandated that all children with disabilities receive a "free appropriate public education" and that it take place in the "least restrictive environment." The least restrictive environment for a particular student would be determined by a group of interested parties including the child's parents, various diagnosticians, and educators from the local school district. Their decisions would be codified in an IEP that would serve as a guide to everyone participating in the child's schooling. An outgrowth of public sympathy regarding the educational needs of many children with disabilities, the EAHCA invited a compliance and process-oriented accountability system because, like so much pioneering civil rights legislation, it combined legal guarantees with ambiguous terminology.

> **The EAHCA invited a compliance and process-oriented accountability system because it combined legal guarantees with ambiguous terminology.**

During the 1970s and 1980s, special education advocates tackled some of the ambiguity by promoting "mainstreaming" as the proper method of educating students with disabilities.[31] This approach again mirrored the civil rights strategy, then popular in advocacy and legal circles, of addressing racial segregation in public schools by integrating them, even using forced busing when necessary. The process-oriented goal was to expose previously excluded classes of students (such as students with disabilities or racial minorities) to the same educational program and environment as their peers. However, just as many minority students were "tracked" within schools in ways that prevented them from being exposed to most of their non-minority classmates,[32] concerns emerged that mainstreamed special-needs students were not truly being integrated into the life of their schools. Therefore, in the 1990s, the emphasis on mainstreaming gave way to an emphasis on inclusion.[33]

Fully including disabled students in all school activities on an equal basis with their peers has not proven to be the clear solution for addressing student needs that was anticipated. In some cases, full inclusion is impossible or even counter-productive. A student with a severe physical disability obviously will not be able to play on the school's football team, although he may be included in the activity as a team manager. Stronger inclusion problems emerge in cases of deaf or severely emotionally disturbed students. Because deafness is a communication impairment, and many deaf people communicate using a distinctive language (American Sign Language), "deaf schools" have persisted as separate places where students can learn in that language and become steeped in their culture, all contrary to the precepts of inclusion. An excellent example of this "celebration of differentness" is Gallaudet University, which operates as an institution of higher education exclusively for deaf and hearing-impaired students, though it is federally funded and overseen by the U.S. Department of Education. Emotionally disturbed students present another case-in-point. Full inclusion of many such children in a regular school would deny them the customized environment and intensive therapy sessions that they need to address their particular disabilities. In such cases, inclusion may mean unequal and ineffective treatment.

> *Fully including disabled students in all school activities on an equal basis with their peers has not proven to be the clear solution for addressing student needs that was anticipated.*

Recently, the process orientation of the compliance model has been challenged by the movement in education circles to emphasize academic standards and results. Standards-based reform in regular education has drawn special education along, as analysts and policymakers confront the compliance model's limitations for ensuring that students with special needs are actually learning. The desire that effectiveness in the special education arena be defined in terms of educational outcomes, and that educators be held accountable for their results, was manifested in the 1997 amendments to the Individuals with Disabilities Education Act (IDEA).

Effectiveness and Accountability Under the IDEA

The mandates contained within the 1997 amendments of the IDEA (IDEA '97) regarding effectiveness are too vague and allow too many exceptions to represent a true "sea change" from previous special education effectiveness mandates. The section of the law that deals with "Performance Goals and Indicators" (P.L. 105-17, Sec. 612(a)(16)) merely requires that: (1) states have "goals for the performance of children with disabilities"; (2) the goals "promote the purposes of this Act"; and (3) the goals be consistent "with other goals and standards established by the State" with the qualifier "to the maximum extent possible." Clearly, states still retain a great deal of discretion in deciding how performance and success are defined for their disabled students.

The reporting requirements of the IDEA (Sec. 612(a)(17)) are heavily qualified and include important loopholes. They require states, for example, either to include special education students in regular statewide assessments (with or without special accommodations) or to develop "alternative assessments" for such students. The one area in which the mandates appear to have real teeth is in requiring that each state make public the following: (1) "the number of children with disabilities participating in regular assessments"; (2) the number opting out via alternate assessments; and (3) the performance of each group on their respective assessments. States are still able to use various means to exempt special education students from standard achievement tests; however, they are now required to report how many of their disabled pupils have been excluded.

Most importantly, the effectiveness and accountability requirements in the IDEA include no rewards and only weak sanctions. There is no explicit mechanism for rewarding states that actually demonstrate significant progress in educating their disabled students. The Secretary of Education is authorized to withhold federal funding from states or localities that are found to be out of compliance with the IDEA but is not required to do so (Sec. 616(a)). Moreover, the IDEA extends the right of appeal to educational jurisdictions that are punished for non-compliance (Sec. 616(b)). Financial sanctions for IDEA violations thus appear unlikely, and we are aware of just one or two instances in which they have even been threatened.

As we read them, the 1997 effectiveness and accountability provisions of the IDEA include elements that could, if strictly enforced, inject a strong measure of results-orientation into the oversight of special education. Yet, many of those provisions are optional or highly discretionary. The fundamental compliance model emphases on *ex ante* procedural prescriptions and *ex post* audits of resources expended and activities conducted remain strong. IDEA '97 includes 13 pages of text describing the intricacies of 13 separate procedural safeguards with which teachers and administrators must still comply (Sec. 615(a-m)). Moreover, the Act specifies seven procedural approaches, described as proven methods for advancing special education, that include "whole-school" intervention, better coordination, greater reliance on classroom aides, and more training for special education teachers (Sec. 601(c)(A-G)). In short, reports of the death of the compliance model of effectiveness and accountability in special education appear to be greatly exaggerated.

> *Reports of the death of the compliance model of effectiveness and accountability in special education appear to be greatly exaggerated.*

IDEA Reforms: The Vision and Process

An express purpose of the 1997 IDEA amendments was to focus the oversight system for special education on educational outcomes (Sec. 601(d)(4)). According to Ronald Erickson of the Regional Resource and Federal Center Network, the performance-based accountability system required by IDEA '97 must include at least 10 critical components.[34] Although Erickson configured them as spokes on a wheel, we have reproduced them in Figure 1 as discreet steps in an implementation flowchart. The first step is to establish consistent standards and outcome targets for special-needs students. Next, curriculum and testing programs must be aligned to the educational standards and goals. Policies must be set for determining which special-needs students must participate in the testing and what accommodations should be provided to them. Procedures must be established for reporting test results, and additional policies must be developed to reward good performers and penalize bad ones. The final three tasks in the flowchart may appear to be improperly placed at the end, as opposed to the beginning, of the process. However, public and legislative support is as often earned at the end as it is granted at the outset of an implementation process. Similarly, expanding access to and revising the content of professional training programs might be more appropriately accomplished after a performance monitoring system is up and running and providing information and feedback to overseers.

To what extent does the post-1997 oversight system designed by the U.S. Department of

Figure 1. Flowchart of Necessary Steps for Results-Based Effectiveness and Accountability Under IDEA '97

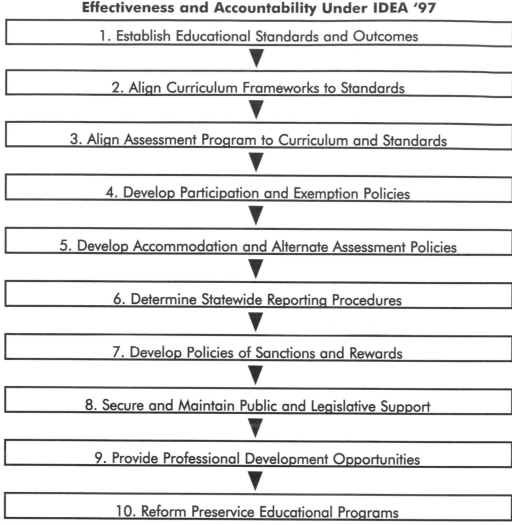

1. Establish Educational Standards and Outcomes

2. Align Curriculum Frameworks to Standards

3. Align Assessment Program to Curriculum and Standards

4. Develop Participation and Exemption Policies

5. Develop Accommodation and Alternate Assessment Policies

6. Determine Statewide Reporting Procedures

7. Develop Policies of Sanctions and Rewards

8. Secure and Maintain Public and Legislative Support

9. Provide Professional Development Opportunities

10. Reform Preservice Educational Programs

Source: Adapted from Ronald Erickson, "Special Education in an Era of School Reform: Accountability, Standards, and Assessment" (Federal Resource Center, January 1998), p. 5.

Education reflect the performance-based model that we have derived from Erickson's work? Unfortunately, the answer is "not very much." The federal government's monitoring system deviates from a well-designed performance oversight system in several important ways. First, in many respects it merely adds a results-based definition of effectiveness to a process-based accountability system. Second, it omits critical components of a results-based accountability system. Third, it leaves the fox in charge of the henhouse. Finally, it still includes certain perverse incentives.

The Department of Education's Office of Special Education Programs (OSEP) has designed an accountability system in response to the 1997 IDEA amendments that appears to pay lip service to standards and testing, while continuing to emphasize procedural compliance. The official OSEP guide to the 2001 monitoring process that is provided to state and local special education administrators is replete with references to "compliance" and "process."[35] The first page of the manual describes how, "In order to ensure *compliance* with IDEA '97...OSEP designed a multifaceted *process*...."[36] Granted, it is described as "an outcome-oriented *process*"[37] that is focused on "improving results."[38] Yet the document suggests to education providers that the self-assessment that drives the accountability system should focus on performance and "adherence to pertinent Federal and State regulations, policies, and procedures."[39] The core of the self-assessment is a series of interviews "to confirm information from the records reviewed and to gather information about local procedures for referral, evaluation, placement, service delivery, and how discussions are made and documented."[40] In short, this important government manual is still designed to prepare state and local officials for compliance-based procedural oversight, not for a results-oriented performance regime.

Several essential components of a results-based effectiveness/accountability model are absent from the OSEP system. These include educational standards and outcome goals, curriculum and assessment alignment, rewards for demonstrated effectiveness, and the reform of pre-service education programs for teachers and other special education staff. Also lacking are consistency in decisions regarding the use of special accommodations and alternative tests for special education students, and predictable consequences for either failing to implement the monitoring system or for adverse results. The last two of these weaknesses especially endanger performance accountability. The testing accommodations provided to special education students can involve variations in the timing, setting, presentation of, or method of responding to the achievement tests. Such policies permit endless variations in possible testing conditions from student to student and year to year, modifications that could yield false signs of performance gains.[41] Regarding sanctions, note the permissive language in the OSEP monitoring manual that:

> *The Office of Special Education Programs' approach to accountability permits the fox to guard the henhouse.*

> If a state does not implement the mandatory components of the improvement plan, or implementation is not effective, OSEP may impose sanctions, which could include OSEP's prescription of corrective actions for compliance, a compliance agreement, withholding funds in whole or in part, or other enforcement actions.[42]

We doubt that such nebulous and uncertain provisions leave special education administrators shaking in their boots.

These weaknesses in the design of the special education accountability system become particularly clear when we contrast Figure 1, on the necessary steps for results-based effectiveness and accountability depicted linearly, with Figure 2, which is the actual monitoring process figure from page 8 of the OSEP manual. Two aspects of Figure 2 are striking. First, as with Erickson's original scheme, the wheel-shape of the figure is intended to signal that the monitoring process is continuous, having no "end" in sight. Second, the hub of the wheel is not the well-being of the special-needs child. Instead, the process is centered around a steering committee. Certainly an accountability system consisting of continuous motion centered around the dictates of a committee was not what reformers envisioned when they crafted IDEA '97!

Figure 2. OSEP Continuous Improvement Monitoring Process

Source: Office of Special Education Policy, U.S. Department of Education, *2001 Monitoring Manual,* p. 8.

OSEP's approach to accountability still permits the fox to guard the henhouse. The Local Educational Agencies (LEAs) that are the "agents" whose performance is to be overseen are themselves allowed to set the agenda, assess their own performance, and recommend data sources and contacts for the external evaluation of their performance.[43] The "self-assessment" that begins the process is planned and executed by the same large steering committee of stakeholders that is literally central to the monitoring process.[44] With the target of the oversight controlling the front end of its own monitoring process, it is unlikely that many criticisms will be forthcoming. As the LEA is being evaluated, OSEP works with it "to plan strategies for validating the self-assessment results...."[45] As with the inspection process of the Occupational Safety and Health Administration in the U.S. Department of Labor, which is often characterized as seriously flawed,[46] OSEP warns the sites that are to be monitored: (1) when inspectors are coming; (2) what they will be asking about; and, (3) that site administrators should select personnel and parents to be interviewed by the overseers.[47] Based on the content of their own oversight manual, OSEP overseers appear to be more "enablers" than "monitors."

Finally, the current "outcome-based compliance system" for special education has the potential for generating perverse incentives. Studies indicate that "high stakes" accountability systems discourage the inclusion of disabled students in testing regimes.[48] Thus, overseers may be forced to choose between encouraging the maximum participation of special-needs students in testing programs by assuring school districts that they will not be punished for poor results, or threatening to penalize poorly performing districts at the risk of encouraging them to exclude special education students from testing. Also, longitudinal gain-scores are more revealing and reliable measures of progress than absolute ability scores, but they are also more costly and difficult to obtain. Not surprisingly, they seldom are the focus of government educational assessments, a practice that continues under IDEA '97.[49]

In sum, the accountability system that has resulted from IDEA '97 appears to hold little promise of solving the "agency problem" in a conclusive or efficacious fashion. The number of regulations in the oversight process and its procedural-compliance focus have not diminished. We are aware of only one significant procedural requirement that was eliminated by IDEA '97—the requirement that students with permanent disabilities, such as blindness, be re-certified as having a disability every three years. Instead, results and performance measurement rhetoric and procedures have merely been grafted onto a barely modified compliance model of accountability. To be sure, redundant and hybrid models of accountability are common in governmental programs. Still, the "outcome-based compliance system" for special education appears to retain the onerous procedural requirements of the previous system—and adds more!—yet omits components that are essential to holding implementors accountable for results. The plethora of regulations implies a strong distrust of agents by their principals; yet the monitoring process is so cooperative and permissive that it implies tremendous trust in agents by principals. In other words, the compliance process is not internally consistent. These weaknesses become clearer when we examine the actual operation of the "outcome-based compliance system."

> *The "outcome-based compliance system" for special education appears to retain the onerous procedural requirements of the previous system— and adds more!—yet omits components that are essential to holding implementors accountable for results.*

IDEA Accountability in Practice

Since 1991, the National Center on Educational Outcomes, a research institute at the University of Minnesota, has been studying the implementation of special education reforms aimed at promoting performance-based accountability.[50] Its December 1999 report (NCEO Report) presents the results of its National Survey of State Directors of Special Education regarding the implementation of IDEA '97. The survey results largely reinforce the central claims of this chapter that performance-based accountability is not yet being achieved in special education.

The Record on Effectiveness

Defenders of IDEA '97 like to define effectiveness in terms of outcomes such as rising test scores. However, the NCEO Report confirms that program overseers still focus on process or output questions such as what percent of special education pupils are being tested and whether they are being educated in the "least restrictive environment."[51] As discussed above, teachers and administrators who work with disabled students often prefer to define success individually, in terms of progress in small, sometimes unquantifiable ways. For example, the students at the private special education school for emotionally disturbed children that we visited are required to work, under direction of student supervisors, to maintain the school's grounds. The purpose is to teach them personal responsibility and interpersonal skills within a work environment. The school staff members view a student's success in completing his maintenance work as an important indicator of progress, despite the fact that it would not fit the standard definition of a results-based accountability indicator. Many educators of special-needs pupils are surely obtaining positive outcomes; however, those positive results are not necessarily induced by or even reflected in the IDEA '97 accountability system.

The Record on Accountability

The NCEO Report confirms our suspicion that the compliance approach to accountability has not been replaced, just supplemented with a testing regime. More special education students are being tested, and most states are reporting the results of those tests (in absolute, not gain-score terms) in compliance with IDEA '97. However, states vary greatly in: (1) the proportion of their special education students who are tested; (2) the proportion who take the

> *States report that the greatest difficulty teachers and administrators face on the ground is aligning IEP goals with state assessment rules and regulations.*

regular test with no accommodations; (3) the proportion who take the regular test with accommodations; (4) the types of accommodations granted to students with similar disabilities; (5) the proportion of students who take an alternative assessment; (6) the nature of the alternative assessments that are given to students with similar disabilities; and, most importantly, (7) the performance standards that are applied to special education students.[52] As opposed to "letting 1,000 flowers bloom," which is the standard justification for permitting state-by-state variation in policy implementation, the type and degree of variation by state that is described here prevent overseers from comparing apples to apples when evaluating the performance garden.

So much paperwork is generated to plan for testing and demonstrate compliance that no one is able to take the time to process or review the data in order to learn what is and is not working and actually hold people accountable for effectiveness and results. State special education directors claim that the lack of resources prevents them from collecting and acting on more accountability data.[53] Most states have issued an elaborate set of rules and regulations regarding IDEA '97 testing that tends to produce paperwork without even achieving consistency. States report that the greatest difficulty teachers and administrators face on the ground is aligning IEP goals with state assessment rules and regulations, Step 3 of the results-based accountability process in Figure 1.[54] Yet 20 of the 34 state directors surveyed still listed "more written policies" as what is most needed to meet IDEA '97 requirements.[55] It would seem that these people are so steeped in the culture of compliance that they have come to view more rules and regulations as an acceptable solution.

At this point, we do not know the extent to which states, localities, and schools are providing excessive or inconsistent accommodations to disabled students who take the regular assessments, or subjecting other special education students to an alternative assessment that is oriented more to input or "process" than to outcomes or "results." The NCEO Report does confirm that special-needs students are excluded from testing mainly due to the perception of administrators that high stakes are involved.[56] Those wary administrators might relax if they examined the OSEP monitoring process manual carefully and saw the many reassuring components of the federal oversight system that we discussed above. Moreover, most states encourage districts and schools to disaggregate test scores into disabled and non-disabled subgroups for reporting and assessment purposes. This practice, which is a component of President Bush's education accountability initiative, would prevent the achievement scores of special education students from dragging down the average score, although it also would generate incentives to classify poorly performing students as suffering from disabilities, even if the reason for their bad performance is motivational or instructional.

Only one third of the states report that they are implementing rewards or sanctions for schools and districts based on disabled students' testing results. Another half of the states say they are developing, revising, or planning such systems.[57] The reward and sanction system being developed in Tennessee appears to hold the most promise to capture performance, as it is to be based on "educational value added."[58] However, two states, Alabama and Connecticut, still reward persistently low-performing districts and schools with more money.[59] We might characterize their accountability systems as based on a "non-performance results model."

> *The "results-oriented compliance" effectiveness-and-accountability system now being implemented in the wake of IDEA '97 appears to be flawed in theory, design, and practice.*

Conclusions

The 1997 IDEA amendments were widely touted as reforms that would extend the results-based effectiveness and performance-based accountability revolution in U.S. education to students with special needs. It was hoped that such a regime shift would complete the transformation of the educational status of disabled youngsters from widespread neglect prior to the 1980s, through general inclusion in the 1990s, to educational achievement in the 21st century. We find that such noble aspirations have yet to be realized.

The extent to which the IDEA '97 oversight system measures up to the requirements for a performance-based accountability system is demonstrated in Figure 3. Just two of the ten necessary steps for performance accountability (darkly shaded) have clearly been accomplished. Reporting procedures have been established in every state, and support for performance-based accountability in special education among the public and policymakers has generally been secured. Some other important components of an effective system may be in place, depending on the state. Yet for four critical steps in the accountability process, little or no progress has been made. At what should be the front-end, educational standards and achievement goals for special education students have not been standardized (possibly because they cannot be), special education curricula have not been modified in light of the (nonexistent) standards, and assessment programs have not been aligned to the curricula and standards (which themselves are moving targets). At the tail-end of the process, the training of special education teachers and administrators has not been modified to account for a shift from procedural accountability under the compliance model to results accountability under the performance model, arguably because no such regime shift has occurred.

**Figure 3. Progress Towards a Result-Based Accountability
System Post-IDEA '97**

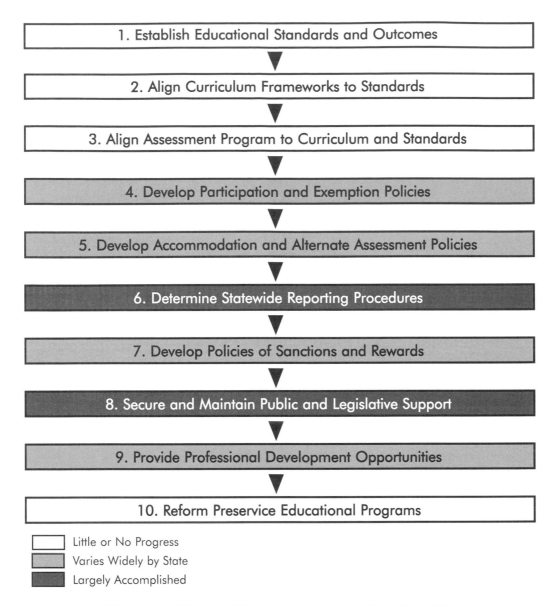

Source: Adapted from Ronald Erickson, "Special Education in an Era of School Reform: Accountability, Standards, and Assessment," Federal Resource Center, January 1998, p. 5.

The "results-oriented compliance" effectiveness-and-accountability system now being implemented in the wake of IDEA '97 appears to be flawed in theory, design, and practice. It is flawed in theory because it still uses oversight practices that assume teachers, schools, districts, and states are untrustworthy, even while trusting them with the keys to the castle during the monitoring process. Teachers or schools that are failing to address the educational needs of students with disabilities can easily escape notice and punishment under the current system. The accountability system is flawed in design because, instead of replacing a rules-driven process with a results-driven oversight system, it merely piles more rules regarding performance assessment onto the process-based compliance system that remains largely intact—and awash in paperwork. The many teachers and administrators who are doing well by their special education students are merely saddled with additional documentation responsibilities that divert their time and resources away from more educationally focused functions. Finally, the system is flawed in practice.

> *The effectiveness and accountability system that has emerged from IDEA '97 does not represent a major shift from the compliance model of the past 25 years.*

For results-based accountability to work, it must set clear goals for performance, clear rules for the measurement of outcomes, and clear consequences for performance and nonperformance. Within those clear guidelines, the system can (and should) allow all kinds of variability in how states, districts, and schools go about meeting their goals. But IDEA '97, viewed as a national program, permits too much state-by-state variability in standards, participation, testing conditions, and rewards/sanctions for the testing of special education students to establish clear results for which we might legitimately hold states accountable. Moreover, states with real teeth in their own results-based accountability systems—commonly called "high stakes" testing—face perverse incentives to exclude special education students or provide them with such generous accommodations that their "success" on the tests is all but assured. Incredibly, some states even reward, with increased funding, local school districts whose special education students are falling further behind.

President Bush's current education initiative holds the prospect of solving one of these problems. His requirement that the scores of students with disabilities who participate in accountability assessments be reported separately could remove the temptation to exclude such children from high-stakes testing.[60] However, a host of additional improvements would need to be made in the accountability system surrounding special education before we could declare it to be an effective results-oriented accountability system.

In short, the effectiveness and accountability system that has emerged from IDEA '97 does not represent a major shift from the compliance model of the past 25 years. Indeed, this new "compliance plus testing" model may offer the worst of both worlds in that it does not even succeed in ensuring compliance with the many rules and regulations that drive it. The traditional incrementalism of policy reform in the United States is still failing to produce a sound accountability system in special education. Could there be a better way? We explore that question in Chapter 14.

---

[1] See Justin Blum, "D.C. Schools Still Neglect Some in Special Education," *Washington Post*, 2 October 2000, sect. A, p. 1.

[2] See Patrick J. Wolf, "Why Must We Reinvent the Federal Government? Putting Historical Developmental Claims to the Test," *Journal of Public Administration Research and Theory* 7, no. 3 (1997): 355, 362.

[3] Patrick J. Wolf, "Authority, Delegation," in *The International Encyclopedia of the Social and Behavioral Sciences*, eds. Neil J. Smelser and Paul B. Baltes (Oxford, England: Pergamon Press, forthcoming 2001).

[4] See Ronald H. Coase, *The Firm, the Market, and the Law* (Chicago, IL: University of Chicago Press, 1988).

[5] See William G. Ouchi, "Markets, Bureaucracies, and Clans," *Administrative Science Quarterly* 25, no. 1 (1980): 129-141.

[6] See Michael Barzelay with Babak Armajani, *Breaking Through Bureaucracy* (Berkeley, CA: University of California Press, 1992).

[7] James Q. Wilson, *Bureaucracy: What Government Agencies Do and Why They Do It* (New York: Basic, 1989), 364.

[8] See Charles L. Schultze, *The Public Use of Private Interest* (Washington, DC: Brookings, 1977).

[9] See John J. Dilulio, Jr., "Principled Agents: The Cultural Bases of Behavior in a Federal Government Bureaucracy," *Journal of Public Administration Research and Theory* 4, no. 3 (1994): 277-318.

[10] See John E. Brandl, "Governance and Educational Quality," in *Learning From School Choice*, eds. Paul E. Peterson and Bryan C. Hassel (Washington, DC: Brookings, 1998), 55-81; and Anthony S. Bryk, Valerie E. Lee, and Peter B. Holland, *Catholic Schools and the Common Good* (Cambridge, MA: Harvard University Press, 1993).

[11] John J. Dilulio, Jr., "Principled Agents," at 277.

[12] See James Q. Wilson, *Bureaucracy*.

[13] See Lynn Olson, "The Common Good," *Education Week in Review*, 27 January 1999, available at <<http://www.edweek.org/ew/vol—18/20access.h18>>; and Diane Ravitch, *Left Back: A Century of Failed School Reforms* (New York: Simon and Schuster, 2000).

[14] See Ben Wildavsky, "A Blow to Bilingual Education," *U.S. News and World Report*, 4 September 2000.

[15] Interview with the principal of a private school for emotionally disturbed students, 27 September 2000.

[16] Interview with the director of a private school for emotionally disturbed students, 27 September 2000.

[17] Interview with the principal.

[18] Ibid.

[19] Ibid.

[20] Interview with a teacher at a private school for emotionally disturbed students, 27 September 2000.

[21] Interview with the director.

[22] Ibid.

[23] Ibid.

[24] Interview with a teacher.

[25] Ibid.

[26] See Herbert Kaufman, *Red Tape: Its Origins, Uses, and Abuses* (Washington, DC: Brookings, 1977); and Robert K. Merton, "Bureaucratic Structure and Personality," in *Reader in Bureaucracy*, eds. Robert K. Merton, et al. (New York: Free Press, 1952).

[27] See Max Weber, "Essay on Bureaucracy," in *Bureaucratic Power in National Politics*, ed. Francis E. Rourke (Boston, MA: Little Brown and Company, 1965).

[28] See John E. Chubb and Terry M. Moe, *Politics, Markets and America's Schools*, (Washington, DC: Brookings, 1990).

[29] There were notable exceptions such as Gallaudet University, America's first institution of higher education for hearing-impaired students, which was established in 1856 and was brought under federal funding and control in 1857.

[30] See Joetta Sack, "Bringing Special Education Students Into the Classroom," *Education Week in Review*, 27 January 2000, available at <<http://www.edweek.org/ew/vol—18/20inclus.h18>>.

[31] See ibid.

[32] See John E. Chubb and Terry M. Moe, "Politics, Markets, and Equality in Schools" (paper delivered at the American Political Science Association Annual Meeting, Chicago, IL, September 1992).

[33] See Joetta Sack, "Bringing Special Education Students Into the Classroom."

[34] See Ronald Erickson, "Special Education in an Era of School Reform: Accountability, Standards, and Assessment" (a product of the Federal Resource Center, Regional Resource and Federal Center Network, January 1998), 5.

[35] See United States Department of Education, Office of Special Education Programs, "Continuous Improvement Monitoring Process: 2000-2001 Monitoring Manual" (Washington, DC: Academy for Educational

Development, n.d.).

[36] Ibid. at 3 (emphasis added).

[37] Ibid. at 4.

[38] Ibid. at 7.

[39] Ibid. at 10.

[40] Ibid. at 33.

[41] See Ronald Erickson, "Special Education in an Era of Reform," at 26.

[42] United States Department of Education, "Continuous Improvement Monitoring Process," at 9.

[43] See ibid. at 24.

[44] See ibid. at 10.

[45] See ibid. at 7.

[46] See Kitty Calavita, "The Demise of the Occupational Safety and Health Administration: A Case Study in Symbolic Action," *Social Problems* 30, no. 44 (1983): 437-448; and John Mendeloff, *Regulating Safety: An Economic and Political Analysis of Occupational Safety and Health Policy* (Cambridge: MIT Press, 1979).

[47] United States Department of Education, "Continuous Improvement Monitoring Process," at 24.

[48] See Ronald Erickson, "Special Education in an Era of Reform," at 7.

[49] See ibid. at 9-10.

[50] National Center on Educational Outcomes, "1999 State Special Education Outcomes: A Report on State Activities at the End of the Century" (December 1999), available at <<http://www.coled.umn.edu/NCEO/OnlinePubs/99StateReport.htm>>.

[51] See ibid.

[52] See ibid.

[53] See ibid. at 39.

[54] See ibid. at 29.

[55] Ibid. at 39-40.

[56] See ibid. at 20.

[57] See National Center on Educational Outcomes, "1999 State Special Education Outcomes," at 33.

[58] Ibid. at 44.

[59] See ibid. at 43.

[60] President George W. Bush, "No Child Left Behind," Summary of the President's Education Initiatives, 23 January 2001, at 8.

Chapter 4

The Moral Foundations of Special Education Law

Mark Kelman

There is little doubt as to where the advocates for special education reform in the 1960s and 1970s—parents, litigators, and legislative activists alike—turned for inspiration. They saw disabled pupils as facing many of the same barriers that had confronted African-American students in the pre-*Brown*[1] era, and they believed that their task, like that of their forerunners in the NAACP, was to dismantle a discriminatory system of education that was both separate and unequal.

> **There are three basic, hotly contested policy issues that should drive today's and tomorrow's debates over special education, and these have little to do with discrimination.**

Like black children living in a regime of *de jure* segregation, children with disabilities faced systematic exclusion from the classroom several decades ago. Impelled by the same sorts of aversive animus towards disabled children and by thoughtless stereotypes about children's limits, local school officials often excluded pupils with physical, cognitive, and emotional disabilities from schooling and segregated them from the regular classroom when they served them at all. Just as African-American families lacked the clout to persuade local school board members that improving achievement levels of black children was as vital a goal as educating their own white kids—an indifference that manifested itself in shorter school years, skimpier facilities, and less well-trained teachers in the segregated black system—so families with disabled kids rightly felt that districts were unwilling to devote the resources needed to educate, rather than warehouse, innumerable children with special needs. The disability-rights movement in education did not just *mimic* the pre-*Brown* civil rights movement; its aims were significantly parallel to those of the ongoing, post-*Brown* movement for black equality. It is not coincidental that a disproportionate number of students victimized by stigmatically separate, underfunded educational "warehousing" programs were African-American pupils labeled mentally retarded.

No one should doubt the nobility of the struggle that pioneer special education activists engaged in, nor should anyone claim that special education policy ought not be motivated in substantial part by the need to eradicate all vestiges of discrimination against pupils with physical, cognitive, and emotional differences. But there are, in my view, three basic, hotly contested policy issues that should drive today's and tomorrow's debates over special education, and these have little to do with discrimination.

First, we must deal with issues of testing accommodation, especially in relation to the burgeoning use of extra time by students with learning disabilities. The significant policy question here is whether the capacity to absorb and respond to written material quickly is worthy of academic reward. If it is, the fact that children with learning disabilities are not "morally" to blame for their inability to read quickly or respond is no more germane than the fact that most kids who are weak in math are not to blame for their incapacity to answer algebra problems on tests.

Second, we must deal with the linked issues of discipline and segregation. It is surely possible that school expulsion and district-enforced efforts to move disabled students to more restrictive environments may be pretexts to restore the old segregated regime, and it is legitimate to question the propriety of expulsion—the use of educational deprivation as a means to achieve some other end. But current federal law skirts the hard questions: When does a student's misbehavior (or even his more benign need for high levels of attention) negatively impact other students? If we believe that the "problematic" student himself would often be better served if he stayed in the mainstream classroom, but his classmates would not, we again face the reality of clashing interests. Certainly, we should deplore and correct a political system that discounts the interests of children with disabilities—because they are "different" or because they are outsiders. We should scrutinize all claims that non-disabled students face disruption, aware that people may unjustly find the very presence of unfamiliar people and behavior disruptive. But we should be equally wary of a system that forbids us from counting the educational interests of "mainstream" students just as worthy as those of pupils with disabilities.

> *We should scrutinize all claims that non-disabled students face disruption, but we should be equally wary of a system that forbids us from counting the educational interests of "mainstream" students just as worthy as those of pupils with disabilities.*

Last, but very important, we face the vexing issue of scarcity: special education costs substantially more per pupil than regular education. We thus must resolve as best we can truly difficult questions of educational policy: Would these resources be better spent on increasing per-pupil spending in "regular" education? Alternatively, or additionally, are there groups or individuals other than the disabled (for example, children of color, children with low IQs who are not dubbed educable mentally retarded, and children facing harsh conditions at home) who might deserve these incremental resources as much or more than those now given priority by federal mandates in the Individuals with Disabilities Education Act (IDEA)?

I now take up these three policy issues in turn.

Accommodations

Should statutes designed to eradicate discrimination force school districts (or universities) to accommodate students with learning disabilities by giving them more time to finish exams? Questions about the propriety of time extensions for students with reading disabilities and attention disorders are most significant in the contexts of standardized college-entrance exams and college and graduate school examinations. The legal regime governing exam accommodations grew up largely under Section 504 of the Rehabilitation Act of 1973, not under the IDEA or its predecessor statutes which largely govern primary and secondary schools. I do not believe testing accommodation issues deserve as much attention as they often receive in the popular press. I discuss them largely to illustrate the broader point that the antidiscrimination norm does little to resolve the important policy question of whether and how more time should be given to accommodate disabled students.

Most disability-rights advocates try to avoid the harsh reality that the case for accommodating some children through time extensions is a complex and ambiguous one. They do so by making unwarranted empirical assumptions. For instance, it is a commonplace argument, although demonstrably false, that nondisabled students would *not* be aided by similar accommodation. Thus, the "good" that disabled students seek is really of no value to others who might claim it; the disabled students have not received a bonus, for they haven't received something that anyone else would value. This is said despite the fact that typical nondisabled test takers complete less than two-thirds of the test items on the SAT; plainly, they, too, would be helped by more time. What one sees far too often in this policy area is just this sort of wishful denial of the reality of conflict and hard choices. Another issue involves the issue of "optimal" integration of behaviorally troublesome children. Advocates try to make the clash of interests disappear simply by declaring that mainstream students will gain huge amounts by learning to deal with classroom diversity, or that distaste for "disruption" should be understood as nothing more than an obsessive and bigoted attachment to certain conventional behavioral styles. But whether these strong empirical assumptions are warranted, rather than convenient, is a far harder question.

> *It is plainly impossible to reward what we ultimately decide is meritorious without implicitly penalizing those who lack the skills and virtues we value.*

Test givers naturally assume that they value and reward skills that are socially significant and relevant. Awareness of the dynamics of subtle discrimination should make us sensitive to the possibility that test-givers overvalue the virtues that their tests reveal and undervalue the virtues of those who work differently. Thus, if examiners claim that rapid reading comprehension is important *per se*, we should certainly be skeptical that they have adequately and self-critically thought through why they believe this. But it is clear that any test must value some set of skills—whether the ability to understand microeconomics, recall formal rules, or absorb complex material quickly—and that all who lack those skills can readily and reasonably be described as disabled to the extent that they lack them. (In the mid-1990s students at Stanford could be classified as "disabled" if they suffered from what was dubbed "Reasoning Deficit," defined as "trouble thinking in an orderly logical way; difficulty prioritizing and sequencing tasks; difficulty applying learned skill to a new task.") Yet it is plainly impossible to reward what we ultimately decide is meritorious without implicitly penalizing those who lack the skills and virtues that we value.

At times, examiners discover that the usual exam administration method poses barriers that preclude a student from being able to demonstrate that he has the skills sought by the examiner. Thus, it is easy to defend the requirement that institutions accommodate an exam-taker in the following sort of "core" case: A blind student cannot be forced to respond to the ordinary written text but must be provided a reader or a Braille copy of the exam. The case for accommodation is easy because (a) the examiner does not view the ability to read hard copy as especially virtuous, compared with being able to read Braille; (b) the blind student will have no opportunity to show that she has many of the virtues the examiner values (such as microeconomic knowledge or memory of rules) if she takes the non-accommodated test; and (c) nondisabled students would not be aided by the accommodation. Thus, the accommodated exam is different, not easier.

> **Whatever one's view of testing accommodations, determinations of what skills are appropriate to test and what can and cannot be justly tested and rewarded are policy issues.**

The dyslexic student seeking extra time, however, cannot rely on any of these arguments. First, the examiner may well value speedy responsiveness. (The fact that exams are usually "speeded" for nondisabled students suggests that this is the case, though exams may, of course, be speeded inadvertently.) Moreover, the learning disabled (LD) student will not be utterly precluded from demonstrating her virtues if not accommodated. Finally, at least some other students would benefit from the accommodation, on at least some occasions. In that sense, the disabled student is seeking an easier, not just a different exam. So the subtler policy point we must ultimately resolve is what to do if we think—quite reasonably—that speed may be a virtue, but that dyslexic students get inadequate opportunity to demonstrate their other virtues unless given additional time. At that point, we would need to resolve the thorny problem of ascertaining what degree of penalty those who work slowly should suffer. (It is also interesting to ask whether we should accommodate all slow workers in the same way as those whose inability to respond rapidly is attributable to a conventionally diagnosed disability.)

My own view on testing accommodation is that there is little justification—other than rather trivial administrative cost-saving—for the general practice of giving speeded exams, and that the right response to the accommodation issue is to make sure that no students take such exams. One virtue of this solution is that it eliminates the pressure we now put on regimes to distinguish students who are eligible for time accommodations from those who are not. The distinctions we draw between the eligible and ineligible are both arbitrary and biased by class, race, and gender. They may also mindlessly drive other poor pedagogic decisions: Students may seek disability diagnoses in order to get exam accommodations but, in doing so, they may siphon off educational resources that could be better used by other poor learners.

My main point, however, is that whatever one's view of testing accommodation, determinations of what skills are appropriate to test and what can and cannot be justly tested and rewarded are policy issues. Casting them as issues of discrimination—do those with disabilities have the opportunity to succeed on tests?—assumes naively that norms against discrimination mandate equality of group outcome, rather than that inequalities be justified by real distinctions in relevant performance.

Segregation and Discipline

There is good reason to believe that mainstreaming physically disabled children has gone well, and that, in the elementary grades, mainstreaming of cognitively impaired kids has been relatively untroubled as well. But there are many cases in which emotionally and behaviorally disordered children have proven disruptive, even when mainstream teachers are tolerant, supportive, and adequately assisted by special education aides. To the degree that this is true, of course, we need to decide how to make vexing trade-offs: higher levels of integration may well improve the educational experience of disabled children but harm nondisabled children.

For present purposes, though, I simply want to make one narrow point. When Gillian Lester and I investigated how districts dealt with the IDEA's mandates,[2] we found that it was not uncommon for them to refuse to classify children with Attention Deficit Disorders (ADD) as eligible for special education services. (Other districts might classify them as "Other Health Impaired" or as "Learning Disabled.") What drove this decision, above all, was the fear that, if a potentially disruptive student were classified as disabled, it would be impossible down the road to suspend or expel him for misbehaving. If such a student's misbehavior were to be deemed a manifestation of his disability, then under the prevailing interpretation of the U.S. Supreme Court's decision in *Honig v. Doe*,[3] expulsion or long-term suspension would not be permitted for most (non-gun) offenses. The other side of the coin is that many kids with ADD would benefit from the services that special educators offer, which puts the administrator into a bind. The statute refuses to recognize conceptual distinctions or priorities among the policy questions: Is it worthwhile to devote extra material resources to this child? Is it sensible to allow this child to stay in school given his behavior? Instead, following the antidiscrimination model, the IDEA forces districts to decide that a person is or is not a member of a protected class, and then attaches certain strong privileges (such as an individualized educational program limited rather loosely by cost and immunity from discipline) to the class status. The administrator may covertly resist the status designation because it might entail more than he thinks is justified.

> *In a world of limited resources, it is plainly not enough to say that children with learning disabilities "deserve" more resources; their claims inevitably compete with claims that could be made by other "deserving" pupils.*

Scarcity and Resource Allocation

The most significant of the policy issues that we must face if we are to rethink the IDEA in a serious way is how to allocate funds among competing claimants, each of whom makes reasonable claims that he or she would benefit from higher spending levels. Answering this question requires us to think carefully both about the diverse principles we might use to allocate opportunities (or funds) and about the empirical difficulties of determining the impact of increased spending on the performance of differently situated students. Let's look at the group Professor Lester and I studied most carefully: students with learning disabilities (typically students with an otherwise unexplained gap between reading performance and "potential," generally measured by IQ tests). Students characterized as learning disabled (rather than, say, "garden variety" poor readers) receive educational help that costs a little more than half again as much as other pupils not dubbed disabled—though these other pupils may well have equally remediable (or preventable) difficulties in reading.

In a world of limited resources, it is plainly not enough to say that children with learning disabilities "deserve" more resources; their claims inevitably compete with claims that could be made by other "deserving" pupils who can be described in a wide variety of ways (such as poor achievers, socioeconomically disadvantaged, and gifted but understimulated).

> **The IDEA currently gives legal force to the position that claims by students with LDs to receive incremental resources have significant priority over claims by students not diagnosed as having a disability.**

The claims that students make upon resources can ultimately be adjudicated using a number of distinct principles. (Some reasonably believe that one principle is dominant while others believe that competing principles must be balanced against one another.) For instance, some would advocate that schools compensate students who have been deprived of stimulation in their home environments; in one such view, the sum of the "educational" inputs that each child receives from home and public sources should be the same. But there is clearly no strong overlap between prior resource deprivation and disability status. Others advocate spending equal sums per pupil, in part because they fear that any system departing from straight democratic equality would permit the state to be captured by the politically influential. Still others believe that the state should spend whatever extra resources are needed to ensure that each pupil is able, if possible, to live independently as an adult, but that there is no other reason to spend more on one pupil than another.

Professor Lester and I are most favorably predisposed toward some variant of what we describe as a "distribution-sensitive" utilitarian principle. This principle is less concerned with rectifying past injustices than looking forward to the consequences of educational interventions. Thus, imagine that we cared about only one educational output, test scores. (My fear is that this has become less of a hypothetical in the last few years, but that's a subject for a different essay!) If one were a utilitarian-consequentialist without concern for distribution, one would simply allocate resources to maximize the aggregate test scores of the affected group. In deciding whether to spend extra dollars on student Y rather than student Z, one would simply ask whether the incremental expenditure would improve Y's score more, or Z's. If one were distribution dependent in one's thinking, the identity of Y and Z might matter. We might think that if Y is a poorer student, for instance, the smaller gains in aggregate test scores would have greater consequences in his life than larger gains might have in Z's life. We might even believe that if Y is a member of a particular social group—African-Americans or people with disabilities, for example—then Y's gains have greater impact on others (in terms of their self-esteem or as a role model for others) than gains made by Z, a member of a socially privileged group. Ultimately, of course, we care about more than test scores; yet, our basic goal within this framework is to allocate education resources so as to maximize the "value" of academic performance, personal adjustment, social attitudes, and other outputs.

Conclusions

The IDEA currently gives legal force to the position that claims by students with LDs to receive incremental resources have significant priority over claims by students not diagnosed as having a disability. The precise legal nature of this claim is complex: formally, districts must provide disabled students with an appropriate education, without explicit reference to cost. The appropriate education, according to prevailing views of the U.S. Supreme Court's decision in *Rowley*,[4] however, is not an education which maximizes disabled students' performance but one which permits them to make reasonable educational progress. Presumably, of course, cost concerns (and trade-offs) are to some extent embedded in the decision not to enforce an obligation to maximize.

This priority is often justified by claiming that, among pupils with learning difficulties, only those with LDs manifest a gap between "potential" and "achievement" and are therefore uniquely able to benefit from discretionary interventions. This is an empirical proposition, however, a fact that is often obscured by fiat or wishful thinking. Learning disabilities are defined, in theory, as an otherwise-unexplained performance-potential gap; the logical conclusion is that those who suffer from LDs have remediable performance deficits. But once one stops treating the argument as a tautology, the assertion is weak. There is considerable evidence that non-LD pupils would also benefit from higher levels of educational inputs, and even stronger evidence that as a group, if not in each and every case, those with diagnosed LDs have been remarkably unresponsive to the costly special education that has been provided them. There is scant evidence, for instance, that dyslexics benefit more from the intervention of a reading specialist than do garden-variety poor readers, either in helping them learn to read or in compensating for their reading problems.

> *Until we see that many of the claims often made in debate over special education policy are important education issues but not civil rights claims, we will not make rational policy in this area.*

We have developed a political culture in which "mere" claims of need count for little. The cries of those who could use our aid seem to fall largely on deaf ears in the courts and the Congress. To get resources, we seem to need to argue that we are members of victimized groups and that the failure to get those resources is further proof that we are being discriminated against. I certainly don't believe that social groups are without meaning; much of the way we perceive ourselves is strongly derivative of the way in which members of our group are treated. But I don't believe that the sole distributive problem is the problem of group equality, either. There is remediable suffering in the world, and those who suffer may not be readily described in terms of group identity. We should be wary, too, of deciding that we must redo local spending decisions because they are contaminated by bigotry. When the IDEA's predecessor statute was enacted, kids with LD labels were richer, whiter, and more likely to be male than their classmates. Do we really believe that their interests were slighted in local political tussles?

The very first time Professor Lester interviewed a campus advocate for students with disabilities, her respondent confidently declared that, "Treatment of the learning disabled is a civil rights matter." But many just claims are not civil rights claims. Among these are claims often made in debate over special education policy: that some students are entitled to remedial actions to ensure they reach their educational potential, that tests should measure genuinely significant skills, and that students should not be disciplined when other viable options may better serve their interests while protecting those of their classmates. Until we see that these are important education issues but not civil rights claims, we will not make rational policy in this area.

---

[1] *Brown v. Bd. of Ed. of Topeka*, 347 U.S. 483 (1954).

[2] See Mark Kelman and Gillian Lester, *Jumping the Queue: An Inquiry into the Legal Treatment of Students with Learning Disabilities* (Cambridge: Harvard University Press, 1997).

[3] 484 U.S. 305 (1988).

[4] *Hendrick Hudson Dist. Bd. of Ed. v. Rowley*, 458 U.S. 176 (1982).

Chapter 5

Special but Unequal: Race and Special Education

Matthew Ladner and Christopher Hammons

Race, Poverty, and Special Education: An Introduction

Congress made special education services a major concern of school districts when it enacted Public Law 94-142, the Education for All Handicapped Children Act, in 1975. That act ushered in an era in which the federal government became active in financing and regulating special education services provided by local districts.

> *It is well known that public schools place a disproportionate number of minority students into special education programs and classes.*

This act, now the Individuals with Disabilities Education Act (IDEA), mandates a "free appropriate public education" for all children with disabilities regardless of the severity. This law also provides parents of a special education student with decisionmaking authority over their child's education, and requires that an individualized education program (IEP) be developed for each child with a disability. The law further requires that students with disabilities receive education services in the least restrictive environment. In 1997, Congress reauthorized the IDEA, requiring states to align more closely the IEPs of disabled students with the standards and curricula of children in general classrooms, and to include regular classroom teachers in the decisionmaking process. The IDEA also requires inclusion of students with disabilities in state and district assessment programs and in setting and reporting performance goals.

On the surface, American school districts and states seem to vary widely in the number of students classified as needing special education services. In 1995-96, Massachusetts certified 17.1 percent of its students in special education programs, while Illinois, New Jersey, and Ohio reported only 4.3 percent, 5.4 percent, and 3.9 percent special education rates, respectively. Variation among individual school districts is even greater.[1]

The federal definition of "learning disabilities" is especially vague, which presumably contributes to variation in diagnosis rates. The referral and identification process varies so much, in fact, that a child could be diagnosed as mildly mentally retarded in one setting but as having no disability in another.[2] Yet the incidence of learning disabilities and more recognizable physical disabilities (for example, blindness and deafness) across states does not differ significantly. In fact, there is slightly greater variance among physical disabilities than learning disabilities.[3]

Whether learning disabilities are randomly distributed across jurisdictions, or the identification process makes them appear to be so, both scenarios suggest a lack of "systemic drivers" to the special education process.[4] If learning disabilities are close to being randomly distributed, we should not expect to find factors such as race or income associated with variance in special education rates. However, if special education rates vary strongly across jurisdictions according to certain demographic variables, then we can conclude that special education diagnosis is not randomly distributed but is influenced by other factors as well. Most special education researchers take this latter position.

Many scholars have identified poverty, for example, as an underlying variable that influences special education rates. Analysts have consistently associated mild mental retardation diagnosis with low socioeconomic status,[5] and research suggests that this may account partially for the disproportionate representation of African-American children in that category, as those youngsters tend to come from lower-income backgrounds.[6]

It is well-known that public schools place a disproportionate number of minority students into special education programs and classes.[7] African-American students accounted for 16 percent of the total U.S. student population in 1992, but represented 32 percent of students in programs for mild mental retardation (MMR), 29 percent in programs for moderate mental retardation, and 24 percent in programs for serious emotional disturbance.[8] A statistical examination of 1978 data from the U.S. Department of Education's Office of Civil Rights found regional differences in the tendency to label minority students as educable mentally retarded (EMR), with the South showing the greatest difference between minority and white EMR designations. Alabama had more than four times as many minorities labeled EMR as whites.[9] Virginia lawmakers recently began an inquiry into overrepresentation of minority students in special education, citing the fact that African Americans represent 20 percent of the state's student population but 28 percent of its special education students, including 51 percent of those labeled EMR. In 1999, the Roanoke, Virginia, chapter of the NAACP asked the Office for Civil Rights to investigate whether the Roanoke schools had violated federal civil rights laws.[10]

In Virginia, African Americans represent 20 percent of the state's population but 28 percent of its special education students, including 51 percent of those labeled educable mentally retarded.

An Analysis of Counties and Districts

The literature on special education leads to the following assumptions: minorities often come from lower socioeconomic backgrounds; poverty is associated with learning disabilities; minorities are disproportionately represented in special education programs; and, as a result, special education rates among minority students are much higher than for white students. We tested these assumptions with county- and district-level data, using standard statistical techniques.

County-level data represent the aggregation of school-district data within counties. District-level data on special education enrollments are unavailable in most states, but county-level data are available from all states. Caution must be employed, however, because relationships between variables at the aggregate level may be the result of the aggregation itself.[11] For instance, a researcher performing a statistical analysis of urban counties alone might conclude that certain variables are unrelated to each other, when, in fact, the aggregating of data from both suburban and urban districts has canceled out the effect. The best strategy to deal with this potential problem is to examine as many levels of analysis as possible. Our analysis looks at both county and district levels, and it shows strikingly similar results. Additional checks at both state and school levels demonstrate a consistent pattern.[12] We conclude, therefore, that the results presented below do not result from aggregation.

Table 1. County-level Analysis of Special Education Rates in Selected States: Percentage of Minority and Free/Reduced-Lunch Eligible Children

Dependent variable: special education rates in all counties of selected states
Independent variables: percentage of minority and free/reduced-lunch eligible children

	Percentage of Minority Students	Percentage of F/R Lunch
California	-.037 (.014)**	.028 (.02)
Colorado	.018 (.030)	-.018 (.023)
Florida	-.058 (.018)**	.058 (.029)*
Georgia	-.037 (.014)*	.06 (.021)**
Maryland	-.046 (.015)**	.079 (.024)**
New York	-.05 (.024)*	.068 (.044)
Oregon	.022 (.030)	-.026 (.052)
Texas	-.079 (.013)***	.056 (.022)**
Wisconsin	.075 (.021)***	.03 (.030)

Note: OLS regression; entries are unstandardized regression coefficients; standard errors are in parentheses. Data source: Mark S. Littman and Deirdre A. Gaquin, *Education Statistics of the United States* (Washington, DC: Bernan Press, 1999).
* $p < .05$ ** $p < .01$ *** $p < .001$

Many states do not have a sufficient number of counties to perform a statistical analysis, and other states have small minority populations. Nevertheless, Table 1 presents regressions from a cross-section of states with county-level data. The dependent variable is the percentage of IEP students; the independent variables are the percentage of minority students and the percentage in a free/reduced lunch program.

The county-level analysis shows that the poverty variable is statistically significant in four of nine states, and behaves according to expectations: Increased levels of poverty lead to higher special education enrollments. The race variable proves to be statistically significant in seven of nine states. The race variable, however, behaves exactly contrary to our expectations. In six of the seven states with a significant relationship between race and special education (California, Florida, Georgia, Maryland, New York, and Texas), counties with *higher* percentages of minority students have significantly *lower* numbers of students in special education on average. Only Wisconsin, where there was a significant positive coefficient associated with higher percentages of minority students, behaved according to expectations with higher minority enrollment leading to higher special education enrollment.

Florida and Maryland organize their school districts on a countywide basis, meaning that the results presented in Table 1 for those states are essentially district-level results.[13] Table 2 presents

---

Table 2. Analysis of Special Education (Dependent Variable), Race, Poverty, and Spending per Pupil in Florida and Maryland School Districts

Independent Variables	Maryland	Florida
Spending per Pupil	-.0008	.0004
	(.000 5)	(.0004)
Percentage of Minority Students	-.034*	-.063**
	(.016)	(.018)
Percentage of F/R Lunch Students	.065**	.057
	(.025)	(.029)
Constant	17.52***	11.97***
	(3.52)	(2.13)
R-Square	.44	.15
N	23	66

Note: OLS regression; entries are unstandardized regression coefficients; standard errors are in parenthesis. Data source: Mark S. Littman and Deirdre A. Gaquin, *Education Statistics of the United States* (Washington, DC: Bernan Press, 1999).* p < .05 ** p < .01 *** p < .001

---

an additional control variable for these two states: spending per pupil at the district level. Is it possible that districts with higher percentages of minority students simply have fewer resources to spend on special education, but these differences are lost in the aggregation of state- and county-level data? Inclusion of a spending-per-pupil control variable will account for this possibility.

Table 2 shows that controlling for spending per pupil fails to achieve statistical significance, while a higher poverty rate (as measured by the level of free/reduced lunch students) raises special education enrollment and an increased number of minority students in a district lowers it. The possible aggregation problem still remains, however. Although Florida and Maryland districts are run on a county basis, they represent the aggregation of many schools into large districts. Dividing Florida into county-size districts ensures, for instance, that wide variations among schools within the same district will wash out at the aggregate level.

District-level data from Texas are the most revealing and lend themselves especially well to analysis. The Texas district-level data contain additional information not readily available in other states, including detailed financial and student information. These data enable us to distinguish among separate categories of minority students, specifying percentages of African-American and Hispanic students, for example. The Texas data also include information on the percentage of school-district revenue raised locally (higher local revenue is a sign of greater property wealth) as well as revenue per pupil and the percentage of economically disadvantaged students. Regressing these independent variables against the percentage of students classified in special education programs shows that they all have significant effects on special education enrollment. The results are presented in Table 3.

The financial variables perform according to expectations: higher proportions of economically disadvantaged students are associated with higher special education rates. Likewise, as the percentage of local revenue increases, special education rates decline: richer districts have fewer students in special education. Total revenue per pupil has a significant yet weak effect on special education rates.

Table 3. Race, Spending, and Special Education in Texas School Districts: District-level Analysis with All Texas School Districts

Dependent variable: percentage of students exempted from the
TAAS accountability exam due to special education status

Independent Variables:

Percentage of Free/Reduced Lunch Students	.090 (.009)***
Percentage of African-American Students	-.073 (.010)***
Percentage of Hispanic Students	-.108 (.006)***
Percentage of Local Revenue	-.045 (.006)***
Revenue per Pupil	.0007 (.00007)***
R-Square	.29
Constant	10.95 (.567)***
N=1059	

Note: OLS regression; entries are unstandardized regression coefficients; standard errors are in parenthesis. Data source: Texas Education Agency, *AEIS Report, 1997-8.*
* $p < .05$ ** $p < .01$ *** $p < .001$

Figure 1 presents the relative effects of various independent variables such as race, revenue, and poverty on special education enrollment in Texas. All factors presented in Figure 1 are statistically significant. The influence of race, however, stands out. In Texas districts, minority enrollment—especially Hispanic enrollment—significantly decreases the number of children in special education programs. Even with separate controls for poverty and revenue, the race variables prove significant.

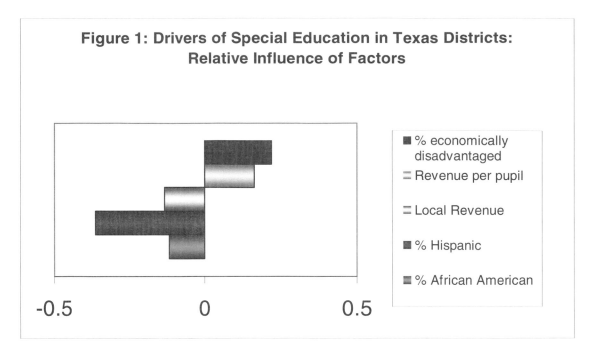

Figure 1: Drivers of Special Education in Texas Districts: Relative Influence of Factors

- % economically disadvantaged
- Revenue per pupil
- Local Revenue
- % Hispanic
- % African American

-0.5　　　　0　　　　0.5

The Relationship Between Minority Student Enrollment and Special Education Certification

Previous literature suggests that minority students are overrepresented in special education, but the analysis presented here suggests that a larger percentage of minority children is associated with fewer students in special education. The relationship between the percentage of minority students and the percentage of students enrolled in special education is all the more mysterious when you consider the fact that minorities overall are more likely than whites to be enrolled in special education.

Why greater percentages of minority students are associated with significantly lower special education rates represents the central paradox of this study. Our research question is: *How can we explain statistics showing that minorities are more likely to be placed in special education when our data indicate that districts with higher percentages of minorities have lower percentages of special education students?* We explore different answers to this question, which we have formulated into four hypotheses. We developed these hypotheses by interviewing officials with expertise in special education. Each hypothesis is independently assessed. The variables developed in the exploration of each hypothesis are included in a summary model from which final conclusions are drawn.

Hypothesis 1—Financial Status: Majority-minority districts provide fewer special education services due to a lack of resources.

Many educators assert that the quality of education is directly related to funding.[14] The poor quality of education in many urban districts, particularly majority-minority districts, is often attributed to insufficient funds. The mantra of many educators is that more money is needed. Given the recurrence of this charge, might it also be the case that enrollment in special education programs suffers in districts with fewer financial resources? If so, we would expect to see lower enrollment in poorer districts and higher enrollment in more affluent districts. We tested this hypothesis by focusing on three related variables.

First, we examined district-level per-pupil spending. Though states typically fund districts on a per-pupil basis, spending per pupil is not always the same across districts. Some larger urban districts have much greater demands on their resources, and available funds are used for a greater variety of expenses. Given our initial findings, however, one might expect to see lower spending per pupil associated with lower rates of special education.

> **Our data reveal no correlation between special education enrollment and per-pupil district expenditures.**

Second, we looked at class size as a function of school resources. The argument is often made that poorer school districts are forced to crowd more students into classrooms. This practice may be a consequence of insufficient facilities and a shortage of teachers. The lower enrollment in special education in less affluent districts, therefore, may be a result of overcrowding in the schools. One educator we interviewed suggested that teachers in larger classrooms may have a more difficult time identifying students with special needs simply because there are so many students of different skill levels.

Third, we examined variations in teacher pay. Salary issues are a recurrent theme in education reform. Critics charge that teacher wages are too low to attract and retain qualified people, a charge with which many educators concur.[15] "The pay for teachers in general is not great," observed Evy Friend, Director of Exceptional Student Education Programs and Services in the Florida Department of Education. "Attracting special education teachers is even more difficult because of low prestige, a disproportionate amount of paperwork, and the increased threat of litigation." Considering this, one might expect to find a statistically significant relationship between teacher pay and special education enrollment.

To determine the relationship of these variables to special education enrollment, we weighted each school district in terms of its relative size compared to all other districts in the sample. A handful of large urban districts with many students would otherwise have a disproportionate influence on the analysis. Dade County, for example, accounts for over 15 percent of all students in Florida. Dade County also has over 85 percent minority students. Hence, thousands of the state's minority students are located in that one district. To resolve this problem, we weighted each district by the proportion of minority students that it has compared to the proportion in the state as a whole.

Table 4 provides correlation statistics between our dependent variable (the percentage of students enrolled in special education courses) and our three independent variables (per-pupil spending, student-teacher ratio, and teacher salary). With regard to enrollment in special education programs, the data reveal no correlation with per-pupil district expenditures. Given the weak effect reported in our previous regressions, this is not entirely surprising.

Table 4 indicates that spending per pupil tends to be slightly greater in districts with more minorities. This may simply reflect greater financial resources because these districts have a larger number of students eligible for aid from state and federal governments.[16] The link

---

Table 4. Percentage of Students Enrolled in Special Education Courses Correlated with Possible Predictors

Correlations

		SPECED % of students in district labeled as special ed	SPENDING district expenditures per pupil 1995	TEACHPUP teacher to pupil ratio	SALARY average salary for teachers 1995	PMS % minority students in district
SPECED % of students in district labeled as special ed	Pearson Correlation	1.000	.027	-.255**	-.401**	-.519**
	Sig. (2-tailed)	.	.367	.000	.000	.000
	N	1126	1126	1126	1126	1126
SPENDING district expenditures per pupil 1995	Pearson Correlation	.027	1.000	-.273**	.202**	.195**
	Sig. (2-tailed)	.367	.	.000	.000	.000
	N	1126	1126	1126	1126	1126
TEACHPUP teacher to pupil ratio	Pearson Correlation	-.255**	-.273**	1.000	.407**	.157**
	Sig. (2-tailed)	.000	.000	.	.000	.000
	N	1126	1126	1126	1126	1126
SALARY average salar for teachers 1995	Pearson Correlation	-.401**	.202**	.407**	1.000	.407**
	Sig. (2-tailed)	.000	.000	.000	.	.000
	N	1126	1126	1126	1126	1126
PMS % minority students in district	Pearson Correlation	-.519**	.195**	.157**	.407**	1.000
	Sig. (2-tailed)	.000	.000	.000	.000	.
	N	1126	1126	1126	1126	1126

** Correlation is significant at the 0.01 level (2-tailed).

---

between funding and quality of education, however, is difficult to establish. "There's little relationship between spending and student performance in those high-poverty schools," says Eric Hanushek, an economist at the Hoover Institution. "If anything, the schools that spend more money have less to show for it."[17]

Table 4 also reveals an interesting pattern. Increased class size is indeed associated with lower rates of enrollment in special education programs. This finding is intuitively appealing because larger classes might make it more difficult to identify the needs of individual students. This assumption was reasserted by many of the educators we interviewed. If overcrowding occurs more often in less affluent districts, which tend to be majority-minority districts, this might help partially explain why districts with greater percentages of minorities enroll fewer students in special education. Table 4 indicates that schools with many minority youngsters also tend to have slightly more crowded classrooms. Although the relationship is modest, it is difficult not to consider class size a contributor to special education enrollment rates.

A third variable of interest is teacher salary. Nationwide shortages of teachers have made pay a hot-button issue for education reform. Average salary for starting teachers in 1999 was roughly $26,000, with great variation depending on the state and district. The educators we spoke with, however, disagreed on whether salary or location is the bigger barrier to attracting good teachers.

"The pay in urban districts is better, but the cost of living is higher, and the classroom discipline problems may be worse," observed Dr. Irene Savary, Director of Exceptional Education Programs for Wakulla County School District in Florida. On the other hand, Catie McRae, Director of Exceptional Student Education in Gadsden County School District, Florida, noted that, "Rural areas typically have a harder time getting qualified teachers because it's harder to find people willing to relocate to these areas. This, coupled with lower pay, makes it hard to recruit and retain good teachers."

Table 4 shows that districts with higher salaries typically have lower enrollment in special education programs; conversely, districts with low pay place significantly more students in special education. We do not contend that variations in salary directly influence the rate at which students are placed in special education programs; rather an examination of salary allows us to look for relationships between a district's resources and its special education rates.

> **Districts with more white teachers have a greater rate of minority enrollment in special education, especially among African-American students.**

At first, it would appear that more affluent districts (with higher salaries) are placing fewer students into special education programs. One possibility is that these numbers must reflect wealthy districts with few minority students. Yet our data indicate that districts with more minorities actually have slightly higher salaries than predominantly white districts. The experts we consulted did not consider this finding unusual, noting that the cost of living in urban areas, where minorities tend to be concentrated, is greater and hence usually translates into higher pay for teachers.

Salary, then, may not be the best measure of district affluence. Poor urban districts may have reasonably well-paid teachers. By contrast, schoolteachers in affluent districts may be less well-paid; recall those communities where students drive much nicer cars than the instructors. A better measure might be to look at differences in urban versus rural settings and to measure per-capita income and poverty levels. We do exactly that in the next section. However, these findings support our initial contention that districts with more minorities place fewer students in special education.

Of the variables examined here, both class size and salary are related to special education rates. To test the relative importance of the two variables, we examine two additional models. It is evident in Table 5 that both variables are significant; neither drops from the equation. The table also indicates that teacher pay is a stronger predictor of special education enrollment than the student/teacher ratio. It is important to remember that the regression model does not imply that one variable *causes* a change in the other. The model only denotes that changes in one variable can predict changes in the dependent variable.

Resources do matter—at least as predictors of special education enrollment. We cannot determine whether they actually influence the process by which students are placed in special education courses. What we can say is that districts with both bigger classes and bigger salaries tend to place smaller percentages of students into special education courses. In the next section,

Table 5. Measuring District Resources: Salary and Class Size as Predictors of Special Education Enrollment

Coefficients[a]

Model		Unstandardized Coefficients		Standardized Coefficients	t	Sig.
		B	Std. Error	Beta		
1	(Constant)	27.872	1.072		25.995	.000
	SALARY average salary for teachers 1995	-4.81E-04	.000	-.401	-14.654	.000
2	(Constant)	28.741	1.092		26.322	.000
	SALARY average salary for teachers 1995	-4.28E-04	.000	-.356	-11.958	.000
	TEACHPUP teacher to pupil ratio	-.158	.043	-.110	-3.691	.000

a. Dependent Variable: SPECED % of students in district labeled as special ed

we examine the possibility that the relationship truly being measured here is one of urban versus rural districts. We will also return to the question of class size and salaries in our final analysis.

Hypothesis 2—District Competence: Urban districts are less competent in identifying special-needs students.

If financial resources do not make a difference in special education enrollment rates, we must look elsewhere for explanations. It may be that special education rates vary between districts as a result of district competence in identifying students with special needs. To this end, lower rates of special education enrollment in districts with greater percentages of minorities could indicate that minority students are poorly served by their school districts, regardless of available finances. We hypothesize that success in identifying learning disabilities might be partially a function of the competency of districts in which minority students are enrolled.

> Our data indicate that the more urban a school district, the lower the percentage of minority students enrolled in special education programs in that district.

Data from the 1990 census show that, in Florida and Texas, urban districts generally have a greater percentage of minority students as part of the total student body than rural districts. This is a national trend as well. It has been estimated that in the mid-1990s, for example, 53.8 percent of urban schools had predominantly African-American student populations.[18] In some cities the number is higher: Milwaukee, 61 percent; Philadelphia, 64 percent; St. Louis, 80 percent; Atlanta, 92 percent; and Birmingham, 94 percent.[19]

Urban districts often come under fire for doing a poor job of educating students, particularly special education youngsters.[20] Our data indicate that the more urban a school district, the lower the percentage of minority students enrolled in special education programs in that district. There are three reasons why this might be the case.

First, urban districts, particularly inner-city schools, under-identify students with special needs because these schools have different priorities. Second, urban schools face a host of problems that preoccupy and distract them.[21] Third, it is not easy to find good teachers who want positions in the inner city. "One of the greatest complaints of new teachers is that the students are terribly behaved and have little respect for authority," says Dr. Savary. "It's one of the reasons so few people want to go into teaching nowadays. And with fear of lawsuits, we basically have to rely on uniformed police to resolve discipline problems."

> *Districts with high percentages of minority students—regardless of whether they are urban or rural, rich or poor—actually tend to place fewer of their pupils in special education programs.*

These factors lead to the possibility that urban districts may be less effective in providing quality education to students in general and particularly those with learning disabilities. It is a hypothesis supported by many national studies that indicate lower test scores, higher dropout rates, and generally poor academic performance in urban districts. Might it also be, then, that efforts to identify students with learning disabilities are simply not as effective in such districts?

According to Diane Johnson, Director of the Florida Diagnostic and Learning Resource System in Tallahassee, that is a real possibility. "Schools vary greatly in the total number of students they refer to special education," says Mrs. Johnson. "The academic standards of the school are an important factor. Schools with low academic standards may fail to identify students who are not performing well on tests because expectations are not high to begin with."

It is difficult to test district competency because no standardized measure exists. However, two surrogate measures are available. First, district dropout rates may provide some indication of the district's general level of organizational competency. Pupil retention is a problem in many districts that struggle to maintain academic standards, and it is a particular problem in urban areas. We use the percentage of students dropping out of the public school system, as measured at the district level in Florida in 1996-1997. We hypothesize that higher dropout rates are associated with lower district competency—that the schools have somehow failed to keep students enrolled. Although retention may be related to factors outside the district's control, our goal is to see if special education rates among minorities suffer as a result of problems related to urban districts, and a high dropout rate is one of these problems.

Second, we use scores on high school math competency exams as an indicator of general academic success. These test scores may provide some indication of the quality of education. Once we account for differences in wealth and race, we can see whether urban schools score lower than non-urban schools, and determine if there is an "urban" effect on education that is independent of the effects of low-income and minority enrollments.

As expected, these variables show some relationship to enrollment in special education. Table 6 reveals that urban areas tend to place a smaller percentage of their students into special education than do rural areas. Districts with higher dropout rates tend to place fewer kids in special education. And districts with higher math scores tend to have higher rates of special education enrollment. In sum, special education rates are lower both in urban districts and in

Table 6. District Competence: Dropout Rates, Math Scores, and Urbanization

Correlations

		SPECED	DROPOUT percent of dropouts, 1997	MATHSCOR % passing HSCT math test	URBAN# 1990 Census
SPECED	Pearson Correlation	1.000	-.292*	.462**	-.718**
	Sig. (2-tailed)	.	.017	.000	.000
	N	67	67	67	67
DROPOUT percent of dropouts, 1997	Pearson Correlation	-.292*	1.000	-.522**	.473**
	Sig. (2-tailed)	.017	.	.000	.000
	N	67	67	67	67
MATHSCOR % passing HSCT math test	Pearson Correlation	.462**	-.522**	1.000	-.497**
	Sig. (2-tailed)	.000	.000	.	.000
	N	67	67	67	67
URBAN# 1990 Census	Pearson Correlation	-.718**	.473**	-.497**	1.000
	Sig. (2-tailed)	.000	.000	.000	.
	N	67	67	67	67

*. Correlation is significant at the 0.05 level (2-tailed).

**. Correlation is significant at the 0.01 level (2-tailed).

areas with lower levels of academic success when measured in terms of retention rates and skills tests.

Table 6 also indicates that lower test scores and higher dropout rates are associated with urban districts. Hence, these districts do not demonstrate the same level of academic achievement as non-urban districts. To this end, one might conclude that urban districts are less successful in educating their students and that, as a result, students with learning disabilities are more likely to be overlooked.

Others might say that the problems of urban districts are not due to lack of competence but to problems beyond the scope of the schools. We examined a number of possibilities:

- the percentage of students on free lunch programs and per-capita income (as indicators of poverty);
- crime rate and district teenage pregnancy rate (as indicators of general urban problems);
- the percentage of minorities in the district; and
- the level of urbanization, measured as the number of people living in cities within the district.

Table 7. District Competence: Community Culture Influences on Special Education Enrollment, Florida Only

Correlations

		SPECED % of students in district labeled as special ed	CAPITA average per capita income 1995	LUNCH % of students on free lunch	UNWED % births in district to unwed teens	CRIME 1995 crime rate per 100,000 people	PMS % minority students in district	URBAN # people in district who live in urban setting
SPECED % of students in district labeled as special ed	Pearson Correlation	1.000	.017	-.362**	.225**	-.595**	-.744**	-.718**
	Sig. (2-tailed)		.720	.000	.000	.000	.000	.000
	N	426	426	421	426	426	426	426
CAPITA average per capita income 1995	Pearson Correlation	.017	1.000	-.544**	-.477**	.146**	.022	.177**
	Sig. (2-tailed)	.720		.000	.000	.003	.651	.000
	N	426	426	421	426	426	426	426
LUNCH % of students on free lunch	Pearson Correlation	-.362**	-.544**	1.000	.565**	.446**	.610**	.391**
	Sig. (2-tailed)	.000	.000		.000	.000	.000	.000
	N	421	421	421	421	421	421	421
UNWED % births in district to unwed teens	Pearson Correlation	.225**	-.477**	.565**	1.000	-.108*	-.075	-.367**
	Sig. (2-tailed)	.000	.000	.000		.026	.124	.000
	N	426	426	421	426	426	426	426
CRIME 1995 crime rate per 100,000 people	Pearson Correlation	-.595**	.146**	.446**	-.108*	1.000	.849**	.811**
	Sig. (2-tailed)	.000	.003	.000	.026		.000	.000
	N	426	426	421	426	426	426	426
PMS % minority students in district	Pearson Correlation	-.744**	.022	.610**	-.075	.849**	1.000	.878**
	Sig. (2-tailed)	.000	.651	.000	.124	.000		.000
	N	426	426	421	426	426	426	426
URBAN # people in district who live in urban setting	Pearson Correlation	-.718**	.177**	.391**	-.367**	.811**	.878**	1.000
	Sig. (2-tailed)	.000	.000	.000	.000	.000	.000	
	N	426	426	421	426	426	426	426

**. Correlation is significant at the 0.01 level (2-tailed).
*. Correlation is significant at the 0.05 level (2-tailed).

Table 7 presents the correlations for these variables. Three of the four have a negative relationship with special education enrollment: the percentage of students in free-lunch programs, the crime rate, and the percentage of minorities in a district. In districts that have high crime, high poverty, and high concentrations of minorities, and also are urban, special education enrollment tends to decline. Unraveling this mystery requires us to determine which of these variables is most important. (Of course, they are all related to some degree.) Is the lower rate of enrollment in special education programs predominantly an urban phenomenon linked to poverty and school climate, or does this occur in other districts as well? To test this question, we use a regression model with the same variables.

The results in Table 8 show that poverty is an important predictor of special education enrollment (Model 1), but it is insignificant once crime is taken into consideration (Model 2). Model 3, however, indicates that once the level of urbanization is also factored in, crime and poverty both become insignificant. Hence, the phenomenon we are studying occurs in urban rather than rural areas.

Table 8. Urbanization, Crime, and Poverty as Predictors of Special Education Enrollment

Coefficients[a]

Model		Unstandardized Coefficients		Standardized Coefficients		
		B	Std. Error	Beta	t	Sig.
1	(Constant)	17.098	1.065		16.056	.000
	LUNCH	-.107	.028	-.433	-3.869	.000
2	(Constant)	18.682	1.006		18.577	.000
	LUNCH	-4.41E-02	.028	-.177	-1.552	.126
	CRIME Crime Rate per 100,000 pop.	-5.21E-04	.000	-.505	-4.417	.000
3	(Constant)	15.863	1.095		14.482	.000
	LUNCH	-2.38E-02	.025	-.096	-.933	.354
	CRIME Crime Rate per 100,000 pop.	-8.81E-06	.000	-.009	-.056	.955
	URBAN# 1990 Census	-2.57E-06	.000	-.663	-4.387	.000
4	(Constant)	14.508	1.103		13.151	.000
	LUNCH	3.241E-02	.029	.130	1.103	.274
	CRIME Crime Rate per 100,000 pop.	2.449E-04	.000	.237	1.481	.144
	URBAN# 1990 Census	-1.13E-06	.000	-.291	-1.601	.114
	MINORITY	-8.61E-02	.027	-.780	-3.244	.002

a. Dependent Variable: SPECED

The most intriguing statistic from Table 8 is in Model 4, which indicates that urbanization, crime, and poverty are all not strong predictors of special education enrollment once the minority composition of the district is taken into consideration. Lower special education enrollment appears to be more determined by the racial composition of the student body than by a district's wealth, school climate, or urbanization.

These findings are in line with the opinions of many educators with whom we spoke, who did not note any real difference between urban and rural districts. Usually their concerns were class size, funding, and classroom discipline, but they did not feel that these issues were exclusive to urban schools. Although there may be some element of urbanism that we have failed to consider—for instance, student morale, school violence, or academic standards—there appears to be little statistical difference between urban and rural districts, or rich or poor districts with regard to special education enrollment.

In sum, the data again indicate that the percentage of minority students in a district is the driving force in determining special education rates. Contrary to the assumption that more students in these districts are enrolled in special education programs, districts with high percentages of minority students—regardless of whether they are urban or rural, rich or poor—actually tend to place fewer of their pupils in special education programs.

Hence the puzzle continues. As shown earlier, the cause does not seem to be a function of finances. Our data also indicate that special education levels seem unrelated to generic urban problems. Instead, there seems to be an effect stemming from the racial composition of the district. Identifying the cause of that effect is the objective of the next two hypotheses.

Hypothesis 3—Parental Attitudes: The finding that districts with a high percentage of minority students place fewer pupils in special education programs can be explained by the fact that minority parents are reluctant to place children in special education programs because they fear that their children will be given lower quality instruction, will never return to the regular classroom, and/or will be stereotyped.

Parental understanding and support are important to any educator, even more so for teachers who work with students with special needs. Parental attitudes could play an important role in determining levels of enrollment in special education programs. Attitudes are difficult to measure, however, and a new survey of parental attitudes was beyond the scope of this study.

> *The possibility exists that varying special education rates may reflect differences in demands placed on schools for such services.*

Still, it seems likely that parental attitude toward placing a child in a special education program is not only important but might be associated with a variety of factors. Determining what these factors are, and how they influence parental support, may help shed light on variations in special education enrollments.

Reluctance to enroll a child in special education may be caused in part by the perception that such a placement will result in a negative label or stereotype. "We often encounter resistance from parents who don't want their kids placed in special education programs," says one high level official on the Florida school system. "The primary reason is that they fear the label. It has a stigma attached to it for some people. The other reason is that they fear [that] once the student is placed in a special education program, they will be in special education for the rest of their schooling."

Researchers have found that such concerns are especially widespread among minority parents, particularly African-Americans, who are said to resist placing a child in special education because they fear that the child will experience academic isolation, that other disabled students will have a negative effect on their child's behavior, and that there will be other implications of the special education label for their child. The fact that our statistical analysis indicates lower special education rates among minority students in districts with a greater percentage of minorities adds empirical support to this hypothesis.

Parental support for placing a child in special education may stem partly from a parent's ability to get answers to questions and gather information. Learning that their child may have special needs can be difficult for some parents. Although it is common for parents to have concerns about placing their child in special education classes, some claim that this concern is fueled by lack of information. Parents who resist enrolling their children in special education programs may do so in part because of inability to find answers to their questions. Special education jargon and labels can be particularly confusing.[22] A desire for information, the patience to navigate a complex bureaucracy, the ability to formulate questions, and the confidence to confront authority figures are critical for parents who seek answers.

This could mean that the educational background of the parent may in part determine his or her success in obtaining information. "Parents who are better educated are usually more aggressive in seeking answers to their questions," according to one district official in Texas. "This does not mean that parents who are not as well-educated are less concerned about their child's education. Parents with less education are often less vocal, less familiar with the lingo, and sometimes feel less secure confronting teachers and administrators."

On the other hand, minority parents may simply be expressing completely rational concerns, given the way special education programs function in their communities. Assessing the source and accuracy of hostility toward special education programs lies outside of the scope of this research. The possibility exists, however, that varying special education rates may reflect differences in demands placed on schools for such services. Simply put, predominantly white communities may have a greater desire for special education services than predominantly minority communities. Such a difference may reflect socioeconomic factors such as education levels or different cultural values.

> *Some of the educators with whom we talked suggested that, because special education students get special treatment, parents often become the biggest supporters of enrolling their child.*

Using data from the 1990 census, we can determine the educational attainment level of any county in the United States. There is great variation. Florida facilitates comparison because of its use of county-level school districts. Using the percentage of people over age 25 who have completed high school as a measure of educational attainment, the range is a low of 54 percent in De Soto County to a high of 85 percent in Leon County. This is not the most accurate measure of education among parents because it does not differentiate among adults with children in school and those without; however, it does allow some general comparisons among school districts and is the best measure available.

We find no relationship between adult educational attainment at the district level and the percentage of minority students in special education, either as a percentage of all students in the district or as a percentage of minority students alone. The relationship is statistically insignificant in both cases, no matter whether we use high school or college graduation as a measure of education. Although both measures are crude, they still reflect the likelihood that a parent will have a high school or college diploma. To this end, we cannot say that lower levels of education among minority parents reduce the likelihood of their child enrolling in special education programs. However, our analysis revealed no relationship between wealth or education among adults in the district and levels of enrollment in special education programs by minority students. This does not mean that these variables do not affect the attitudes of some parents toward special education programs, only that such effects do not show up at the district level. A study of parent attitudes using survey data may reveal different relationships.

It is interesting to note that many districts make great efforts to reach out to parents regardless of race, income, or education. Such has been the advice of many special education reformers and researchers.[23] Their intent is to reduce any anxiety parents may have regarding special education programs and involve them more in the decisionmaking process.

"Parents are a big part of the equation," contends Teresa Williamson, Special Education Director for Fort Worth Independent School District in Texas. "It's really important to offer parents as much information as they need to make informed decisions." The Texas Education Agency has established a Parent's Information Hotline that parents may call to ask questions, express concerns, or lodge complaints if they do not have success at the district level. According to Claudia Knowles, a veteran TEA specialist who oversees the hotline, "We get calls from parents of all races and backgrounds. It doesn't seem to be limited to one particular group."

> **Districts with more white teachers have a greater rate of minority enrollment in special education, especially among African-American students.**

Some of the educators with whom we talked suggested that, because special education students get special treatment, parents often become the biggest supporters of enrolling their child. According to Catie McRae of the predominantly black Gadsden County School District in Florida, "Word gets out that these programs can be a great help to students who are struggling in school. Many parents actually encourage the placement of their kids into these programs. The kids get more attention and it gives them more opportunity to jump some of the barriers that traditionally get in the way of students, such as retention tests." In this sense, special education may be seen as a means of advancement, rather than a barrier to academic success. Such perceptions, it should be noted, vary widely according by community.

Hypothesis 4—Social Segregation: The finding that districts with a high percentage of minority students place fewer pupils in special education programs can be explained by the fact that predominantly white districts place a higher percentage of their minority students into special education services than do predominantly minority districts.

Evidence that minority students are placed into special education programs at higher rates than white students is nothing new.[24] What is new is our counter-intuitive finding that districts with the highest concentration of minorities tend to have the lowest rates of special education enrollment, not the highest, despite the fact that minorities are enrolled in special education at higher rates than whites. In attempting to explain this paradox, we have focused intently on minority districts, looking at such factors as district revenues, district competency, and parental attitudes to explain why special education enrollment is so much lower in minority districts.

One area we have so far neglected is the racial composition of the district itself. Although districts with higher proportions of white students may have greater percentages of students in special education programs than minority districts, it does not necessarily follow that white districts place higher percentages of *white* children in these programs. Districts with higher percentages of white students may simply be placing more of their *minority* students into special education programs. Such a phenomenon could help explain the fact that districts with higher

Table 9. District Composition and Special Education Enrollment

Correlations

		MSPED minorities in special ed as % of minorities in district	PWS % of white students in district	SPECW White students in special ed as % of all white students
MSPED minorities in special ed as % of minorities in district	Pearson Correlation	1.000	.247**	.150**
	Sig. (2-tailed)	.	.000	.000
	N	1043	1043	1042
SPECW White students in special ed as % of all white students	Pearson Correlation	.150**	-.011	1.000
	Sig. (2-tailed)	.000	.715	.
	N	1042	1118	1118
PWS % of white students in district	Pearson Correlation	.247**	1.000	-.011
	Sig. (2-tailed)	.000	.	.715
	N	1043	1126	1118

** . Correlation is significant at the 0.01 level (2-tailed).

percentages of white students also have higher special education rates, even as minority students demonstrate greater special education rates in the aggregate.

To test this possibility, we divided special education students into minority and non-minority groups. For purposes of our analysis, minority students consisted of black, Hispanic, and Asian students. (Native-Americans were such a small percentage of the population that they did not alter the analysis.) Table 9 reveals a direct relationship between the racial composition of the student body and the racial composition of students placed in special education. Districts with a greater percentage of white students place a slightly higher *percentage* of their *minority* students into special education compared to primarily minority districts.

The correlation between the percentage of white students enrolled in special education and the percentage of white students in the district is insignificant. If predominantly white districts simply enrolled a larger number of special education students in general, we should see an increase in enrollment in both white and minority rates. However, what we see is an increase only in the rates of enrollment among minority students. This would seem to indicate that, in predominantly white districts, minority students are treated differently.

To explore the impact of ethnicity in special education, we plotted the enrollment rate of different ethnic groups in special education programs against the percentage of the student body that is white. The results are presented in Figure 2. Two things are immediately evident.

- *First, white districts enroll a greater percentage of minority students in special education than majority-minority districts.* Enrollment rates for all ethnic groups are highest in

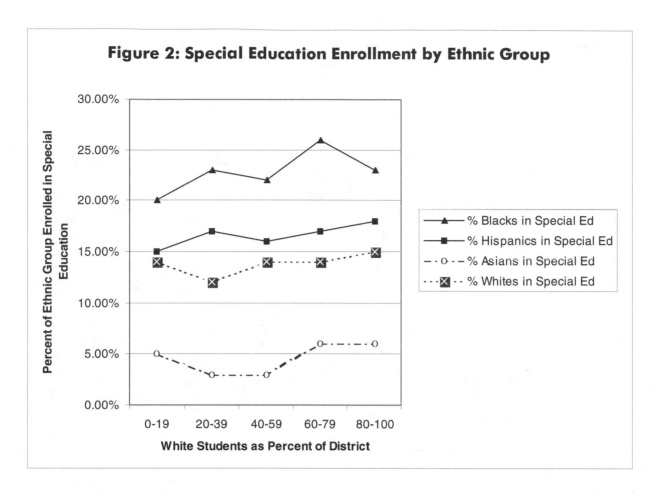

Figure 2: Special Education Enrollment by Ethnic Group

primarily white districts, and enrollment rates seem to vary most for blacks and Hispanics in predominantly white districts (60 percent white or greater).

- *Second, a greater percentage of black students are placed in special education programs than any other racial group.* Black students have a much higher special education rate than Hispanic and white students in every category. Similar trends have been reported elsewhere.[25] In predominantly white districts, special education enrollment among blacks is 9-10 percent higher than in other districts. Although this difference may not appear significant, it means that in predominantly white districts, almost one in every four black students is in special education. It also represents an enrollment rate 50 percent higher than that of white students. Hispanic student enrollment is consistently a few percentage points higher than white students but lower than black students.

There is some evidence, then, that in districts with predominantly white students, minority students—particularly black students—are treated differently. One could say that the disparity in rates of enrollment reflects little more than differences in academic standards among the districts. That is, perhaps minority students have a more difficult time in white districts because such districts maintain more rigorous academic requirements than inner-city districts. Academic difficulties of a minority student may be interpreted as a learning disability because the student is "slow" or not on the same learning level as his or her white peers.[26]

Table 10. Correlations of Faculty, Race, and Racial Composition of Students in Special Education

Correlations

		BTEACHER % of teachers in district that are black	HTEACHER % of teachers in district that are hispanic	WTEACHER % of teachers in district that are white	SPECBLAC African-Americans in special ed as % of all black students	SPECHIS Latinos in special ed as % of all Hispanic students	SPECW White students in special ed as % of all white students
BTEACHER % of teachers in district that are black	Pearson Correlation	1.000	-.077**	-.500**	-.211**	-.274**	-.076*
	Sig. (2-tailed)	.	.010	.000	.000	.000	.011
	N	1126	1126	1126	1033	1118	1118
HTEACHER % of teachers in district that are hispanic	Pearson Correlation	-.077**	1.000	-.824**	-.137**	-.076*	-.012
	Sig. (2-tailed)	.010	.	.000	.000	.011	.700
	N	1126	1126	1126	1033	1118	1118
WTEACHER % of teachers in district that are white	Pearson Correlation	-.500**	-.824**	1.000	.245**	.225**	.059
	Sig. (2-tailed)	.000	.000	.	.000	.000	.050
	N	1126	1126	1126	1033	1118	1118
SPECBLAC African-Ameicans in special ed as % of all black students	Pearson Correlation	-.211**	-.137**	.245**	1.000	.613**	.169**
	Sig. (2-tailed)	.000	.000	.000	.	.000	.000
	N	1033	1033	1033	1033	1032	1032
SPECHIS Latinos in special ed as % of all Hispanic students	Pearson Correlation	-.274**	-.076*	.225**	.613**	1.000	.136**
	Sig. (2-tailed)	.000	.011	.000	.000	.	.000
	N	1118	1118	1118	1032	1118	1113
SPECW White students in special ed as % of all white students	Pearson Correlation	-.076*	-.012	.059	.169**	.136**	1.000
	Sig. (2-tailed)	.011	.700	.050	.000	.000	.
	N	1118	1118	1118	1032	1113	1118

**. Correlation is significant at the 0.01 level (2-tailed).

*. Correlation is significant at the 0.05 level (2-tailed).

There are two problems with this highly controversial assertion. First, our previous analysis of Hypothesis 2 indicated that the racial composition of the school is more important than variables that we might associate with the school's academic standards (dropout rate, test scores, spending, and level of urbanization). To this end, the quality of the school seems unrelated to, or to have little influence on, enrollment once the racial composition of the student body is taken into account.

Second, our analysis indicates that race is important not only in terms of the student body, but also the faculty. Table 10 reveals that districts with more white teachers have a greater rate of minority enrollment in special education, particularly for African-American students. The correlation for African-Americans is almost the same as for Hispanics. Special education rates for white students are unaffected by the racial composition of the faculty. Again, it seems that minority kids are singled out, but this time the data point toward the race of faculty members as an explanation for higher minority student enrollment in special education.[27]

Conclusions

The data indicate that minority students are treated differently in predominantly white districts than in predominantly minority districts. Districts with predominantly black teachers, for example, have lower special education rates for all students, but particularly for African-American and Hispanic students. That is, the data reveal that in districts with a predominantly black faculty, minority students see a reduction in special education enrollment that is three to four times

Table 11. Final Model: Class Size, Salary, Student Body, and Spending as Predictors of Special Education Enrollment

Model Summary

Model	R	R Square	Adjusted R Square	Std. Error of the Estimate
1	.632[a]	.400	.397	2.2812

a. Predictors: (Constant), % of students on free lunch, teacher to pupil ratio, district expenditures per pupil 1995, average salary for teachers 1995, % minority students in district

Coefficients[a]

Model		Unstandardized Coefficients		Standardized Coefficients		
		B	Std. Error	Beta	t	Sig.
1	(Constant)	15.203	1.267		11.997	.000
	% minority students in district	-9.22E-02	.005	-.847	-18.426	.000
	average salary for teachers 1995	-1.46E-04	.000	-.121	-3.983	.000
	teacher to pupil ratio	-5.29E-02	.040	-.037	-1.325	.186
	district expenditures per pupil 1995	7.685E-04	.000	.151	5.801	.000
	% of students on free lunch	6.926E-02	.007	.443	10.499	.000

a. Dependent Variable: % of students in district labeled as special ed

greater than the reduction seen by white students. This does not mean that minorities have lower special education rates than whites in these districts, only that these rates drop greatly in districts with minority faculty while those of white students experience only a slight decrease. This is illustrated in Figure 2, where the difference among black, Hispanic, and white students is lowest in districts with less than 20 percent white faculty (that is, predominantly minority districts).

These findings indicate that enrollment in special education might be determined in part by race—not only of the student but also of the student's teachers and/or fellow students. Table 11 presents a final comprehensive model combining district-level data from Texas and Florida, weighted by population (districts with high populations are given a higher weight). Our dependent variable is again the number of students enrolled in special education in each district, and the key independent variable of interest is again the percentage of minority students in each district. Control variables include those that demonstrated some influence in our four major hypotheses—teacher salaries, teacher-to-student ratio, spending per pupil in the district, and the percentage of students eligible for a free or reduced lunch.

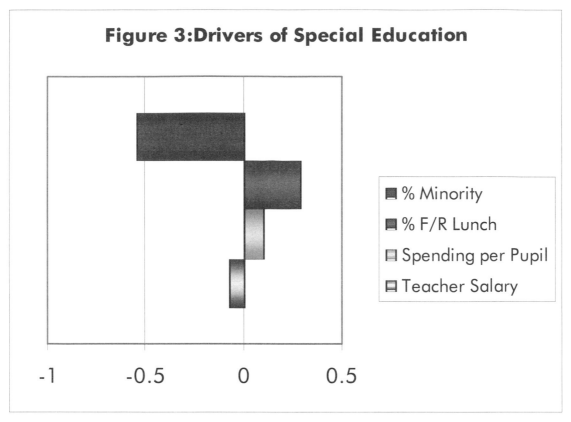

Figure 3: Drivers of Special Education

Legend:
- % Minority
- % F/R Lunch
- Spending per Pupil
- Teacher Salary

X-axis: -1   -0.5   0   0.5

The control variables behave according to expectations. The spending-per-pupil variable is significant and positive: more spending leads to more special education. The class-size variable is negative but not statistically significant. Poverty (as determined by free- or reduced-lunch eligibility) proves strongly significant and positive, with higher percentages of low-income children leading to higher rates of special education. *Race, however, impacts special education rates far more than any other variable.* Figure 3 presents the relative size of the impacts for the statistically significant variables in the model. The percentage of minority students in the district is the strongest driver of special education enrollment in our model. In fact, the effect is nearly double that of the next highest variable and has a greater overall impact than the other three combined. The racial composition of the district, therefore, is a key predictor of special education enrollment.

One argument advanced by commentators is that the educational system is inherently racist and classist.[28] Rather than claiming outright bigotry on the part of the faculty, these researchers contend that faculty are trained to teach white, middle-class kids. Students who fall outside this teaching paradigm suffer.

Other researchers contend that minority children often bring to the class different language patterns that might not be compatible with those of white teachers. Others argue that minority students excel under certain teaching styles but tend to suffer under the teaching methods used in predominantly white schools.[29] Still other researchers contend that minority children are socialized differently and hence develop different perspectives on authority and how to relate to the teacher.[30] One of the most common assertions is that the content of the traditional curriculum is incongruent with the experiences and lives of minority students.[31]

The short version of these commentators' arguments is that many public schools, designed to serve white middle-class students, pose an additional challenge for minority students. White teachers, according to many researchers, often are untrained in recognizing and dealing with these differences or remain unaware of them. The result is that many teachers evaluate lack of progress or differences in learning among minorities as deficiencies. Minority students are compared against a standard model based on white, middle-class norms.

When asked about this hypothesis, a top official in one of the largest districts in Texas commented that any time a student is placed in a situation where the other students and faculty are of different cultural groups, there is going to be a problem. "What we find is that in many cases, these children self-select themselves out of the school, and essentially refuse to participate in the learning process. Self-selection may take the form of withdrawing from classroom activities and becoming increasingly introverted, to behavioral problems and attempts to disrupt the learning process." Because these students often perform poorly in terms of academics, they are more likely to meet the legal requirements for special education enrollment. This might explain why we see a pattern of increased minority special education in predominantly white districts and increased white and black enrollment in predominantly Hispanic districts. The numerical minority gets marginalized.

> **We simply have no way to know what the special education rate "should be" in any district or any state. What we do know is this: Race plays a powerful role in the placement of children in special education.**

State and district officials voiced two recurring themes for this pattern in our interviews. First, some officials suggested that some white parents may attach less stigma to special education and may be more willing to litigate—or threaten litigation—if students do not receive the help they need. One district official even speculated that white parents might prefer that their child receive a special education label rather than be identified as simply a poor student. The result of these pressures may be that white districts have a tendency toward overclassifying white children as special education-eligible. However, this cannot explain the discrepancy between the negative coefficients for our race variables and the fact that minorities are enrolled in special education at a disproportionately high level. The phenomenon described in these interviews relates only to white parents wanting special education services for their own children rather than to minority parents in predominantly white districts.

In our interviews, district and state officials noted great reluctance among minority parents to place students in special education. Administrators claim that special education is often viewed by minority parents as a failing that reflects on the family and signals that there is something "wrong" with the student. Alternately, minority parents may have rational concerns about placing their students in special education because such programs fail to yield benefits. Unfortunately, it is impossible to "prove" any of these theories because no objective measure of a "norm" for special education exists.

We simply have no way to know what the special education rate "should be" in any district or any state. *What we do know is this: Race plays a powerful role in the placement of children in special education*. The evidence presented above goes beyond the finding that children of different racial groups are placed into special education at varying rates. It shows that the influence of race survives the inclusion of a variety of control variables and plays the most powerful role.[32]

The results demonstrate conclusively that school districts do not make special education placements in a color-blind fashion. Commentators have noted the expansion and possible abuse of special education designations. If one suspects that over-diagnosis occurs, then logic dictates that it is happening primarily in predominantly white districts where special education rates, especially among minorities, are much higher. The most positive interpretation of these data might explain the disparate rates as a function of parental demand; minority parents in primarily white districts may be more likely to want their children placed in special education, and they therefore may be receiving the services they want for their children with special needs. Perhaps, however, these findings represent racial bias: that special education is, in part, a de facto method for intra-district and intra-school racial segregation. In all probability, there is likely no single overarching explanation that applies to all districts. The fact that the special education process is glaringly impacted by race, however, surely warrants both concern and further research.

[1] Mark S. Littman and Dierdre A. Gaquin, *Education Statistics of the United States*, 1st ed. (Washington, DC: Bernan Press, 1999).

[2] See Donald MacMillian, "Development of Operational Definitions in Mental Retardation: Similarities and Differences with the Field of Learning Disabilities," in *Better Understanding Learning Disabilities: New Views from Research and Their Implications for Education and Public Policies*, ed. G. Reid Lyon (Baltimore, MD: Paul H. Brookes Publishing, 1993), 117-152.

[3] See Mark Kelman and Gillian Lester, *Jumping the Queue: An Inquiry into the Legal Treatment of Students with Learning Disabilities* (Cambridge, MA: Harvard University Press, 1997), 67-75.

[4] A "systemic driver" is an independent variable (such as the percentage of Hispanic students in a state's school districts) that has a statistically significant effect on the dependent variable (such as special education enrollment).

[5] See M. Yeargin-Allsopp, C. D. Drews, P. Decouflé, and C. C. Murphy, "Mild Mental Retardation in Black and White Children in Metropolitan Atlanta: A Case-Control Study," *American Journal of Public Health* 85 (1995): 324-328.

[6] See United States Department of Education, "Factors Associated with the Provision of Special Education to Students with Disabilities in Inner Cities." Internet document available at <<http://www.ed.gov/pubs/OSEP96AnlRpt/chap4b.html>>.

[7] See Jane Burnette, "Reducing the Disproportionate Representation of Minority Students in Special Education," *ERIC/OSEP Digest* #E5661998 (Reston, VA: ERIC Clearinghouse on Disabilities and Gifted Education, 1998).

[8] See P. Robertson and M. Kushner, et al., "An Update of Participation of Culturally and Linguistically Diverse Students in Special Education: The Need for a Research and Policy Agenda," *The Bilingual Special Education Perspective* 14 (1994): 3-9.

[9] See Jeremy D. Finn, "Patterns in Special Education Placement as Revealed by the OCR Surveys," in *Placing Children in Special Education: A Strategy for Equity*, ed. Kirby A. Heller, et al. (Washington DC: National Academy Press, 1981), 334-342.

[10] See "Committee Studies Over-Representation of Blacks in Special Ed," *Newport News*, 20 September 2000.

[11] See Gerald H. Kramer, "The Ecological Fallacy Revisited: Aggregate Versus Individual Level Findings in Economics and Elections, and Sociotropic Voting," *American Political Science Review* 77 (1983): 92-111.

[12] Additional regressions were performed on both the state level of analysis, and on the level of schools. The fact that information was only available from 36 states limits the utility of the state-level analysis, although the same relationship between race and special education appeared at the state level as at county and district levels. Similarly, a sample of 600 individual schools from Texas demonstrated a very similar relationship between variables as was found at the county and district levels. After examining the state, county, district, and school levels of analysis, we concluded that our findings are not the result of ecological fallacy.

[13] Florida includes gifted-and-talented students in figures, but these students have been removed from Florida data employed in this paper.

[14] See Michael S. Knapp, Patrick M. Shields, and Brenda J. Turnbull, "Academic Challenge in High-Poverty Classrooms," *Phi Delta Kappan* 77 (1995): 770-776; and Allan Odden, David Monk, and Yasser Nakib, "The Story of the Education Dollar: No Academy Awards and No Fiscal Smoking Guns," *Phi Delta Kappan* 77 (1995): 1-12.

[15] See Ann Bradley, "If I Were a Rich Man," *Teacher Magazine* 11 (2000): 14-15.

[16] See Richard J. Herrnstein and Charles Murray, *The Bell Curve* (New York: Free Press, 1994); and James M. Kauffman, "Historical Trends and Contemporary Issues in Special Education in the United States," *Handbook of Special Education*, eds. James M. Kauffman and Daniel P. Hallahan (Englewood Cliffs, NJ: Prentice Hall, 1981).

[17] Quoted in John Tierney, "Money Per Pupil Is an Incomplete Response," *New York Times*, 21 June 2000, sect. B, p. 4.

[18] See Michael Nettles and Laura W. Perna, "Schools and Staffing Survey, 1993-1994," in *The African-American Education Data Book, Volume 11: Preschool Through High School Education* (Fairfax, VA: Frederick D. Patterson Institute of The College Fund/UNCF, 1997).

[19] See Jerome E. Morris, "What is the Future of Predominantly Black Urban Schools? The Politics of Race in Urban Education Policy," *Phi Delta Kappan* 81 (1999): 316-319.

[20] See Ted Gotsch, "Urban Disabled Children Lay Behind Non-City Peers," *Education Daily* 33, no. 77 (2000): 1-2.

[21] See Cynthia Esposito, "Learning in Urban Blight: School Climate and Its Effect on the Performance of Urban, Minority, Low-Income Children," *The School Psychological Review* 28 (1999): 365-377; and E. Kelley, J. Glover, J. Keefe, C. Halderson, C. Sorenson, and C. Speth, *School Climate Survey (Modified) Form: Examiner's Manual* (Reston, VA: NASSP, 1986).

[22] See H. Mehan, A. Hartwick, and J. L. Meihls, *Handicapping the Handicapped: Decisionmaking in Students' Educational Careers* (Stanford, CA: Stanford University Press, 1986).

[23] See Thomas C. Lovitt and Suzanne Cushing, "Parents of Youth with Disabilities: Their Perceptions of School Programs," *Remedial and Special Education* 20 (1999): 134-142; Pamela Pruitt, Donna Wandry, and Diane Hollums, "Listen to Us! Parents Speak Out About Their Interactions with Special Educators," *Preventing School Failure* 42 (1998): 161-166; and A. P. Turnbull and H. R. Turnbull, *Families, Professionals, and Exceptionality: A Special Partnership* (Upper Saddle River, NJ: Prentice Hall, 1997).

[24] See A. J. Artiles and S. C. Trent, "Overrepresentation of Minority Students in Special Education: A Continuing Debate," *The Journal of Special Education* 27 (1994): 410-437; B. Harry, *The Disproportionate Representation of Minority Students in Special Education: Theories and Recommendations* (Alexandria, VA: National Association of State Directors of Special Education, 1994); and Eugene C. Valles, "The Disproportionate Representation of Minority Students in Special Education: Responding to the Problem," *The Journal of Special Education* 32 (1998): 52-54.

[25] L. M. Dunn, "Special Education for the Mildly Retarded—Is Much of it Justifiable?" *Exceptional Children* 35 (1968): 5-22; and J.E. Keulen, "Why Is There an Overrepresentation of African Americans in Special Education Classes?" *College of Education Review* 7 (1995): 76-78.

[26] See K. Holt, "Why Must We Pluralize the Curriculum," *Educational Leadership* 49 (1992): 12-16; T. Lucas, R. Henze, and R. Donato, "Promoting the Success of Latino Language-Minority Students: An Exploratory Study of Six High Schools," *Harvard Educational Review* 60 (1990): 315-340; and F. Stevens, "Closing the Achievement Gap: Opportunity to Learn, Standards, and Assessment," in *Closing the Achievement Gap*, ed. B. Williams (Alexandria, VA: ASCD, 1996).

[27] Faculty and student-body compositions tend to mirror each other, making any definitive conclusions about the impact of faculty versus student populations difficult to reach.

[28] See E. W. Gordon and C. Yowell, "Cultural Dissonance as a Risk Factor in the Development of Students," in *Schools and Students at Risk*, ed. R. Rossi (New York: Teachers College Press, 1994); and Marleen Pugach and Barbara Seidl, "Associate Editors' Exchange Responsible Linkages Between Diversity and Disability: A Challenge

for Special Education," *Teacher Education and Special Education* 21 (1998): 319-333.

[29] See L. Delpit, *Other People's Children* (New York: New York Press, 1995); and J. Irvine and D. York, "Learning Styles and Culturally Diverse Students: A Literature Review," in *Handbook of Research on Multicultural Education*, ed. J. Banks and C. M. Banks (New York: Macmillan, 1995).

[30] See S. Heath, *Ways and Words: Language, Life, and Work in Communities and Classrooms* (Cambridge: Cambridge University Press, 1983); and L. A. Vogt, C. Jordan, and R. G. Tharpe, "Explaining School Failure, Producing School Success: Two Cases," *Anthropology and Education Quarterly* 18 (1987): 276-286.

[31] See M. Asante, "Afrocentric Curriculum," *Educational Leadership* 49 (1991): 28-31; and M. D. Harris, "Afrocentrism and Curriculum: Concepts, Issues, and Prospects," *Journal of Negro Education* 63 (1992): 301-316.

[32] Several of our findings agree with those presented at a recent Capitol Hill forum releasing findings in a series of papers commissioned by Harvard University's Civil Rights Project. The papers' findings show that African-Americans make up 16 percent of the student population but over 25 percent of students labeled emotionally or behaviorally disturbed, and that African-American students in wealthy suburban schools are more likely to be labeled mentally disabled than those in poorer urban schools. See Ted Gotsch, "Tracking Urged to Stem Racial Gap in Special Ed," *Education Daily* 34, no. 43 (2001): 3-4. Drafts of several of the papers discussed at this forum are available at <<http://www.law.harvard.edu/civilrights/conferences/SpecEd/moreinfo.html>>.

Chapter 6

Special Education at Coles Elementary School

Robert Cullen

Marge Scheflen's classroom at Coles Elementary School in Manassas, Virginia, is an unusual one, reflecting the unusual nature of the teaching she does. It's smaller than the normal classrooms at Coles, and it does not have the standard collection of small desks for the pupils and one large desk for the teacher. Instead, it has two tables, one rectangular and one circular, and an odd collection of bookshelves that divide the remaining space into smaller nooks and carrels. Still less standard is the range of instructional material posted on the walls. There are placards on one wall depicting letters of the alphabet and words they initiate—"A is for Apple." Close by is a chart describing how a plot turns in a work of fiction, a chart only slightly less sophisticated in its approach than material you might expect to see in a creative writing class for high school students. The setting makes two things quickly apparent. This is a classroom designed to teach children individually and in small groups. And it is designed to teach children with an irregular range of aptitudes, children who may well be capable of analyzing the plot in the movie they watched over the weekend but at the same time be incapable of writing the word "plot" correctly.

> **Mrs. Scheflen's classroom is designed for children deemed to have normal intelligence and abnormal needs.**

Ms. Scheflen teaches special education, and that is the nature of special education at Coles Elementary, as at other schools. Her classroom is designed for children deemed to have normal intelligence and abnormal needs. But that formulation, although true, oversimplifies the complexity of the problems faced by special education students, their parents—and the teachers and school systems that serve them. This chapter chronicles what I observed during a few days visiting Coles Elementary and suggests how formidable those problems are.

Inside a Special Education Classroom

Ms. Scheflen's pupils are part of the fastest-growing segment in the special education population—children diagnosed with learning disabilities. They range from second graders to fifth graders. They come to her and her aide, Colleen Isbell, in groups of four, five, and six throughout the day. Some come for only an hour. Some spend most of their day in special education with Ms. Scheflen or another teacher. Ms. Scheflen responds to them all with a calm and patient warmth, rarely criticizing them for failures, rarely getting effusive when they succeed.

She tries, of course, to give them chances to succeed. On one fairly standard day in 2000, she organized a little learning game for six fourth graders. Two were girls and four were boys, a fairly typical division between the genders in special education. The children stood in line and tried to spell a word from their weekly spelling list. Then they tossed a soft white bath sponge into a waste can six feet away. They could get one point for spelling their word correctly and one point for making a basket.

"'Best, Roger',"[1] Ms. Scheflen challenged a ten-year-old boy with a mop of dirty-blond hair hanging over his forehead. "Spell, 'best.'"

"B-e-a-d," Roger replied.

Gently, Ms. Scheflen corrected him. He tossed the sponge in the basket and got his consolation point. He marked it on the blackboard next to his name. Part of the game is adding up and keeping track of the scores.

A chubby boy named Peter took his place at the head of the line.

> **The ratio of students to staff in Ms. Scheflen's room, never more than 3:1 or 4:1, was at this time 1:1. This suggests why special education is costly.**

"Together," Ms. Scheflen said.

Peter cast an eye at the blackboard, where among the names was that of a classmate, Heather.

"T-o-g-e-a-t-h-e-r," Peter spelled.

This time, Ms. Scheflen tried to help him with a mnemonic, a memory aid. "If you want to be together with a girl, you have to get her first," she said. "To-get-her. Together."

Peter nodded and shot his basket.

A bell rang, and four of the children left for a physical education class. That left only two, a boy named Benjamin and a girl named Dorothy. (This suggests why special education is costly. The ratio of students to staff in Ms. Scheflen's room, never more than 3:1 or 4:1, was at this time 1:1.) Mrs. Isbell began to work with Benjamin on a paragraph he was trying to write. Ms. Scheflen sat down with Dorothy for some one-on-one reading.

Dorothy, a painfully shy, quiet girl with a variety of problems relating to language, began to read aloud from a passage in a book about ghost towns. She came to the word "thousands" and stopped, unable to decipher it.

Ms. Scheflen wrote the word on a piece of paper. She underlined the last five letters, "sands."

"Do you know that?" she asked Dorothy.

Dorothy did.

She circled the letters "t" and "h" at the beginning of the word. Dorothy quietly made the appropriate sound.

Ms. Scheflen circled the letters "o" and "u." She reminded Dorothy of the sound they made. Slowly, Dorothy pieced together the word: "Thousands."

Ms. Scheflen nodded her approval, and they went on.

This scene, repeated countless times, is the essence of special education at Coles Elementary. Though English is normally their first language, Ms. Scheflen's kids respond to written English words as if they were in a foreign language they were just beginning to study. Little comes easily. When they read a difficult word, it is as if they are peeling it off the page, letter by letter. The rhythm of the written language is beyond them.

Sometimes, Ms. Scheflen tries an alternative way of getting a child to master spelling or reading a word, like the mnemonic she used with Peter. But more often, she does what she did with Dorothy. She drills her pupils in the standard reading techniques that their more fortunate peers picked up by the end of first grade—associating sounds and letters, deciphering diphthongs, assembling phonemes.

> *Though English is normally their first language, Ms. Scheflen's kids respond to written English words as if they were in a foreign language they were just beginning to study. Little comes easily.*

Reading Instruction for the Learning Disabled

Coles Elementary teaches reading by a method called "guided reading strategies." The school's principal, Candace Rotruck, describes it as a blend of phonics and the whole-language method that doesn't stress one or the other. Dorothy had heard all the phonics information Ms. Scheflen was giving her in first and second grade, but it didn't register. She had strong visual and artistic aptitudes, but a blind spot for reading. And being shy, she did not ask for help. She sat quietly and politely. She repeated the first grade, but it didn't seem to help her. When she was lagging two years behind her peers, she was referred for a special education evaluation and diagnosed with a variety of learning disabilities. Ms. Scheflen's job is to help her try to catch up.

Another bell rang, and a new group of pupils entered Ms. Scheflen's room. One was a fidgety, bespectacled, tow-headed second-grade boy named Eddie in a red T-shirt with a logo for Wilson, the sporting-goods company. He had been reading a barnyard story.

"Where does this story take place?" Ms. Scheflen asked when it was Eddie's turn for tutoring.

"Outside," Eddie replied. He drummed a pencil against the underside of the table.

"What's the name of a place that's outside, that has fields and animals and a barn?" Ms. Scheflen asked him.

"I don't know," Eddie said. He didn't seem obstreperous. He appeared unable to get his mind around Ms. Scheflen's question.

"A farm," she told him. He nodded, vaguely.

Ms. Scheflen tried to get Eddie to tell her what happened at the beginning and end of the story he'd been reading. He was supposed to have drawn a picture of the story's beginning and another of its end, a device Ms. Scheflen uses to improve comprehension. But Eddie couldn't respond. He continued to drum his pencil against the underside of the table. He squirmed.

> *About 18 pupils at Coles Elementary take Ritalin or another drug intended to improve their concentration and ability to focus.*

"Eddie, did you take your medication this morning?" Ms. Scheflen asked. About 18 pupils at Coles Elementary take Ritalin or another drug intended to improve their concentration and ability to focus. Eight of the 18 are in special education. Eddie is among them; he is supposed to get his dose at preschool day care.

"I don't know," Eddie said.

Ms. Scheflen persisted for a moment, trying to ascertain whether Eddie's inability to concentrate was more a chemical problem than an attitudinal one. Eddie insisted he could not remember whether he got his medication or not.

"Well, do the best you can," Ms. Scheflen finally said.

Another bell, another group of children—this time fifth graders. Ms. Scheflen had one of them draw a slip of paper from a hat full of slips. Each slip had a writing topic on it. The selected topic for the day turned out to be "A musical instrument I would like to play." Ms. Scheflen set out to help her pupils write a paragraph on that topic, beginning with a freckle-faced, snub-nosed boy named Andrew, who was a few days shy of his eleventh birthday.

Andrew sat down next to Ms. Scheflen and without hesitation told her he would like to play the drums.

"You play the cello now, don't you?" Ms. Scheflen asked.

"I don't like it," Andrew said.

"Why would you like to play drums?"

Drums, Andrew said, would be more fun. He wouldn't have to lug them around as he has to lug the cello. Maybe he could form a band with a friend of his and make some money. He could make a lot of noise and let out some of the anger he feels. And, he said with evident relish, "it would drive my sister insane."

Ms. Scheflen nodded and asked Andrew to write a "web," a writing tool in which ideas are gathered like spokes around a wheel. It helps pupils organize their thoughts before writing an actual paragraph.

"Fed. [sic.] 4, 2000," Andrew wrote on his paper. Then he started to write down his reasons for playing drums. He wrote nothing about the anger of which he spoke. That may have been too frightening to commit to paper. But he did remember his sister. He wrote that playing the drums would "bive my sister in shain."

The County's Perspective

To paraphrase Tolstoy, every special education student is special in his own way. There is no perfectly typical case, and there is no perfectly typical school. But Andrew and Coles Elementary, judging by the national data, fall within the normal range of special education pupils and programs.

Coles Elementary is about 30 years old, built of red brick, with a parking lot to one side and an athletic field in the back. Inside the front door, the usual array of plaques and awards is mounted on the wall. The school has a program for the hearing-impaired which serves several neighborhoods, but other than that, its special education offerings are no different from those at other schools in the area.

> *To paraphrase Tolstoy, every special education student is special in his own way. There is no perfectly typical case, and there is no perfectly typical school.*

Prince William County, where Coles Elementary is located, is an area in transition from rural South to standard American suburb. Stonewall Jackson's statue stands guard at the Bull Run Battlefield about ten miles from the school, and the two-lane blacktop roads in the neighborhood still wind past four-room, clapboard farmhouses in the midst of modest pastures and fields. But the roads nowadays also wind past new cul-de-sacs and subdivisions of larger, more expensive homes with chimneys and two-car garages and sun decks. Prince William is becoming a bedroom community for the burgeoning high-tech industries of Fairfax County to the north. In 1997, the Census Bureau reported a population of 254,464—up from 215,000 in 1990.[2] Of that, 82.5 percent were white and 12.8 percent black. About six percent identified themselves as Hispanic. The median household income was most recently estimated at $55,276, and the number of families living in poverty was estimated at 5.4 percent.

The Prince William County Schools are administered from an old Nike missile base in a wooded area eight miles west of Interstate 95; the base was once part of the air defense system for the nation's capital. The military left a series of small, temporary buildings, and Prince William County school administrators shuttle between them for meetings like students shuttling between temporary classrooms. The director of special education for the county is Tom Carter, a burly North Carolinian who came to Prince William 32 years ago and has occupied his present post since 1990.[3]

From Carter's perspective, special education is a constant battle between the demand for service and budgetary constraints. Since he began his career, he has seen special education grow from a program that served a limited population—primarily the deaf, the blind, the mute, and the severely retarded—into one that wants every year to consume more of the county's educational resources. That's in large part because of the identification of new disability categories.

"In 1973, we had about six percent of our students in special education and there was no such thing as a learning disability," Carter said in an interview. "We didn't recognize Attention Deficit Disorder [ADD] until 1990. Now about 12.7 percent of our students are in special education. At least half of those are diagnosed with learning disabilities or Attention Deficit Disorder. We have 12 to 13 percent of our students using 25 percent of our budget."

> *The law states that a child's environmental disadvantages cannot be used as a qualification for special education.*

Carter does not think there are more children with disabilities now than there were when he was a young teacher. He thinks that the system has changed so as to identify more students as disabled. One reason, he thinks, is that parents today see no stigma in the label. They may even want a child to be identified as disabled.

"It's an acceptable handicap," he said. "It's a perfect excuse for why a child isn't performing."

Carter feels that some percentage of the county's special education population—he doesn't know precisely what percentage—is getting extra help for questionable reasons. Essentially, they are children whose parents had the knowledge and wherewithal to determine that special education might be a good deal for their children and then pushed to make certain they got it.

They can do that, Carter said, because the criteria for defining special education eligibility are subject to interpretation and vulnerable to manipulation. "A lot of cases are not perfectly clear as to whether the child should be eligible," Carter said. "You could test the child five times, and three of the testing panels would say yes, and two would say no."

The county would prefer to use an objective yardstick. It has devised an evaluation rule that attempts to make objective the somewhat vague federal and state laws on eligibility. To be entitled to special education in Prince William County, a child should have an IQ twenty-three points higher than his performance on a similarly scaled test of academic achievement. This is not the only criterion the county uses, but it is, perhaps, the most important.

A parent who disagrees with the verdict of the tests can hire psychologists and lawyers to dispute it. Occasionally (though no statistics are kept on the subject), the school system is forced to give in. This, Carter feels, tends to bias the system in favor of children from middle- and upper-middle-class homes. Their parents are more likely to have the resources to fight the school system than are blue-collar and poor parents. In addition, the law states that a child's environmental disadvantages cannot be used as a qualification for special education. This, again, tends to favor a child from a comfortable home. If he or she is not achieving, there can't be environmental factors behind it. But a child from a trailer park or public housing?

How Special Education Is Funded in Prince William County

Carter would not mind so much, except that the pie for education in Prince William County is finite, and every dollar spent on special education is a dollar that won't be spent on children deemed by the law to have no special needs. Virginia's education funding system aggravates the problem. The state provides a basic aid sum per pupil to Prince William County schools, which amounted to $2,120 in the most recent fiscal year. On top of that, it makes a blanket grant of $146 per pupil to Prince William to cover special education. This grant is paid regardless of how many of the district's children are enrolled in special education classes. Thus, in Virginia, a district in which few pupils are diagnosed with special education needs will find that the state funds a higher proportion of its special education budget than the state does in a district where a higher percentage of children are diagnosed with disabilities. Put another way, if Prince William had one-tenth of all its pupils in special education classes, its state aid for special education would come to $1,460 per pupil in the program. If the special education population rises to roughly one child in seven, the state aid drops to $1,000 per pupil in the program.

> *Special education in Prince William County is a classic case of unfunded mandates falling on the shoulders of local taxpayers.*

The federal government provides Prince William County with about $3.5 million annually to cover the cost of extraordinary cases, such as a child whose disabilities require the services of a full-time, one-on-one aide. But that, Carter points out, is a paltry percentage of the roughly $90 million that Prince William spends annually on special education, especially in view of the fact that so much of the spending is mandated by federal law.[4] Special education in Prince William County is a classic case of unfunded mandates—in this case from both the federal and state governments—falling on the shoulders of local taxpayers.

The county calculates that special education costs, on average, a little more than twice the education of an average student, which is about $6,500. The bottom line is that every time a child is diagnosed with learning disabilities in the Prince William County school system, the diagnosis costs the county thousands of dollars in annual expenditures.

As a result, Carter and the school administration press principals like Ms. Rotruck to stick to the guidelines in determining whether a pupil is eligible for special education. The administration doesn't want pupils made eligible until and unless they show that 23-point gap between intelligence and achievement. The administration is trying to slow the increase in the special education population and make certain that only those who meet the eligibility criteria are certified. This policy may make some fiscal sense, at least in the short term, but it also has an educational impact. Principals and teachers may notice that a child has special learning problems in kindergarten or first grade. They can and do try to provide such a child with remedial help. But it may take a couple of years for that child's learning disability to cause the requisite 23-point gap. Until it does, the child is not eligible for special education services, and he or she may not get the full-scale early intervention that could minimize the impact of a learning disability.

On top of that, Carter noted, there is the paperwork generated by special education. Each child's case quickly accumulates a thick file of forms generated at teacher discussions, evaluation sessions, and meetings with parents to work out the required Individual Education Plan for each pupil. Simply assessing a pupil to determine his eligibility for special education can cost $5,000-$7,000.

As a result, Carter said, the county Board of Education and the school administration have begun to feel that "special education is out of kilter." The Board, in its legislative policy statement for 2000, asked Prince William County's representatives in Richmond to oppose any measure that would make Virginia's special education requirements exceed those already mandated by federal law, particularly in ways that give parents additional rights. Carter thinks this is part of a predictable reaction against the growing cost of special education. "There will be a backlash," he said. "I just don't know when it's coming."

> *The needs of individual children, an abstraction in the system's offices, become concrete concerns in the school setting.*

The View from the School

If you leave the Prince William County Board of Education compound and drive the five miles to Coles Elementary School, the perspective changes and so does the perception of special education. For one thing, the budget dynamic is much different from the point of view of a school, its principal and teachers, and its parents. For another, the needs of individual children, an abstraction in the system's offices, become concrete concerns in the school setting. Some 70 of the 530 children at Coles are in one special education program or another. They stop being numbers on a spreadsheet. They all have faces and names.

Candace Rotruck, the principal at Coles, is a kindly woman in her late forties. Ms. Rotruck grew up in West Virginia in the era before federal laws mandating special education programs. She can remember peers who had trouble reading. But in those days, that was considered dullness rather than a disability, and there were still many places in society for people who couldn't read well. One high school classmate who was barely literate, she recalled, became a policeman.[5]

By the time Ms. Rotruck finished her training at West Virginia University, special education was being woven into the fabric of American schools, thanks to federal legislative mandates. Ms. Rotruck had had a summer job as a lifeguard teaching mentally retarded children to swim. She had loved the work. Upon graduation, she got a full-time job teaching the mentally retarded. Over the years, she also taught children with severe speech problems and learned some American Sign Language. Then she moved into administration, becoming a principal in 1995.

One thing her experience gave her is an appreciation for the paperwork burden imposed on special education teachers. (Ms. Rotruck has two large milk crates on the floor of her office containing forms that must be filled out as part of the evaluation process for each child who is a special education candidate. She has file cabinets full of folders, each one several inches thick, on the school's special education students.) She tries to ease the paperwork burden on her staff by doing a lot of it herself, often on weekends. And she has one special education teacher who does not meet with students until 10:30 each morning, giving her two hours to work on the communal red tape. Partly as a result, Ms. Rotruck said, Coles Elementary does not have the problems with burnout and teacher turnover in the special education program that plague other schools in Prince William County.

Eighteen of Coles Elementary's 50 staff members are involved in special education. Some are teachers of children with learning disabilities, like Ms. Scheflen. Some are aides, like Mrs. Isbell. Some are interpreters and specialists assigned to the program for hearing-impaired students at the school, which serves deaf children from several surrounding neighborhoods. There is a speech therapist and a part-time psychologist. By contrast, children at Coles Elementary who are simply slow learners, but do not meet the special education criteria, have a relatively small number of staff devoted to their needs; one reading specialist works with anyone in the early grades who is having trouble reading.

Yet Ms. Rotruck does not see Coles Elementary's special education population as a financial burden. To the contrary, she said, "Special education keeps a small school like ours afloat."

That is because of the county's budget formula. It allocates to Ms. Rotruck's budget $2,650 for each normal child; special education student may get an allocation of as much as $8,000.

> **Eighteen of Coles Elementary's 50 staff members are involved in special education.**

Using all the funds allocated to her, Ms. Rotruck is responsible for hiring staff. She must do this within fairly tight guidelines, assigning teachers and aides where the law requires them. But, she said, "It's like a family. All the money goes in one big pot." The money for special education gives her some flexibility in other areas of the school.

So, although the growth of special education seems like a potential fiscal disaster from the county's perspective, it does not seem that way to a principal or to teachers. They have no financial incentive to limit the number of special education students.

But it would be a mistake to suggest that the identification of special education students at Coles Elementary is driven by budgetary considerations. It is driven, rather, by pupils' problems and the desire of teachers and parents to do something about them. This was the case with Andrew, Ms. Scheflen's 11-year-old fifth-grade student.

The Learning-Disabled Student

Andrew is the second of three children; he has a sister who is twelve and a brother who is six. His mother, who did not complete college, runs a store that sells honey-glazed hams. His father, who has a degree in wildlife management, owns a lawn-care service.[6] His father, in an interview, suggested that he, too, might have some undiagnosed learning disabilities. He called himself "scatterbrained" and said he had had trouble focusing on tasks as a boy. He also had trouble reading and required six years to finish college.

Andrew's father was not a special education student, though in his boyhood fewer children were. He may, in fact, have received an informal version of special education. He remembered that, when he was roughly Andrew's age, his parents sent him to spend the summer with a grandmother in Vermont. This woman decided that her grandson needed tutoring. She handed him a copy of *The Bounty* trilogy and insisted that he read some of it with her every morning. By the end of that summer, Andrew's father had finished the trilogy, and his reading was much improved.

Both his parents recalled that Andrew was slow to read. But his older sister was slow as well, and her problems seemed to diminish around the third grade. They assumed Andrew's would as well. Their efforts to read to him and get him to read back to them did not have happy results. Andrew could not perform. His parents, particularly his father, chastised him for not trying hard enough, for not paying attention. Reading sessions at home often ended with books being hurled across the room in frustration. This may account for some of the anger of which Andrew spoke in his conversation with Ms. Scheflen. "We were hard on him," Andrew's mother recalled in an interview. "We had no idea what a reading disability was."

> *The difficult special education eligibility cases are the ones where a child does have a learning disability and does need special education, but the child's scores don't show the required 23-point gap.*

Andrew's performance in first grade was unsatisfactory, but his parents and teachers decided to wait to see if he would grow out of his problems. They thought that perhaps he was reacting badly to the birth of his younger brother, Tyler, and would eventually adjust. Second grade, though, saw no improvement. Andrew's problems spread to behavioral issues. He talked back to his teacher. He showed anger and frustration. His second-grade teacher, toward the end of the year, suggested that he be evaluated for learning disabilities. His parents agreed.

Andrew's parents never hired their own lawyers or psychologists. They relied on the school system's evaluation. The process took about six weeks. A Coles Elementary evaluation for special education eligibility begins with a meeting among Ms. Rotruck, the child's teacher, and the school's psychologist. They fill out an evaluation form and advise the child's parents that the process is underway. "It should not be a surprise to them," Ms. Rotruck notes. "By the time it reaches this stage, a child has usually been having significant difficulties, and the parents are already concerned."

During the process, a diagnostician comes to the school to test the child's achievement level in reading, math, or written language. The psychologist tests the child's IQ. A visiting teacher meets with the parents at the child's home or in school, trying to gauge the child's environment and behavior outside of school. Ms. Rotruck sits in on the child's class for a few hours, observing. The speech specialist screens for hearing problems. The child takes a simple vision test. When all of this is done, the diagnostician, psychologist, principal, and child's teacher meet. They vote on whether the child is eligible for special education. The child's parents are entitled to attend and vote at this meeting. Usually, Ms. Rotruck says, the vote is unanimous one way or another. The difficult cases, she feels, are the ones where she believes a child does have a learning disability and does need special education, but the child's scores don't show the required 23-point gap. She can try to have a child declared eligible in such cases, but if she does, she knows she will likely get a stern letter from the county school administration asking her to justify the decision.

When Andrew's testing process was over, his parents went to the meeting. They were told that Andrew had a disability having to do with reading and writing. Ms. Rotruck told them he might also suffer from ADD. This combination is not infrequent, and ADD can exacerbate the reading disorder. Andrew, for instance, has a tendency to transpose b and d. If he could focus his attention better, more intensely, he might be able to fight that tendency more effectively. But he has difficulty focusing.

As far as his parents know, that is as specific as Andrew's diagnosis got. "You go to a meeting, and they ask if you have any questions," Andrew's mother recalled. "But you have a million questions, and it's hard to come up with one."

Andrew's father compared the experience to going to a mechanic and being told that your car has a complicated and costly problem. You may not completely understand the diagnosis, or agree with it. But unless you know more about the car than the mechanic does, you have little choice but to trust his judgment and tell him to go ahead and make the repairs he suggests.

> *"I was glad to know it was something,"* Andrew's mother said. *"It was a relief to know that there was a problem, that we could get help."*

The only outside specialist Andrew's parents have consulted is the family pediatrician, who said Andrew might have ADD or might have a mere developmental delay that will cure itself. He did not urge Andrew's parents to put him on medication, and they did not do so.

For Andrew's parents, the diagnosis was an occasion for mixed emotions.

"I was glad to know it was something," his mother said. "It was a relief to know that there was a problem, that we could get help."

There was also a burden of guilt. "I felt very guilty because of the way I'd treated him [prior to the diagnosis]," Andrew's mother said. "Telling him he could do it if he paid attention. Accusing him of not trying hard enough." Andrew's parents had given him a fair amount of intellectual stimulation outside of school. He took cello lessons. He was in the Cub Scouts. He played youth soccer and baseball. He and his father took occasional fishing trips. Still, there was a nagging fear that they had not done enough.

To Andrew's mother, the diagnosis was a positive step in that it changed her son's status from a child who wouldn't try to read to that of a child who had a disability that prevented him from learning to read in the normal way.

At first, Andrew's mother felt little or no stigma attached to the label of special education. Andrew went willingly to the special education classes. He showed some improvement in school.

After a couple of years, however, she started to notice other things. There was Back-to-School Night at the beginning of Andrew's fifth-grade year. All the pupils had work posted on the bulletin board, including Andrew. His was a picture of a chicken, except that the word "chicken" underneath it was so badly misspelled that it was hard to figure out what he had intended to write. His mother remembered feeling embarrassed for her son.

She said she had noticed that Andrew has fewer friends than her older child, who is not in special education. She was uncertain whether this was caused by a social stigma attached to special education or simply by Andrew's personality. If other boys were in the house playing video games, she said, Andrew might quickly get bored, leave them, and go off to do something by himself. "And he still, to this day, sucks his thumb," she sighed.

> "I really don't understand learning disabilities," Andrew's father said. "But I've come to grips with the fact that he has a problem."

Ironically, considering he was the parent who had reading problems as a child, Andrew's father resisted the disability diagnosis. "I thought maybe he hadn't gotten enough attention from us, compared to his older sister and younger brother. I thought maybe his classes were too big—maybe 29 or 30 kids in first grade. I thought maybe the county was trying to do whole-word recognition instead of phonics. I didn't think it was a disability," he said. He smiled, self-deprecatingly. "Maybe it's an ego thing—you don't want your boy to be called disabled."

"I really don't understand learning disabilities," he went on. "I mean, how can he sit down and do a 200-piece jigsaw puzzle, or put together an elaborate Lego toy, and not be able to read? But I've come to grips with the fact that he has a problem."

The major concern Andrew's parents expressed about the program at Coles Elementary is the time he spends in Ms. Scheflen's classroom. While other fifth-graders take social studies or science, Andrew works with Ms. Scheflen on reading and writing. His parents are concerned that, when he gets to middle school, Andrew will be too far behind in those subjects to catch up. Andrew has an aunt who's an archaeologist, and he's expressed interest in that profession; he also likes watching documentaries about animals on television. As a result, science is one professional career track Andrew's parents think he might have a chance to pursue. Science is important to them.

But Ms. Scheflen and Ms. Rotruck have persuaded them that unless Andrew catches up in reading, he won't be able to grasp science or history. On the other hand, if he does catch up in reading, he ought to be able to make up fairly quickly the science he is missing now.

Parents' Perception of a Special Education Child's School and District

Andrew's mother said she was aware of the fact that some school districts would assign Andrew to a regular science class with a co-teacher to help him and other special education students keep up. But she has not asked Ms. Rotruck to do that for Andrew. For one thing, it would mean rocking the boat. For another, she has a sense that it "wouldn't be fair" to ask for so much special assistance for one child.

But perhaps the main factor in the disinclination of Andrew's parents not to insist on a mainstream science class for their son is the relationship they have developed with Ms. Rotruck and Ms. Scheflen. They believe both women have Andrew's best interests in mind. They trust both women. In fact, Ms. Scheflen, who has a daughter in the same class as Andrew's older sister, has become a family friend.

This reflects a common pattern at Coles Elementary that does not seem to make its way into many media reports on special education. Those reports tend to focus on disputes between parents who insist on mainstream classroom experiences for their children and school districts that refuse to provide it on grounds that the child is too severely handicapped. Sometimes, the people in these stories become caricatures—the ego-driven, overeducated parents who are prepared to game the system for all it is worth to get what they want, or the callous bureaucrats in the skinflint school system.

At Coles Elementary, there are few, if any, bitter disputes and no caricatures. No one is callous. Rather than see the teachers and principal as adversaries, the parents of special education students by and large see them as expert advisers and rely on their judgment. And parents tend to listen to their children, to be guided by what the children have to say.

> *At the national level, advocates for the disabled tend to push hard for an integrated classroom experience for nearly all special education students.*

One of the parents on Coles Elementary's Curriculum Advisory Council, a sort of informal board of trustees for the school, is JoAnne L. She has a daughter who is considered to be "E.M.R.," or educable mentally retarded. In an interview, Mrs. L. said she had brought her daughter to the school uncertain whether she should be placed in a mainstream classroom or a separate program for the retarded. The school at first placed the child in a regular class, but the girl didn't like going to school. She told her mother she felt stupid. Ms. Rotruck had the child evaluated and determined that she was eligible for special education services for the retarded. Mrs. L. and Ms. Rotruck agreed to transfer the child to a class for the retarded. The child's attitude toward school and her performance both improved.[7]

Although at the national level, advocates for the disabled tend to push hard for an integrated classroom experience for nearly all special education students,[8] parents at Coles Elementary seem to make decisions on the basis of what they perceive is best for their child. And that may be a separate class, like Ms. Scheflen's or the one Mrs. L's daughter is in.

In fact, Ms. Rotruck said, in the 1999-2000 term, there were almost no core academic classes at Coles Elementary in which learning-disabled students were taught side-by-side with their non-disabled peers. All the pupils at the school take physical education, art, and music together. But for reading and math, special education services are delivered separately, in classes like Ms. Scheflen's.

Three factors are involved in Coles Elementary's movement away from mainstreaming the learning disabled. One is the budget formula. In the 1998-99 school year, the school had some third-grade classes which were taught by both regular and special education teachers, with the pupils mixed. But this year's third grade did not have enough special education pupils to justify hiring full-time co-teachers. A second factor is the absence of parental insistence on mainstreaming. If a parent does insist, Ms. Rotruck's policy is to be accommodating. But they rarely insist. The main factor, though, is the preference of Ms. Rotruck and her staff. "I'm not convinced," she said, "that co-teaching works." In her experience, kids with learning disabilities, especially those with ADD, do better in separate classes, where they have fewer distractions and can receive more individual attention. That is what she tries to give them.

The Physically Disabled

The learning disabled are not the only special education pupils at Coles Elementary, and some of the others are mainstreamed. The school has a special program for the hearing-impaired, which draws children from several surrounding neighborhoods. Three of the hearing-impaired kindergartners spend part of their day in a regular class.

> *In Mrs. Rotruck's experience, kids with learning disabilities, especially those with ADD, do better in separate classes, where they have fewer distractions and can receive more individual attention.*

This trio—Billy, Joey, and Luke—started a typical February day in Dawn Voysey's kindergarten class with perhaps 20 other pupils. The three boys wore "phonic ears," an apparatus carried by all the hearing-impaired children at the school. It consists of a power pack clipped to their belts and a set of headphones. The teacher or interpreter wears a microphone tuned to the boys' frequency. The idea is that the headset filters out any ambient noise and allows in only the sound the teacher is making, thus making it easier for the pupils to use what hearing they have. But it's not clear what, if anything, Billy, Joey, and Luke can hear. They appear to get along by responding to a multitude of cues.

Mrs. Voysey knows some rudimentary American Sign Language, but she relied on an interpreter to do most of the signing for the three deaf boys, who sat directly in front of her. Mrs. Voysey led the class in a song about a groundhog. The three boys appeared to enjoy it, but they didn't sing along. None of them can speak very well.

Mrs. Voysey moved on to a calendar lesson, and there the hearing-impaired boys had a chance to shine. It was the third day of February, and Luke got to pin the numeral three to the big calendar on the wall. It was also the 89th day of the current school term, and Mrs. Voysey asked if anyone knew what numerals are in the number "89." Luke raised his hand. Mrs. Voysey called on him. He made the signs for nine and eight and proudly sat down again. The class counted to 89. Billy, Joey, and Luke signed along.

The class did an alphabet recital, and Billy got to aim the pointer at the letters as Mrs. Voysey recited them and the children repeated after her. Then it was time for a numbers game. Mrs. Voysey held up a jar with a jumble of tickets inside. Each child guessed how many tickets he or she thought were in the jar. Joey guessed 22. Billy went along with Joey. When all the guesses were in, Mrs. Voysey counted the tickets. There were 23. Joey and Billy came closest. They exchanged high fives.

Joey and Billy are exuberant boys who seem almost unaware of their handicaps. Luke is quieter by nature and more reserved. They all, however, appeared to enjoy their time in Mrs. Voysey's class and to be accepted readily by the other children in it. Several of the hearing children have picked up some of the signs for numbers, and they signed along with Billy, Joey, and Luke during the counting games.

> **The speech therapist's job is to find ways for hearing-impaired students to learn to make sounds they cannot hear.**

After an hour the three boys were gathered by Linda White and escorted upstairs to the second floor of the school. Mrs. White, the school's speech therapist, works in a small, windowless room that was probably a storage closet when the school was opened in 1969. There is barely enough space for her chair and a small, curved table at which the boys sat.

Mrs. White's job is to find ways for the boys to learn to make sounds they cannot hear. It's not easy. She opened her mouth wide so the boys could see her lips and tongue move as she pronounced the "luh" sound of the letter "l." Then she held a mirror in front of each boy's mouth so he could see his own lips and tongue move as he tried to duplicate the sound. She put Billy's finger to her lips so he could feel the expulsion of breath as she made the sibilant sound for "s." She took his hand and put his fingers to his own lips to let him compare what came from his own mouth when he tried to imitate the sound.

The boys have varying degrees of speech ability. Joey, who has some residual hearing, can say words like "go" and "big" in a mechanical way, though putting words together into a sentence is beyond him at this stage. Luke is still working on sounds. Billy's speech is closer to Joey's than Luke's.

Mrs. White tried to integrate the speech work with their work on American Sign Language. She made the signs for each sound, letter, or word she asked the boys to say. She and the three boys seemed to be communicating on three levels—with sound, with signs, and with lips. The boys, far from being reticent about using their voices, seemed to delight in it. They cheered for one another's successes, calling out, "Yay!"

After speech therapy, the three boys returned, not to the mainstream class in which they had begun the day, but to a kindergarten class for the hearing-impaired. This class has eight children—seven of them boys. Several of them have additional problems. Joshua is autistic as well as hearing-impaired. David, in addition to being deaf, has cerebral palsy, which kept him from walking until he was nearly kindergarten age. He walks now with a stiff, clumsy gait, and he has not been toilet-trained. David also has a habit of biting. An additional aide has been assigned to the class to look after David. Juan and Lorenzo are children of Salvadoran immigrants. In addition to being hearing-impaired, they know no English, and their parents do not know sign language. All of the children in this class, like Billy, Joey, and Luke, wear the phonic ear apparatus.

If Billy, Joey, and Luke were put off by any of these problems, they showed no signs of it when they joined the class. Within seconds, they were in the midst of a play period, running around the room, scrawling on chalkboards, playing with toys. After a couple of minutes, the teacher, Teresa Wyrick, signaled that play time was over. She brushed her hands together, the sign for "clean-up." Mrs. Wyrick, a woman in her late twenties dressed in sweat clothes, hears normally. She chose to go into education for the hearing-impaired and got a master's at Gallaudet University in Washington, D.C.

Most of the boys, but not all, responded to Mrs. Wyrick's signal and started dumping toys in boxes. David joined in the clean-up, and Mrs. Wyrick signed "thank you" and "good" to him. David beamed.

Mrs. Wyrick began a lesson on the days of the week. "Yesterday was Tuesday," she said, speaking into the microphone mounted on her headset. At the same time, she made the signs for "yesterday" and "Tuesday." She pointed to the word, "Tuesday," on a wall display.

> **Joshua's autism tends to keep him out of sync with the rest of the class, and Mrs. Wyrick watches him closely most of the time, trying to keep him with the group.**

"Today is Wednesday," she went on. Mrs. Wyrick is a warm, enthusiastic woman with an engaging smile. She was easily able to make a group of five-year-old boys believe that Wednesday is the best of all possible days of the week, and it seemed likely that on the following day they would think Thursday was just as swell. Joey obviously thought so. He smiled back at her, repeated the sign for Wednesday, and did his best to say the word aloud as well.

On to numbers. Mrs. Wyrick let Joey hold the pointer and point to each number as she led the boys in counting to 50 by fives and to 100 by tens. She moved closer to Joshua during this exercise, giving him a light hug, trying to help him to pay attention to the numbers. Joshua knows the numbers. But his autism tends to keep him out of sync with the rest of the class, and Mrs. Wyrick watches him closely most of the time, trying to keep him with the group.

She asked the children to sit on swatches of carpet and conducted a coin game. The boys, in turn, took coins and put them in envelopes posted on the bulletin board underneath large pictures of each coin and a number indicating its worth—one, five, ten, twenty-five, and fifty cents. Joshua, however, began to play with his coin like a wheel on the floor, seemingly lost in a reverie. Mrs. Wyrick noted that he was sitting on a floral carpet pattern instead of a plain one. The pattern, she said, can distract Joshua, taking his attention away from the class. She replaced Joshua's floral carpet swatch with a plain beige one. Joshua didn't rejoin the coin game, but he seemed, momentarily, to be paying attention again. David deposited his coin properly, but then he hobbled over to Joey and got in his face, making loud, incoherent sounds. Joey, perhaps because of his hearing impairment, did not seem to mind, and one of Mrs. Wyrick's aides took David by the hand and returned him to his carpet swatch.

Mrs. Wyrick deftly switched the boys to a game of alphabet lotto; none of her class activities lasts more than about ten minutes. The boys used cards with letters and signs, working on their mastery of the American Sign Language (ASL) alphabet. Joshua, however, got obstreperous. He spat at Juan. Mrs. Wyrick, like a hockey referee, responded by putting Joshua in the penalty box—a chair set by itself in front of the teacher's desk, in the middle of a red box outlined in tape on the floor. Using a kitchen timer, she set the clock to tick off Joshua's penalty: five minutes. One of the aides moved over toward Joshua and prodded him gently back into the box whenever he tried to leave.

Mrs. Wyrick made certain to include Joshua prominently in the next segment, a counting exercise, and Joshua displayed the mix of ability and disability characteristic of autism. With his attention engaged, he counted to 48, higher than anyone in the class. Then he lapsed into another reverie.

Mrs. Wyrick decided it was time to reward the boys, and she let Joey pass out the treat—a single piece of candy for each. The boys patiently waited their turn to grab their treats and eat them. "It's an accomplishment that they all don't try to grab at once," Mrs. Wyrick said.

The candy consumed, Mrs. Wyrick decided to burn a little of the energy her charges had ingested. She set up an obstacle course around the perimeter of the room, pulling two small desks into the path along one wall, laying two ropes on the floor along the next wall, and placing a soft Nerf soccer ball along the third wall. Then she showed the boys how to run the course. She slithered under the desks (this, presumably, is why kindergarten teachers wear sweat clothes), jumped up, and hopped over the pieces of rope. Jogging around the corner, she got to the soccer ball and kicked it toward the smiling boys. One by one, they imitated her, waiting eagerly for her signal to start.

> *Mrs. Wyrick deftly switched the boys to a game of alphabet lotto; none of her class activities lasts more than about ten minutes.*

When each boy had made two or three circuits, she had them sit at their desks and work on writing their names. Then they drew shapes on pieces of paper. Toward the end of the day, the class had a library period. They joined another hearing-impaired kindergarten class and started walking toward the library. David, for some reason he could not communicate, did not want to go. When his aide tried to take his hand and lead him, he bit her, puncturing her skin. The class was delayed while the aide found some disinfectant and a Band-Aid and patched herself up.

In the library, the two classes gathered around the librarian. Their teachers joined them. So did the aides and an ASL interpreter. It was another display of the cost of special education: seven staff members were attending thirteen children. The librarian read a picture book about Abraham Lincoln. The interpreter signed. Some of the children seemed engaged by this; Billy did not. He wanted to converse with Joey. Hearing-impaired children can sometimes get away with this, since they make no noise when they engage in ASL conversations. But this time, Billy was caught. An aide banished him to a chair in the back row, and Billy sat there, face flushed, tears of shame dripping from his eyes.

The story ended, and the children had a few minutes to look at some of the books on the shelves. Joey, an elfin boy who plows through life with a smile on his face, pulled two books out as if he knew exactly where they would be. One was about trains, and the other was about alligators. He sat happily on the floor, leafing through the books one at a time, absorbing the pictures.

Alligators and trains are two of Joey's passions. Both of Joey's parents hear normally. His mother worked in a bank but quit shortly before Joey was born. His father has a job handling computer security for Prince William County Schools. Joey has two siblings, an eleven-year-old sister and a six-year-old brother. They, too, hear fine.

Joey's parents do not know precisely what caused his deafness. They believe he was born hearing normally. But when he was about a year old, he fell suddenly and mysteriously ill. He vomited and couldn't hold his head upright, though he had no fever. Joey's mother took him to the hospital, where the doctors couldn't find anything specifically wrong with him or say what had caused his illness. After a two-and-one-half day hospitalization, Joey seemed back to normal. The doctors sent him home.

> *Joey's parents, like the parents of Andrew, the boy with learning disabilities, dealt with a burden of guilt.*

But as the months passed, Joey's parents noticed that he wasn't normal. He didn't speak. He didn't respond to sounds, such as the ringing of the doorbell, that stimulated his older brother. He didn't respond to his parents' voices when they spoke to him from behind. They had him tested and learned that he had a moderate-to-severe hearing impairment. His doctors guessed that it was caused by the bout of illness when he was a year old. Retroactively, they diagnosed it as encephalopathy, a catch-all term for illnesses of the brain.

"It was devastating," Joey's mother recalled in an interview.[9] "You don't ever think it will happen to you. You sit and wonder, 'What do I do with a disabled child?'"

Joey's parents, like the parents of Andrew, the boy with learning disabilities, dealt with a burden of guilt. "Because no one could say for sure why this had happened to him, you think, 'Did I do something wrong when I was pregnant with him? Did I get him to the hospital in time?'" she recalled. With time, those questions fade into the back of a parent's mind. But they never go away.

Joey's grandmother played an important, supportive role in this crisis. "She kept reminding us that Joey was a very normal boy. He's stubborn, headstrong. He's not very conscious of his disability. He wants to learn, wants to be a part of things. And he makes sure he is."

Joey's family adjusted. His parents continued to read stories to him. They watched movies and television together. They continued to talk to him, taking care to speak up and make sure he could see their faces when they wanted to communicate. They took a class in sign language and learned the basic signs appropriate for a young child. His older brother shared a room with Joey, and the two boys developed a rough, effective way of communicating, mixing signs, words, and a bit of shoving. Joey's mother has noticed, with gratitude, that when the boys go outside, his brother and sister look out for him, trying to protect him from being teased or picked on.

For all that, Joey still faces limitations and challenges. His mother sees that he has been slower to read and write than his older brother. The older boy plays video games and takes Tae Kwon Do lessons. Joey, thus far, is content to watch. He can be a bit reclusive at times. And, of course, his mother constantly worries about the oncoming car that Joey won't hear.

Discovering the preschool program for the hearing-impaired at Coles was a relief to Joey's parents, in part because he took to it immediately and well. He began at the age of two. "He loved being there," his mother recalled. "He was so much happier around other hearing-impaired kids."

Like Andrew's parents, Joey's parents developed an alliance with the special education teachers they found at Coles, depending on them for expertise and advice. Joey's teacher in preschool was Jill Burns, a young woman who is herself hearing-impaired. Joey's parents asked her opinion about a cochlear implant for him. Many members of the deaf community oppose cochlear implants (Ms. Rotruck has heard it compared to trying to change the color of one's skin), and Ms. Burns advised Joey's parents against the operation. They took her advice and have not pursued the issue.

> *Down the road, Joey's parents know he will have to make choices between the hearing world and the deaf world. Which classroom he prefers will be one of the first of those choices.*

Similarly, they have accepted the recommendations of the school staff about mainstreaming Joey. During preschool, Joey stayed in a special class for the hearing-impaired. When he began kindergarten, Ms. Rotruck and her staff recommended that Joey spend a small part of the day in a Mrs. Voysey's mixed class with an interpreter. But he spends the bulk of his day in the hearing-impaired class with Mrs. Wyrick.

That was fine with Joey's parents. "We were worried about putting him in a mainstream kindergarten class," his mother recalled. "But the teachers said he would do all right, and he has. We aren't worried now."

All other things being equal, his parents would like to see him spend more time in mainstream classes as his education progresses. But, says his mother, "It's not the principal issue. Joey has to be where he does the best he can. If that turns out to be a hearing-impaired class, fine. As long as it's determined on the basis of his interests."

She expects that she and her husband will be swayed, in part, by Joey's own preferences. For the moment, he seems to like both his hearing-impaired class and his mainstream class equally well. Down the road, they know he will have to make choices between the hearing world and the deaf world. Which classroom he prefers will be one of the first of those choices. But that choice is in the future.

At present, they are guided both by what they perceive to be Joey's best interests and by the advice of the teachers at Coles Elementary. That suggests a continuing, cautious, and undogmatic experimentation with the mainstream class. Ms. Rotruck says she is pleased with how Billy, Joey, and Luke are doing with Mrs. Voysey. She will probably recommend more time in a regular class in first grade.

Evaluating the Program

Joey's adulthood, of course, is still just a speck on the horizon, and it is impossible to predict how well his eventual dreams and aspirations will be served by the special education program at Coles Elementary. But that is true of everyone in the special education program. Evaluating precisely how well the program serves them is difficult.

> *Children with broken legs usually, in time, get rid of their crutches, and walk more or less normally, perhaps even run. Special education students by and large will always have the equivalent of a limp.*

Andrew, for example, came to Ms. Scheflen roughly two years behind his peers in key reading and writing skills. Ms. Scheflen thinks that, after two years of special education, he's made up about half that gap. But he still has persistent, basic problems, like his tendency to mix up the letters b and d. How well he will do in middle school or beyond is open to question.

For Andrew, it may not matter. His father noted that Andrew has often expressed an interest in taking over the family lawn-care business, and his mother can always use help at Christmas time in the honey-glazed ham business. Andrew may find a niche in the economy that doesn't require first-rate reading skills. Such niches, say some of the special education teachers at Coles Elementary, are where they've seen a lot of their pupils wind up over the years. "I would say that 80 percent of the special education students go into fields where they don't have to use absent skills," Ms. Rotruck said.

There are occasional pleasant exceptions. Ms. Rotruck recalled a girl named Mandy who had problems with reading and written language. Mandy was in a mainstream class for math, but she got special education in language arts. "We pushed Mandy pretty hard," Ms. Rotruck said. "We gave her a lot of positive reinforcement, we taught her how to manage things, to compensate." Mandy learned. Not long ago, Ms. Rotruck said, Mandy dropped by for a visit and informed her that she was working on a book.

But Mandy was unusual, Ms. Rotruck added. For the most part, "There is no magic to special education. The program doesn't resolve a child's disability." She compared a child with a learning disability to a child with a broken leg. Special education may provide such a child with the equivalent of a crutch that helps him or her get up and get around.

But there the analogy to a broken leg tends to break down. Children with broken legs usually, in time, get rid of their crutches, and walk more or less normally, perhaps even run. Special education students by and large will always have the equivalent of a limp. They may find ways to get around, but they do not become sprinters.

Statistics to back up the anecdotal evidence offered by teachers like Ms. Rotruck are hard to find. Prince William County's Board of Education has tried to evaluate the special education program, according to Board president Lucy S. Beauchamp.[10] But would-be evaluators run into an immediate snag. It's difficult to measure the effectiveness of the program without a control group of pupils with disabilities who did not receive special education. Such a control group would be inconceivable—to say nothing of illegal.

Mrs. Beauchamp said the Board of Education in Prince William County has nevertheless commissioned a consulting company to audit the special education program and see how it's doing. "We want to be delivering services that improve the students' performance," she said. "We don't want to run a baby-sitting service."

Statewide statistics collected by the Virginia Department of Education, though, suggest that for a significant number of learning-disabled students, the ideal paradigm—normal children who perform normally after receiving a little special help—is a myth. In the 1999 statewide Standard of Learning test for third graders, for instance, 39 percent of all students failed the reading and writing test. For students with learning disabilities, the failure rate was about twice as high—75

> *It's difficult to measure the effectiveness of the program without a control group of pupils with disabilities who did not receive special education. Such a control group would be inconceivable— to say nothing of illegal.*

percent. Roughly the same pattern prevailed for all grade levels tested. Among all fifth graders, the failure rate on the reading SOL test was 31 percent; among students with learning disabilities, it was 64 percent. Of all eighth graders, 33 percent failed the reading test; among eighth graders with learning disabilities, the failure rate was 73 percent. Among high school seniors, the reading failure rate was 25 percent, but for learning-disabled students it was 67 percent. The data suggest that in Virginia, learning-disabled students generally don't catch up.[11]

Virginia has had to make accommodations for special education students in its graduation requirements. Some 25 percent of special education students statewide opt out of trying to pass the tests for a standard diploma and instead get a "special diploma." The state is also discussing whether to add a third option, a "basic diploma" for special education students who demonstrate competency in reading, writing, and math and complete some occupational training.[12]

Some Thoughts on Reform

Regardless of how many of its students will go on to pass the SOL tests, Coles Elementary School suggests several important observations about special education that are often ignored and occasionally distorted in media reports dealing with the subject.

First, the teachers who deliver special education services are an extraordinary group. On a daily basis, they display patience, skill, enthusiasm and concern—even love—for pupils who are, on many occasions, hard to love.

Second, the problems that bring students into special education are real. There may well be some cases at Coles Elementary where pupils with nearly identical abilities received different diagnoses, with one being sent to special education and the other branded as "slow" and left in a regular class. But there are probably not many. And there appear to be no students in the school's special education classes who don't need help. This may not be the case further up the educational ladder, however, where there may be growing numbers of students seeking accommodations such as extra time on tests for questionable learning disabilities. But it is true at Coles Elementary School.

Third, although it is no doubt true, as Tom Carter suspects, that there are occasions when parents can push the system to admit a child with a marginal learning disability into special education, parental pushing does not seem to be a common route into the program. It is far more likely that the child's first- and second-grade teachers, noticing a lack of progress, initiate the evaluation. The parents then go along with the school's decision. Parents may dream of the day their child graduates from college, or scores a winning touchdown, or takes over the family business. But it seems safe to say that few parents, on their way home from the maternity hospital, dream of their child's first day in special education.

Fourth, the intense emphasis placed by advocates for the learning disabled on the least restrictive environment for a child—which usually means a mainstream classroom— seems oddly divorced from the reality of a school like Coles Elementary. So does the media attention given to lawsuits by parents of disabled pupils who insist on mainstream class rooms for their children. The reality at Coles Elementary is that parents rely on the teachers and the principal for advice, and that advice often sends the child to a separate class with the consent of all concerned.

> **As matters now stand, local government, the entity which bears the funding burden, has little or no control over which and how many students receive services.**

A fifth and final observation flows from the first four; if Coles Elementary is any indication, there are no quick or easy solutions to the financial and educational problems posed by learning disabilities.

Certainly, a few days spent at Coles Elementary School suggested that the special education system needs examination and improvement. There is much room for debate about the funding mechanism—which separates the primary responsibility for raising money from the responsibility for setting admissions criteria and selecting students for evaluation. As matters now stand, local government, the entity which bears the funding burden, has little or no control over which and how many students receive services. That authority rests with federal and state governments, which determine the rules, and with parents and teachers, who have the most influence in selection. It's a system seemingly designed to grow in cost each year. And it may, in Virginia at least, tend to delay the delivery of special education services for children who need them, until they can demonstrate a "23-point gap" that, as is required in Prince Williams County, in turn may mean that children stay in special education longer, make less progress, and wind up costing the system more money.

There is also room to question whether the selection process is too arbitrary at the margin, selecting some students and not others based more on the quirks of parents, teachers, and psychologists on objective measures of aptitude and performance.

There is much room for improvement in monitoring the results the system produces, although more detailed monitoring might conflict with another desirable reform, a reduction in time and money devoted to paperwork and red tape.

Last, there is room for debate on whether the agenda of professional advocates for the disabled, which puts such a premium on mainstreaming and least restrictive environments, is the right one for disabled students, particularly those with learning disabilities. It may well be that professionals like Ms. Rotruck are correct in thinking that many such children do best in separate classes.

But Coles Elementary also suggests that would-be reformers of special education ought to be careful about how much they promise. It suggests that there is a substantial population of children who, under any rational evaluation system, will be found to have learning disabilities. They require and deserve special help. And that help cannot be inexpensive.

---

[1] The names of all Coles students in this paper were changed to protect their privacy.

[2] Data from U.S. Census Bureau at <<http://www.census.gov/statab/USA98/51/153.txt>>.

[3] Interview with Tom Carter, January 19, 2000.

[4] Funding data from a telephone interview with David Cline, director of finance, Prince William County Schools, February 22, 2000.

[5] Interview with Candace Rotruck, February 2, 2000.

[6] Andrew's parents were interviewed separately on February 14 and 16, 2000.

[7] Interview with Mrs. JoAnne L., February 16, 2000.

[8] See, for example, the report to President Clinton by the National Council on Disabilities, January 25, 2000, entitled "Back to School on Civil Rights—Advancing the Federal Commitment to Leave No Child Behind" at <<http://www.ncd.gov/newsroom/publications/backtoschool_1.html>>.

[9] Interview with Joey's mother, February 14, 2000.

[10] Telephone interview with Lucy S. Beauchamp, February 17, 2000.

[11] Taken from unpublished raw data files provided by the Office of Special Education and Student Services, Virginia Department of Education.

[12] "New Diploma Proposed for Special-Ed in Va.," *The Washington Post*, February 3, 2000, page B-2.

Chapter 7

How Special Education Policy Affects Districts

Anna B. Duff

When I started calling school districts to see if they would talk to me for this study, I mentioned to the secretary of one special education office that Congress would soon be looking to reform the Individuals with Disabilities Education Act (IDEA). "Oh great," she said. "More forms."

From the perspective of school districts, this casual perception of how the IDEA works is not far off the mark. In trying to make sure that special-needs children get an education, federal and state governments have created a massive procedural maze that frustrates teachers, parents, and administrators alike.

> *In trying to make sure that special-needs children get an education, federal and state governments have created a massive procedural maze that frustrates teachers, parents, and administrators alike.*

Not long before the conference that preceded publication of this volume, I spoke with Dr. A. Andrea Witkowski, special education director for the Garden City Public Schools in Michigan. A team of federal and state compliance monitors had recently visited her district, as is typical every three years.[1]

What changes did the regulators request? New forms. Specifically, they required this district (and others in the county, Witkowski later discovered) to print new forms for the individualized education program (IEP) that all special education students receive.

The changes required did not seem likely to do much to improve education for these students; rather, they asked for changes in wording that might make it easier for regulators to determine compliance. For example, the old IEP form asked when a student was to be in general education classes and when a student was not. The new form had to ask when a student was to be in general education for academics and when a student was not to be in general education for academics, and when a student was to be in general education for nonacademic classes and when a student was not to be in general education for nonacademic classes.

Aside from the direct cost of having to print new forms (not insignificant in a district with little if any money to spare), are such changes anything more than a nuisance? The example serves to illustrate the extent to which federal and state laws addressing the education of special-needs children are focused on procedure and regulatory compliance. This focus may help ensure that children with disabilities have access to education, but it is not likely to improve the quality of their education.

Some 6,000 rules govern special education in Michigan, according to one official who spoke with me. Special education offices at school districts are often little more than a few desks surrounded by walls of file cabinets storing files needed not only to organize the delivery of special education services, but also to prove, if need be, that the districts are following the rules.[2]

School districts in Michigan provide special education under a set of state laws that precede the federal ones and exceed the federal mandate of a "free appropriate public education" (FAPE). In Michigan, state law requires districts to educate students with disabilities to their "maximum potential." It is also a state where special education is more stringently regulated than it is in many other states.

There is an elephant in the room that no one is talking about, largely for fear of being accused of lacking commitment to educating the disabled. It is the rising cost of special education.

In both Michigan districts studied here (Troy School District and Garden City Public Schools), special education programs had generally good reputations beyond their compliance with laws. Administrators took pride in their programs, sincerely believing they did well by these children in terms of trying to make their school experiences productive and enjoyable. Both special education directors often referred to their district's special education students as "my kids."

But there are problems with special education as many school districts see it. The main ones? Too many rules, too many lawyers, and not enough money. Some argue that there is no real limit on what districts may be required to spend on special education, and that increasing costs are forcing them to dip further and further into their general education budgets. What may be even more pressing, though, is the sense that districts are able to do little more than hold a finger in the dike—that with the threat of increasing litigation a future deluge is all but certain. And although some districts may want Michigan and Washington to loosen their stringent regulations, they believe that doing away with the regulations could do away with what little protection they have from lawsuits.

There is also an elephant in the room that no one is talking about, largely for fear of being accused of lacking commitment to educating the disabled. It is the rising cost of special education. Even districts with healthy per-pupil funding say it requires them to make tradeoffs, as will be discussed below. But the arguments focus on who should pay what share—not on the fact that the law puts no real limits on what districts have to spend to fulfill a student's rights.

Two Michigan Districts in Brief

The Troy School District sits at the edge of wealthy Oakland County in what was, two decades ago, an outlying area. It's now home to a ritzy shopping mall, several major corporations, and brand-new subdivisions of increasingly large homes populated mostly by professionals, more than 70 percent of whom have completed at least some college according to Census Bureau statistics. In 1997-98, the district had a K-12 enrollment of 12,047 and per-pupil funding of $7,996, well above the state average of $6,063, according to the Michigan Department of Education's *1999 Michigan School Report*. Just over 9 percent of its students are in special education, which cost the district $10.6 million last year, including transportation costs, a sum equaling approximately 15 percent of district spending, according to the Michigan Department of Education.

The Garden City Public Schools cover a middle- to working-class bedroom community in Wayne County. The bungalows and small ranch homes are average-priced, typically less than $150,000. Just one in three Garden City residents has continued his education past high school. The school district's funding for its 5,412 students stood at $6,145 last year. Just over 20 percent of Garden City's students are in special education, although that high share is partly due to its Burger School, the largest public-school autism program in the nation. (It enrolls students from all over Wayne County). If the district had a more typical number of autistic children, it would still have about 16 percent of its students in special education, higher than the state average of 12 percent. For Garden City, special education costs amounted to about $16 million last year, including transportation, or close to 40 percent of all its spending. The funds for the Burger School alone amount to approximately $10 million of that, all of which is paid for by the county. Not counting those expenses, special education takes up 15 percent of the budget.

> **Ask the director of special education in any school district how students are identified for special education, and you are likely to get the same answer. The law sets out a clear set of steps from which districts deviate at their legal peril.**

Referral to Special Education

For all their differences, the ways that the districts identify and place students in special education are much the same. In fact, ask the director of special education in any school district how students are identified for special education, and you are likely to get the same answer. The law sets out a clear set of steps from which districts deviate at their legal peril.

The procedure goes as follows: When a student is referred as potentially in need of special education, the district has ten school days to get a parent's okay to test the student to see whether the child has a disability. Within 30 school days, the district has to convene a Multidisciplinary Evaluation Team (MET), whose members are defined by Michigan law based on the suspected disability. The MET conducts the tests and any observations needed to determine whether the child is eligible for special services.

Once the test results are in, within that same 30 days (more if the district and parents agree), the district will convene an IEP team whose members are also defined by law. They include (at minimum) the student's parent(s), regular teacher, a special education teacher, a representative of the district, and any specialists based on the possible nature of the disability—for example, a speech pathologist, if the disability seems to be speech- and language-impaired. At least one member of the MET shows up at the initial IEP meeting to present that team's report. They decide whether the tests and observations were properly conducted, look at what the preponderance of evidence points to, and make a determination on eligibility.

If a child is certified for special education, the IEP team will discuss what services are needed; the state provides a form with a checklist of things to discuss. Once eligibility for specific services is determined, those services have to start within 15 school days. Such services include academic assistance as well as transportation, physical therapy, speech therapy, psychological counseling, occupational therapy, social work and services, and technological aids.

What does vary between these two districts is what happens before a referral to special education is ever made. The law states that, to get special education services, a student must need those services to overcome his or her disabilities. Differing emphasis on whether students are perceived to need special education services, therefore, can play a big role in how many students are eventually certified for the program.

By the time children reach school age, those with more severe mental impairments, obvious physical disabilities, and speech and language impairments are usually already in special education. Since the passage of its own special education law in 1971, four years before the federal legislation was passed, Michigan has required its districts to serve special-needs children from birth. In both of these districts, such children are usually brought to the attention of the district by a parent, often on the advice of a doctor or social worker.

> *The law states that, to get special education services, a student must need those services to overcome his or her disabilities. Differing emphasis on whether students are perceived to need special education services, therefore, can play a big role in how many students are eventually certified for the program.*

School-age children are nearly always referred for evaluation by a teacher, primarily because they are struggling to keep up. Some critics of Michigan's special education law point out that, taken literally, it requires districts to give special education services to anyone not living up to his or her potential, even if that student is doing okay. In neither of these districts did that question arise. Special education was seen as a service for those who were well behind their peers. "If a student wasn't struggling, you'd never recognize there was a problem," said Dr. Lawrence Selaty, director of special education in the Troy School District.

Persistent behavior problems might also trigger a referral. In one elementary school, a child born to a crack-addicted mother was in the process of being evaluated for emotional impairment due to uncontrollable behavior.

Resources Outside of Special Education

What happens before a referral ever takes place depends a lot on what resources a district has to devote to remedial help outside of special ed education.

In Troy, that means a fairly substantial intervention. Initially the district encourages general education teachers to try to adapt their instruction informally to the learning style of the student in question. Partly for that purpose, the district has about a dozen teacher consultants that general education teachers can call on for help. The district also has a Reading Recovery program—an expensive one-on-one tutoring program—for struggling readers. "Our focus is on the general ed classroom," Selaty said. That focus has kept unnecessary—and costly—evaluations to a minimum. More than four in five students who are referred for testing are eventually certified for special education, a high percentage. However, using special education as a last resort after many options are tried is an approach that can frustrate parents of children who are eventually certified for special education. One mother of a learning-disabled child said her child entered first grade unable to read and failed to make progress in reading for a whole year before being certified. She felt that valuable time had been lost in addressing her child's needs.

> *"It used to be there was more of a stigma [to being classified as needing special education services]," said a district special education director. "Now, if this is the way you get help [for learning disabilities], then this is what you do," she said.*

Garden City has fewer such resources for extra help outside of special education. In the past, many struggling students would have gotten one-on-one help through the federal Title I program for districts with a high share of poor students. Prior to 1994, that program required schools to pull students out of class for extra help, so the district could show that Title I funds were only being used to help eligible students. In 1994, however, Congress changed the law to permit districts the flexibility to use Title I funds to help pay for schoolwide improvement programs. Garden City embraced the schoolwide approach.

That change has sent special education referrals in Garden City Schools soaring, noted Dr. Witkowski, the district's director of special education, even though the rate at which students are actually certified isn't increasing any faster than in the state as a whole. Because of the Title I changes, the district doesn't have funds to pay for the one-on-one reading help that some students need. As a result, teachers may seek to place students needing special attention in reading in special education, where such help is still available.

Neither district reported much resistance from parents when it came to certifying children for special education. When parents did resist, neither district seemed likely to fight them. When a problem was severe enough the parents would eventually agree to the certification, district officials said. Ironically, the district often has more trouble certifying students for more serious and obvious disabilities than for lesser learning disabilities. "It used to be there was more of a stigma," Witkowski said. "Now, if this is the way you get help [for learning disabilities], then this is what you do," she said.

In fact, some teachers pointed out that they believed that some parents were trying to "work the system" in favor of their child, wanting the child to be identified with a mild disability that would garner some accommodations and extra help, but little or no stigma.

Much of the nationwide growth in the special education population has come in the category of specific learning disabilities—one of the twelve categories that Michigan requires districts to identify—and the Garden City and Troy school districts show no exception to that trend.[3] Both report steady, slow increases in the learning-disabled population over the past 15 years.

"Learning disabled" is also the special education category open to the most interpretation. For its other categories, Michigan leaves little discretion in terms of how to classify students. For example, a student is supposed to be classified as educable mentally impaired when his score on an intelligence test is two to three standard deviations below the mean, and when he scores within the lowest six percentiles on standardized tests of reading and math.

With learning disabilities, however, the state's definition leaves some flexibility to local districts. A student has to show a "severe discrepancy" between his ability on an intelligence test and his score on an achievement test, among other factors. Local districts can define "severe" as they see fit.

Both the Troy and Garden City school districts cast a wide net when it comes to this definition, using a 15-point, or one-standard-deviation, gap between scores on intelligence and achievement tests. And in Troy, such a wide gap is not a necessary condition if other evidence suggests special education is needed. In Garden City, Dr. Witkowski recently looked at the test scores of each student with learning disabilities (LD) to see whether requiring a larger point gap would reduce the size of that category of the special education population. She found that every one of the district's LD students had at least a 20- or 25-point (one-and-a-half to two standard deviations) gap in at least one academic area.

The goals listed on a student's IEP are also supposed to be determined individually. In reality, they typically follow recommendations from Michigan's outcome guides, developed by teams of special education experts for the state.

Public insistence on higher academic standards has led to the elimination of nonacademic tracks in both districts over the past two decades. And both districts point to that development as a major factor in the increasing LD population—especially at the high-school level—over that same period. "There used to be things like general math that kids who were not headed for college would take," Witkowski said. "Now that's gone—the lowest math class we have in high school is an algebra/geometry class—but the kids are not gone. They don't have options like general math or auto shop so they're in special ed. It's the only game in town to get out of a strictly academic curriculum," she said.

As the district has made its general education more difficult over the past decade, Selaty points out, referrals and certifications for learning disabilities have increased steadily. "You'll see more students who aren't making it as the curriculum becomes more difficult," he said, "so you'll have more being referred."

From IEP to the Classroom

Once a student is certified for special ed, the IEP team takes over, planning long- and short-term goals for the student and delineating the services needed to meet them. As its name suggests, the IEP is determined on an individual basis, in theory without regard to cost or what's actually available in the district.

In reality, what the law requires will usually translate into services that look very much the same from district to district, even though the curricula that is used may differ. For school-age children with disabilities like speech and language impediments or mild learning disabilities, a child will almost always be placed in a general education classroom and be pulled out for special help in a resource room. Children with severe disabilities will be placed in a special class or program, and they may be "pulled in" to a general ed class (most often art or physical education) or a lunch period for mainstreaming.

> *Like the federal IDEA, Michigan's special education law emphasizes inclusion, or placing the student in the "least restrictive environment" in which he or she can benefit educationally.*

The goals listed on a student's IEP are also supposed to be determined individually. In reality, they typically follow recommendations from Michigan's outcome guides, developed by teams of special education experts for the state. These guides outline in detail what students of different disabilities and grade levels should be expected to accomplish in academics and other life skills. For example, the "Special Education Program Outcomes Guide: Educable Mental Impairment" lists six different categories of expected outcomes—academics, social competence, community integration, personal growth and health and fitness, vocational integration, and domestic living environment. (For educable mentally impaired (EMI) students, even the "academic" goals primarily relate to daily living.) Each category has subcategories—19 in all—each with a detailed list of "selected educational considerations" for a given grade level.

For example, the academic category lists three subcategories:

- to "communicate effectively through oral language";

- to "integrate the use of print material into daily living"; and

- to "respond productively to mathematical problems encountered in daily living."

Some of educational goals for EMI students that are listed under the subcategory concerning the use of print materials are as follows:

- students exiting third grade should "have the skills to write a letter";

- students exiting fifth grade should "have the skills to read at 2.5 grade level";

- students exiting eighth grade should "have the skills to complete simple forms requesting basic personal data and answers to questions that are familiar"; and

- students exiting twelfth grade should "have the skills to read and respond in a written manner to application forms, health forms, surveys, school forms, legal contracts etc."

On a student's IEP, then, the goals typically follow these state-level templates, with some changes based on the student's individual case.

Determining Placement

Like the federal IDEA, Michigan's special education law emphasizes inclusion, or placing the student in the "least restrictive environment" in which he or she can benefit educationally. IEP teams are supposed to keep children in general education classes unless they can't be taught there even with supplementary aids and services, and those teams are supposed to see that disabled children are educated to "the maximum extent appropriate" with the nondisabled. To the greatest extent possible, the law requires IEP teams to keep children as close as possible to home, ideally in the school they would go to if they weren't disabled. The only caveat mentioned is that the IEP team is supposed to consider the potential harm to the students or quality of services they get when placing them in "the least restrictive environment."

> *As a practical matter, inclusion is adding to the demand for greater spending from parents and teachers. The law's focus has created an expectation on the part of parents that their children can be mainstreamed no matter the cost.*

That means just about every school—in these districts, at least—has either a resource room or a room for basic programs. It's a bureaucratic distinction—the difference is the amount of time students can spend in them under Michigan regulations. A resource room is for students who spend less than half the school day in special education, and who need at most two instructional areas taught by the resource room teacher. "Basic program" rooms can take students for up to the full day. (Those are also the rooms often used by each district's traveling coterie of special education personnel, including teacher consultants, assorted therapists, and counselors.)

Not all elementary and middle schools have special education classes because each school does not necessarily have enough students to justify its own class for each category. The district typically assigns those classes to whatever schools have extra space. (Michigan regulations stipulate minimum square footage for each type of special class.) This means many students in special classes are transported—often at very high cost—somewhere other than their neighborhood school. The Troy School District's superintendent, Janet Jopke, said that special education students in that district are transported to at least 31 different sites around the county, at a minimum cost of $22 per hour, per bus.

A speech- and language-impaired student might be pulled out for an hour per day of therapy. Balancing the need for the individualized attention of "pull-out" classes with the need to not miss too much of general education classes is a constant challenge. In elementary school, most administrators try to schedule pull-out services during science or social studies, although in many cases the time for therapy is the time an itinerant teacher can be at the school.

For example, say an elementary school student has a learning disability that interferes with math skills. If his normal class would spend an hour per day on math, the student's IEP might call for 5 hours per week of special education math assistance. High schools can offer separate special education classes in different subjects like science or government.

In both districts, special education students who spend most of their time in general education can graduate with a regular diploma. They offer a separate diploma or certificate for those with more severe disabilities who are taught almost entirely in special education.

Inclusion

The worry that too many special education students, especially those with minor learning disabilities, were missing too much of the general education curriculum has led to changes in laws that mandate a focus on inclusion. That focus is often expressed in the saying, "Special ed should be a service, not a place." Both districts are following the law's focus on inclusion. No administrator I spoke to raised any doubts about the merits of that focus. As a practical matter, however, inclusion is adding to the demand for greater spending from parents and teachers. The law's focus has created an expectation on the part of parents that their children can be mainstreamed no matter the cost. And general education teachers—especially those at the elementary level—want more help in the classroom as they contend with special education paperwork and attempt to individualize instruction in classes of 20-30 students. In theory, the accommodations that enable inclusion are supposed to focus on the delivery of the curriculum, not the content itself. Examples might be acquiring computer technology that allows a visually impaired student to take notes or arranging for an LD student to sit in the front of the class. In practice, however, many accommodations are beginning to change what gets taught.

> *Inclusion requires that general education teachers play an increasingly active role in IEP meetings and in the extensive paperwork associated with special education.*

For Garden City students in the autism program, "mainstreaming" rarely means inclusion in a general education class because the program is housed in its own building. A large part of this education program, however, focuses on getting students comfortable with operating in the world outside of school. That includes things like trips to the grocery store and other community experiences. In some cases, however, a high IQ autistic student might return to his or her home school district each afternoon for some academic classes.

Troy students in the district's program for the trainable mentally impaired spend the better part of their days in a special class within the district's schools. In their case, mainstreaming typically means joining general education students for a gym class or lunch period.

The mainstreaming of physically impaired students also appears to be relatively straightforward.

"It used to be that a child with cerebral palsy would get sent off to a center somewhere," Witkowski said. "Now the ability to walk is not a criterion you need to be in the regular school. We just get the student an amigo, an elevator, and maybe a health aide."

Questions tend to arise with respect to inclusion when general education teachers have a special education student who can't keep up with the rest of the class. In more limited circumstances, general education teachers worry about coping with special education students with behavior problems. Even in Troy, which has a relatively large staff of teacher consultants to help general education teachers adapt their classes to special ed students, the push for inclusion has proven to be easier said than done.

"It's one of the areas where I get the most questions," said Ruth Augustine, president of the Troy Education Association. "Teachers don't always feel they have the help or training they need, and they're worried about what their liabilities are." She cited one example of a high-school special education student whose behavioral difficulties included wandering off between classes; the student was once found off school grounds in the middle of a busy street. Teachers worried that they were not able to prevent such occurrences and still pay attention to their other duties, and that they could be held liable if something happened.

> *Increasingly, as special education students spend more time in general education classes, general education teachers are asking for additional aides to help them manage their classes.*

Inclusion also requires that general education teachers have to play an increasingly active role in IEP meetings and in the extensive paperwork associated with special education. In Troy, the union unsuccessfully filed a grievance against the district to try to prevent IEP meetings from taking up teachers' planning periods. Having a special education student in a general education class means the teacher needs to spend even more time on planning in order to individualize instruction, and on documentation of progress or problems. That extra work appears to be creating pressure from teachers for the district to hire more instructional aides and contributing to a sense that classes need to be smaller.

Instructional, or teacher's, aides are one of the rapidly growing categories of paraprofessionals in demand to help provide special education services. Another is the category of health aides.

The requirements for an instructional aide are fairly low. An aide to teachers of students with severe mental impairments must have a high school diploma and some postsecondary training either in a community college or daycare center. The state sets no standards beyond a high school diploma for instructional aides in LD classrooms. For a long time, aides were most often deployed in special education classes or resource rooms to help the special education teachers handle a larger class. For example, a special class for severely mentally impaired (SMI) students can have 12 students with one teacher and two instructional aides, or up to 15 students with a teacher and three instructional aides. Increasingly, as special education students spend more time in general education classes, general education teachers are asking for additional aides to help them manage their classes. Aides might help attend to students when the class is doing group work, prompt a student to take notes at important parts, and so on.

"All the parents want aides" for their children, one Troy teacher told me, a sentiment that was echoed by many of the parents and teachers with whom I spoke. "To me, full inclusion means that my child will be in a regular classroom with a [paraprofessional] to help him," one mother of a learning-disabled child said. "But I would never ask for that because then they'd have to do it for everybody."

A district's reluctance to assign aides to special-needs students concerns more than cost, although the cost of one instructional aide for each student would overwhelm even the healthiest district balance sheet. "We have a real concern that kids will become dependent on the aides," one special education teacher said. Another added that the promise of one-on-one attention from an aide may not work as well as extra help in a special education class given the fact that aides typically do not have much training in helping students deal specifically with their disabilities.

> *The focus on inclusion is not only changing the way the general education classroom works, it is creating two important pressures on school districts: the potential for rising costs due to the demand for paraprofessionals, and the potential for conflict with parents as to the degree to which inclusion can be attained.*

Districts set their own standards for health aides, who attend to the physical needs of disabled students, such as helping them go to the bathroom. The number of aides in this category has increased sharply in recent years because courts have expanded the definition of services deemed educationally necessary to include attending to such physical needs. For instance, the Supreme Court's 1999 decision *Cedar Rapids Community School District v. Garret F.*[4] expanded the definition to include nursing care.

Teacher Training

In both districts, new teachers receive training in how to create "differentiated" instruction, so that special-needs children can be educated alongside the average and the gifted. In-service training is also directed to these areas.

In Troy, teachers are trained in the SAALE model (Systematic Approach for Adapting the Learning Environment), created by Dr. Judy Wood of Virginia Commonwealth University. Carried to its farthest, that model would make special education a thing of the past for all but youngsters with severe disabilities. For example, in *Adapting Instruction to Accommodate Students in Inclusive Settings* (3rd edition),[5] Wood presents alternatives to writing book reports for struggling students. Some include illustrating a book jacket, writing to the author, or writing and performing rap songs about the book.

Even sincere proponents of inclusion and the adaptive classroom expressed doubts that adapting instruction can always be done without watering down the curriculum. "This is a question I ask myself every day," one teacher—and parent of a gifted student—said. Another teacher implied that the adaptive classroom did not always work the way it was intended for special-needs students either; that they were simply not expected to do the same work. "We're told it doesn't matter if Jimmy can't take the test in social studies, that it's okay for him to benefit just by being there."

Districts also sense that the expectations of parents for full inclusion are rising faster than the districts' ability to include special-needs students, in some cases rising well beyond what the districts think is appropriate. The mandate for "least restrictive environment" and the ideology surrounding inclusion have created an impression for some parents that pull-out services are second best. In fact, they are often exactly what is needed. "Sometimes these kids really just need some one-on-one attention," Witkowski said.

In one situation in Troy, the parents of an autistic child insisted that their child attend a general education class because they felt their child functioned well enough academically to keep up. The situation turned out to be disruptive for the whole class, and it was not helpful for the child in question. Halfway through the year, the district hired an instructional aide to do what one teacher described as "babysitting" the student, making sure the student followed directions and otherwise regulating the child's interactions with other students. This year, the child was placed in a special class.

> "Districts are now in a terribly untenable position. They cannot ignore or take lightly physical or other aggressive behavior," but the current law provides them little recourse in situations involving special education students, says a Detroit law partner.

In sum, the focus on inclusion is not only changing the way the general education classroom works, it is creating two important pressures on school districts: the potential for rising costs due to the demand for paraprofessionals, and the potential for conflict with parents as to the degree to which inclusion can be attained.

Discipline and IDEA 1997

Neither district reported specific incidents in which a special education student committed an act that administrators felt should be punished but could not be due to the restrictions on discipline under the IDEA. If such an event were to happen, however, neither district seemed to feel that recent changes to the law, intended to enable administrators to discipline special education students more easily, would make much difference.

A suspension, being sent home from school, or a forced trip to the principal's office can constitute a change in placement for a special ed student, and, therefore, districts are required to figure out whether a student's actions are the result of his disability. Officially, the district may not "change the placement" for more than 10 days without an order from a hearing officer. (In the past, it took a federal court injunction.) Informally, such "changes in placement" seem to happen with parental consent. One teacher told me that an elementary school special education student with a fairly severe mental impairment was sent home for the day after hitting a teacher, not so much as a punishment but as a way to diffuse the situation. No committee was convened to determine whether the offense stemmed from the nature of the student's disability because the parent agreed it was best for everyone to take the child out of school for the day.

If a student's offense does allow for disciplinary action, the law provides that disciplined special education students be provided the same educational services as they were getting before, but in an "alternative" setting. Exactly what constitutes such an "alternative" setting was not clear to special education administrators or, for that matter, to the county-level regulators who monitor them or the lawyers who defend districts in court.

"We're really flying blind here," said Greg Gwisdalla, director of special education for the Oakland Intermediate School District (OISD), which oversees all of Oakland County's local school districts including Troy. He said that he didn't know what such an alternative setting would actually look like, as there has been little case law to define it. Troy School District's Lawrence Selaty went a step farther: "That kind of setting simply does not exist in Oakland County," he said. OISD officials were also worried that the issues surrounding discipline of emotionally impaired students, in particular, were making its local districts reluctant to sponsor programs for them.

> *In Michigan, local governments turn their property taxes for education over to the state, which then redistributes those and other funds in a way that aims to equalize funding among districts over time.*

"In the real, everyday world for a school district, you can't write this stuff in books and have it work," said Beverly Burns, a partner at the Detroit law firm of Miller, Canfield, Paddock and Stone. "Districts are now in a terribly untenable position. They cannot ignore or take lightly physical or other aggressive behavior," she said, but the current law provides them little recourse in situations involving special education students.

Spending on Special Education

Funds for special education come from federal, state, and local sources.

State funds. First a word on how school funding operates in Michigan. Since the 1994 passage of Proposition A, all funds for a school district's operating expenditures come from the state. Local governments turn their property taxes for education over to the state, which then redistributes those and other funds in a way that aims to equalize funding among districts over time. The state now bars local districts such as Troy and Garden City from raising local funds for school operating expenses.

For each of its students, a local district gets a "foundation allowance" from the state. On top of that, districts also get a "special education foundation allowance." The latter amount is derived by multiplying the regular foundation allowance by the full-time equivalent of special education pupils—and then multiplying the result by 28.6 percent, the state's court-mandated share of special education costs (the court case that established this share will be discussed in greater detail below). For Troy School District, that special education foundation allowance amounted to $1.98 million in 1999-2000. In Garden City, it was $3.65 million. In addition to this per-pupil funding, districts submit to the state a gigantic expense report for special education, listing nearly everything they spend on special education (except for capital outlays). The state pays back 28.6 percent of these costs, and 70 percent of special education transportation costs. For Troy School District, that amounted to $1.38 million in 1999-2000, and in Garden City the amount was $1.1 million.

Federal IDEA funds. Federal funds come in part from grants under Part B of the IDEA, and they take a circuitous route to get to districts like Troy and Garden City. The federal government hands IDEA funds over to the Michigan state government, which then disburses the funds to countywide school districts, called Intermediate School Districts (ISDs) or Regional Educational Service Associations (RESAs). These countywide districts (Troy belongs to the Oakland ISD and Garden City to the Wayne County RESA) exist in part to allow local districts to join together to provide special education programs for students with low-incidence disabilities. The ISDs and RESAs distribute IDEA grants as they see fit. In the Wayne RESA, Part B grants are combined with other federal and county funds to reimburse local districts directly for their programs for low-incidence disabilities. In the Oakland ISD, federal funds are distributed on a per-capita basis, amounting to about $500,000 for the Troy School District.

> *As courts have expanded the services that districts are required to fund, districts have become very aggressive in seeking out Medicaid payments to cover some special education expenses.*

Federal Medicaid funds. Since 1988, districts have been able to get reimbursed from Medicaid—the federal health care program for the poor—for some special education expenses. The ISDs and RESAs submit expenses to the Michigan Department of Community Health, which submits the expenses to the federal Health Care Financing Administration (HCFA). The HCFA then reimburses the state, which reimburses the districts. An example of something that Medicaid would cover might be physical therapy or a health aide for a Medicaid-eligible student.

As courts have expanded the services that districts are required to fund, districts have become very aggressive in seeking out Medicaid payments. Medicaid now spends some $2.3 billion in school-related expenses, an amount that has risen more than five-fold in the past five years, according to an April 2000 General Accounting Office report.[6] The report also criticized school districts for charging Medicaid millions of dollars too much, and for paying accounting firms a contingency fee. In the wake of this report, the U.S. Department of Health and Human Services simply refused many reimbursement claims. What's more, the federal government launched a fraud investigation of Michigan school officials, on grounds that the state used money intended for districts improperly and that school officials accepted what amounted to bribes from accounting firms for their business. As of this writing, no charges have been filed, but $103 million in Medicaid funds to the state have been frozen. The stop in Medicaid reimbursements has thrown the Troy School District's budget into deficit. It had budgeted for about $350,000 in Medicaid expenses, but only received about half. The district dipped into its rainy-day fund to make up the shortfall.

County funds. As mentioned above, Michigan's local school districts can no longer levy taxes for school operating expenses. But the countywide ISDs and RESAs may still do so for special education expenses, a funding source that both the Oakland ISD and the Wayne RESA tap. The Oakland ISD uses some of that money to fund its own programs—one for autistic students and one for hearing-impaired preschoolers and toddlers. After those programs are paid for, it distributes the rest to local districts on a head-count basis, amounting to about $2.85 million for the Troy School District. Oakland's local districts then contract with each other for services to benefit students with low-incidence disabilities.

> *In most districts, half or more of special education students are learning disabled. So even a fairly low per-student cost of additional educational services can add up to a huge sum.*

The Wayne RESA pools its local tax money with federal funds to pay directly for regional "center programs" for low-incidence disabilities, such as Garden City's Burger School. Yet in Wayne County, these funds do not always cover the entire cost of all of the center programs. In that case, the RESA bills local districts for the balance, based on the number of disabled students they have. Local districts pay for these so-called charge-backs however they can—with rainy-day funds or program cuts. The level of recent charge-backs is the main reason why the Garden City Public School's budget lurches in and out of deficit from year to year. It has to cover the cost of charge-backs with spending cuts in other areas.

The problem of charge-backs sending local districts' budgets into deficit was the main reason why Oakland ISD began providing funds on a more predictable head-count basis three years ago. Before 1997, its funding mechanism was much the same as that still used in Wayne County. Oakland ISD officials also believed that funding center programs directly was skewing school officials' placement decisions. Because it was essentially free to send students to those center programs, many students were not being served in their home district when they could have been.

High—and Rising—Costs

It is close to impossible to know how much it costs to educate any given special-needs student because a precise figure would depend on knowing the exact blend of services provided for in the student's IEP. But a recent study by the Michigan Department of Education made some estimates of the average cost in 1996-97 of educating students with different disabilities.[7] Researchers estimated that the cost of educating students full-time in special education classes ranged from $6,646 for the pre-primary impaired (a category for children from birth to age three with developmental delays that do not fall into one of the other categories) to $46,987 for a visually impaired student. For the learning disabled, full-time placement in a special class costs an average of $15,423. For students with speech and language impediments, who spend all day in a regular classroom but then receive speech therapy, the average cost was $1,911 above what was spent in a regular classroom. Learning-disabled students needing only the services of a teacher consultant cost $5,576 on average above what was spent on students in a regular classroom.

In short, even the costs of educating students with low-incidence disabilities can be astronomical. As courts continue to expand what is considered educationally necessary, as in *Garret F.*, districts expect those costs to go even higher. But in most districts, half or more of special education students are learning disabled. So even a fairly low per-student cost of additional educational services can add up to a huge sum. With the push for inclusion and the corresponding demand for more paraprofessionals, smaller classes, and improved classroom technology, those costs are also expected to rise.

The day I spoke with the superintendent of Troy School District, the transportation managers had just informed her that they needed three new buses with lifts to handle special education pupils. And the parents of one student with an auditory processing problem were appealing the results of a due process hearing to federal court, trying to get a full-time transliterator so their child could go to a general education class instead of a special program.

Even the seemingly trivial changes in IEP forms requested by regulators can create major pressure for new spending, Garden City Public Schools director of special education Witkowski pointed out. One recent change to the IEP forms added a box that the IEP team has to check once it has informed the parent that some students with disabilities may have the school year extended to as many as 230 days. The old form had no mention of the availability of an extended year, which is intended to prevent students with severe impairments from regressing over the summer. On the basis of tests administered to Garden City's special education students, Witkowski estimates that about a third of special education students need such help. But now that mention of an extended school year is on everyone's form, parents of students with fairly mild learning disabilities—who were not part of the group targeted by this policy—are asking for what amounts to year-round tutoring.

> *Many districts nationwide, including the two studied here, believe one of the biggest problems associated with special education is lack of adequate funding from state and federal governments to help meet rising costs.*

There are few ways that districts can contain costs. "Without all the 'guidelines,' I think we could get a lot more bang for our buck," Witkowski said. Extensive and sometimes conflicting regulations from federal and state governments can stifle innovation. For example, changes to the IDEA allow districts to use special education funds in a way that might also benefit students up to age nine who are not certified for special education. And Witkowski thinks it would be more efficient, without being less effective, for each school to have a speech teacher and a reading teacher to help any student. Yet state rules governing class size and caseload restrictions on special education teachers mean that such efforts would have to come on top of the special education services that already exist, not instead of them, making it too costly. Michigan does permit districts to apply for waivers to these regulations under certain circumstances; as a practical matter, however, parent committees and teachers' unions prevent these waivers for anything other than short-term issues.

Unfunded Mandate

According to research by the Michigan Association of School Administrators, special education costs grew at a 9 percent compounded annual rate during the 1990s, while overall school revenues grew at just a 3 percent rate. Many districts nationwide, including the two studied here, believe one of the biggest problems associated with special education is lack of adequate funding from state and federal governments to help meet rising costs. This so-called unfunded mandate, districts say, forces them to shortchange their general education programs because they are bound by the courts to fund special education fully, even as general education enjoys no such legal protection. "At the start of the year, my programs will be fully staffed and fully funded because they have to be," Witkowski said. "My kids will get bus service, although their brothers and sisters (who are not in a special education program) may not."

> *The issue of cost is not just one of underfunding. From the perspective of school districts, increasing litigation of special education claims threatens what little ability they have to control costs.*

The tradeoffs resulting from high special education costs and the ostensible lack of state funding are the subject of the Durant litigation in Michigan—a two-decades-long series of lawsuits brought by school districts against the state to force it to devote more funds to special education.

"This is a very severe problem," said Dennis Pollard, an attorney who is representing the school districts. "School districts can only absorb these costs for so long, and then they don't have any choice but to start cutting off general programs." Both Garden City and Troy have joined nearly 200 other Michigan school districts in the third round of Durant litigation, which seeks at least $460 million from the state.

The Durant lawsuits stem from the 1979 Headlee Amendment to the Michigan Constitution, which bars the state from imposing unfunded mandates. For all mandates in existence at the time the amendment passed, including special education, the state's required contribution was to be fixed at its 1979 level. This is why Michigan is now required to pay 28.6 percent of districts' special education costs and 70 percent of special education transportation costs.

The school districts won the first round of the lawsuits after 17 years, during which the state unsuccessfully argued that it was not liable for a higher share of special education costs because special education was ultimately a federal mandate. Both sides claimed victory in the second round, when the courts awarded no new funding to the school districts but told the state that special education monies had to be kept in a separate funding stream. In the current (third) dispute, districts are suing on two grounds: (1) first, that the state has raided other education funds to pay for its share of special education costs; (2) second, that the state actually owes even more than 28.6 percent. In the years since the Headlee Amendment passed, districts argue, the state imposed new regulations on special education—such as stricter class-size limitations—for which it should bear the full cost.

The state denies that it is raiding other education funds to pay for its special education obligations, pointing to a huge increase in education spending throughout recent years.

The issue that paying for special education may mean shortchanging general education is hardly confined to Michigan. In fact, economist Richard Rothstein has argued in a series of studies for the Economic Policy Institute that this has been a national trend. In a detailed look at nine school district budgets from 1967-1996, Rothstein found that overall spending rose substantially. Even so, the amount going to general education barely budged. The share of the districts' budgets going to general education fell from 80 percent in 1967 to 58.5 percent in 1991, and then to 56.8 percent in 1996. By contrast, the share going to special education rose from 3.6 percent of school budgets in 1967, to 17.8 percent in 1991 and 19 percent in 1996.[8]

Full Funding?

As school districts hold out hope for "full funding" of special education, taxpayers might have a different view. In reality, the dollars for special education come from taxpayers, no matter which level of government does the taxing. From their perspective, the actual costs of special education might be the more salient issue. "Full funding" from state and federal governments is important to local school districts because it allows them to get more money without having to ask local taxpayers for it. And in Michigan, now that districts can't raise taxes, "full funding" from the state government may well be the only way they can get more money at all—especially wealthy districts where the state equalization formula is producing only meager year-to-year increases.

> *Districts often feel that it's better to accommodate parents than face the uncertainty of a due process hearing.*

Litigation

The issue of cost is not just one of underfunding. From the perspective of school districts, increasing litigation of special education claims threatens what little ability they have to control costs. Litigation is also a cost in its own right for school districts—not only in cases that reach administrative hearings or federal court, but also in terms of what districts feel they must do to avoid legal challenge.

Lawsuits and other challenges to local special education services are hardly new. But these school districts report that the number of parent-initiated hearings and eventual court cases is on the rise. (To appeal an IEP decision, parents may first request a local due process hearing. Then the losing party may appeal to a hearing at the state level. After that, an appeal can go to court, most likely federal.)

In the Troy School District, there have been eight hearings since the start of 1995, only one of which the district initiated. By contrast, in the 15 years from 1979-1994, the district faced just three hearings, illustrating the extent to which litigiousness is on the rise. In the district-initiated case, the district successfully challenged a parent's continuing requests for independent testing to confirm the results of the district's tests. "Every time we had to test the child, it cost us a few thousand dollars a pop," director of special education Lawrence Selaty said. "Just to double check our results. They never found anything we hadn't."

In the Garden City Public Schools, there has been only one due process hearing in 15 years. "When you look at the big picture, it's just not worth a fight so you cave," Witkowski said. "This morning I was in an IEP meeting with the parent of an autistic four-year-old who's not ready for a full day at school. Only the parent can't find a baby-sitter who can deal with an autistic child. So if push comes to shove, I'll just put the child in a class for a full day, three days a week." Witkowski emphasized that the conflicts that lead parents to seek hearings are in many cases "good" ones, meaning that parents have a legitimate difference of opinion with the district.

"I know a lot of people who threaten [to use] lawyers to get what they want," one parent told me. A special education teacher pointed out a growing sense that IEP teams are becoming more and more likely to defer to parents. "I've sat in these meetings when a parent brings in an advocate and an attorney," he said. "Pretty quickly there's a shift from what's educationally sound to what's politically sound."

Districts often feel that it's better to accommodate parents than face the uncertainty of a due process hearing. When matters go to a hearing, each party puts forth two or three names of potential hearing officers that they would consider acceptable. If there's any overlap, then that will be the hearing officer. If, as is more likely, no names overlap, the state Department of Education appoints one at random. That process, Selaty says, is a major source of the uncertainty. "It can be a real crapshoot," he said. "There are some that tend to think parents are unreasonable, and others that think all school districts are evil."

> "The best defense to any claim is very careful attention to procedure," said Detroit attorney Beverly Burns. "There was a time when those things weren't as important as long as the intent and the result were there, but today you had better follow procedure rigidly, or your program could be derailed down the road."

And then there are the costs of the hearings themselves. Districts bear all of the administrative costs—the fees of the hearing officer, their own attorney fees, and the cost of substitutes for any school personnel needed in the hearing, as well as the other side's attorney fees if they lose. One parent came to the Garden City district wanting a different curriculum for a dyslexic child from the one provided by the district. "If we had fought that, it could easily cost us $50,000 if we lost," Witkowski said.

So for any individual case, the cost of yielding is usually lower than the cost of fighting. As Selaty puts it, "There's a saying: Do you want to be wrong for $10,000 or right for $100,000?" Yet the cost of acceding to demands eventually adds up in a way that threatens to break a district's bank.

Networking among parents is also fueling demands for the simple reason that parents are becoming more aware of what the district has done in other cases.

Districts perceive that many of the information sources parents are turning to—in particular on the Internet—are helping to create a more contentious atmosphere between parents and administrators. "I go to these workshops myself, and I look at the websites. They are all set up in an adversarial mode," Selaty said. "We have this medical model for problems," he continued. "If you have a broken arm, you go to the doctor, get an X-ray, and get it set. With a lot of these disorders, though, you're dealing with things that are never really going to go away. But there's this concept that we can fix it, that we have the cure and just don't want to pay for it."

The IDEA lets attorneys for parents recoup their fees if they win a case, and Selaty thinks that fact is fueling much of the litigation. The potential for an attorney to be awarded fees has created an industry of lawyers urging parents to challenge districts, he believes.

"It is just too easy to bring a lawsuit," Selaty said, noting that the one change he believes would make the biggest difference in the IDEA would be to do away with awarding attorney fees to the successful party. "It's getting to the point where every disagreement turns into a bad divorce case," he said. "If someone sends us a positive letter, we save it just in case."

> **The same procedures that shield districts from litigation can also act as a ceiling on the efforts of school districts to provide special education.**

Michigan's law requiring districts to educate special-needs students to their "maximum potential" sets a more substantive rather than procedural standard than the IDEA, which requires a "free appropriate public education." Yet that does not change the fact that both court battles and due process hearings tend to focus on procedure in Michigan as elsewhere. In theory, there is little that cannot be said to contribute to a child's "maximum potential." But courts and hearing officers generally do not try to reinvent an education program from the ground up, and parents usually have to find a procedural misstep on the part of a district in order to get a hearing at all.

"The best defense to any claim is very careful attention to procedure," said Detroit attorney Beverly Burns. "There was a time when those things weren't as important as long as the intent and the result were there, but today you had better follow procedure rigidly, or your program could be derailed down the road." Increasingly, that means having teachers who are trained in special education law and willing to document just about every detail of a student's educational progress. "Teachers aren't going into special education anymore because they don't get to work with kids," Witkowski said. "They study all these years, and then they get a Ph.D. in paperwork."

Attention to procedure is also clearly what federal and state regulators want to see, as evidenced by the example cited above in which regulators asked for additions to IEP forms. "When you tell them, 'come on, use your common sense; we are doing this,' they'll say 'well, no, not exactly,'" Witkowski said. Dealing with county monitors is somewhat easier, she finds. "They know these kids, and they know what we're trying to do," she said. "The system really breaks apart in terms of monitoring because (federal and state regulators) don't have a clue what we do on a daily basis, and it's not something you can put on paper."

The state has also urged districts to survey parents about special education. Yet the questions it wanted districts to ask were almost exclusively focused on procedure. For example, the state wanted to know whether districts informed parents of their upcoming IEP meetings. Only one question of 11 had anything to do with substantive matters, and that asked for an overall grade for special education programs.

> *Several basic, but important, questions have never been clearly answered by the legislators who mandate special education or by the administrators who implement the program.*

In short, litigation and regulation burden school districts tremendously. Yet districts find that the burdens of procedure are in fact their most reliable defense in court.

Does Special Education Work?

Administrators in both districts studied here were proud of their special education programs. Their complaints had mostly to do with cost pressures and what they viewed as obstacles to putting their programs into effect or improving them.

Both districts have good reputations for special education. In the Troy School District, for example, at least some special education students will go on to higher education. As a minimum requirement for graduation with a special education diploma, the district also requires students to have at least ten weeks of successful employment experience. This means that even students with fairly severe mental impairments leave the district with letters of recommendation for employment, surely an important sign of success.

"The number of people in Wayne County who make complaints about special education is well below a half of one percent," Witkowski said. "I would think that would be proof in the pudding that we are doing a good job." In terms of officially lodged complaints, this is true enough, and neither district has run afoul of the law. These, however, are better measures of compliance with procedure than of results.

It is not hard to see how the same procedures that shield districts from litigation can also act as a ceiling on the efforts of school districts to provide special education. "It can be easy for districts to lose sight of what they're really there for," said Detroit law partner Beverly Burns.

Currently, there is little the public can do to measure the success of special education. Success is currently measured by how well students meet their IEP goals; however, the nature of the goals themselves are sometimes vague and unmeasurable. For example, one IEP that I saw belonging to an LD student said that he was to "develop self-editing skills." There is no absolute way to determine when this goal has been achieved. The other problem with measuring the success of special education is that IEP goals are confidential. Not only is the public barred from knowing anything about an individual student's IEP, but the "individual" nature of the IEP makes it hard to render any aggregate judgment on the system as a whole.

Several basic, but important, questions have never been clearly answered by the legislators who mandate special education or by the administrators who implement the program:

- **Who should and who should not be expected to master the general education curriculum?** For some students, the answer to this is fairly obvious—for example, the student whose disabilities are largely physical, or the student whose mental impairments are quite severe. Yet the largest group of special education students, the learning disabled, exists somewhere in the middle. The 1997 amendments to the IDEA that mandate "access to" and "progress in" the general curriculum seem to imply that these students might be expected to master it, but they stop short of actually saying so. In neither district is it clear how many current special education students might be expected to do this, and how many of those achieve it.

- **In what cases can special education students be expected to leave special education?** In the districts studied here, only students in the speech and language category (which make up about a fifth of special education students statewide) would normally be expected to leave special education after therapy. That the overwhelming majority does so is seen as a sign of success. In neither district is the failure of other students to leave the special education system in significant numbers seen as a sign of failure.

- **Is the growing need for special education the result of failure on the part of the schools themselves?** Both districts seemed to be trying to improve early reading instruction in part as a way to reduce future special education referrals. But I detected no sense on the part of special education administrators or teachers that the students currently in special education were there for any reason other than true impairment, nor any inclination that students may have been sent to special education because of poor teaching methods in general education.

> *Including students with disabilities in Michigan's testing regime will at the very least provide everyone—parents, students, teachers, and districts—clearer information about what is actually being achieved in special education, particularly as it relates to the general curriculum.*

Answers to these questions might well provide concrete evidence that these districts do have quality special education programs. But at this point, it is hard for the observer to say. The advent of the testing regime mandated in the 1997 IDEA amendments may help change this.

In Michigan, the new testing regime will be fully implemented by the end of the 2001-2002 school year, although parts are being put into place this year. According to the law, IEP teams will determine whether a student is capable of taking the statewide tests known as the Michigan Educational Assessment Program (MEAP) either with or without accommodations. If an IEP team determines that a student should not take the MEAP tests at all, it must outline how the student will be tested. The state is developing alternate assessments that districts can use.

The State Board of Education in 1998 created four levels of performance expectations for students with disabilities: full independence, functional independence, supported independence, and participation. IEP teams will use these in deciding whether and which alternate assessments are to be used. (These levels cross categories; therefore, autism-impaired students, for example, might be found at any of these levels).

The state test proposals clearly anticipate that any student who can be expected to achieve full independence in life (for example, LD students and those with physical disabilities) will take the MEAP tests. Districts will have to include in their reporting of test scores to the state and the public the scores of any student who receives at least half of his or her English or reading instruction in general education.

For the other three levels of performance expectations, the state is developing alternate assessments. The proposals anticipate that these will be used for students with moderate to severe cognitive deficits, with educable mental impairment being the least severe condition that might qualify for one of the alternate tests. These students amount to about 15 percent of the special education population. The assessments themselves will cover the full range of goals—academic to life skills—that are set out for these students in Michigan's outcome guides. They will likely include extensive teacher observations in place of more traditional test questions.

This testing is an important first step in informing the public—and parents—about the actual performance of special education students. As such, it may eventually help improve special education. And with access to information about how special education students are doing, the public may begin to discern answers to some of the questions outlined above.

> *If school districts could say to parents, "This is our program; take it or leave it," and parents could, in fact, leave it, a measure of peace might be attained.*

Still, people looking to use this data to judge a district on its special education programs may be disappointed. The number of students taking alternate tests in a given district may be so small that it would violate their privacy rights for the district to report the results to the public. (This information will be available on a statewide basis). Nor is it clear whether the public will have any access to data about students who take the MEAP but who get less than half of their English or reading instruction in a general education class.

Including students with disabilities in Michigan's testing regime will at the very least provide everyone—parents, students, teachers, and districts—clearer information about what is actually being achieved in special education, particularly as it relates to the general curriculum. More information may prove a valuable weapon with which to demand improvements.

Recommendations

Rising costs and greater inclusion are creating important dilemmas for school districts. In particular, less-wealthy districts often have to meet an increase in special education costs with a decrease in spending elsewhere. In some cases, including a disabled student in a general education classroom can impact the education of the rest of the class, such as when an autistic child's behavior disrupted a kindergarten class for half a year.

Districts have little room to weigh such considerations when making decisions about individual special education programs. This fact creates the potential for unlimited demands on a special education program, whereas real-world resources are limited.

From the perspective of school districts, "full funding" of special education from state and federal governments is an obvious solution to the cost dilemma. Not only would it ease districts' budgeting squeeze, but it would do so without their having to convince local taxpayers to pay higher taxes.

From the taxpayers' perspective, however, the level of government that does the taxing to pay for special education doesn't make much difference. Rather, it is the total cost that is at issue. Without addressing the underlying cause of the problem—the fact that districts can not refuse to pay for a given special education program on grounds that it is too expensive—it is unlikely that schools will be able to rein in special education costs.

> *If policymakers tackle some of the hard questions surrounding special education, they might get beyond access and compliance—and improve quality.*

Likewise, making it marginally harder for parents to sue school districts—by eliminating payments of attorney fees under the IDEA—might marginally ease the pressures that districts face. Once again, though, this would fail to address the underlying sources of conflict.

The law currently binds parents to the district in which they live, and the school district to all students who live there. When parents want something and the district says no—or vice versa—someone either has to capitulate or initiate legal action for the conflict to be resolved. This is not a recipe for peace. Strengthening the role of parental choice might provide a way out. Currently, parental choice for a special education placement is subject to veto power on the part of school districts. And district programs are subject to potentially endless negotiation and new demands. If school districts could say to parents, "This is our program; take it or leave it," and parents could, in fact, leave it, a measure of peace might be attained. This, however, would also depend on whether school districts could expect funding that reflected the actual cost of education in order to ensure that they had the means to provide quality programs.

The new testing regime for special education students provides a clear opportunity not only to improve special education, but to do so in a way that eases some of the obstacles faced by school districts. By using information from new testing regimes, Washington might grant states waivers from regulations in exchange for proven results. Likewise, states with more stringent regulations than the federal government requires, such as Michigan, could do the same with their districts.

In the two districts studied here, one thing I did not see was much innovation or experimentation. Any new program had to come on top of what already existed and also conform to regulations, which means it would add significant costs and probably end up looking a lot like what was already being done. Trading regulations and compliance for results would make it possible to foster much more innovation.

The providers of special education programs face many tradeoffs and obstacles to doing their job well. Existing laws serve mainly to guarantee access to public schools and assure procedural rights. If policymakers tackle some of the hard questions surrounding special education, they might get beyond access and compliance—and improve quality.

[1] The interviews and visits on which this report is based were conducted in person and by phone between August 2000 and October 2000. The author wishes to thank the administrators, parents, and teachers who agreed to be interviewed. Any conclusions drawn from their valuable input, however, are the author's alone.

[2] Just before this volume went to press, the state of Michigan proposed substantial changes to its rules governing special education. The proposals are intended to align Michigan's regulations with the federal government's, as well as give districts some flexibility with class sizes, teacher caseloads, and the determining of IEPs. At this writing, the proposals are still in a public comment period, which has generated a great deal of controversy among parent groups. They have yet to be adopted.

[3] The others categories, in order of their statewide incidence, are speech and language impaired (23.7 percent), emotionally impaired (8.5 percent), educable mentally impaired (8.5 percent), physically and otherwise health impaired (6.6 percent), trainable mentally impaired (2.6 percent), autistic impaired (1.9 percent), hearing impaired (1.8 percent), severely multiply impaired (1.8 percent), preprimary impaired (1.6 percent), severely mentally impaired (0.7 percent), and visually impaired (0.5 percent). The learning disabled make up 42 percent of Michigan's special education population.

[4] 19 S.Ct. 992 (1997).

[5] Judy W. Wood, *Adapting Instruction to Accommodate Students in Inclusive Settings*, 3rd. ed. (Upper Saddle River, NJ: Prentice Hall, 1997).

[6] See U.S. General Accounting Office, *Medicaid in Schools: Improper Payments Demand Improvements in HCFA Oversight* (Washington, DC: General Accounting Office, 2000).

[7] See Michigan Department of Education, *Comparison of Regular Education and Special Education Costs for the 1994-95 School Year* (Lansing, MI: Michigan Department of Education, 1997).

[8] See Richard Rothstein, *Where's the Money Going: Changes in the Level and Composition of Education Spending, 1967-91* (Washington, DC: Economic Policy Institute, 1995); Richard Rothstein, *Where's the Money Going: Changes in the Level and Composition of Education Spending, 1991-96* (Washington, DC: Economic Policy Institute, 1997).

Chapter 8

How Federal Special Education Policy Affects Schooling in Virginia

Frederick M. Hess and Frederick J. Brigham

Introduction

Federal special education legislation has an honorable heritage and a laudable purpose. Unfortunately, the manner in which Congress and the executive branch have pursued that purpose now impedes the ability of state school systems to serve children in both general and special education.

> The current system of oversight and resource allocation focuses less on educational attainment and more on procedural civil rights.

The current system of oversight and resource allocation focuses less on educational attainment and more on procedural civil rights. Problems result from the federal government's use of this legalistic approach. In most areas of education, Washington offers supplementary funding as a carrot to encourage desired state behaviors. The challenge of compelling states to abide by federal dictates in special education, however, has produced a reliance on procedural oversight with deleterious effects for the federal-state partnership in education.

Under the present system, educators are restricted in their ability to make decisions regarding how best to assist children with disabilities. Instead, in response to federal dictates, states press school districts toward a defensive posture in which educators may spend more time attending to procedural requirements than to students' instructional and behavioral needs. Most discussions of reforming special education at the federal level ask what policy changes would alleviate this problem of excessive proceduralism. We suggest that such an approach is too narrow, that over-reliance upon procedural regulation actually arises from Washington's attempt to compel behaviors with insufficient incentives or guidance.

While seeking to get states to do its bidding with respect to children and youths with disabilities, Congress has provided neither inducements for them to cooperate nor flexibility in how they comply with federal direction. Lacking the capacity to implement special education policy on its own—considering that it does not operate public schools or employ their teachers—Washington has instead relied upon micro-managing state procedures and using the threat of legal action as a primary enforcement tool.

Lacking explicit federal direction or support, state officials cope by crafting their own muddled guidelines. This permits the state, like the federal government, to forestall messy conflict over details regarding program eligibility and services by pushing such questions down to districts and schools. Principals and teachers complain that the nested levels of governance deepen the confusion as the rules grow more convoluted and cumbersome at each stage.[1]

In this chapter, we explore how federal special education policy affects schooling in the Commonwealth of Virginia. The data were collected from official documents; interviews and discussions with more than 50 educators, policymakers, and other individuals involved with special education; and observation of state meetings and hearings. The research was conducted between June and October 2000.

> *Under the IDEA, a satisfactory program is defined as one that adheres to due process, regardless of its results.*

The Federal Role in Special Education

The federal government shapes special education policy through both the Individuals with Disabilities Education Act (IDEA) and Section 504 of the Rehabilitation Act. We shall briefly review both, discuss the role of litigation in enforcing special education requirements, and then explore the consequences for schooling in Virginia. The discussion focuses on key dimensions of policy and practice. In the first half of the paper, we discuss how special education's "free appropriate public education" (FAPE) and "least restrictive environment" (LRE) requirements are implemented in Virginia, how special education affects state education funding, and how special education services are monitored. In the second half of the paper, we discuss how these policies affect school practice in terms of individualized education programs (IEPs), discipline policy, and state education standards.

The IDEA

In making special education law, Congress and the executive branch have relied heavily upon judicial precedents rooted in the Equal Protection and Due Process Clauses of the 14th Amendment. Whereas most federal legislation is framed as a compromise between competing interests and claims, this more absolutist orientation means that special education policies turn on endowing claimants with an inviolable set of rights. That mindset is illustrated by the "inclusion" proponent who prominently argued, "It really doesn't matter whether or not [full inclusion] works...even if it didn't work it would still be the thing to do."[2]

Under the IDEA, a satisfactory program is defined as one that adheres to due process, regardless of its results. Critics suggested that this orientation fed lower expectations for students with disabilities. In response, the 1997 IDEA reauthorization sought to emphasize academic performance by insisting upon "meaningful access to the general education curriculum to the maximum extent possible" for students with special needs. It is too early to judge the overall impact of these recent changes, though we will discuss some of their effects later in the paper.

Section 504

In theory, states are free to disregard the IDEA. The only federal sanction is the ability of the Office of Special Education Programs (OSEP) to withdraw IDEA grants. These grants amount to less than ten percent of state special education spending. This apparent freedom is illusory, however, because any state that fails to comply with the IDEA's requirements would still be liable under Section 504 of the Rehabilitation Act of 1973. Section 504 is designed to protect individuals with "a physical or mental impairment which substantially limits one or more...major life activities." The initial regulations implementing Section 504 explained that the statute was intended "to eliminate discrimination on the basis of handicap in any program or activity receiving Federal financial assistance." Although it supplies no funding, Section 504 applies to any entity receiving any federal funding, meaning that all states must abide by its directives. Because the courts have interpreted Section 504 as implying the same responsibilities as the IDEA,[3] schools would be required to fulfill the same federally imposed obligations even if they were to spurn IDEA funding.

Although the IDEA offers guidelines regarding various disability conditions, the provisions of Section 504 are so nebulous that it becomes extremely difficult to distinguish students entitled to special education services from those not entitled. As one administrator said, "In my opinion, IDEA is much more precise, much more specific....504 is the same as saying, 'you have a problem here.' [Anybody can identify some problem] 'substantially limits' [a life activity]....What's the line there? So you're wide open."[4]

Special Education in Virginia

Special education comprises a substantial share of Virginia's K-12 educational expenditures. Between 1995 and 1998, special education students made up 13 percent to 14 percent of the state's student population, while the special education budget consumed 23 percent to 25 percent of the state's education budget. (See Figure 1.)

Figure 1. Sources of Special Education Funding in Virginia, 1992-99

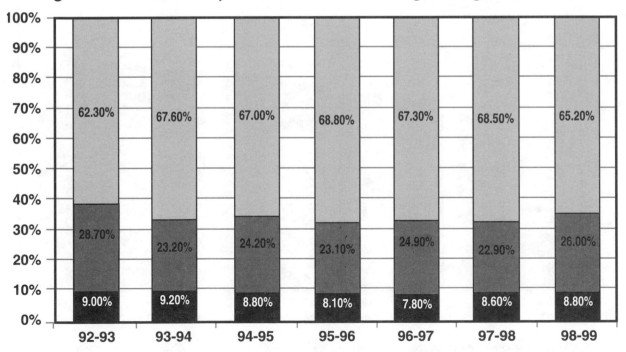

Source: Virginia Department of Education, "Local School Division Reported Expenditures for Special Education," available at <<http://www.pen.k12.va.us/VDOE/Instruction/Sped/by_percent.pdf>> (August 20, 2000).

During the 1990s, Virginia's special education student enrollment grew at a pace that outstripped the general education population. Special education enrollment grew 38 percent between 1990 and 1998, from 111,000 to 153,000. (See Figure 2.) During that same period, overall K-12 enrollment grew only 12 percent, from 1 million to 1.2 million.

From 1995 to 1999, costs for special education grew at roughly the same rate as for general education. (See Figure 3.) As general education spending per pupil grew by 17 percent during that period (from $4,858 to $5,675), special education spending grew by 18 percent (from $10,035 to $11,874). In other words, special education spending remained at approximately twice the level of general education spending.

In Virginia, federal special education directives are interpreted and implemented by a designated group of professionals in the state Department of Education (DOE). Within the larger DOE, headed by the state Superintendent of Education, is a directorate for special education headed by a Director of Special Education and Student Services (SESS). Historically, the directorate for Special Education did nothing else. In 2000, DOE merged "Special Education" with "Student Services," the unit responsible for activities such as school health and safety. Despite this reorganization, Special Education remains relatively isolated from the other areas of the DOE. In January 2001, SESS included 23 positions devoted to oversight of special education. These individuals include specialists in learning disabilities, emotional disturbance, mental retardation, early childhood, and severe disabilities. Not one member is explicitly charged with coordinating policy with the other parts of the DOE.

Figure 2. Virginia's Increasing Special Education Enrollment, 1990-98

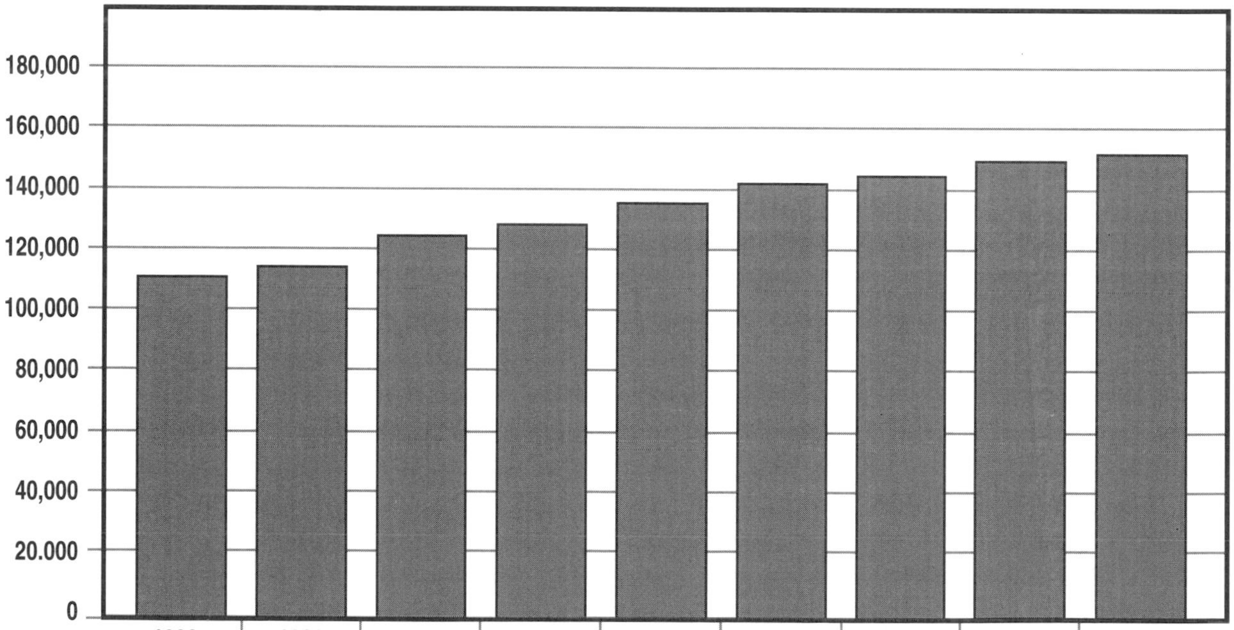

	1990	1991	1992	1993	1994	1995	1996	1997	1998
N Students	110,777	115,823	122,849	128,326	135,710	141,351	144,210	148,368	153,379

Source: Virginia Department of Education, *Report of Children and Youth with Disabilities Receiving Special Education,* available at <<http://www.pen.k12.va.us/VDOE/Publications/SPED_child_count/total98.html>> (August 15, 2000).

Figure 3. Virginia's Per-Pupil Costs for General and Special Education, 1995-99

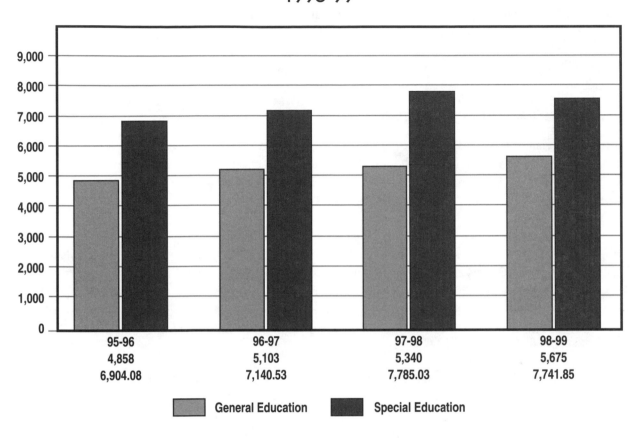

	95-96	96-97	97-98	98-99
General Education	4,858	5,103	5,340	5,675
Special Education	6,904.08	7,140.53	7,785.03	7,741.85

■ General Education   ■ Special Education

Source: Virginia Department of Education, "Cost Comparison for Students Receiving Special Education Versus Students Not Receiving Special Education," available at <<http://www.pen.k12.va.us/VDOE/Instruction/Sped/compare_expend.pdf>> (August 20, 2000).

Virginia's DOE essentially runs parallel school systems, one staffed by special educators for students with disabilities, the second staffed by general educators for everyone else. Each side exhibits distrust and frustration with the other. A local special education administrator observed, "People in general education don't listen to us or even ask us about the kids in our caseloads." A state-level administrator said, "We have consistent problems with some of our districts," explaining that the state deals with such challenges by using legal and administrative sanctions to coerce general educators into "playing ball." General educators voice reciprocal concerns. One administrator spoke for many, saying, "I have all I can handle right now without attending to students with wildly varying educational and behavioral needs." A high school teacher reported similar frustration, relating, "I remember trying to teach history to one kid who had to pass the SOL [Standards of Learning] test, and all he was doing is [sic] sitting there and calling me a bitch. And, because he's in a special education program, there's nothing I can do about it and nothing that anybody else is willing to do about it."

The current structure ensures that special education policy decisions are mostly made by people removed from actual school practice and from the general decisionmaking process for K-12 curriculum and instruction. This makes it less likely that services for students with special needs will be integrated or coordinated with the larger educational program. Meanwhile, general educators and board members are suspicious of special educators, worrying that they fail to recognize how their policies and actions impact the general student population. The structure of the DOE helps to divide general and special education personnel, while encouraging professionals to think differently about different categories of children, despite Congress' insistence that its goal is to eliminate distinctions among students.

Special Education Litigation

Despite the visibility of special education cases that reach the courts, such actions are relatively rare in Virginia. The most common legal or quasi-legal actions are complaints and due process hearings. The Commonwealth devotes considerable time and energy to these. Due process hearings are a quasi-judicial, adversarial procedure overseen by part-time hearing officers trained by the DOE.

Between 1992-93 and 1999-2000, 799 due process requests were filed with the DOE (see Table 1), roughly 100 a year.[5] All such requests require formal notification to the Department that the plaintiff is exercising his right to a due process hearing. Ninety-three percent of these requests were filed by parents. The remaining 7 percent were filed by school districts, usually when the district was concerned that parents were refusing to allow it to provide the services it

Table 1. Due Process Hearing Requests, Sources, and Outcomes in Virginia, 1992-2000

School Year	Due Process Hearing Requests	% Initiated by Parent	Hearings Concluded*	No. of Decisions Rendered	% Decisions Wholly Favoring LEA		% Decisions Favoring Parent in Part or in Whole**	
1992-93	66	97%	50	20	80%	(16)	20%	(4)
1993-94	102	91%	73	29	90%	(26)	10%	(3)
1994-95	120	90%	111	42	67%	(28)	33%	(14)
1995-96	96	92%	64	20	90%	(18)	10%	(2)
1996-97	84	Not reported	53	15	80%	(12)	20%	(3)
1997-98	104	Not reported	66	9	22%	(2)	78%	(7)
1998-99	114	Not reported	79	16	75%	(12)	25%	(4)
1999-00***	113	Not reported	90	26	60%	(15)	28%	(7)
Total	799	93%	586	176	75%	129	25%	(44)

* Actions may be concluded by settlement prior to the hearing, a hearing decision, or the withdrawal of the hearing request by the party who filed it.

** Includes spilt decisions where findings for both parties were yielded. Data reported only for cases filed and concluded in the same academic year.

*** The 1999-2000 column totals equal only 88 percent because the data include the number of cases that went forward to hearing but were dismissed (3 cases, 12 percent).

Source: Virginia Department of Education, *Annual Report for Special Education Due Process Hearings and Special Education Complaints* (Richmond, VA: Virginia Department of Education, various years).

deemed appropriate. These figures indicate that formal legal proceedings may be less of an issue than critics sometimes fear.

Of those 799 cases filed, 586 were resolved in the same year.[6] Of the 586, 176 (30 percent) led to decisions by a hearing officer while the rest ended through withdrawal of the complaint or settlement prior to a hearing. Of the 176 decisions rendered, three-quarters were resolved wholly in favor of the school district. The other 25 percent either favored the parent or split the difference between parent and district.

There are at least two ways to interpret these outcomes. One is that a substantial percentage of the requests filed lack merit. A second is that some schools respond to parental concerns only when faced with the threat of legal sanctions. A significant number of hearing requests are withdrawn after districts make concessions. As one attorney active in special education noted, "Most of the cases I deal with involve discipline. IDEA requires schools to act proactively on behalf of students with behavior problems rather than expelling them. If they do not, the law affords families a way of ensuring their children will be educated."

> *The larger problem of the due process system is not the number of formal complaints or their resolution, but the incentives that this legalistic mechanism creates for local educators.*

Critics of the due process system have asserted that many complaints and hearing requests are produced by the same small group of disgruntled parents. As one district administrator said, "When you look at who is doing the complaining, usually you find it is the same person over and over again. One angry parent can use IDEA mechanisms to make schools look like they are much worse than they really are." However, the data do not provide evidence for this contention. In 1999-2000, for example, 113 due process hearing requests were filed in Virginia. Just four parents filed more than one request; in each case, they filed two.

The larger problem is not the number of formal complaints or their resolution, but the incentives that this legalistic mechanism creates for local educators. Presently, the desire to avoid legal sanctions and officer-ordered costs and services is the clearest incentive for schools to make extraordinary efforts to serve students with disabilities. Such efforts may cause the district to divert resources from other worthy purposes. Educators have cause to focus on what services and accommodations will forestall complaints, rather than on which are cost-effective and educationally appropriate. The result is that districts are caught between a desire to "cut corners" on special education expenditures and the impulse to provide services in order to avoid the threat of legal action. By encouraging schools and parents to adopt adversarial roles, the legalistic emphasis makes cooperative solutions more difficult and shifts the focus of decisionmaking from educational performance to the avoidance of potential liability.

The Institutional Shape of Special Education

Here we examine three key program dimensions used by the federal government to define special education and to ensure that it is delivered in an acceptable manner. These policies address the key statutory provisions of FAPE and LRE, education funding, and special education monitoring.

FAPE and LRE

The key IDEA mandates affecting instruction and student placement are FAPE (free appropriate public education) and LRE (least restrictive environment). FAPE addresses the elements of a student's education program, although LRE addresses the integration of disabled students into the general education system. Often, the two mandates embody contradictory impulses. Legal scholar Anne Dupre has observed, "The friction between 'appropriate' education and 'appropriate' integration has baffled the courts and led to a confusing array of opinions on inclusion."[7] While educators must attend to both considerations, in Virginia it appears that the balance is tipped in favor of inclusion, even at the cost of effective education. An attorney who often represents parents of children with disabilities said, "[t]he intensity of the programs offered for students with mild disabilities fell after the push for more inclusion. Now we more often have to pursue formal action to get these students the services they need."

> *For students with less obvious disabilities, program appropriateness ought to take into account curricular demands on the student as well as the larger educational context of the school.*

The most difficult aspect of FAPE involves the meaning of "appropriate," which is clearer for some disabilities than others. Few question the need for Braille tests for students who are blind or ramps for those with limited mobility. For students with less obvious disabilities, however, program appropriateness ought to take into account curricular demands on the student as well as the larger educational context of the school.

In Virginia, the nature of appropriate services has changed dramatically with the recent institution of the state's "Standards of Learning" and accompanying assessment program. Teachers, principals, schools, and entire districts are to be judged based upon the aggregate scores attained by their students on the new state tests. One Virginia professor recalled traveling to a district to conduct training on how to support students with disabilities in general education curricula. He was introduced to the faculty by a school administrator who announced, "If your scores do not rise every year, you will most likely lose your job." It is hardly surprising, given such pressures, that general education teachers are often wary of being held responsible for students with behavior difficulties and histories of low achievement.

Although the challenge of validating the appropriateness of a given student's educational program is daunting, it is overshadowed by the problems surrounding the LRE requirement. Few areas of special education are as controversial. Much effort is invested in determining the LRE for individual students, closely watched by a group of educators and advocates who call for "full inclusion" of disabled youngsters in regular education classes.

The IDEA signals that general education settings are preferred for students with disabilities because they are the least restrictive. Indeed, at first glance a general education class may seem to meet the requirements of LRE by affording maximum contact with other children. Yet programs conducted in such settings may fail to deliver necessary treatments with sufficient frequency or intensity to meet the needs of individual students, at least without substantial alteration.[8] There is also evidence that students with mild disabilities fare better in more specialized settings.[9]

In Virginia, as a result of the push for "inclusion," many of the services formerly available to students with mild disabilities (such as resource rooms and partial-day special education) have

> **The current approach to FAPE and LRE fails to resolve the tension between maximizing achievement and maximizing integration.**

been cut back or eliminated. Such programs frequently have been replaced by "collaborative" or "consultative" models, in which students with special needs are enrolled full-time in general education classrooms. One result has been that a continuum of placement options has been replaced with a starker choice between intensive (for example, self-contained) classes and limited services (for example, enrollment in general education programs). This shift has left both general and special education teachers with fewer ways to respond to the needs of students, which reduces their ability to make effective professional judgments about what works for children in their schools.

This change has pushed students with mild disabilities out of specialized programs and into general education classrooms, even as research suggests that some of them would be better served by more intensive programs. One member of the Virginia State Special Education Advisory Committee (SSEAC) said,

> Here's my concern with the way that LRE is interpreted. I'm thinking of one private residential facility for students with behavioral disorders. It's one of the most effective facilities I have ever seen. However, school personnel report pressure to move students out of the facility due to IDEA's emphasis on children attending the school that they would attend if not handicapped. LRE requirements have sometimes been interpreted to suggest that a general education is always least restrictive. But every environment is restrictive of something, and this particular environment is restrictive of unacceptable behavior. The students I see in this school are learning and supporting pro-social behavior among themselves. Such a program is simply not possible in a general education setting.[10]

The current approach to FAPE and LRE fails to resolve the tension between maximizing achievement and maximizing integration, leaving these competing desiderata to be worked out by administrators, teachers, and parents without clear guidelines. Yet educators are blocked from using their professional judgment in weighing these two imperatives and are subjected to administrative or judicial review and sanction if deemed to have proceeded in an inappropriate manner. In other words, district officials are granted an ambiguous autonomy and expected to make appropriate decisions but are prevented from relying upon their professional determinations of efficiency and efficacy in reaching those decisions. The system is faintly redolent of a star chamber in which one is not sure the criteria to which one is being held.

Funding
One of most significant impacts of FAPE is on state education funding. Because Congress has

imbued disabled children with particular rights, the state is legally required to give budgetary priority to their needs. States are legally vulnerable to charges that they have failed to provide adequately for students with special needs, while parents of general education students cannot make similar claims. The consequence is that states have a difficult time making the case against the provision of even very expensive special education services and tend to fund these by dipping into the pool that would otherwise fund general education.

Because the rights of a child with special needs are hard to delimit, tensions also characterize efforts to distribute resources fairly within the special-needs population. Consider a pilot program in Fairfax County that serves ten preschoolers with autism. The two-year-old program offers each child 30 hours per week of one-on-one home instruction at an annual cost of $30,000 apiece. Meanwhile, Fairfax spent $8,200 on the average pupil in 1999-2000. Researchers have found the autism program promising and suggest that it may generate substantial savings in the long-term. Yet, it raises obvious issues of allocative justice. These ten children are receiving resources that could provide for full-time music or art teachers in several elementary schools or for intensive reading tutoring for hundreds of children.

> **Because the rights of a child with special needs are hard to delimit, tensions also characterize efforts to distribute resources fairly within the special-needs population.**

The program is costly enough that Fairfax County does not even offer it to all preschoolers with autism. At least 40 children who might benefit from the program are placed in more conventional programs. This decision has provoked heated complaints. Said one bitter parent, "They're ruining children and ruining families." Meanwhile, Fairfax officials report that the ten students were selected based on the severity of their autism or other clinical factors, and the superintendent has pointed out that expanding the program would require the system to forego other expenditures. Given limited resources, the pressing question for administrators is how to ration them.[11]

Recall earlier Figure 1 illustrating how special education costs were apportioned among federal, state, and local governments from 1992 to 1999. During this period, the federal share of funding was 8 percent to 9 percent and the state share ranged between 23 percent and 29 percent. Sixty-five percent, or nearly two-thirds, of total spending incurred on behalf of special education students was borne by local districts.

The federal government gave states about $1,045 per IDEA student in 1998-99. Even this modest figure overstates the actual extent of federal support to local districts because up to 25 percent of these dollars may be retained by states to help defray the costs of IDEA-mandated monitoring and enforcement. As one local administrator working on the state special education advisory committee argued, "Here we sit doing all this work mandated by the feds, and they can't even be bothered to pay the share that they think *they* owe us."

Given that special education students attract additional federal and state funding, one might wonder whether districts over-identify children as disabled in order to obtain state revenues or whether they over-identify students for services that are reimbursed by the state at a relatively high dollar value. Two factors render such gamesmanship unlikely.

First, selectively identifying students for more generously reimbursed services is no longer a viable strategy for resource-hungry districts, due to 1997 IDEA amendments requiring that states provide "placement neutral funding."[12] These changes mandated that states fund every special education student equally. Thus states are not to use funding plans that encourage one service delivery model (for instance, self-contained classes) over another (for instance, part-day programs). States are not permitted to give schools money on the basis of how much it costs to operate a particular program but must use a standard formula that funds all special education students equally. In promoting this change, reformers reasoned that schools would be more likely to place students in more restrictive—and costlier—programs if such students were funded more generously. The state wanted to discourage such activity because it would violate the IDEA's LRE rule. If anything, therefore, there is now a financial incentive for districts to identify special-needs students for less costly services such as resource rooms or consultative support.

> *Selectively identifying students for more generously reimbursed services is no longer a viable strategy for resource-hungry districts, due to 1997 IDEA amendments requiring that states provide "placement neutral funding."*

Second, although it is theoretically possible that Virginia districts over-identify low-cost special education students so as to reap additional federal and state largesse, the actual costs involved make such a strategy unlikely, even counterproductive. In 1998-99, the typical special education student cost a Virginia district about $6,200 more than the average general education student. Meanwhile, the maximum special education funding supplied by state and federal sources totaled about $4,100 per student. In other words, the typical special education student costs districts about $2,100 above and beyond the attached state and federal aid. Thus, districts generally lose money by identifying students as eligible for special education. As one district administrator said, "We want to offer these programs to as many children as possible, but we simply cannot afford to provide them to everyone. They just place a tremendous strain on our budget." In Virginia, at least, there is little to recommend over-identification as a money-making strategy.

Monitoring Special Education

In theory, federally inspired monitoring ensures that special education programs provide an appropriate education to all eligible students. In reality, the monitoring focuses more on procedural compliance than on either the appropriateness or effectiveness of the education being delivered. Given the lack of evidence that procedural compliance equates to more effective services, it is not clear that federal monitoring is effectively promoting quality special education. Moreover, such an emphasis undermines teacher professionalism by forcing educators to invest significant time in managing procedures and documenting processes, rather than on instruction.

OSEP's policy, adopted after the 1997 IDEA amendments, monitors states predominantly by requiring them to conduct self-studies. A key problem in this process is that the reporting requirements are both complex and vague. For example, the phrase "free appropriate public education" sounds straightforward and easily implemented, but a closer look proves otherwise.

Assuming that "free" means no cost to the parents, interpreting this part is straightforward. But, what does "appropriate" mean? In order to define this term, one must first determine the goals of the education program and ask the question, "Appropriate for what?" The IDEA is silent on that point, meaning that this question must be revisited in the case of each student. OSEP plainly is unable to monitor the "appropriateness" of a given decision in the case of a particular child. Therefore, it winds up monitoring processes and procedures—for example, the way that the decision was made. In practice, the guidelines are daunting, elaborate, and time-consuming even for many special education professionals—let alone the parents and students they are intended to protect. As one state official commented, "Monitoring used to be a part of my job, now it's all I do. Running the monitoring program has become my whole job."

> *The phrase "free appropriate public education" sounds straightforward and easily implemented, but a closer look proves otherwise.*

Virginia's SSEAC, which is supposed to identify critical issues and advise DOE on carrying out special education programs, scrapped its entire agenda for 2000-2001 in order to concentrate on the issue of program monitoring. The state DOE has had to add additional staff to handle these responsibilities.

In early January 2001, the SSEAC met to discuss the self-study that comprises the initial stage of Virginia's federal monitoring. At the beginning of the meeting, a facilitator asked each committee member why he or she had given up the time to attend this particular meeting. The most common response was to attain closure on the process. The facilitator pointed out that the federal monitoring process, being continuous, could never result in closure.

Reports were presented regarding programs for both school-aged and preschool children. Each report was several hundred pages long. After the meeting, several parent representatives remarked that they saw little connection between the activities conducted through the federal monitoring and discernible improvements in the educational services offered to their children. The best that can be said of the self-study is that it allows parents and special educators to voice their concerns. However, there is little reason to suspect that this unfocused airing of grievances is likely to produce substantive improvements in special education. More likely, because the state officials who led the self-study procedure were diverted from their responsibilities to monitor and support local education agencies (LEAs), the federal monitoring program is likely to result in decreased attention to the problems faced by children and youths with disabilities, their families, and the schools that serve them.

The Practice of Special Education

In this section, we focus on the practical impact of special education policy in Virginia, especially the role of IEPs, school discipline, and the manner in which special education interacts with Virginia's emphasis on academic standards and accountability.

IEPs

As originally conceived, IEPs were to be a flexible tool for creating specialized programs responsive to student needs as well as parental and school concerns. However, Virginia practice emphasizes *pro forma* compliance with IEPs in order to protect educators from administrative and legal actions. A typical IEP form offers 45 boxes for committees to check off before they even begin to describe the student's own education program. Rather than a flexible pedagogical tool, the IEP is often a ritualized document. As one special education administrator said, "Of course, all of our special ed students have IEPs. But how relevant are [the IEPs] to what our teachers are doing on a day-to-day basis? Not very."

Parents are not alone in their dissatisfaction. Teachers often complain that IEPs do little but absorb time and repeat platitudes. One veteran teacher who moved to special education after more than 15 years of general education teaching remarked, "The IEPs for all of my students say the same thing. The 'current level of performance' indicates that they have 'processing disorders.' There is no indication of what kind of processing disorders or what that might mean in, say, an English or a math class. The accommodations are all about test-taking, and they pretty much all say the same thing. My training tells me that [this vagueness] is bad educational practice, but my department chair tells me that it is the way we do things. Lots of little boxes appear on the placement pages, and they have been appropriately checked, so the due process stuff is evident. But that doesn't help anyone teach."

> **IEPs have historically reflected a given student's particular instructional regimen, rather than providing a road map for helping that child accomplish the general education goals promulgated by the school or state.**

IEPs have historically reflected a given student's particular instructional regimen, rather than provided a road map for helping that child accomplish the general education goals promulgated by the school or state. A result is that they are often written with little input from general education teachers and scant regard for the standards of general education programs. Conscientious teachers who make a good-faith effort to deal with these additional burdens often find themselves marginalized in the planning process and frustrated by the demands placed upon them.

Until 1997, the IDEA did not even require regular classroom teachers to be involved in the construction of a student's IEP. The result was that, in some districts, IEP teams would design programs that demonstrated scant awareness of classroom conditions and instructional realities. One teacher explained, "If I'm part of the team, I know exactly what I need to do. I know a child's weaknesses. If not, I'm shooting in the dark."[13]

The 1997 amendments required that general education teachers be included in IEP meetings and that IEPs yield "meaningful access to the general education curriculum." Unfortunately, both changes appear to hold only limited promise. So long as special education policy is driven by rights and legalisms, inserting general education teachers into IEP planning sessions is unlikely to produce significant changes in practice. As for "meaningful access to the general education curriculum," the phrase is so nebulous as to serve no real purpose, while creating yet one more interpretive minefield for school personnel.

The trouble with most efforts to improve IEPs is that they fail to address the contradiction at the heart of the process. On the one hand, professional educators are charged with designing flexible programs that respond to the needs of each student with disabilities. On the other hand, these plans are devised and implemented in a context shaped by compliance-based rules and marked by legal peril. The result is that IEPs cease to be useful pedagogical tools.

Discipline Policy

The IDEA requires the development of distinct disciplinary policies for students with disabilities. Some of these distinctions make sense. It is unreasonable to discipline a wheelchair-bound student for failing to stand during the national anthem. The IDEA prevents schools from punishing students in such situations (although we see no evidence that Virginia schools, left to their own judgment, would engage in such practices). The IDEA requires a "zero reject" model that extends special education services to *all* students with disabilities. Under this logic, schools may not interrupt or withhold services for any such students save for infractions involving guns or possession of drugs. Such interruption of services has been deemed to violate the IDEA's procedural safeguards.[14] These requirements have little direct impact at the state level—the DOE simply passes the federal regulations through to LEAs that must take responsibility for compliance—but many district educators suggest that they present significant challenges at the district level.

> *As for "meaningful access to the general education curriculum," the phrase is so nebulous as to serve no real purpose, while creating yet one more interpretive minefield for school personnel.*

IDEA regulation of discipline may serve a legitimate purpose. It is well established that students with disabilities are frequently "over-punished" for behavior infractions.[15] Many parents of children with disabilities report that their children feel singled out by school officials for behavior that rarely leads to sanctions for other students. One distraught mother said, "My son is sent to detention for things that I see other kids doing. He's in trouble almost every week." School officials acknowledge that her child was frequently disciplined. However, while other students occasionally break rules, they reported that the aforementioned student was constantly provoking conflicts due to his impulsiveness and poor social judgment. Although the school had no systematic plan for teaching social behavior, officials admitted that such an effort might be useful. The IDEA regulations seek to encourage such planning and instruction.

Unfortunately, the IDEA also has a number of undesirable disciplinary consequences. School officials must determine the extent to which an act of misbehavior results from a disability. Judgments regarding the motivation of a specific act have eluded philosophers and psychologists through the ages, yet are required by the IDEA. Such deliberations are bound to yield variable results, even as they consume substantial time. Effective disciplinary procedures require that acts and consequences be closely linked in time and consistent over time if they are to have the desired effect. The IDEA's procedural mandates make such practices doubly difficult when the child has any sort of disability.

The IDEA's requirements can work against the child's interests, too. Many educators report that schools are reluctant to identify or properly classify students with behavior disorders. One teacher explained, "Because the school thinks that it can discipline LD [learning disabled] kids but not SED [seriously emotionally disturbed] kids, we call everyone LD, no matter how serious their problems are." A high school principal reported that some peers "drag their heels" when it comes to referring students with behavior problems. The principal sympathized, noting, "Once a kid is identified as SED, you can't really get rid of him, no matter what he does."

Fair or not, there is a perception among school personnel that the IDEA simply blocks discipline for any student with an IEP. One elementary principal tells of a recent case where a student receiving speech and language intervention was caught with narcotics on school grounds. The principal said, "They...determined that the drug-holding was related to disability...that the student had low self-esteem rooted in his speech and language deficits, and that the student became involved in drug use in an effort to obtain peer approval." The principal continued, "Anybody that has a little bit of social difficulty can be said to be misbehaving as a result of that problem. Under this approach, such behavior has to be accepted in school, no matter how unacceptable in the community at large."

> **The disparity in disciplinary approaches gives rise to concerns about a double standard and the perception that special education students are a privileged class.**

The disparity in disciplinary approaches gives rise to concerns about a double standard and the perception that special education students are a privileged class. The assistant principal of a large elementary school articulated this concern, saying, "The problem arises when you have a kid with a disability who does something to a kid with no disability. Parents outside of the special education system expect the school to administer the sanctions for things like fighting, to maintain the kind of order that they recall from their childhood. If the kid who beat their kid up is suspended, they are usually satisfied. The explanation that no suspension could be made because the kid had behavior problems doesn't carry much weight with most people and creates a terrible PR problem for us."

Despite the frequent voicing of such concerns, the IDEA constraints do not actually result in many disciplinary measures being challenged or overturned in Virginia. In 1998, for example, there were just 18 complaints and three hearing decisions relating to discipline. Still, the fear of such a challenge reportedly causes many teachers and administrators to shy away from punishing students with disabilities for infractions for which others would be disciplined. One district special education director explained, "IDEA's restrictions on discipline don't come up formally very much, but that's because everyone in the schools is bending over backwards to make sure they don't. The problem is that when we've got principals who are trying to maintain order in schools with big special education populations, they feel like they can't discipline those kids, and this means that the other kids are regularly seeing misbehavior go unpunished." The perception in Virginia that the IDEA creates a class of students licensed to "terrorize schools and teachers" undermines public trust in school safety and support for special education.

State Education Standards

Special education has had a significant effect on Virginia's push for educational standards. Virginia's SOLs are a high-stakes standards, testing, and accountability regime adopted to ensure that all students master a specified body of content and set of skills before graduating. Starting in 2004, students who fail to pass the specified exams will not receive a high school diploma.

Much special education practice draws heavily on the philosophy of progressive education, emphasizing notions of personal relevance more heavily than traditional academic skills and knowledge. However, this tradition clashes with today's emphasis on "core curricula."[16] The IDEA's ethos of individualized instruction is at odds with systems of standards-based accountability that seek to improve education by requiring all students to perform at a measurably high level on a specified set of objectives.

> *Much special education practice draws heavily on the philosophy of progressive education, emphasizing notions of personal relevance more heavily than traditional academic skills and knowledge.*

In the past, this conflict was often accommodated by exempting special education students from standardized assessments. In the 1990s, however, special educators began to assert that such policies caused disabled students to be denied effective and equitable instruction. Consequently, the 1997 IDEA amendments mandated that students with disabilities be included in testing programs to the maximum feasible extent. As a result, students with special needs now participate in Virginia's SOL testing regime.

This change places schools and districts in an awkward position, as the state simultaneously asks them to raise test results and to include students who have shown historically poor performances on standardized assessments. The IDEA requires educators to take greater responsibility for the achievement of students with disabilities. However, the law can also encourage educators to look for loopholes to relax the standards for students who are unlikely to fare well on high-stakes assessments. An example of this tendency was the SSEAC recommendation in early 2000 that the state extend the category of "developmental disabilities" up to the federal maximum age of nine so that more students would be afforded special accommodations on the SOL tests. The nature of this request suggests the fundamental tension between special education provisions and the push toward high uniform standards.

Even with such accommodations, some students with disabilities will fail to perform at an acceptable level in a high-stakes testing regime. Given the twin desires to maintain high standards and avoid creating insuperable barriers for students with special needs, Virginia policymakers have sought an array of accommodations and alternatives for such youngsters.

In lieu of a standard diploma, schools in Virginia are empowered to issue two other kinds of documents testifying that a student has completed an education program. A "certificate of attendance" is usually issued to individuals who have left the education system because they are no longer eligible for school services due to their age or because they chose to exit the system before completing the requirements of any specific program. An "IEP diploma" is issued to students who have completed the educational requirements established by their own IEPs but are not eligible for a regular diploma. Some districts indicate in their printed high school graduation programs which type of document is being awarded to each student. This practice formally acknowledges the kind of academic differentiation and categorization that the IDEA mandates sought to eliminate.

Such problems are exacerbated by Virginia's emphasis on test-based validation of high school credits. Large numbers of students are expected to have trouble passing Virginia's high-stakes assessment. Many of these students have disabilities. For those unable to pass the SOL test, Virginia has proposed a new "basic diploma" for students who demonstrate basic competency in reading, writing, and math. The new diploma would represent more advanced accomplishment than the "IEP diploma," but it triggers two concerns. First, it may disadvantage special-needs students as they seek employment or continue their education. Second, it may create perverse incentives in which low-performing students or their families agitate for special education identification so that the student can receive a diploma without satisfying the requirements of the SOLs. This situation presents risks for both the individual student and the integrity of the educational system.

> An "IEP diploma" is issued to students who have completed the educational requirements established by their own IEPs but are not eligible for a regular diploma.

A further approach adopted by Virginia is to alter the SOL test for some students. In general, two approaches are employed for addressing students with disabilities in standardized tests: the test "accommodations" and the use of different tests. Accommodations leave the target skills (for example, explaining the origins of the American Civil War) unaltered but change the "tool skills" (for example, presenting work orally rather than in a written essay). Extended time on tests is a frequent accommodation as well. For some students, however, the content of the test is clearly inappropriate. In such cases, alternative assessments or tests of different target skills are necessary.

Sometimes accommodations lead to questions of test reliability and validity. In order to understand the potential conflict, it is important to differentiate between changes that level the playing field but leave the target skill unaltered (accommodations) and changes that alter the skill in some way. For example, if the target skill were a discussion of three causes of the American Civil War, one could reasonably argue that either a written essay or an oral presentation could tap that information. However, if the target skill were writing an essay, then an oral presentation would clearly assess a different skill. Test accommodations, done properly, do not alter the essential parts of the test. Altering the essential parts of a test results in a different test.

Virginia has adopted a variety of SOL accommodations. Some produce scores that are still regarded as official but carry a notation that the student received a "nonstandard accommodation." One example is that the reading comprehension test can be read aloud to some students with disabilities. Although some "nonstandard" accommodations are minor, listening to a text obviously does not measure the ability of a student to read that text. This poses real difficulties in terms of test validity and raises the possibility that families or schools might seek to identify students as having disabilities in order to help them pass the state test.

Under the IDEA, students with disabilities must be included in state or local accountability systems, yet some students with disabilities are being taught skills and/or content that are substantially different from what the assessments measure. Virginia has also developed an alternative assessment for such students. The 2000-2001 school year marks the first time that students with disabilities in Virginia may use the alternative assessment. This option is provided to students who (1) have an IEP, (2) demonstrate significant cognitive impairments and adaptive skills deficits, and (3) need extensive direct instruction and/or intervention in a variety of settings. Rather than the paper-pencil academic test administered to students in the standard curriculum, the alternative assessment will consist of a "Collection of Evidence" (COE) that measures student progress on IEP objectives by using a variety of indicators. Still, special educators anticipate that more than 90 percent of students in special education will take the standard SOL exams with appropriate accommodations.

> **Perhaps the central dilemma for states pursuing high-stakes accountability is how best to serve those students with mild disabilities who find attaining acceptable levels of performance a daunting challenge.**

Perhaps the central dilemma for states pursuing high-stakes accountability is how best to serve those students with mild disabilities who find attaining acceptable levels of performance a daunting challenge. On the one hand, it is sensible to hold these students and their teachers to the same high level of expectations to which we hold others. On the other hand, these students may find assessments frustrating or insurmountable and may drop out of school altogether. This bifurcation is partly a function of the Virginia SOL's virtually exclusive focus on academic preparation. Although this emphasis is understandable, it leads to de-emphasis of programs such as vocational education and the arts that can provide other forms of useful instruction and skill-based learning for students with mild or moderate disabilities.

Conclusion

Surveying the six dimensions of policy and practice in which special education poses significant challenges, we can see that the key problems have much in common. FAPE and LRE demand that educators abide by open-ended and ill-defined directives, even as the court-enforced right of a select group of children to "free and appropriate education" prohibits measured decisions regarding the allocation of resources. The monitoring of special education relies upon documentation and paper trails, requiring much time and effort and forcing educators to base program decisions upon procedures rather than determinations of efficiency or effectiveness. IEPs intended as flexible instruments of learning have evolved into written records of compliance with formal requirements. In the area of school discipline, protections afforded to special education students have caused educators to look askance upon these children and have made it more difficult to enforce clear and uniform standards in schools. And in jurisdictions such as Virginia, which have moved to a standards-based curriculum and a results-based accountability system, the question arises of how to track the progress of disabled students and whether they will be treated as part of the reformed education system or (reminiscent of pre-IDEA discrimination) as a separate educational world.

Reformers have sought to tackle one or another of these issues in isolation, acting in the belief that incremental policy shifts could remedy the particular problem. For example, the 1997 IDEA reforms sought to emphasize outcomes by requiring schools to test all students and enhancing schools' ability to discipline disabled students who misbehave. Such efforts have not worked very well, however, because they fail to recognize that the enumerated problems are symptomatic of a deeper tension at the heart of the federal-state relationship.

In sum, special education policy today is unwieldy, exasperating, and ripe for rethinking. Congress has demanded that states and schools provide certain services, but it has refused to pay their costs. States are obliged to deliver special education, yet lack substantive control over its objectives and policy design and the nature and shape of its services. But Washington does not actually run the program, either. Instead it tells states, albeit in ambiguous terms, what they must do, no matter whether these requirements are in the best interests of children, schools, or the larger education enterprise. Whatever the cost of compliance, states and districts are obliged to pay it, regardless of the effect on other children, programs, and priorities. The result is a hybrid reminiscent of the "push-me, pull-you" that accompanied Dr. Doolittle in Hugh Lofting's legendary children's tales. Like that mythical two-headed creature, the special education system is constantly tugged in opposite directions. To compel state cooperation with its directives, Washington relies upon a rights-based regimen of mandated procedures and voluminous records, enforced by the specter of judicial power. Yet because states and districts end up paying most of the bill for special education, Congress is hesitant to order the provision of particular services or to demand specific results. The consequence is that educators must interpret vague federal directives while operating under the shadow of legal threat.

> *Special education policy today is unwieldy, exasperating, and ripe for rethinking.*

Arguably, this produces the worst of two very different policy regimes. If special education were an outright federal program, like the National Park Service, the Weather Bureau, or Social Security, Washington would run it directly, in uniform fashion, with all bills being paid via Congressional appropriation. If it were a state program, Congress might contribute to its costs but states would determine how best to run it. Today, however, it is neither, and the result is not working very well.

There are two obvious solutions. The first is for Congress to pay for the special education services that it wishes to provide disabled children. The second is for Washington explicitly to decentralize special education, granting substantive authority to states, districts, and schools.

Either remedy, of course, would bring its own new problems. Full federal funding, for example, may encourage local overspending. Similarly, decentralization raises the likelihood that substantial variation will occur between states.

Yet these problems are likely to be less vexing than those we now face and apt to be more amenable to solution. The intergovernmental confusion would diminish. Those setting policy would be directly in charge of those delivering services. And a shift away from today's emphasis on rights and procedures will increase flexibility and foster innovations responsive to the distinctive needs of individual students, the judgments of expert educators, the preferences of parents, and the priorities of communities. This, we believe, would be good for children. And that, we believe, is the main point.

---

[1] See Margaret J. McLaughlin and Deborah A. Verstegen, "Increasing Regulatory Flexibility of Special Education Programs: Problems and Promising Strategies," *Exceptional Children* 64 (1998): 371-384.

[2] The quote is taken from the concluding remarks presented in the videotape *Regular Lives*, produced in 1987 by Syracuse University, Syracuse, New York.

[3] Section 504 of the Rehabilitation Act reads, "No otherwise qualified individual with disabilities...shall solely by reason of his disability, be excluded from participation in, be denied the benefits of, or be subjected to discrimination under any program or activity receiving federal financial assistance." A person with a disability is defined in Section 504 as: "Any person who (i) has a physical or mental impairment which substantially limits one or more of such person's major life activities, (ii) has a record of such an impairment, or (iii) is regarded as having such an impairment." Major life activities, as defined in Section 504, include the following: "Caring for oneself, performing manual tasks, walking, seeing, hearing, speaking, breathing, learning and working."

[4] See Mark Kelman and Gillian Lester, *Jumping the Queue: An Inquiry Into the Legal Treatment of Students with Learning Disabilities* (Cambridge, MA: Harvard University, 1997), 114; see ibid. at 37-42 for an overview of Section 504.

[5] In addition, informal complaints are frequently lodged with the Virginia Department of Education. Officials estimate that, in the typical school, there are about twice as many informal complaints as formal hearing requests. However, because the criteria for determining what constitutes an informal complaint are vague, and because Department record-keeping on such matters is uneven, a more systematic discussion of these complaints is not possible here. Department records do suggest that "frequent complainers" may be slightly more likely to lodge informal complaints than to file multiple due process requests.

[6] The other cases either stretched over more than one year or have not yet been resolved.

[7] Anne Dupre, "Disability, Deference, and the Integrity of the Academic Enterprise," *Georgia Law Review* 32 (1998): 394-473.

[8] For discussion, see Margaret Weiss and Frederick J. Brigham, "Co-teaching and the Model of Shared Responsibility: What Does the Research Support?" in *Advances in Learning and Behavioral Disabilities*, ed. T. E. Scruggs and M. A. Mastropieri (Greenwich, CT: JAI Press, 2000); and Naomi Zigmond and Janice M. Baker, "Is the Mainstream a More Appropriate Educational Setting for Randy? A Case Study of One Student with Learning Disabilities," *Learning Disabilities Research and Practice* 9 (1994): 108-117.

[9] See Beverly R. Guterman, "The Validity of Categorical Learning Disabilities Services: The Consumer's View," *Exceptional Children* 62 (1996): 111-124.

[10] A further irony: Students with sensory disabilities, physical disabilities, or mental retardation often respond less positively to more intensive special education services. In other words, children who we might suppose would be best served by intensive special education programs instead benefit most from inclusion. Their needs are more easily managed in the general education environment. After all, children with sensory and physical disabilities are most often learning the same curriculum, only with modifications in presentation and accommodation. Meanwhile, it is vital for children with mental retardation to learn to manage social interactions. Obviously, one is better able to learn social skills when presented with more social opportunities. There is reason to question how including these students in general education classrooms may affect the learning of their peers, but that does not negate the point regarding how best to serve these populations.

[11] See Victoria Benning, "Fairfax Autism Program Ignites Battle Over Access," *Washington Post*, 30 June 2000, sec. A, p. 1.

[12] Prior to the 1997 amendments, most states took actual program costs into account when reimbursing districts. This, of course, raised its own set of problems, particularly the concern that districts might be more likely to

place children in more intensive settings because of the associated increases in funding.

[13] "What IDEA Means to You," *Virginia Journal of Education* 91 (1998): 7-10.

[14] The courts have ruled that long-term suspensions and expulsions constitute *de facto* "changes of placement" and therefore require schools to abide by IDEA procedures related to program placement.

[15] See Gretchen Butera, Holly Klien, Lynn McMullen, and Brenda Wilson, "A Statewide Study of FAPE and School Discipline Policies," *The Journal of Special Education* 32 (1998): 108-114.

[16] See Diane Ravitch, *Left Back: A Century of Failed School Reforms* (New York: Simon & Schuster, 2000) (for a discussion of accountability); and E.D. Hirsch Jr., *The Schools We Need and Why We Don't Have Them* (New York: Doubleday, 1996) (for a discussion of the concept of a core curriculum).

Chapter 9

The Rising Costs of Special Education in Massachusetts: Causes and Effects

Sheldon Berman, Perry Davis, Ann Koufman-Frederick, and David Urion

Introduction

Over the past decade states across the nation have seen rapid increases in the number of children requiring special education services. They have also experienced significant increases in the cost to school districts for these services. In states where additional funding has been provided to support education reform and school improvement, the rising costs of special education have consumed a disproportionate share of these funds, thereby compromising school-based and state-based efforts to support reform.

> *The rising costs of special education have consumed a disproportionate share of new funds for school reform and school improvement.*

The causes of these increases, however, have been mis-diagnosed as the result of district policy and practice. In this case study of cost increases in Massachusetts, we determine that the increases schools have been experiencing have not been caused by school district policy and practice. In fact, just the opposite has been the case. School district policy and practice have been effective in containing and even reducing the percentage of children who require special education services in Massachusetts. Nonetheless, costs in Massachusetts have continued to increase. These cost increases have been primarily due to the increased numbers of children with more significant special needs who require more costly services.

As this chapter will show, the root causes of these increases have been factors beyond the control of schools, such as advances in medical technology, the deinstitutionalization of children with special needs, privatization of services, and economic and social factors including increases in the number of children in poverty and the number of families experiencing social and economic stress. Although the focus of this paper will be on Massachusetts, national data on special education reveal that these factors are also influencing the increased number of special education children across the country.

The National Context

National Enrollment

For the past 21 years the Department of Education has collected data on the number of infants, toddlers, and preschoolers receiving special education services and the number of children ages 6 through 21 served under the Individuals with Disabilities Education Act (IDEA). The U.S. Department of Education's Office of Special Education Programs (OSEP) reports that in 1999 almost 5.5 million students ages 6 to 21 with disabilities were served by schools under the IDEA.[1] The average increase among these students over the past 10 years was 29 percent. During this period, the annual data reported by states indicate that both the number of disability categories and the number of children receiving services increased. A state-by-state comparison of changes in the percentage of children ages 3 to 21 served under the IDEA from 1987-1988 to 1998-1999 indicates that the average increase was 36.5 percent. The states in the top quartile ranged from Nevada with the highest increase at 120 percent, to Florida with an increase of 77.7 percent, to New York with a 49.9 percent increase.

> *We believe that continued growth of the special education preschool population reflects medical, economic, and social factors that are producing actual increases both in the number of children with disabilities and the severity of those disabilities.*

The U.S. Department of Education's 1999 Annual Report to Congress shows that each year in the last decade experienced an increase in the numbers of infants, toddlers, and preschoolers with disabilities receiving special education services through the Department's Early Intervention Program and Preschool Grants Program. From 1988-1989 to 1997-1998 the cumulative increase in special education preschool enrollment for ages three through five was 58.5 percent. This was a significantly larger increase than the 29.4 percent increase in children ages six and older served under the IDEA (see Table 1). The report suggests that continued growth of the special education preschool population reflects increased and more effective outreach at the state level, as well as continued improvement in reporting

TABLE 1: NATIONAL SPECIAL EDUCATION AND SPECIAL EDUCATION PRESCHOOL ENROLLMENT, 1989-1998						
YEAR	AGES 3-5			AGES 6-21		
	Enrollment	% Increase	Cumulative % Increase	Enrollment	% Increase	Cumulative % Increase
1988-89	360,281			4,173,512		
1989-90	385,587	7.02%	7.02%	4,253,018	1.91%	1.91%
1990-91	394,766	2.38%	9.57%	4,361,751	2.56%	4.51%
1991-92	420,403	6.49%	16.69%	4,499,824	3.17%	7.82%
1992-93	455,449	8.34%	26.41%	4,625,574	2.79%	10.83%
1993-94	491,685	7.96%	36.47%	4,779,359	3.32%	14.52%
1994-95	522,709	6.31%	45.08%	4,907,511	2.68%	17.59%
1995-96	548,593	4.95%	52.27%	5,078,951	3.49%	21.69%
1996-97	557,152	1.56%	54.64%	5,230,740	2.99%	25.33%
1997-98	571,049	2.49%	58.50%	5,401,292	3.26%	29.42%
Source: U.S. Dept. of Education, *Twenty-first Annual Report to Congress* (Washington, DC: DOE, 1999).						

procedures.[2] However, we believe that this growth also reflects medical, economic, and social factors that are producing actual increases both in the number of children with disabilities and the severity of those disabilities.

The 1999 Annual Report concluded that the number of students with disabilities served under the IDEA continued to increase at a rate higher than both the general population and school enrollment.[3] Based on estimated enrollment (preK-12) for 1990-1991 through 1998-1999 the percentage of children served under preschool special education services increased faster than the percentage of children in regular education. There were increases at all levels, among children ages 0- to 2-years-old, 3- to 5-years-old, and 6- to 17-year-olds; but the greatest percentage increase occurred among children ages 3 to 5, with a 1.4 percent increase. Increases for children ages 0 to 2 were .4 percent, and increases for school age children were 1.3 percent.

> **Research by the U.S. Department of Education concludes that special education costs for individual children with disabilities is 2.28 times the average regular education expenditure.**

The National Center for Education Statistics (NCES) confirms the data reported in the 1999 Annual Report. NCES reports that, from 1988 to 1999, public school enrollment for grades 1 through 12 increased by 17 percent, reaching 43 million in 1999. Enrollment is projected to increase through the first half of this decade to an all-time high of 44.4 million students in 2006. Enrollment trends calculated by NCES also show that the numbers and proportions of children being served in programs for the disabled increased over the last decade.[4]

The Center for Special Education Finance reports that, "special education enrollment has experienced continual growth in numbers and as a percentage of total school enrollment since the implementation of IDEA. It is, therefore, not surprising that special education expenditures have also continually risen and that based on various estimates, it appears that per-pupil expenditures for special education are growing faster than for general education."[5]

National Expenditures on Special Education

Since Congress passed the Education for All Handicapped Children Act of 1975 (EAHCA), special education expenditures have been shared among federal and state governments and local school districts. In 1988, the federal government eliminated the requirement that states provide information on special education expenditures. Therefore, it is difficult to answer the tough questions about how much is being spent on special education at the state and local levels. When EAHCA was originally enacted, the federal government made a commitment to pay 40 percent of the excess cost of its special education mandate. The Center for Education Finance reports that over the years since 1975, however, federal appropriations have ranged from 7 percent to 12 percent of the total excess cost. The national average for federal, state and local expenditures for FY94, the last year for which the Center has data, was 7 percent federal, 53 percent state, and 40 percent local.[6]

The best estimates of dollars currently spent on special education annually across the nation range from $30.9 billion to about $34.8 billion.[7] Although national expenditures on special education are not really known, various calculations support that these expenditures are rising at a faster rate than those for public education as a whole.[8] Research by the U.S. Department of Education concludes that special education costs for individual children with disabilities is 2.28 times the average regular education expenditure.[9] The national average of state special education expenditures as a percent of total K-12 expenditures was 12.2 percent. Expenditures for special education in the top quartile of states ranged from 21.2 percent for Illinois to 13.4 percent for Minnesota. Therefore, these states were spending considerably more per pupil on special education than the national average.

Updated and more accurate special education expenditure information and its relationship to general education is critical. Because this information has important policy implications, over the next four years the U.S. Department of Education's Office of Special Education Programs (OSEP) is funding the Special Education Expenditure Project (SEEP, www.seep.org/seep). SEEP research will investigate the average expenditures across states, districts, schools, and students. The project will address expenditure issues relating to inclusion, consolidation, and assessment, with an emphasis on the relationship between general education and special education. Beginning in December 2001, expenditure data from SEEP will be available to the public.

> *The Massachusetts Special Education Task Force found that the financial challenges facing districts as a result of rising special education costs were exacerbated by Massachusetts' new education reform funding formula.*

In the interim, special education enrollment and spending in Massachusetts can serve as a case study in the causes and effects of increased enrollment and expenditures in special education.

A Case Study: Massachusetts

In the spring of 1996, the Massachusetts Association of School Superintendents (MASS) established a task force to study rapidly increasing special education costs across the state. These cost increases were significantly impacting school districts' ability to implement the state's education reform program. This task force was co-chaired by Sheldon Berman and Perry Davis, two of this chapter's authors. Drs. Berman and Davis, both Massachusetts district superintendents, co-authored the 1997 MASS study reporting the task force's findings.[10] This study has been updated with new data in 1999 and 2000, and again for this paper.

The MASS Special Education Task Force concluded that the increase in special education costs had not been a result of school district policy and practice. Instead it had been due to such medical, economic, and social factors as advances in medical knowledge and technology, the deinstitutionalization of special-needs children, the consequences of a higher percentage of children living in poverty, and the increase in families experiencing social and economic stress. Due to these factors, more children with more severe special needs were entering public schools.

In addition, the task force found that the financial challenges facing districts as a result of rising special education costs were exacerbated by Massachusetts' new education reform funding formula. This formula was built on the inaccurate assumption that school district policy and practice were responsible for the cost increases and that the state could force school districts to change their practices by under-representing the costs of special education in the formula. Not only did the formula set unrealistically low percentages for students in special education, but also it allocated less than half of what would be required to pay for services for these students.

Finally, the task force found that increases in the numbers of children and severity of disabilities in early intervention programs serving 0- to 3-year-olds and special-needs preschool programs serving 3- to 5-year-olds indicated that costs would continue to increase in the future.

Special Education Services in Massachusetts

Massachusetts has 350 separate school districts. The vast majority are town-based and serve students within a particular town. A second group of school districts are regional districts that serve two or more towns. These tend to be in rural or suburban areas of the state. Only three school districts—Boston, Worcester, and Springfield—serve more than 15,000 students. The median size of a Massachusetts school district is approximately 2,000 students with only 9 districts having enrollments that exceed 10,000. The majority of school districts serve between 1,000 and 4,000 students.

> *Special education law in Massachusetts enables parents to request an alternate placement if they feel that their child is not being well-served by a district or collaborative program.*

The structure of Massachusetts' school districts has a direct impact on special education service delivery. Due to the small size of most Massachusetts school districts, it is difficult to provide specialized programs for children with significant disabilities within a district. To reduce costs, school districts join legally approved collaboratives that share these programs among the participating districts. Virtually all local school districts in Massachusetts are members of a collaborative. However, the incidence of a particular disability may still not economically justify the creation of a collaborative program. In order to serve these low-incidence special-needs students, they are placed in private special education schools either as a day placement in which the student returns home in the evening or as a residential placement. In general, the large cities have sufficient student populations to create special programs within their districts, although they, too, place some students in collaborative and private programs.

Special education law in Massachusetts enables parents to request an alternate placement if they feel that their child is not being well-served by a district or collaborative program. In these cases, parents often seek placements in private programs. In general, student placements within a district or through a collaborative are more cost-effective for a district than placement in a private setting.

There are two factors that have been important in determining a child's qualification for services and the nature of his or her program in Massachusetts. The first is the eligibility standard set for a student to qualify for special education services. The second is the standard by which the student is to be served. In September 1992, the state implemented a new set of eligibility guidelines. Prior to 1992, schools needed only the presence of a disability to place children on an IEP. Starting in 1992, schools were to use two criteria to determine eligibility: (1) the presence of a disability; and (2) determination that a child was not making effective progress in regular education. These two standards were to be used by evaluation teams to determine whether a disability was affecting the student's educational performance. In terms of standard of service, Massachusetts is one of two states that had a standard higher than the federal standard of "free appropriate public education" (FAPE). This standard, usually referred to as "maximum feasible development," has existed since 1972. Due to legislation passed in July 2000, Massachusetts will revert to the federal standard as of January 2002.

> *The special education components of Massachusetts' education reform funding formula were built on the assumptions that school districts did not effectively contain costs and that they identified more children than necessary as having special needs.*

For state reporting purposes, Massachusetts special education placements are categorized into eight categories. The first four categories represent classifications of students who are served within a school district as follows: (1) regular education program with modifications; (2) regular education with up to 25 percent time out; (3) regular education with up to 60 percent time out; and (4) substantially separate program with more than 60 percent time out and with access to regular education, or a substantially separate special education program, run by the public school, in a facility other than a public school regular education facility. The fifth classification, known as a "private day placement," indicates students served in private settings that specialize in that disability. The sixth classification indicates "residential placements" for students served in private settings who require 24-hour care. The seventh classification represents students who reside in hospital or home settings. School districts do not have responsibility for the costs of such placements. Finally, the eighth classification indicates preschool children.

Almost all special education students are the financial responsibility of their local school district. For some private placements, the Department of Social Services shares the cost with the school district. Currently, the state pays 50 percent of all residential placements. The state also assumes responsibility for students in hospital settings and students who are incarcerated. In the early 1970s, the state managed a number of institutional settings for children with disabilities; however, by 1995 all of these children were deinstitutionalized and put under the care of their local school district.

The Massachusetts financing formula for special education was changed in July 2000 and will go into effect for the 2002-2003 school year. In this formula, the state will assume a larger share of the financial responsibility for children with disabilities. Although the new funding formula provides for a modest increase in state resources, it is still far from the formula recommended by MASS and many other groups working on special education reform in Massachusetts.

Data Collection

The MASS Special Education Task Force collected and reviewed Massachusetts Department of Education data on school expenditures and enrollments, as well as data from the state Department of Public Health, the Department of Social Services, and the office for Educational Services in Institutional Settings. Massachusetts has a comprehensive and consistent system of collecting data from each school district on district finance and enrollment. Each school district files an end-of-year report documenting expenditures by program and function. Each district also reports enrollment data as of October 1 of each year and special education data as of December 1. These reports are entered into a computer database which was made available to the task force. In addition, the task force was also able to review data on child maltreatment, enrollment in early intervention programs for 0- to 3-year-olds, and placement in foster homes.

The task force reviewed data on all school districts in the state. However, the analysis that follows does not consider vocational-technical, trade, or agricultural schools. These schools usually draw from ten or more feeder districts and their special education expenditures are not comparable to other districts. Therefore, the task force's findings and recommendations are based on data from the state's 300 city, town, and regional academic districts.

The Reality of Special Education Costs in Massachusetts

The special education components of the state's education reform funding formula, known as the foundation formula, were built on the assumptions that school districts did not effectively contain costs and that they identified more children than necessary as having special needs.

> *Massachusetts schools have rigorously applied eligibility standards and provided regular education and inclusive programming for children as alternatives to special education services.*

Specific elements of the formula were designed as disincentives to these practices. For example, in all areas other than special education actual enrollment within a district is used to build the foundation budget. Additional allocations are provided for the number of students who are from low-income families or who are in bilingual or vocational programs. In contrast, allocations for special education are based on a preset percentage of children in special education set at a rate lower than the state average. In addition, the cost allocations for providing services to in-district preschool, in-district K-12 students, and out-of-district placements are set at levels well below the actual costs that districts incur for these students. These disincentives were designed to cause districts to be more rigorous in their use of the eligibility standards and to encourage more cost-effective placement of students.

Analysis of Massachusetts enrollment data shows that these assumptions are not accurate. In fact, schools have done a good job containing costs. They have rigorously applied eligibility standards and provided regular education and inclusive programming for children as alternatives to special education services.

Special education enrollments as a percent of total enrollment reached a high in FY92 of 17.4 percent. (See Chart 1.) After that, new eligibility standards were implemented statewide. Beginning in FY93 and continuing through FY97 districts applied these new standards, and enrollment declined to a low of 16.6 percent. With the exception of a "spike" in FY99, special

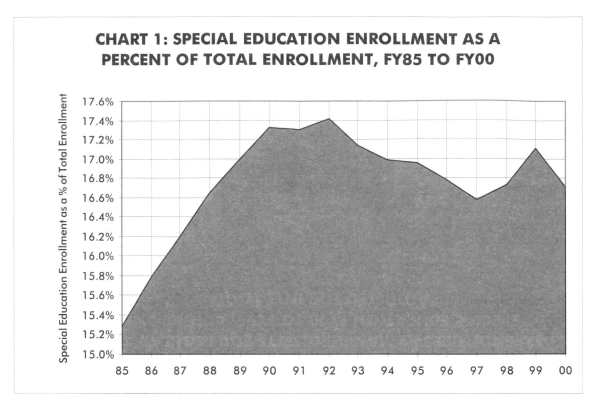

education enrollment has remained relatively steady at approximately 16.7 percent.

Massachusetts special education enrollment increases are also well below national trends. Between FY89 and FY98, special education enrollment in Massachusetts grew at less than half the rate of growth nationally (31.7 percent growth enrollment nationally compared to 13.3 percent growth in Massachusetts). (See Table 2.)

In its 1997 study, the Massachusetts Special Education Task Force observed sharp increases in special education preschool enrollments and predicted that these would impact enrollments and

TABLE 2: NATIONAL VS. MASSACHUSETTS SPECIAL EDUCATION ENROLLMENT, 1989-1998

YEAR	NATIONAL			MASSACHUSETTS		
	Enrollment	% Increase	Cumulative % Increase	Enrollment	% Increase	Cumulative % Increase
1988-89	4,533,793			140,326		
1989-90	4,638,605	2.31%	2.31%	143,373	2.17%	2.17%
1990-91	4,756,517	2.54%	4.91%	144,707	0.93%	3.12%
1991-92	4,920,227	3.44%	8.52%	147,732	2.09%	5.28%
1992-93	5,081,023	3.27%	12.07%	147,727	0.00%	5.27%
1993-94	5,271,044	3.74%	16.26%	149,431	1.15%	6.49%
1994-95	5,430,220	3.02%	19.77%	151,843	1.61%	8.21%
1995-96	5,627,544	3.63%	24.12%	153,912	1.36%	9.68%
1996-97	5,787,892	2.85%	27.66%	155,128	0.79%	10.55%
1997-98	5,972,341	3.19%	31.73%	159,042	2.52%	13.34%

Source: 21st Annual Report to Congress 1999, U.S. Dept. of Education and Massachusetts Dept.

costs in future years. In fact, current special education increases are indeed being driven by significant increases in special education preschool enrollment. Between FY89 and FY00, special education preschool enrollment in Massachusetts rose by 83.8 percent, while other special education enrollments increased by only 13.1 percent and total enrollment by 17.8 percent. School districts continue to contain costs and effectively apply the eligibility standards but are seriously pressed by a greater number of children entering school districts at age 3 with a disability diagnosis. This sharp increase in preschool enrollment is also present nationally; overall enrollments of children ages 3 to 5 are growing at twice the rate of children ages 6 to 21 (see Table 1).

Costs continued to increase over the past decade as districts enrolled a greater number of children with more serious needs. The task force found that between FY90 and FY99 per-pupil expenditures in special education increased by $3,574 from $6,675 to $10,249, while they increased by approximately one-third as much, $1,384, in regular education-from $4,103 to $5,487. During this period, special education expenditures grew by 53.5 percent, increasing at almost twice the rate of regular education expenditures, which grew by 33.7 percent. The difference is even more significant when adjusted for inflation. In 1990 dollars, per-pupil regular education expenditures grew by only $186 or 4.5 percent, while per-pupil special education expenditures grew by $1,336 or 20 percent. (See Chart 2.)

The Education Reform Act of 1993 resulted in the addition of $1.2 billion in state aid to local school districts. However, special education costs statewide increased by $476 million during

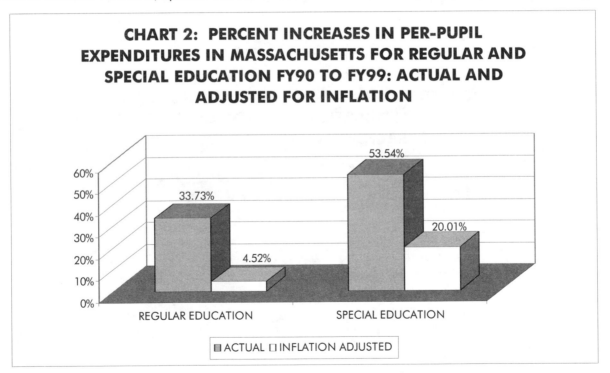

CHART 2: PERCENT INCREASES IN PER-PUPIL EXPENDITURES IN MASSACHUSETTS FOR REGULAR AND SPECIAL EDUCATION FY90 TO FY99: ACTUAL AND ADJUSTED FOR INFLATION

those years, an equivalent of 38 percent of all the additional aid from 1993 to 1999.

The statewide impact of these increases has been dramatic, as shown in Chart 3. As a percent of total school expenditures, special education expenditures increased from 17.2 percent in

FY90 to 19.5 percent in FY99. This represented almost $140 million in additional expenditures for special education in just FY99. Special education has continued to consume an ever-larger percentage of school district budgets throughout the past decade, while expenditures on regular education as a percent of total expenditures declined from 52.3 percent to 48.6 percent between FY90 and FY99.

Impact at a District Level

The majority of school districts in Massachusetts have experienced significant increases in special education costs. Between FY90 and FY99, expenditures for special education increased at a greater rate than expenditures for regular education in 88 percent of Massachusetts school districts. In only 1.3 percent of the districts was there a decline in special education expenditures between FY90 and FY99.

> *Between FY90 and FY99, expenditures for special education increased at a greater rate than expenditures for regular education in 88 percent of Massachusetts school districts.*

These increases have been particularly acute in approximately one-quarter of all districts. Between FY90 and FY99, 78 districts, or 26 percent of the non-vocational districts, spent more than 30 percent of all new funds—local as well as state—on increases in special education. Of these, 60 spent between 30 percent and 40 percent, 12 spent between 40 percent and 50 percent, 5 spent between 50 percent and 75 percent, and 1 spent 80 percent of all new funds on special education.

The impact on education reform is clear when one compares the additional state aid provided

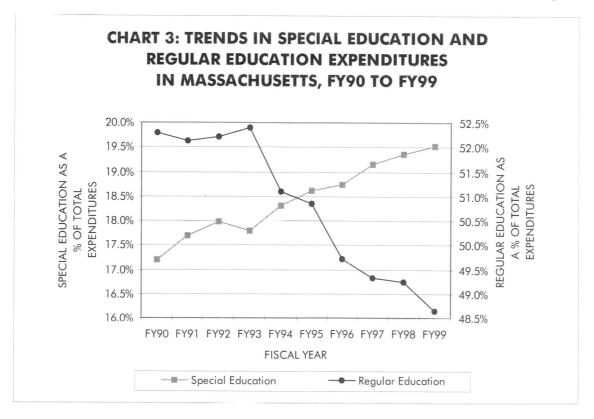

CHART 3: TRENDS IN SPECIAL EDUCATION AND REGULAR EDUCATION EXPENDITURES IN MASSACHUSETTS, FY90 TO FY99

to communities for education reform with the additional special education expenditures in those communities. The increases in special education exceeded the amount received in new state aid between FY93 and FY99 for 88 of the 300 school districts. For 36 more school districts, special education increases equaled between 75 percent and 99 percent of additional state aid. And for another 44 school districts, special education increases equaled between 50 percent and 74 percent of new state aid. This means that 56 percent of Massachusetts school districts spent the equivalent of 50 percent or more of new state aid on special education. There is no consistent pattern among these districts. They vary in size, wealth and region.

Chart 4 compares increases in regular and special education in five communities between FY90 and FY99. Brookline is a suburb of Boston that has become highly urbanized. Median household income from the 1990 census was $45,598. Brookline enrolls almost 6,000 students preschool to twelfth grade. Between FY90 and FY99, Brookline's total budget grew by 38 percent. Special education costs grew by 108 percent while regular education expenditures grew by 34 percent. The increased expenditures on special education represented 42 percent of all new dollars added to Brookline's budget, including additional local funds as well as additional state aid. In FY90, Brookline devoted 14.8 percent of its budget to special education; by FY99, the percentage had grown to 22.3 percent. Although education reform brought the district an additional $2,198,210 in aid between 1993 and 1999, the additional special education costs of $3,867,659 were almost double that amount. For Brookline, the additional state aid, meant

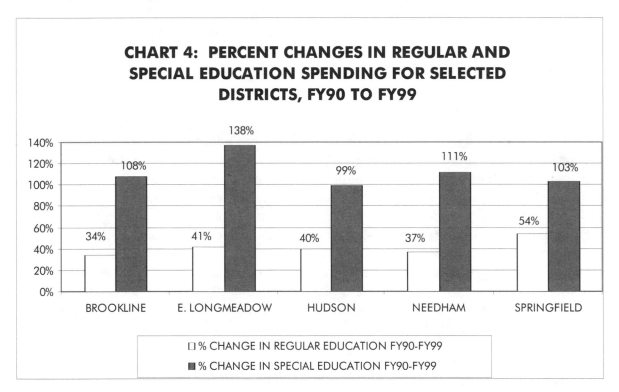

CHART 4: PERCENT CHANGES IN REGULAR AND SPECIAL EDUCATION SPENDING FOR SELECTED DISTRICTS, FY90 TO FY99

□ % CHANGE IN REGULAR EDUCATION FY90-FY99
■ % CHANGE IN SPECIAL EDUCATION FY90-FY99

primarily to help Brookline implement education reform, simply offset a portion of the increased special education costs.

East Longmeadow is a rural community in western Massachusetts with a student population of approximately 2,600 and a median family income of $41,372. Between FY90 and FY99, East

Longmeadow experienced a 138 percent increase in special education costs, with the equivalent of 37 percent of all new funds going to special education. In contrast, regular education expenditures increased by only 41 percent. In FY90, special education represented 16.4 percent of East Longmeadow's total budget; by FY99, this had grown to 24.3 percent. As in Brookline, increases in the costs of special education between FY93 and FY99 exceeded all new aid to the district. East Longmeadow received $1,241,054 in new aid and experienced special education cost increases of $1,539,676.

Hudson is an industry-based community in central Massachusetts. Median household income is $43,600 with a student population of approximately 2,800. Special education expenditures increased by 99.4 percent between FY90 and FY99 while regular education expenditures increased by 40.2 percent. The special education cost increases were equivalent to 32 percent of all new dollars added to Hudson's budget, and special education expenditures increased from 13.9 percent of its budget to 19.4 percent. Special education cost increases almost matched all new education reform aid between FY93 and FY99. Hudson received $1,445,134 in new state aid but spent an additional $1,259,662 on special education during those years.

Needham is a middle-income suburb on the outskirts of Boston with a median household income of $60,357 and a student population of approximately 4,300. Special education expenditures increased by 111 percent between FY90 and FY99 while regular education expenditures increased by only 37 percent. New special education expenditures were equivalent to 50.6 percent of all new funds, driving special education's percent of the total budget from 12 percent to 20 percent. As a wealthier suburb, Needham received less aid than more urban or poorer communities. Between FY93 and FY99 Needham received $1,525,975 in new aid, while its special education expenditures grew by $2,182,409.

Springfield is the third largest city in Massachusetts with a student population of almost 25,000 and a median household income of $25,656. Massachusetts education reform was designed to bring equity to school funding, and Springfield, like many urban areas of the state, received a large percentage of new education reform aid. However, even with this new aid, special education cost increases had an impact. Between FY90 and FY99, special education expenditures grew at almost double the rate of regular education expenditures. Regular education grew by 54 percent; special education expenditures increased by 103 percent and were equivalent to 28 percent of all new dollars invested in education in Springfield. This meant that Springfield was spending 25.8 percent of its budget on special education in FY99 in contrast to 23.6 percent in FY90. Springfield received $63,546,973 in new education reform aid between FY93 and FY99. Special education expenditures increased by $26,163,228, or 41 percent of the total new aid to Springfield.

An examination of the internal costs over time within a single district reveals the extent to which districts have attempted to reduce costs by creating inclusive programs. The Hudson Public Schools spend the largest portion of the district's budget on special education instructional services that include special education teachers, teacher assistants, nursing and psychological services, and such contracted services as physical therapy and occupational therapy. (See Chart 5.) As a district of 2,800 students, the district cannot provide in-district programs for some students. Tuition and transportation costs for the 28 students placed in out-of-district settings represent approximately 32 percent of the district's special education budget.

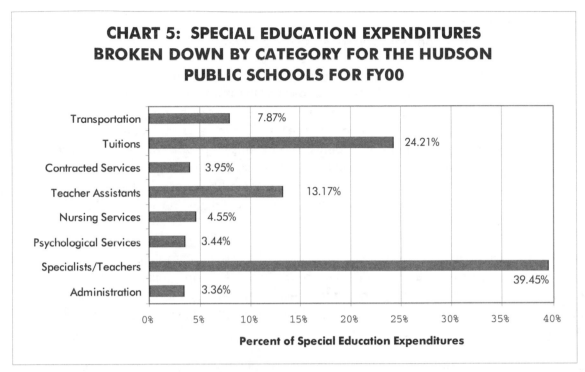

CHART 5: SPECIAL EDUCATION EXPENDITURES BROKEN DOWN BY CATEGORY FOR THE HUDSON PUBLIC SCHOOLS FOR FY00

Hudson's effort to contain costs through in-district services is shown in Chart 6. Expenditures on teacher assistants (special education aides) between FY94 and FY00 increased by 279 percent. Physical therapists and occupational therapists contracted by the district to serve students who would otherwise be in out-of-district placements increased 144 percent. The additional students served within the district also required additional psychological and nursing services. (The increase in nursing services is understated in this chart due to a grant subsidizing 30 percent of

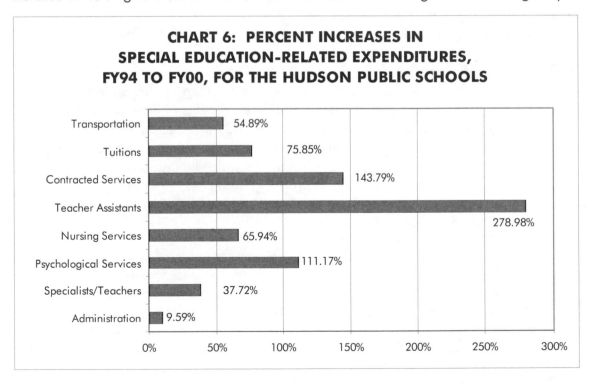

CHART 6: PERCENT INCREASES IN SPECIAL EDUCATION-RELATED EXPENDITURES, FY94 TO FY00, FOR THE HUDSON PUBLIC SCHOOLS

Hudson's nursing budget.) Although the number of out-of-district placements decreased from 45 to 28, the increased severity of disabilities of these out-of-district placements resulted in tuition increases of 76 percent and transportation increases of 55 percent.

For most districts, the three primary causes of increased costs are students moving into the district with IEPs requiring private placement, increases in the number of preschool children requiring special education services, and increases in the number of foster placements within the community requiring significant special-needs services. In fact, one factor in declining costs in some districts has been the movement of students with expensive private placements to another community. In all these districts, compromises have been made regarding implementation of education reform initiatives due to budget constraints presented by special education cost increases. Making headway on education reform is extremely difficult in the face of such increases.

Given the limited funds available to districts, even those districts with smaller increases in special education expenditures have had their education reform efforts compromised by a disproportionate share of new funds allocated to special education. In fact, the data the task force has provided may understate the problem. Most of the increases in regular education expenditures have simply covered the cost of inflation.

Significant increases in special education have the potential for starting a vicious cycle. Increases reduce the funds available for regular education classrooms, causing increases in class size and reduction in support services. These in turn make it more difficult for teachers to address the range of student needs in the regular classroom, producing more referrals to special education. This increases costs again, perpetuating the cycle. (See Chart 7.) For many Massachusetts districts, education reform funds have prevented the perpetuation of this cycle by providing the infusion of new funds necessary to maintain regular education programs at a time of increasing special education costs. However, the price has been little improvement in regular education services for those districts—the original intent of the funding.

Associated Health Costs

Another cost trend impacting school districts is the increase in health and nursing expenditures. Over the past six years many school districts have experienced significant increases in the number of medically involved students who require nursing and other health-related care. These children are not necessarily classified as special education students, although they often receive extensive services. Many are classified under "504" plans for which the Massachusetts Department of Education does not collect data. However, in analyzing the data on statewide health expenditures for school districts, we found that costs increased by 114 percent between FY90 and FY99, from $24.6 million to $52.7 million.

A portion of these costs pay for health educators, but the remainder pays for nursing services. Health education costs funded through the state's Health Protection and Smoking Cessation grants are not included in this data. At this point, we have not been able to secure data on how much has been expended for health education versus nursing services. However, we believe that the primary driver of costs in this area is the increasing number of students who need medical attention. This was not anticipated when the foundation formula was developed and remains an area of serious underfunding in the formula.

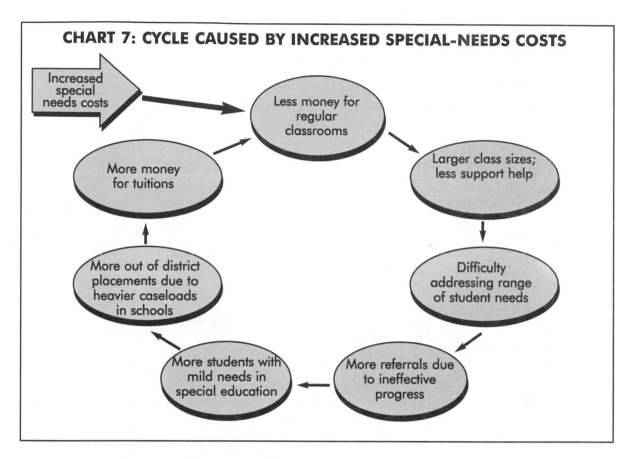

CHART 7: CYCLE CAUSED BY INCREASED SPECIAL-NEEDS COSTS

Medical and nursing-related costs could increase in the future, not only in Massachusetts but throughout the nation. On March 3, 1999, the U.S. Supreme Court announced its decision in *Cedar Rapids Community School District v. Garret F,*[11] a case involving a medically fragile student who had constant medical needs. In its decision, the Court clearly established the need for school districts to provide any and all necessary health services to qualified students with disabilities. The only services that school districts do not need to provide are those that can be performed only by a licensed physician. Analysts examining the implications of this case on special education in public schools have concluded that this decision will result in higher costs for school districts.[12] This did not concern the Court in *Garret F.*: "[T]he district may have legitimate financial concerns, but our role in this dispute is to interpret existing law, [our] concern was whether meaningful access to public schools will be assured."

Ominous Trends

Based on increases in preschool and early intervention enrollments as well as trends in medicine and social services, we believe that special education costs will continue to increase well into the future. A significant factor in the increase in costs over the past decade has been the rapid rise in the number of children with moderate and serious disabilities who require special-needs preschool programs. Between FY89 and FY99, regular education enrollment rose by 17.8 percent. (See Chart 8.) During this period, special education enrollment in all categories excluding preschool rose by 13.1 percent. However, special education preschool enrollment increased by 83.8 percent.

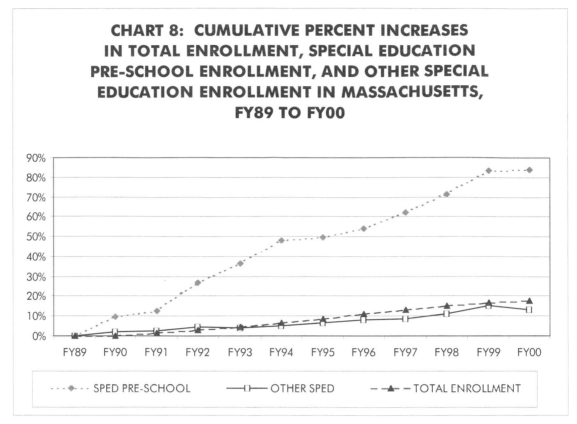

CHART 8: CUMULATIVE PERCENT INCREASES IN TOTAL ENROLLMENT, SPECIAL EDUCATION PRE-SCHOOL ENROLLMENT, AND OTHER SPECIAL EDUCATION ENROLLMENT IN MASSACHUSETTS, FY89 TO FY00

Preschool enrollment nationally has been growing at twice the rate of other special education enrollments. The increases in the Massachusetts preschool population parallel this trend. (See Chart 9.)

Many districts reported to the MASS Special Education Task Force that not only were the number of children requiring special-needs preschool programs continuing to increase, but these children had more significant disabilities. These reports are confirmed by data provided by the Department of Public Health regarding children in early intervention programs. (See Chart 10.) In FY92, 9,809 children were served by early intervention, with 59 percent of these children considered to have moderate or severe delays. By FY99, the number of children being served had increased by 105 percent to 20,075. However, the more ominous trend is that in FY99, the percent of children with moderate or severe delays had increased to 86 percent. Therefore the number of children with moderate to severe delays almost tripled during those years, from 5,818 to 17,290.

> *Increases in the numbers and severity of disabilities of children served by early intervention and special education preschool programs indicate that trends toward rising costs will only escalate further in the future.*

There are other trends among young children that lead us to believe we will soon see a burgeoning of special education costs as these children enter preschool and K-12 programs. For example, between FY84 and FY97, there was a 50 percent increase in the number of children placed into foster care by the Department of Social Services,

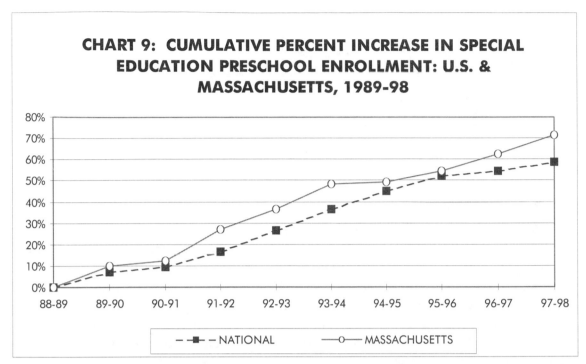

CHART 9: CUMULATIVE PERCENT INCREASE IN SPECIAL EDUCATION PRESCHOOL ENROLLMENT: U.S. & MASSACHUSETTS, 1989-98

increasing from 8,579 children in FY84 to 13,877 in FY94 and then declining to 12,850 in FY97. (A decline between 1996 and 1997 was due to a tightening of foster home requirements and a reduction in the number of available placements.) The Department of Social Services also reports that between 1987 and 1994, the greatest increase in placement was among children age 6 and under. This age group increased 106 percent as opposed to a 40 percent increase

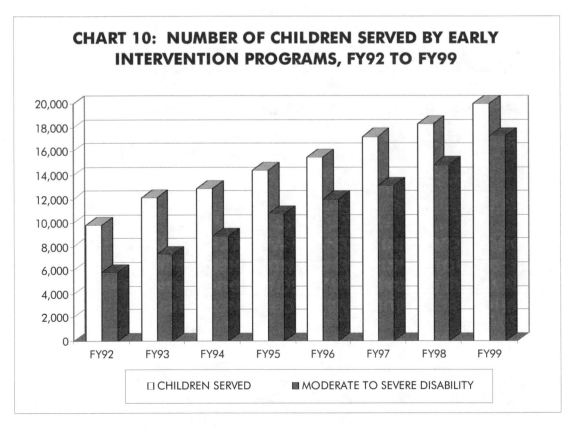

CHART 10: NUMBER OF CHILDREN SERVED BY EARLY INTERVENTION PROGRAMS, FY92 TO FY99

for children age 7 and older.

Increases in the numbers and severity of disabilities of children served by early intervention and special education preschool programs also indicate that the cost trends of the past decade will only escalate further in the future.

Major Causes of Rising Special Education Costs

Rather than school district policy and practice, the increases in special education costs are due largely to medical, economic, and social factors.

Changes in Medical Practice

Medical technology has advanced to such a degree that children who would not have otherwise survived due to prematurity or disability are now surviving. In addition, those whose disability would previously have placed them in hospital or institutional settings are now able to enter public schools or private special education schools. The medical profession has also become increasingly aware of disabilities and is better able to diagnose them at an earlier age. Special education services are often recommended at infancy, and children are placed in early intervention programs. At age three, the responsibility for providing special education services is referred to the school district.

In particular, neonatology, the specialty of newborn medicine, has triumphed over the past decades. The last 20 years have seen increasingly premature infants survive at ever-lower mean birth weights. Table 3 shows that absolute numbers of premature infants with low birth weights increased over the last two decades. Due to advances in medical technology, survival of children at a birth weight below 3.3 pounds has increased from 52 percent twenty years ago to 73 percent ten years ago to 90 percent today. Although this development is laudable, it has left us with consequences. Multiple studies have shown a close correlation between prematurity/low birth weight and subsequent developmental outcome.[13] Many premature infants are left with

TABLE 3: SURVIVAL RATES OF INFANTS BORN WEIGHING LESS THAN 3.3 LBS.

Birth Years	Approximate Number of Infants Born Weighing <3 1/3 Lbs.	% Surviving to 5 Years of Age	Approximate Number Surviving at 5 Years of Age
1980 – 1985	35,000	52%	18,200
1985 – 1995	46,000	73%	33,600
1995 – current	55,000	90%	49,500

lifelong developmental and neurological problems.

Of infants born at birth weights less than 3.3 pounds, approximately 10 percent will develop classic cerebral palsy with seizures, severe spastic motor deficits, and mental retardation. All of these children, approximately 4,950 annually over the last five years, will have multiple medical issues that will necessitate the expansion of medical and nursing capabilities within the schools responsible for them. (See Table 4.)

Fifty percent of children born weighing less than 3.3 pounds will have significant cognitive difficulties without spastic motor problems. Half of these, or approximately 12,375 annually over the last five years, will have measured intelligence in the borderline to mentally retarded range.

TABLE 4: DISABILITIES ASSOCIATED WITH SURVIVING INFANTS BORN WEIGHING LESS THAN 3 1/3 POUNDS

Birth Years	Approximate Number with Cerebral Palsy	Approximate Number with Mental Retardation	Approximate Number with Learning Disabilities
1980 – 1985	1,820	4,550	4,550
1985 – 1995	3,360	8,400	8,400
1995 – current	4,950	12,375	12,375

The other half will have significant to severe learning disabilities.

The actual number of children with disabilities resulting from prematurity, therefore, has increased markedly over the past 20 years. In fact, those numbers have almost tripled as medical technology has improved.

Two decades ago, there was a 35 percent risk of death in the newborn period after asphyxia. Now nearly all these infants survive, and all come to school with significant to severe motor and cognitive deficits.

Prematurity and its consequences are not evenly distributed across society. The children of poor and marginalized populations are more likely to be born prematurely and suffer greater difficulties from this than children of middle- and upper-income families. Various studies suggest that maternal poverty increases the risk of poor developmental outcome from prematurity by factors ranging from 1.5- to 3-fold. Multigenerational poverty has been noted to be particularly associated with poor developmental outcomes in premature infants.[14] Thus, the social and economic burden of educating children with significant developmental problems resulting from their premature births is not evenly or equitably distributed across communities. Urban and rural communities bear a disproportionate share of poverty and a greater share of the disabilities resulting from prematurity.

Medical advances have enabled other populations of students to attend school who would not have been able to do so 20 years ago. For example, two of every 1,000 full-term infants are born asphyxiated because of various medical events in the delivery process. This number has been very stable over the last two decades. Two decades ago, however, there was a 35 percent risk of death in the newborn period after asphyxia. Now nearly all these infants survive, and all come to school with significant to severe motor and cognitive deficits.[15]

Another example is children born with epilepsy. Increasingly effective anti-seizure medications have allowed larger numbers of children with epilepsy to attend school on a regular basis. Although only 60 percent of school-age children with epilepsy were able to attend school without significant interruptions 20 years ago, now more than 95 percent are in school full-time. One percent of the school-age population has epilepsy; 85 percent of these children have significant special education needs. Given the treatment regimens that allow for full-time schooling, essentially all will require nursing supervision of their anti-seizure medications in school.

> One of the factors impacting costs has been the deinstitutionalization of special-needs children and the privatization of special education services over the past decade.

Children with autism represent another population that is increasingly able to attend school. Autism spectrum disorders (frank infantile autism and pervasive developmental disorders) appear to be present in roughly 2 percent of the population. It is not clear whether the apparent increase over the last 20 years represents an absolute increase in numbers or increased recognition. However, increasingly effective medical treatments for elements of behavioral dyscontrol in children with autism, coupled with more effective behavioral treatment modes, have allowed a larger percentage of children with autism to be educated in public school or consortium environments. These children generally require extensive and costly services within the school environment.

Twenty years ago, roughly two percent of the school-age population had a medical diagnosis that impacted upon their ability to function in school, both from an academic/cognitive as well as physical standpoint. Currently, conservative estimates suggest that 7.5 percent of the school-age population have a medical diagnosis that has such impact that these children cannot expect to prosper in school without significant multimodal academic and medical assistance in the school setting. The burden is placed disproportionately upon communities that have less access to contemporary treatment and intervention strategies.

The research necessary to implement effective treatments that prevent disabilities associated with prematurity, birth asphyxia, epilepsy, and autism is only now in its very earliest stages. As a result, the number of students with these disorders attending schools and requiring extensive services is likely to continue to climb for at least the first two decades of this century.

Deinstitutionalization and Privatization

A second factor impacting costs has been the deinstitutionalization of special-needs children and the privatization of special education services over the past decade. The best example is the Bureau of Institutional Schools (BIS). The Bureau of Institutional Schools was established within Massachusetts special education law to provide special education services for children residing in facilities under the control of the Departments of Mental Health, Retardation, Public Health, and Youth Services and the County Houses of Corrections. However, in 1974, BIS primarily served two populations in state institutions. The first group was children with mental retardation;

the second was children in hospital settings due to psychiatric or medical problems. BIS institutions and services for these populations were supported by state rather than local funds.

The number of children served by BIS, which has been reorganized as Educational Services in Institutional Settings (ESIS), has increased only slightly since 1974. However, the population is dramatically different from those served in 1974. Children with mental retardation are served directly through school district funds, either in programs within the district or in private or residential placements. This population, representing the majority of children served by BIS in 1974, is now the complete financial and educational responsibility of public schools. In addition, some children in hospital settings, who would have previously been served by BIS, especially those receiving psychiatric treatment, are also the responsibility of school districts. Currently, two-thirds of ESIS's caseload are incarcerated or detained youth served by the Department of Youth Services and the County Houses of Corrections, with the remainder coming from Departments of Public Health and Mental Health programs.

The shift away from state institutions toward a reliance on local school districts and collaborative or private placements is a positive one. It provides better services within a less restrictive environment. However, the financial resources to fund this shift have not come with the children.

Another example is a shift in policy at the Department of Social Services (DSS), especially in the new Commonworks Program. This program is designed to respond to the needs of hard-to-reach adolescents with multiple problems through out-of-home care. DSS typically has responsibility for out-of-home care but has sought to increase school districts' financial responsibility for children in the program. The Commonworks Program removes children from services they are receiving within a district and places them in private day or residential placements due to non-educational, family-related circumstances. School districts are then expected to share the cost of these placements. The request for proposals for lead agencies of the Commonworks Program contained specific references to the expansion of special education services, with DSS referring to school districts as a partner in paying for education services. DSS only set funding in place for educational services for 20 percent of the youth enrolled in Commonworks, however, creating an expectation that 80 percent of the youth enrolled in Commonworks would receive their educational services under cost-sharing agreements with school districts. The reality is that school districts lack the funding to support this new demand for services.

> *A single foster home taking one special education foster child can require a school district to pay for an out-of-district tuition of over $30,000 plus daily transportation.*

A third example is the increase in the number of children who are state wards placed in foster homes. These children receive services in public schools. However, the placement and movement of these children is controlled by DSS and the foster parent. The dilemma presented by the placement process is the large number of children placed in foster homes in some communities. In addition to the financial strain on these school districts, they are given late notification that a student with special needs will be placed in their community. A single foster home taking one special education foster child can require a school district to pay for an out-of-district tuition of over $30,000 plus daily transportation. The state does provide some additional funding for state wards, but no funding is available until the year after the costs are incurred. Plus, the funding is usually less than actual costs.

The children in both Commonworks and foster care deserve the services and education they receive. The problem is that both programs shift cost and responsibility from state level departments to local districts. Together with the deinstitutionalization of many children in ESIS, the financial and educational responsibilities now fall primarily on local communities without the funding to provide for these children.

Economic and Social Factors

A third cause of special education cost increases has been a higher percentage of children living in poverty. There is a correlation between poverty and special needs.[16] During the 1980s and early 1990s, there was a significant increase in children living in poverty nationally and in Massachusetts. The Massachusetts Committee for Children and Youth reported that the poverty rate for Massachusetts children under age 18 increased throughout the 1980s to highs of 17 percent to 19 percent between 1990 and 1993.[17] With improvement in the economy in 1994, poverty among children declined slightly, but the rate for Massachusetts rose again in 1995 to 17.1 percent. This means that between 17 percent and 19 percent of Massachusetts children in primary grades lived in poverty for their early years.

The national data on children in poverty reveal that the percentage of children under six years of age living in poverty rose significantly during the 1980s and early 1990s to a high of 25.7 percent in 1993.[18] The rate has steadily declined since 1993 and was approximately 18 percent in 1999. (See Chart 11.) The high national level of children living in poverty since the 1980s may account for a portion of the increase in special education enrollments throughout the last two decades.

Adding to the impact of poverty is the increase in families experiencing social and economic stress. Many communities and school districts have seen increases in such indicators as child

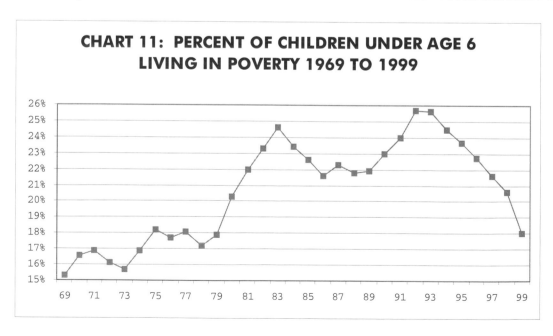

CHART 11: PERCENT OF CHILDREN UNDER AGE 6 LIVING IN POVERTY 1969 TO 1999

abuse and neglect, alcoholism and drug use, and dysfunctional family environments that lead to increases in children requiring special education services.

> **The major causes of districts' cost increases are advances in medical technology, deinstitutionalization and privatization of services, and increases in children in poverty and families experiencing social and economic stress.**

According to the Massachusetts Department of Social Services, reports of child maltreatment were more than two and half times higher in 1999 than in 1983, as was the number of cases of confirmed maltreatment through supported investigations. (See Table 5.) DSS's report *Child Maltreatment Statistics 1995* states that "families reported for child maltreatment displayed the following characteristics: substance abuse, poverty, economic stress (and the associated problems of poor housing and limited community resources), and a lack of specific parenting skills."[19] In cases of children found to be maltreated in Massachusetts in 1997, 82 percent involved neglect, 24 percent involved physical abuse, 5 percent sexual abuse, and 2 percent emotional maltreatment.

If the Commonwealth of Massachusetts and other states wish to address the financial dilemma presented by special education, they need to recognize that the major causes of cost increases are not school district policy and practice. Instead, they are advances in medical technology, deinstitutionalization and privatization of services, and increases in children in poverty and families experiencing social and economic stress.

TABLE 5: CHILD MALTREATMENT: NUMBERS OF REPORTS AND INVESTIGATIONS, 1983-1999*

Year	Maltreatment Reports	Investigations	Supported Investigations
83	36,258	28,204	12,518
84	46,393	34,326	16,515
85	49,320	35,971	18,203
86	51,759	35,085	18,291
87	52,391	33,832	17,356
88	61,506	37,229	18,957
89	70,713	42,590	22,532
90	82,831	52,492	28,621
91	88,748	52,853	28,048
92	89,592	47,960	24,601
93	93,752	47,587	24,186
94	97,210	51,452	26,325
95	96,255	51,285	25,375
96	101,180	54,403	27,219
97	103,533	58,743	29,815
98	97,108	52,899	27,559
99	98,799	56,335	30,349

Source: Massachusetts Department of Social Services.

The Foundation Formula

Rather than helping school districts adequately address special education cost increases, Massachusetts' education reform foundation formula exacerbates the problem by underestimating the percentage of children in special education programs as well as the cost of these programs. For example, in FY99 16.7 percent of the total student enrollment statewide was being served in special education programs. However, the foundation formula locked in a figure of 14 percent of student enrollment being served 25 percent of the time in special education programs. The formula adds an additional 1 percent for out-of-district placements. Locking in a 1 percent limit for out-of-district placements is particularly problematic. Given the small size of many Massachusetts districts, enrollment can vary widely, especially high-cost out-of-district placements. Out-of-district placements, in fact, can vary between 1 percent and 3 percent with smaller districts—those that can least afford it—experiencing the greatest variation. The formula makes no accommodations for these variations between districts.

> *Massachusetts' failure to fund adequately the costs of educating students with severe disabilities is compromising school districts' ability to implement the kinds of instructional improvements intended in the state's Education Reform Act.*

More significant, the formula underestimates the cost of services for these students. For example, the formula provided $2,384 for a special education preschool student in FY99, yet the statewide average cost was $9,988. The formula allocated $17,269 for tuition costs of an elementary-age special education student enrolled in a private day or residential placement; however, the FY99 statewide average cost was $35,509 for a private day placement and $46,275 for a residential placement. In fact, only 11.9 percent of the state's FY99 foundation budget was allocated to preschool, in-district, and out-of-district special education costs while actual expenditures from school district budgets averaged 19.54 percent.

As special education costs continue to rise, the low estimates built into the formula remain inflexible and unresponsive to these changes. Consequently, they produce unrealistic estimates for districts' foundation budgets and provide no additional state aid to address the problem. Massachusetts' failure to adequately fund the costs of educating students with severe disabilities is compromising school districts' ability to implement the kinds of instructional improvements intended in the state's Education Reform Act.

Changes in Special Education Law and Policy

Based on the concerns raised in the Massachusetts Special Education Task Force study issued by MASS, as well as concerns expressed by many municipal officials and school board members, the state legislature enacted reforms in special education in July 2000.

The final FY01 State Budget contained a number of outside sections that changed the Massachusetts Special Education Law. Many of the changes were intended to bring this law into alignment with the federal IDEA. Most significant, the legislature adopted the federal standard of "free appropriate public education," replacing the more expensive standard of "maximum feasible benefit." However, because Massachusetts will maintain its own special education law, it is not clear how this change will bring Massachusetts into full alignment with the IDEA. Special education advocacy groups have indicated they will test in court any changes made by school districts to meet the new perceived lower federal standard. Ultimately, courts will determine the benefits intended by the new Massachusetts law.

The state also moved closer to federal definitions of a disability and federal requirements for independent evaluations. However, the legislature chose to adopt provisions that were still more expansive than the federal standards in these areas. The Massachusetts law only adopted the federal definition of specific learning disability and emotional disability. This leaves other disabilities subject to Massachusetts standards that may be interpreted as different from the federal IDEA definitions. This will cause some confusion for school districts.

> *The increases in serious disabilities within the population in general and the increase in the number of young children with moderate and severe disabilities will require greater expenditures in special education.*

Two new provisions of the law attempted to address the financial issues facing school districts. The first was an attempt to provide financial relief to a school district for unanticipated special education placements by creating a shared risk pool to which districts contribute much like an insurance policy. However, the risk pool provides relief only in the first year of expense. The local school district will need to budget for the expense in future years.

The second provision provided some relief from out-of-district costs by creating a new formula in which the state shares a greater percentage of these costs with districts. In the past, the state paid 50 percent of the cost of all residential placements but none of the costs for other special education students. The new legislation drops this provision and provides financial assistance to a district when costs for an in-district student exceed three times the per-pupil average of the foundation formula and when costs for an out-of-district student exceed four times the per-pupil average. For an in-district student the state will provide 80 percent of the costs above this point, and for an out-of-district student the state will provide 65 percent. For FY2000, the per-pupil average was $6,700; consequently, a school district would incur the complete cost for the first $20,100 for an in-district student and the first $26,800 for an out-of-district student. Although this provision appears to be beneficial to districts, in actual operation most districts will receive only very modest relief in the range of 1 percent to 3 percent of their total special education budget. Some districts will actually receive less financial assistance than they did through the 50 percent provided by the state for residential placements.

In reviewing the financial aspects of special education, the state legislature commissioned a study to determine if there would be any savings produced by changing to federal disability definitions and the federal standard of "free appropriate public education." The study, completed by McKinsey and Company, concluded that changing the eligibility rules and criteria could result in up to 30,000 fewer students enrolled in special education and could free up approximately $125 million from local special education budgets.[20]

Despite the McKinsey analysis, we do not anticipate that the school districts will be able to realize this degree of savings. The estimate of savings was derived from a comparison of the percentage of students in special education in Massachusetts versus the percentage of students in special education nationally. Based on this, McKinsey assumed that changing the eligibility criteria would enable the state to lower the percentage of students in special education. There are two problems with this analysis. First, school districts have already rigorously applied the existing eligibility standards to such a degree that the rate of growth in special education in Massachusetts is less than half the rate of growth nationally. Second, the study did not take into account the rapidly rising percentage of children in special education nationally. Finally, children who might no longer qualify for special education services still have educational issues that will need to be addressed. Although these would theoretically be addressed through additional regular education rather than special education services, they would still represent a cost similar to what the school district was paying through special education services. There will be some savings realized in the change, especially in the cost of bureaucratic red tape associated with special education, but the savings will be modest.

> *The long-term solution lies in addressing the underlying causes of the special-needs increases—the medical, social, and economic issues that cause increasing numbers of children to require special education.*

The study also concluded that adjusting the Massachusetts special education standard to the federal standard could, at full implementation, shift between 2,200 and 35,000 students into different educational environments and could save between $8 million and $36 million. It provided this wide range of savings because there was no definitive evidence as to whether or not the current state standard of maximum feasible benefit plays a role in keeping children in the least restrictive environment. Again, we believe that the savings will be very modest and may be consumed by expensive litigation in the short term. Districts have done their best to provide in-district programs for children, and we do not anticipate a great decline in out-of-district placements. Again, there may be a benefit to the change in that it provides school districts with a better chance to design effective in-district programs for children; however, it will not produce significant savings.

Although many of the legislative changes may have a positive benefit for school districts, the legislation does not address the essential problem. The increase in cost is not due to district policy and practice and will not be solved by legislating changes in these practices. The increasing numbers of more severely disabled children entering school have required the allocation of additional resources to educate and care for these students. The state and the federal government need to recognize that these increases are real and the only way to address them is to provide additional relief to districts. MASS originally recommended that the state pay 90 percent of the cost of special education placements, whether in-district or out-of-district, beyond three times the per-pupil average within the foundation formula, with direct payment for the out-of-district placement by the Massachusetts Department of Education. This would ensure real relief to districts and a shared responsibility between local communities and the state.

Recommendations

Based on the data in this chapter, we conclude that policymakers should be realistic about the rising costs of special education. The increases in serious disabilities within the population in general and the increase in the number of young children with moderate and severe disabilities will require greater expenditures in special education. Even though districts in Massachusetts are making their best efforts to provide regular education programs and services as an alternative to substantially separate special-needs programs, these regular education programs and services require additional resources. Learning disabilities do not disappear just because a child is not classified as a special education student. These are realities that policymakers need to face.

The long-term solution requires that the state and federal government support school districts in meeting the responsibility for special education. Communities, especially smaller communities,

> *It would be tragic if education reform, increased funding, and public education in general were declared failures when, in fact, the experiment was never really tried.*

cannot meet the needs of children who cost the district over $20,000 each without compromising other programs, but, under current law, communities pay the bill. This places an unfair burden on local communities when the responsibility for these children is best addressed through the collective efforts of all citizens within the state and throughout the nation.

One proposal for addressing the increasing costs is to have the local community pay the educational costs and the state or federal government pay for medical, psychiatric, physical therapy, and/or occupational therapy services. Although schools should not be required to address medical problems, it is so difficult to define which service is educational and which is medical that we believe that the only effective approach is to increase both the state's and federal government's financial responsibility for special education.

On a federal level, the landmark Education for All Handicapped Children Act of 1975 established a federal commitment to pay for 40 percent of the excess cost of its special education mandate. This mandate has never been met, and the federal government currently contributes approximately a modest 12 percent of the costs of special education. Additional resources provided at a federal level would help relieve the burden on states and local school districts.

Conclusion

We face a challenging dilemma. Children are entering our school systems with significantly greater special needs, and these needs are often identified at a very early age. The increased cost of special education services is seriously compromising regular education programs and education reform in states throughout the country. We need a solution that addresses the financial crisis emerging in many districts while at the same time meeting the real and substantial needs of these children. In addition, we need a solution that does not blame the children or those working with them and does not pit regular education against special education.

The Massachusetts Education Reform Act set ambitious new standards and dedicated significant funds for the improvement of education. However, for the majority of districts the increase in special education spending has meant that little of the new funds have been available for the improvement of regular education. For all too many districts the situation is critical. The long-term interest of children with disabilities will not be served by pulling resources from regular education classrooms. Action on the part of the state of Massachusetts and the federal government is imperative so that the needs of both regular education and special education children can be well-served and the goals of education reform realized. It would be tragic if education reform, increased funding, and public education in general were declared failures when, in fact, the experiment was never really tried.

The long-term solution lies in addressing the underlying causes of the special-needs increases—the medical, social, and economic issues that cause increasing numbers of children to require special education. We need to invest in medical research directed toward the prevention of disabilities in premature infants. We also need to invest in reweaving the social and economic support systems for families. These are difficult problems to solve, but we encourage our state and federal legislators to work toward these long-term solutions.

---

[1] See U.S. Department of Education, *Twenty-first Annual Report to Congress on the Implementation of the Individuals with Disabilities Education Act* (Washington, DC: U.S. Department of Education, 1999), table II-2.

[2] See ibid. at table II-34.

[3] See ibid. at table II-44.

[4] See National Center for Education Statistics, *NCES Fast Facts-Enrollment Trends* (Washington, DC: National Center for Education Statistics, 1999), tables 3-1, 3-2 (also available at <<www.nces.ed.gov/fastfacts/display.asp>>).

[5] J. G. Chambers, T. B. Parish, J. C. Lieberman, and J. M. Wolman, "What Are We Spending on Special Education in the U.S.?" *CSEF Brief* (1998): 8.

[6] See Center for Education Finance, "Frequently Asked Questions" (available at <<www.csef.air.org>>).

[7] See National Center for Education Statistics, *What Are We Spending on Special Education in the U.S.?* (Washington, DC: National Center for Education Statistics, 1998) (also available at <<nces.ed.gov/edfin/faqs/speced1.asp#table1>>).

[8] See T. B. Parrish, *Special Education Finance: Past, Present, and Future* (Policy Paper 8) (Palo Alto, CA: Center for Special Education Finance, 1996); T. B. Parrish and J. M. Wolman, *Escalating Special Education Costs: Reality or Myth?* (Palo Alto, CA: Center for Special Education Finance, 1996) (also available at <<www.csef.air.org>>); and R. M. Rothstein and K. H. Miles, *Where's the Money Gone? Changes in the Level and Composition of Education Spending* (Washington, DC: Economic Policy Institute, 1995).

[9] See M. T. Moore, E. W. Strang, M. Schwartz, and M. Braddock, *Patterns in Special Education Service Delivery and Cost* (Washington, DC: Decision Resources Corporation, 1988).

[10] See Task Force on Special Education, *The Impact of Special Education on Educational Reform* (Boston, MA: Massachusetts Association of School Superintendents, 1997).

119 S.Ct. 992 (1999).

[12] See A. Katsiyannis and M. L. Yell, "The Supreme Court and School Health Services: *Cedar Rapids v. Garret F.,*" *Exceptional Children* 66, no. 3 (2000): 317-326.

[13] See, for example, A. A. Fanaroff, L. L. Wright, and D. K. Stevenson, "Very Low Birth Weight Outcomes of the National Institute of Child Health and Human Development National Research Network, May 1991 Through

---

December 1992," *American Journal of Obstetrics and Gynecology* 173 (1995): 1123-1141; C. L. Fawer, S. Besnier, and M. Forcada, "Influence of Perinatal, Developmental, and Environmental Factors on Cognitive Abilities of Preterm Children Without Major Impairments at 5 Years," *Early Human Development* 43 (1995): 151-164; C. L. Halsey, M. F. Collins, and C. L. Anderson, "Extremely Low Birth Weight Children and Their Peers: A Comparison of Preschool Performance," *Pediatrics* 91 (1993): 807-811; L. Jain, C. Ferre, and D. Vidyasagar, "Cardiopulmonary Resuscitation of Apparently Stillborn Infants: Survival and Long-term Outcome," *Journal of Pediatrics* 118 (1991): 778-782; C. H. Leonard, R. E. Piecuch, R. A. Ballard, and B. A. Cooper, "Outcome of Very Low Birth Weight Infants: Multiple Gestations Versus Singletons," *Pediatrics*, 93 (1994): 611-615; M. C. McCormick, S. L. Gortmaker, and A. M. Sobol, "Very Low Birth Weight Children: Behavior Problems and School Difficulties in a National Sample," *Journal of Pediatrics* 117 (1990): 687-693; A. Majnemer, B. Rosenblatt, and P. S. Riley, "Influence of Gestational Age, Birth Weight, and Asphyxia on Neonatal Neurobehavioral Performance," *Pediatric Neurology* 9 (1993):181-186; M. E. Msall, G. M. Buck, and B. T. Rogers, "Risk Factors for Major Neurodevelopmental Impairments and the Need for Special Education Resources in Extremely Premature Infants," *Journal of Pediatrics* 119 (1991): 606-614; J. Roth, M. B. Resnick, and M. Ariet, "Changes in Survival Patterns of Very Low Birth Weight Infants from 1980 to 1993," *Archives of Pediatrics and Adolescent Medicine* 149 (1995): 1311-1317; S. Saigal, L. A. Hoult, and D. L. Streiner, "School Difficulties at Adolescence in a Regional Cohort of Children Who Were Extremely Low Birth Weight," *Pediatrics* 103 (2000): 325-331; S. Saigal, P. Szatmari, and P. Rosenbaum, "Cognitive Abilities and School Performance of Extremely Low Birth Weight Children and Matched Control Children at 8 Years: A Regional Study," *Journal of Pediatrics* 118 (1991): 751-760; K. Stjernqvist and N. W. Svenningsen, "Extremely Low Birth Weight Infants Less than 901g Growth and Development After One Year of Life," *Acta Paedtrica Scandinavica* 82 (1993): 40-44; A. J. Thomson, M. Searle, and G. Russell, "Quality of Survival After Severe Birth Asphyxia," *Archives of Diseases of Childhood* 52 (1977): 620-626; C. M. Thompson, S. S. Buccimazza, and J. Webster, "Infants of Less than 1250 Grams Birth Weight at Groote Schuur Hospital: Outcome at 1 and 2 Years of Age," *Pediatrics* 91 (1993): 961-968; N. Veelken, M. Schopf, O. Dammann, and F. J. Schulte, "Etiological Classification of Cerebral Palsy in Very Low Birth Weight Infants," *Neuropediatrics* 24 (1993): 74-76; N. Veelken, K. Stolhoff, and M. Claussen, "Development and Perinatal Risk Factors in Very Low Birth Weight Infants: Small Versus Appropriate for Gestational Age," *Neuropediatrics* 23 (1992): 102-107; U. Wariyar, S. Richmond, and E. Hey, "Pregnancy Outcome at 24-31 Weeks Gestation: Neonatal Survivors," *Archives of Diseases of Childhood* 64 (1989): 678-686; N. Weisglas-Kuperus, H. M. Koot, and W. Baerts, "Behavioral Problems of Very Low Birth Weight Children," *Developmental Medicine and Child Neurology* 35 (1993): 406-416; and N. Wood, N. Marlow, K. Costeloe, A. T. Gibson, and A. W. Wilkinson, "Eurologic and Developmental Outcome After Extremely Preterm Birth," *New England Journal of Medicine* 343 (2000): 378-384.

[14] See Fawer, Besnier, and Forcada, "Influence of Perinatal, Developmental, and Environmental Factors"; Veelken, Stolhoff, and Claussen, "Development and Perinatal Risk Factors"; and Wariyar, Richmond, and Hey, "Pregnancy Outcome at 24-31 Weeks Gestation."

[15] See Jain, Ferre, and Vidyasagar, "Cardiopulmonary Resuscitation of Apparently Stillborn Infants"; and Thomson, Searle, and Russell, "Quality of Survival After Severe Birth Asphyxia."

[16] See G. T. Fujiura and K. Yamaki, "Trends in Demography of Childhood Poverty and Disability," *Exceptional Children* 66, no. 2 (2000): 187-199.

[17] See Massachusetts Committee for Children and Youth, *State of the Child 1996* (Boston, MA: Massachusetts Committee for Children and Youth, 1996): 5.

[18] See <<www.census.gov/income/histpov/hstpov21.txt>>.

[19] Massachusetts Department of Social Services, *Child Maltreatment Statistics 1995* (Boston, MA: Massachusetts Department of Social Services, 1996): 2.

[20] See McKinsey and Company, *Special Education in Massachusetts* (Boston, MA: Massachusetts Legislature Joint Committee on Education, Arts and Humanities, 2000).

Chapter 10

Nasty, Brutish . . . and Often Not Very Short: The Attorney Perspective on Due Process

Kevin J. Lanigan, Rose Marie L. Audette, Alexander E. Dreier, and Maya R. Kobersy

Introduction

This paper presents an attorney perspective regarding certain effects of impartial due process hearings on the larger special education system and the persons who populate that system. Views and conclusions expressed in this paper are based primarily on the particular experiences of Hogan & Hartson attorneys[1] in representing parties on both sides of special education disputes, rather than on empirical analyses of broader data. (Indeed, for the most part, few data are collected on a nationwide basis regarding many of the interesting issues addressed here.) The authors' experience in this field derives mostly from work in large urban school districts that face a high volume of special education disputes; this experience is not necessarily representative of due process proceedings nationally. Nevertheless, our experience—gained in school districts across the country—has been extensive and substantial and warrants this reflection upon our "lessons learned."

> *The federally mandated due process hearing is one of the most visible and unique features of the U.S. system for providing special education.*

We begin with a digression on the law.

Historical Background

One of the most visible and unique features of the U.S. system for providing special education and related services to students with disabilities is the federally mandated impartial due process hearing. Although the federal government provides substantial aid to state and local school systems in a variety of areas other than special education, apparently nowhere else in K-12 education does the federal government tie its aid (in part) to the provision by state and local authorities of an administrative procedure conducted by an independent third party for resolving individual grievances.[2]

The federal government has not always mandated impartial due process hearings in special education; in fact, the mandate did not exist at all in the early years of Congress' intervention in the field. In 1970, Title VI of the Elementary, Secondary, and Other Education Amendments of 1969, Pub. L. No. 91-230, 84 Stat. 121 (1970), created the Education of the Handicapped Act (EHA), the true progenitor of the current Individuals with Disabilities Education Act (IDEA), 20 U.S.C. § 1400, *et seq.*, through which Congress consolidated and expanded upon several earlier discrete initiatives relating to the education of children with disabilities. One stated purpose of the EHA was to relieve the growing financial burden on local school districts (via supplemental federal funding) of providing educational services to students with disabilities, an obligation that state and federal courts were imposing on constitutional grounds even in the absence of federal legislation. At first, and through its early years, the EHA said nothing about impartial due process hearings.

> **When Congress first imposed the special education due process mandate in 1974, and for a decade thereafter, federal law was silent on the issue of attorneys' fees.**

Four years after enactment of the EHA, however, at the behest of the U.S. Senate, the impartial due process hearing became a feature of the nation's special education system. It was Title VI of the Education Amendments of 1974, Pub. L. No. 93-380, 88 Stat. 484 (1974), that for the first time required states accepting federal special education funds to provide:

> procedures for insuring that handicapped children and their parents or guardians are guaranteed procedural safeguards in decisions regarding identification, evaluation and educational placement of handicapped children including, but not limited to (A) ... (ii) an opportunity for the parents or guardians to obtain an impartial due process hearing..., and (iv) provision to insure that the decisions rendered in the impartial due process hearing required by this paragraph shall be binding on all parties subject only to appropriate administrative or judicial appeal....

Id., § 614 (b).[3]

Starting from this highly general mandate, Congress added increasing specificity to its due process requirement. Current law now contains a "procedural safeguards" section substantially devoted to laying out the IDEA's specific requirements regarding impartial due process hearings (see 20 U.S.C. § 1415), a section so long and detailed that simply setting it forth here—not to mention its extensive fabric of implementing regulations[4]—would fill half of this chapter.

Yet establishing the impartial due process hearing is really only part of the story. Also critical to creating the current due process environment was Congress' decision a decade later that prevailing *parents* in these cases—but *not* prevailing school districts—would be entitled to an award of attorneys' fees and expenses from a losing school district (and/or state).

When Congress first imposed the special education due process mandate in 1974, and for a decade thereafter, federal law was silent on the issue of attorneys' fees. Many attorneys for prevailing parents nevertheless argued—with mixed results in the courtroom—that their clients were entitled to attorneys' fee awards under *other* federal statutes. In 1984, the Supreme Court, in *Smith v. Robinson*, 468 U.S. 992 (1984), resolved this debate among the lower federal courts.

Characterizing the EHA as a "comprehensive scheme set up by Congress to aid the States in complying with their constitutional obligations to provide public education for handicapped children[,]" *id.* at 1009; finding that Congress had "intended handicapped children with constitutional claims to a free appropriate public education to pursue those claims through the carefully tailored administrative and judicial mechanism set out in" the EHA, *id.;* noting that, under the so-called "American Rule," attorneys' fees are awarded by courts to prevailing parties "*only* when statutory authority so provides[,]" *id.* at 1002 (emphasis added); and further noting that the EHA "does *not* provide for the payment of attorneys' fees," *id.* at 995 (emphasis added),[5] the Supreme Court held that parents who prevail in special education litigation over denial of their children's right to a "free and appropriate public education" were *not* entitled to an award of attorneys' fees and expenses. *Id.* at 1021.

One year later in 1985, Congress effectively overruled the Court's decision in *Smith v. Robinson* by enacting the "Handicapped Children's Protection Act," amending the EHA to provide (for the first time) an award of attorneys' fees and expenses to prevailing parents in special education cases. As a result, it has been clear since 1985 "that under this section, parents and guardians will select their own attorneys and that to the extent the parents or guardians prevail, the attorneys' fees and other expenses of the litigation may be awarded by the court." H.R. Rep. No. 99-296, at 6 (1985).

> **Under the IDEA, states—and, indirectly, school districts—that accept federal funds for serving children with disabilities must, in return, provide all disabled children with a "free appropriate public education."**

The Statutory and Regulatory Framework of the Impartial Due Process Hearing

Let us now examine how current law is designed to work.

Under the IDEA, states—and, indirectly, school districts—that accept federal funds for serving children with disabilities must, in return, provide all disabled children with a "free appropriate public education" (FAPE). The regulations define FAPE as "special education and related services that—(a) Are provided at public expense, under public supervision and direction, and without charge; (b) Meet the standards of the [state education agency] . . . ; (c) Include preschool, elementary school, or secondary school education in the State; and (d) Are provided in conformity with an individualized education program (IEP) that meets the requirements of §§ 300.340-300.350." 34 C.F.R. § 300.13 (2000).

To ensure that a FAPE is provided, Congress established what the Supreme Court has termed "elaborate and highly specific procedural safeguards."[6] Additional procedural and substantive requirements are found in state laws and federal and state-level regulations. Overall, such safeguards require school districts to keep parents informed about their child's education, involve them in decisionmaking about special education evaluations and placements, and then guarantee an impartial due process hearing in a neutral forum in which parents may challenge school district actions (or seek reimbursement if they unilaterally place their child in a private setting). The IDEA also requires schools to tell parents how to initiate impartial due process hearings and of their right to recover attorneys' fees if they prevail.

Not surprisingly, many parents do file complaints and seek due process hearings, often represented by attorneys who specialize in such cases. Ultimately, special education litigation under the IDEA boils down to two questions: Did the school district comply with procedural safeguards? And did it provide a FAPE?

Triggers to Due Process Hearings

The IDEA and its implementing regulations contain many provisions that trigger—and perhaps encourage—litigation.

Much special education litigation revolves around alleged deficiencies in a child's Individualized Education Program ("IEP"), or in the meetings at which the IEP was developed. Every child with a disability must have an IEP in effect at the beginning of the school year, and the IEP must be reviewed at least annually. 20 U.S.C. § 1414(d)(4); 34 C.F.R. §§ 300.342, 300.343. The IDEA specifies several categories of information that must be included in the IEP, such as the child's current level of educational performance and measurable annual goals for that child's progress. 20 U.S.C. § 1414(d)(1)(A).

> *Ultimately, special education litigation under the IDEA boils down to two questions: Did the school district comply with procedural safeguards? And did it provide a FAPE?*

The school district is responsible for initiating and conducting meetings to draw up an IEP. For example, an initial IEP meeting must be convened within 30 days of a determination that a child needs special education services. 34 C.F.R. § 300.343. Generally, the district must take steps "to ensure that one or both of the parents of a child with a disability are present at each IEP meeting or are afforded the opportunity to participate." Id. at § 300.345(a). Thus, the parent must be adequately notified in advance of IEP meetings (with the notice satisfying regulatory requirements), and meetings must be scheduled at mutually convenient times and places. Id. at § 300.345(a). If the school district is unable to get the parent to attend, it may go forward with an IEP meeting, but it must keep a detailed record of the steps taken to obtain the parent's attendance. Id. at § 300.345(d).

Because the IDEA specifies who must be included in the "IEP team," 20 U.S.C. § 1414(d)(1)(B); 34 C.F.R. § 300.344, an IEP meeting often includes six or more people—typically the parent, a special education teacher, a regular education teacher, the IEP chair, a psychologist or counselor, as well as the parent's attorney, whose presence may, in turn, prompt the presence of an attorney for the school district. (This latter dynamic also can work in the opposite direction, but in our experience rarely does.) With attorneys present, the meeting can come to be dominated by strategic positioning for expected litigation to come, with one or both sides seeking advantages, making a record, or perhaps obtaining some early discovery, as well as (hopefully) devising a reasonable solution to the child's special education needs.

The IDEA also dictates a detailed battery of procedures for discipline of special education students. 20 U.S.C. § 1415(k). If suspension or a change of placement is contemplated, parents must be notified and informed of procedural safeguards. An IEP meeting must be convened for some types of discipline and to determine whether the behavior prompting the discipline was "a manifestation of such child's disability." Id. at § 1415(k)(4). (Expedited due process hearings are required for some disciplinary actions.)

Schools must provide parents with "written prior notice" not only of IEP meetings, but also whenever the school proposes (or refuses) to start or change a special education identification, evaluation, or placement. *Id.* at § 1415(b)(3). This "written prior notice" must explain the school's proposed action or inaction; describe other options; explain any other relevant factors; *and*—very important for purposes of impartial due process hearings—tell parents that they have procedural rights and provide either a "Procedural Safeguards Notice" or information on how to obtain that detailed notice. *Id.* at § 1415(c). The "Procedural Safeguards Notice" must give "a full explanation of the procedural safeguards" under the IDEA, written "in an easily understandable manner." *Id.* at § 1415(d)(2); *see also* 34 C.F.R. § 300.504(b). The notice must inform parents of their rights regarding independent educational evaluations, parental consent, due process hearings, civil actions, attorneys' fees, and more. And this Procedural Safeguards Notice must be provided repeatedly—when a child is referred for evaluation, upon reevaluation, when notifying parents of an IEP meetinssg, and when a complaint is registered. 20 U.S.C. § 1415(d).

> **Schools must provide parents with "written prior notice" not only of IEP meetings, but also whenever the school proposes (or refuses) to start or change a special education identification, evaluation, or placement.**

Two important aspects of the current IDEA scheme make it economically feasible—and sometimes even economically *beneficial*—for parents to file due process claims.

First, a court, at its discretion, may award attorneys' fees to a parent who is the "prevailing party." *Id.* at § 1415(i)(3)(B). There is *no* provision, on the other hand, for a prevailing school district to recover fees. Parents' counsel may be awarded fees for work in the due process administrative proceeding and in any civil action. Pursuant to relatively recent amendments, no attorneys' fees are to be awarded for an attorney's IEP meeting attendance (unless a hearing officer or court ordered the meeting). *Id.* at § 1415(i)(3)(D)(ii). In awarding attorneys' fees, the court must consider the parties' conduct. For example, the school district may avoid (or reduce) liability for attorneys' fees if parents reject a settlement offer without substantial justification. *Id.* at § 1415(i)(3)(D) and (E). An attorneys' fees award may also be reduced if parents "unreasonably protracted" proceedings or failed to provide adequate information in the initial complaint—unless the district itself is deemed to have delayed resolution or violated some procedural requirement. *Id.* at § 1415(i)(3)(F) and (G). These provisions create incentives for much finger-pointing regarding responsibility for delays.

A second important feature of IDEA economics is the so-called "stay-put" provision. During any due process proceeding, the child must remain in "the then-current educational placement" unless parents and district agree to some other placement or certain disciplinary exceptions apply. *Id.* at §§ 1415(j), (k). If application is being made for initial admission to public school, then the child is to be placed in that school until proceedings are complete. *Id.*; 34 C.F.R. § 300.514(b). If the parent succeeds in convincing the administrative hearing officer, or subsequent state reviewing officers or courts, that a change in placement is appropriate, then *that* placement—including a private school placement—becomes entitled to "stay put" protection through the remainder of the administrative proceedings and civil appeals. *Id.* at § 300.514(c).

The Impartial Due Process Hearing

A due process hearing is initiated when a parent makes a complaint about his or her child's education (or, more rarely, when the school does so because, for example, a parent refuses to consent to a special education evaluation). Many kinds of school actions (or inactions) may be the subject of due process hearings. The IDEA guarantees "an opportunity to present complaints with respect to *any* matter relating to the identification, evaluation, or educational placement of the child, or the provision of a free appropriate public education to such child." 20 U.S.C. § 1415(b)(6) (emphasis added). When parents make a complaint, the IDEA guarantees them the right to an "impartial due process hearing." *Id.* at § 1415(f). The IDEA requires that parents or their attorney specify the nature of the problem and propose a resolution when they file a complaint. *See* 34 C.F.R. § 300.507(c)(2)(iv) and (v). But while school districts at times complain that parents' requests for hearings are vague, the regulations bar school officials from denying or delaying a due process hearing on such grounds. *See id.* at § 300.507(c)(4).

> *Many school officials believe that the IDEA is one-sided in protecting parents and students on the one hand, while burdening schools on the other.*

Many school officials believe that the IDEA is one-sided in these and other respects in protecting parents and students on the one hand, while burdening schools on the other. To the extent that this is so, the basic rationale has been that it is school officials—and not parents or students—who have both primary responsibility for and greater expertise in developing and implementing special education programs.[7]

Since 1997, the IDEA has also included provisions to encourage mediation. When a complaint is filed, the district must provide an opportunity for voluntary, confidential, and free mediation "conducted by a qualified and impartial mediator who is trained in effective mediation techniques." 20 U.S.C. § 1415(b)(5), 1415(e). The district may further require parents not choosing mediation to meet with a disinterested parent group or alternative dispute resolution group "to encourage the use, and explain the benefits, of the mediation process." *Id.* at § 1415(e)(2)(B). However, the school district may not use mediation "to deny or delay a parent's right to a due process hearing" or to other rights under the IDEA. *Id.* at § 1415(e)(2)(A).

The structure of due process hearings depends on a combination of the IDEA requirements and state-adopted procedures. States are authorized to establish either a "one-tier" or "two-tier" system for due process claims. *Id.* at § 1415(f). Under a one-tier system, a neutral hearing officer under the auspices of the state education agency conducts the due process hearing, with appeal to the courts available by filing a civil action. Under a two-tier system, the initial hearing is conducted by a hearing officer acting under the auspices of the local or intermediate education agency, with an "impartial review" available from a neutral reviewing officer for the state agency, after which appeal is possible by filing a civil action in the courts. Under both the one- and two-tier systems, selection of the hearing officer is left to state procedures. The IDEA requires, however, that any hearing officer be "impartial," and thus not an employee of the state education agency or the child's school district. *Id.* at § 1415(f)(3).

IDEA-dictated deadlines drive a fairly quick pace for due process hearings, though in practice the deadlines often are not met. IDEA regulations require that, unless either party requests otherwise, the hearing officer's final decision must be made and mailed to the parties within 45 days of the *request* for a hearing. *See* 34 C.F.R. § 300.511(a). In a two-tier process, the state-level review decision must be made and mailed within 30 days after receipt of the request for review. *See id.* at § 300.511(b).

The hearing officer usually communicates with the parties to set the time and place of the hearing and must satisfy the federal requirement that the hearing be held at a time and place "reasonably convenient" to the parent and child. *See id.* at § 300.511(d). (There is no corresponding requirement that the hearing be convenient for the school district.) The hearing officer may require—or the parties may request—a pre-hearing conference to consider any preliminary motions and to discuss hearing procedures and whether the issues can be narrowed by agreement. One important requirement is that exhibits and witness lists must be exchanged five *business* days in advance of the hearing; otherwise, the opposing party has the right to prohibit the introduction of evidence not so disclosed. *See id.* at § 300.509(a)(3).

> **IDEA-dictated deadlines drive a fairly quick pace for due process hearings, though in practice the deadlines often are not met.**

Due process hearings have many of the trappings of, but usually less formality than, a court proceeding. The hearing may take place in a state agency hearing room or around a conference table at the school district. The IDEA permits parents to represent themselves or be represented by an attorney or by "individuals with special knowledge or training" related to children with disabilities, *see id.* at § 300.509(a)(1), which means parents may be represented in the administrative proceeding either by an attorney or by a lay advocate. Although the full scope of the rules of evidence does not apply, the IDEA guarantees both sides the power to subpoena witnesses, present evidence, and cross-examine witnesses. *See id.* at § 300.509(a)(2). Even when counsel represents parents, the hearing officer often takes an active role in questioning witnesses. A verbatim record is usually made because parties have the right to a written transcript or (at the parents' option) an electronic record of the hearing, provided at no cost to the parent. *See* 20 U.S.C. § 1415(h)(3); *see also* 34 C.F.R. § 300.509(a)(4) and (c)(2).

Once convened, due process hearings follow the general outline of a civil trial. The hearing officer usually states for the record how the hearing will proceed and summarizes any agreement on the hearing's scope. The parties usually have an opportunity to make opening statements. Then the parties present their witnesses and other evidence, with the school district often going first because it has the burden of proving that it made a FAPE available to the child. At the close of the evidence, the parties may make oral closing argument or request a written briefing in its place. The hearing officer may make an oral ruling on the record or reserve judgment until he or she issues a written opinion.

The Civil Action

The hearing officer's decision (or, in a two-tier system, the state-level reviewing officer's decision) is final unless a party elects to file a civil action in state or federal court, which is essentially an appeal of the due process outcome. *See* 20 U.S.C. § 1415(i)(2). (The vast majority of IDEA civil actions are brought in federal court.) An important converse requirement normally applies: Parents cannot bring a civil action under the IDEA unless they first have invoked the IDEA's administrative procedures in a timely manner and exhausted those procedures. The civil action must also be filed within the applicable statute of limitations, which is not established by the IDEA but borrowed from state limitations periods for similar claims.

In *Board of Education v. Rowley*, 458 U.S. 176 (1982), the Supreme Court held that a court's focus in an IDEA case consists of two inquiries. "First, has the State complied with the procedures set forth in the Act? And second, is the individualized educational program developed through the Act's procedures reasonably calculated to enable the child to receive educational benefits?" *Id.* at 206-07. If these questions are answered affirmatively, the Court stated, then the school district has satisfied its obligations. The IDEA directs the court reviewing a due process decision to hear "additional evidence" if requested by a party, to base its decision on the "preponderance of the evidence," and to grant "such relief as the court determines is appropriate." 20 U.S.C. § 1415(i)(2)(B).

> *The IDEA directs the court reviewing a due process decision to hear "additional evidence" if requested by a party, to base its decision on the "preponderance of the evidence," and to grant "such relief as the court determines is appropriate."*

The losing party in an IDEA civil action, whether parents or school officials, may appeal the decision of a federal or state trial court through normal appellate procedures.

Anatomy of a Case: How Due Process Hearings and Special Education Litigation Really Work

So much for theory. Now, for real life.

What ultimately would become the case of *Angela Jones v. Big School District*[8] started with questions and informal expressions of concern. Beginning during the fall 1997 semester, Angela's mother, Ms. Jones, expresses to her daughter's teachers her dissatisfaction with various aspects of Big School District's placement of her 14-year-old daughter, who is mentally retarded and has behavioral problems. When she was younger, Angela spent some time "mainstreamed" with regular education children. But for several years—partly because of Angela's increased acting out and the greater difficulty in controlling tantrums that accompanied her physical growth—Big School District has paid her tuition at Special Kids School, a full-time, private special education day school.

Ms. Jones, however, wants more. Now, she has suggested to her Big School District placement specialist that Angela should be placed in a full-time *residential* facility at public expense.

Angela can be difficult for her mother to control at home, destroying property and physically threatening her family. Ms. Jones also says her daughter is not getting enough educational attention to prepare her for adulthood. But there is no formal dispute yet: Ms. Jones has not yet filed a complaint or requested a due process hearing; however, she has hired attorney Repeat Handler, who specializes in bringing special education actions against school districts in the area. The stakes are high because round-the-clock residential placements are expensive—anywhere from $60,000 to twice that much per year, depending on the particular program—and, if found necessary to provide Angela with a FAPE, Big School District might need to provide such a placement for seven more years, until Angela is 21.

Attorney Handler also does not yet file a complaint requesting a due process hearing. Instead, he attends Angela's annual IEP review meeting with Ms. Jones, but only after the meeting is rescheduled several times around Mr. Handler's schedule. By the time they actually meet in May 1998—just as the school year is coming to a close, and months after Big School District *first* attempted to convene this meeting—the IEP chairperson has prepared for the meeting and Angela's teacher has had to arrange classroom coverage on three different dates. The IEP chairperson leads the group through discussion of Angela's current placement, educational progress, and proposed goals. Staff persons who work with or monitor Angela report that she recognizes a few more words, counts a little more accurately, and has been able to do simple chores in housekeeping; they recommend that the current placement continue.

> **The IEP chairperson leads the group through discussion of Angela's current placement, educational progress, and proposed goals.**

Attorney Handler states that he is not surprised: he says he *knew* the IEP team would never recommend a residential placement. He spends the meeting apparently focused on cross-examining Angela's teachers and Big School District's special education staff on discipline incidents and shortcomings in Special Kids School—seemingly (at least to the Big School District IEP team) more interested in setting up and preparing for a due process hearing that has not yet been requested than in attempting to work cooperatively toward an agreement on placement.

There appears to be a clear dispute here: Ms. Jones has refused to sign the IEP or agree to the placement, yet Attorney Handler still does not request a due process hearing. Big School District staff members suspect he is waiting for a more tactically advantageous time—such as when some incident at Special Kids School may make that placement seem less effective—as well as when a hearing would best fit into Attorney Handler's crowded calendar. (This is a real issue for Mr. Handler; his small, three-lawyer firm does not provide him with a lot of back-up when scheduling conflicts occur.)

The new school year begins, and Angela appears to be doing fine at Special Kids School (where Big School District is still paying her tuition, notwithstanding Ms. Jones' refusal to sign Angela's IEP). Then one day in the fall—nearly a year since Ms. Jones began talking about a residential placement—Angela acts out. Attorney Handler moves quickly, filing a request for a due process hearing to be held within the following two weeks. The complaint is completely generic, stating only that Big School District's placement of Angela, as shown in her May 1998 IEP, has denied

Angela a FAPE.

Now the due process machinery—and more delays—kick in. Big School District forwards the complaint to the state Department of Administrative Hearings, which immediately assigns it a case number and hearing officer. Big School District proposes mediation, which Attorney Handler refuses. Counsel for Big School District—Outside Law Firm—files a response asking for a prehearing conference to clarify the issues and proposing several different hearing dates. (Outside Law Firm is a much larger firm than Mr. Handler's; with more attorneys it is able to be more flexible when it comes to scheduling.) The hearing officer sets a date for the prehearing conference via telephone conference call, which (seemingly like everything else) ultimately is rescheduled several times to accommodate Attorney Handler's schedule. During the prehearing conference, the hearing officer takes a "no nonsense" approach but also seems inclined to

> *Now the due process machinery—and more delays—kick in.*

give parent's counsel a lot of leeway. To preserve as many options as possible, Attorney Handler is very vague on what is deficient with Angela's current placement. Is it lack of effective discipline? Is the teacher inadequate? Is Angela not making educational progress? No specific answers are forthcoming. By letter, the hearing officer sets the hearing for two weeks later— which will be a month after the complaint was filed.

Outside Law Firm starts preparing for the hearing as soon as the complaint comes in, reviewing Angela's educational file, interviewing her recent regular and special education teachers and members of her IEP teams for the last several years, and investigating whether any expert witnesses will be needed. All this is made much more difficult (and expensive) and must cover all conceivable subjects and persons with knowledge about Angela because Attorney Handler has managed to avoid specifically itemizing his complaints.

Nevertheless, and as required by the IDEA, five business days before the hearing (and just four days after the prehearing conference), Big School District faxes its "five-day disclosure" to Attorney Handler, including a list of potential witnesses and all the documents it may use at the hearing, including Angela's IEPs, psychological and educational assessments, discipline reports, and more. All this work has required a lot of time by Outside Law Firm attorneys and has run up a significant bill for Big School District before the hearing has even started.

Instead of making his own five-day disclosure, however, Attorney Handler sends a letter to the hearing officer withdrawing the complaint, claiming he was unaware of the hearing date. Big School District staff members suspect, however, that other concerns actually prompted this withdrawal. This case may be conflicting with another of Handler's many active special education cases, and the Big School District placement specialist who regularly deals with the particular residential program that Ms. Jones appears to prefer has heard that it lacks space right now for Angela. Outside Law Firm moves for the complaint to be dismissed with prejudice, but the hearing officer refuses.

Several weeks later, Attorney Handler files a second due process complaint, asking for a hearing on one of three dates over the succeeding three weeks. Again, Outside Law Firm requests a prehearing conference and prepares for the hearing by gathering recent information on Angela and re-interviewing witnesses. (This prehearing conference is just as unhelpful as the first one in terms of extracting any sort of "bill of particulars" from Attorney Handler.) The School District again makes a timely five-day disclosure. And, once again, Attorney Handler withdraws the complaint, this time asserting in a letter that he is trying to settle the case with Big School District's counsel. That is news to Outside Law Firm; its attorneys have heard nothing from Attorney Handler. Again, Big School District staff suspects that tactical posturing is behind the most recent dismissal, especially when Mr. Handler fails ever to initiate settlement discussions. Outside Law Firm thus sends Mr. Handler a letter warning that it will seek to dismiss any new complaint based on his lack of good faith in filing and withdrawing complaints.

Months pass. Big School District begins to think that Ms. Jones has decided that Angela's placement at Special Kids School is acceptable after all. Then, in January 1999, Repeat Handler requests an "emergency" IEP meeting on grounds that Angela's performance has deteriorated and an emergency residential placement is necessary. The IEP team meets and finds no emergency exists and no change is warranted. A week later, a third due process complaint is filed, demanding a hearing the next week. Hearing preparations kick off yet again, but this time Outside Law Firm also files a motion to dismiss the complaint, arguing that Repeat Handler and Ms. Jones have acted in bad faith by twice before filing and withdrawing the complaint and never pursuing settlement. Although the hearing officer chides Mr. Handler for claiming he intended to explore settlement and never doing so, and finds that there is no factual support for Mr. Handler's claim that he did not receive notice of the first hearing date, she nevertheless allows the hearing to go forward. This due process complaint involves new facts, the hearing officer finds: the alleged recent deterioration in Angela's school performance. Moreover, the most important thing, she rules, is that Big School District must show it is providing Angela with a FAPE—and she won't deprive Angela of her due process rights solely because her attorney may have acted disingenuously. The hearing is set for two weeks later, in March 1999, a month after the third complaint is filed, but more than ten months after the last full IEP meeting.

> *Big School District staff suspects that tactical posturing is behind the most recent dismissal, especially when Mr. Handler fails ever to initiate settlement discussions.*

Big School District again makes its five-day disclosure; this time, Repeat Handler does too. As potential witnesses he lists Angela, Ms. Jones, a special education expert, all of Angela's teachers, and all IEP team members. He also produces a handful of discipline notes sent home by the school. It appears the hearing really is going forward.

The hearing convenes, as scheduled, in a conference room at Big School District. There is no court reporter present, but a tape recorder sits in the middle of the table, and throughout the hearing, the hearing officer is very careful about turning it on and off, stating the case number, the date and time, and who is present. The hearing officer announces the case and asks if there are any preliminary matters. Immediately, Repeat Handler announces (for the first time) that this case will take at least *four* days of testimony and that he has conflicting cases over the next several days. The hearing officer says she is tired of delays. She instructs everyone to pull out their calendars and then finds four available days over the next month and a half. Angela's case will be heard in fits and starts.

The parties outline their case in opening statements. Even though Big School District has the ultimate burden of proof, the hearing officer decides that it will be most efficient for Angela's attorney to go first (and thus finally reveal specifically what he alleges is inappropriate about Angela's IEP and/or current placement at Special Kids School). Attorney Handler argues that the evidence will show that Angela needs round-the-clock attention to make educational progress and that her out-of-control behavior at home means she is not meeting the "social skill" goals in her IEP. Big School District counters that Angela is making some educational progress at school and that that is what the IDEA requires, not that the District *maximize* Angela's progress.

> *As the first witness, Angela's counsel calls the IEP chair to set the stage with information on Angela's disabilities, placements, and evaluations.*

Then the witnesses begin, sprinkled over four hearing dates with only three to four hours devoted to the hearing each day, largely due to Attorney Handler's continuing schedule conflicts. As the first witness, Angela's counsel calls the IEP chair to set the stage with information on Angela's disabilities, placements, and evaluations. Then Ms. Jones testifies, with vivid details about Angela's difficult behavior and her desire for Angela to become self-sufficient.

More witnesses follow: Angela's current teacher, a prior teacher, her after-school provider, a counselor, Angela's Big School District caseworker, and dueling experts on appropriate expectations for educational progress of a child with Angela's disabilities.

Numerous sub-themes develop: Did the District improperly fail to provide summer school? Was an in-home assessment required? What exactly do Angela's IEP goals require? Is Angela taking her medications at home? Why were some IEP meetings delayed? Has Angela's mother adequately cooperated with her school? Is the residential placement proposed by Angela's mother well run? And is Angela actually so dangerous in the home that child welfare should get involved?

On the third hearing day, Repeat Handler angles for an immediate ruling and placement in a residential facility. An emergency has arisen, he asserts, and recalls Angela's mother to testify. The incident she describes—a thrown glass, a pinched social worker—sounds no more severe than others, and the hearing officer refuses to act precipitously.

On the final hearing date, just one witness is heard. Attorney Handler asks for the opportunity to submit written post-hearing briefs in lieu of offering closing oral argument then and there; Big School District does not object. This will delay the decision, but because it is requested by the parties, the hearing officer agrees and works out a schedule: Briefs are due in four weeks, and the parties will then respond to each other's opening briefs in simultaneous reply briefs to be filed three days later.

Four weeks after the reply briefs are filed (two days late, in Mr. Handler's case), in July 1999 the hearing officer issues her decision. The hearing officer rules that Angela is making educational progress and that therefore Big School District is providing a FAPE. The decision carefully describes all the witnesses and exhibits entered into evidence. Big School District doesn't agree with all the characterizations of events but is generally satisfied with the result.

Over a year has passed since Angela's May 1998 IEP meeting that produced the IEP and placement decision that had been the subject of these proceedings. It now is approaching two years since Ms. Jones first began talking about a residential placement. While Repeat Handler and Outside Law Firm were completing the due process hearing, another annual IEP meeting occurred in May 1999, continuing Angela's placement at Special Kids School.

Big School District waits for the next shoe to drop. Will Ms. Jones appeal the hearing officer's decision to federal or state court? Will she file a *new* due process claim based on the May 1999 IEP meeting? Months go by with no action. Angela remains at Special Kids School. Eventually, Outside Law Firm boxes up the files on Angela's case and sends them off-site. As for Big School District, it is still busy with Angela's regular evaluations, IEP meetings, and providing her with special education.

> *Impartial due process hearings can be an imperfect tool to efficiently enforce the IDEA's mandate of a free appropriate public education for students with disabilities.*

Big School District has prevailed for now, but at huge cost. It has paid substantial attorneys' fees for multiple trial preparations and a lengthy hearing. Special education staff members have spent days away from classrooms and normal duties—for scheduled and rescheduled IEP meetings, interviews with the district's attorneys, and several trial days during which they waited to, and did, testify. Angela remains in her same placement and is living at home with her mother.

The Efficacy of Due Process and Litigation for Enforcing the IDEA

As the foregoing description of Angela's case suggests, impartial due process hearings can be an imperfect tool to efficiently enforce the IDEA's mandate of a free appropriate public education for students with disabilities. Summarized below are several specific areas in which we believe due process has tended to work well, or not so well, in our experience.

From the Perspective of School Districts

One clear benefit to school districts from the due process system is identification of special education problem areas, including service gaps. Due process hearings can be a source of valuable information in this respect; responsible districts closely monitor the outcomes of due process hearings and special education litigation and move quickly to correct any deficiencies that may be contributing to adverse outcomes. This, in turn, enhances the overall quality of the districts' special education program and their ability to meet the needs of the children they serve.

At the same time, due process hearings cost money and consume other resources that are thus unavailable to educate children. In 1984, the Supreme Court concluded that this was the reason

Congress had not previously provided for an award of attorneys' fees to prevailing parents in the EHA,[9] the next year, Congress "corrected" that omission.

Of course, it is not merely the prospect of having to pay attorneys' fees to prevailing parents that districts must assess in determining how to handle a parent request for due process—it is the district's *own* attorneys' fees as well because it has no prospect of reimbursement, even if the parent complaint is completely frivolous. In our experience, districts have at times agreed to parental demands, asserted through due process complaints, for changes to IEPs and placements that the districts genuinely believed to be completely inappropriate simply because its own costs in attorneys' fees to defend the cases would likely be greater than the costs of the requested changes. It is unlikely that such skewing of resources toward the "squeaky wheels" is what Congress intended.

> *The current due process regime is very complex and technical, and thus difficult (if not nearly impossible) for parents to navigate successfully without legal representation or well-trained parent advocates.*

Finally, although this wasn't illustrated by Angela's case, the IDEA's "stay-put" provision is subject to serious abuse. Once a child has been placed in a private placement—either directly by a school district or indirectly by order of a hearing officer or judge after a parent's unilateral placement—any effort by a district to move the child back into a public placement (including designing and implementing a new and entirely appropriate program) can be frustrated *for years* by many of the same kinds of delays that took place in Angela's case. College basketball long ago implemented a 40-second clock to put some reasonable limits on versions of "stall ball." There is no comparable mechanism in the IDEA; running out the clock is a strategy that remains alive and well in special education due process proceedings.

From the Perspective of Parents and Students

Having counseled and represented parents as well as school districts in special education litigation, we can attest that one definite benefit of due process hearings is to ensure, as a last resort, the provision of appropriate IEPs and placements. There are indeed children with disabilities in this country who have received a FAPE only due to the intervention of due process hearing officers and judges.

Moreover, although we have not seen comprehensive data on the issue, it is undoubtedly true that many parents have obtained legal representation in special education due process proceedings and litigation only because of the attorneys' fees provision enacted in 1985. Although it often appears to district staff that affluent parents are more likely to take advantage of the due process procedure, this trend undoubtedly would increase in the absence of the IDEA's fees provision.

Still, the current due process regime is very complex and technical, and thus difficult (if not nearly impossible) for parents to navigate successfully without legal representation or well-trained parent advocates. This is particularly true for less sophisticated parents. That is likely not what Congress intended. Indeed, it may well be that the recent (1997) requirement that states and districts offer mediation as an alternative to due process was the result of Congress' recognition of the increasing complexity and expense, as well as the time-consuming nature, of due process.

Breakdowns in the System Common to (and Unhealthy for) Both Sides

In our experience, due process has proven in two additional respects to be imperfect for efficiently enforcing the IDEA's FAPE mandate.

First, such proceedings tend to foster mutual perceptions of dishonesty between the parties and often result in deep suspicion and hostility between parents and school officials. While litigation is inherently adversarial, the level of antipathy in post-due process relationships appears to us generally to be much higher than in relationships between parties in other areas of our education practice. Perhaps this is due, in part, to the relative absence of mechanisms in the statute and regulations that would inhibit "gaming" of the system, some of which was described above in Angela's story.

Second, due process does not lend itself to quick resolution of any dispute, unless both parties genuinely desire such a resolution. This is unfortunate (and can have tragic consequences) when a child is being denied adequate services while the dispute remains unresolved. The IDEA's relatively new mediation mechanism, to the extent it is used and actually resolves disputes, may fill the need for a quick, informal dispute resolution process that does not require attorneys—which due process itself probably was initially intended to provide.

> **Due process does not lend itself to quick resolution of any dispute, unless both parties genuinely desire such a resolution.**

Recommendations—and Tradeoffs

In a perfect world, all these problems would be fixed. Any fix, however, will bring with it unintended (as well as intended) consequences. Moreover, we recognize that features of the system that we have described as problems based on our experience actually may not be problems on a national scale.

More Data Are Needed

Our ability to prescribe improvements in the system is limited by the absence of comprehensive data on many of its key features. Much research has been published regarding some aspects of the IDEA and other federal special education directives,[10] such as trends in the rate and category of placements of students with disabilities[11] and qualitative studies of factors affecting such trends.[12] Furthermore, some districts and states collect certain due process data such as numbers and percentages of due process claims filed, mediated, settled, and decided by a hearing, the final disposition of such claims, and the schools from which they arise.[13] However, we are unaware of recent national data on many of the questions raised in this paper.[14]

Specifically, data regarding three broad issues would be useful to policy makers and advocates as Congress moves toward the 2002 IDEA reauthorization:

• **Which students and parents make use of the process?** Data regarding the profiles of students and parents most and least likely to file due process claims and to prevail in such claims (including, for example, those seeking private placements) would help policy makers assess not only the extent to which the procedural aspects of the IDEA are being implemented equitably, but also how specific provisions—such as the fee-shifting provision—might contribute to outcomes.[15]

• **What are the costs of due process litigation—and who bears them?** School districts that receive many due process requests from sophisticated parents represented by experienced counsel spend substantial resources, including administrative and instructional staff time and attorneys' fees, in processing and responding to these requests and litigating the claims. On the other hand, districts that receive few claims, of which many are resolved informally, commit relatively fewer resources. Research quantifying the costs of due process litigation under the IDEA would be useful in determining whether the system is working efficiently and in assessing the costs of alternatives. Such research could also be used, for example, to determine whether and to what extent school districts are diverting resources from other programs to respond to due process claims and in what proportions the costs of litigation are borne by parents, districts, and states.

> *Congress' attention will be focused on amending the IDEA when the Act comes due for reauthorization in 2002.*

• **Is mediation serving its stated purpose?** Pursuant to the 1997 amendments, the IDEA now requires states to make mediation available to parents who file due process requests. Some school districts with which we are familiar have seen as many as one-half of all disputed placements resolved through mediation. Such cases tend to involve disputes over issues entailing relatively low financial stakes, such as the amount of time that certain related services are to be provided to a student. Higher-stakes issues, such as whether the school district will fund an expensive private placement, appear *not* to be resolved by mediation. Data regarding the extent to which, and the kinds of cases in which, mediation is used, and the results that follow, also would be useful to policy makers in assessing whether the mediation provision has served its intended purpose of providing a streamlined, inexpensive, and fair alternative to due process hearings.[16]

Possible Amendments to the IDEA

Congress' attention will be focused on amending the IDEA when it comes due for reauthorization in 2002. Notwithstanding the current dearth of national data on many of the questions we have raised, several amendments that have been proposed in the past, or are currently being discussed among advocates, commentators, and key congressional staff, are of interest.

Limiting attorneys' fees. One possible reform, presented in a bill introduced in Congress several years ago, would bar the award of attorneys' fees for due process hearings by limiting such awards to actions brought in state or federal court.[17] This proposal apparently reflects the view that due process hearings can be made less formal and thus less expensive and time-consuming by limiting the participation of parents' attorneys. This proposal would have a disproportionate impact on low-income families who cannot afford to retain an attorney.

Establishing an IDEA statute of limitations. Another proposal, establishing a relatively short period within which due process claims under the IDEA must be filed, would likely reduce the number of claims filed. It is not clear, however, that such a measure would bar frivolous claims any more than meritorious claims.

Trained judges as hearing officers. The IDEA gives states broad discretion to design their own systems for reviewing due process claims by parents of students with disabilities, including, for example, the selection of hearing officers. In Maryland, district officials report that an amendment to state law requiring that hearing officers be administrative law judges[18] has produced more consistent application of legal standards, and therefore more predictable outcomes and overall fairer hearings. Based on these officials' and our own experience, we believe inclusion of a similar requirement in an amended IDEA or the adoption by other states of a law similar to Maryland's, with the added requirement that hearing officers receive training in special education, could produce significantly more equitable, consistent and efficient due process systems.

> *Due process is a blunt, costly, time-consuming, and otherwise imperfect instrument to accomplish its assigned task.*

Limiting the duration and scope of the process. Other proposals designed to reduce the duration, expense, and "legalization" of due process under the IDEA have included limiting (a) the length of hearings (e.g., to not more than a single trial day), (b) the types of issues from which an appeal may be taken (e.g., to "purely legal" issues), or (c) state and federal courts' ability to hear additional evidence not presented in the hearing.[19] Amendments of this kind would likely reduce the cost of due process hearings and litigation. They also—if applied inflexibly—would result in a real sacrifice of due process rights for litigants in some cases. This is an area in which additional data would shed needed light on the proper balance between seeking to ensure fairness for the parties and managing the cost and efficiency of the process.

Conclusion

As attorneys who have represented both sides in these cases, we can vouch for the following:

- Special education staff members in the public schools devote their professional lives to educating children with disabilities, are truly dedicated to the endeavor, and genuinely want to provide appropriate special education and related services to the students they are charged with educating. Yet school resources are not unlimited, budget pressures are real, and the IDEA allows districts to take program costs into account *only* so long as they still are meeting the FAPE requirement. This is the fundamental source of school district conflict with parents.

- Parents (and other guardians) who devote their lives to raising children with disabilities genuinely want to make sure that their children receive *at least* appropriate special education and related services. In truth, however, what these parents *really* want—indeed what *all* parents want—is an education that will allow their children to maximize their potential. The IDEA does not require this. This is the fundamental source of parents' conflict with school officials.

In its wisdom, Congress has decided that when conflicts occur (and—now—cannot be resolved through mediation), they must be resolved through due process. Due process is a blunt, costly, time-consuming, and otherwise imperfect instrument to accomplish its assigned task. The IDEA's 2002 reauthorization may well provide our best opportunity to improve it.

---

[1] The authors are attorneys at Hogan & Hartson L.L.P., one of the few "national" law firms representing education institutions as a focus of its practice. The firm represents school districts; colleges, universities, and other post-secondary institutions; national education associations; and corporations and foundations with an interest in education. Hogan & Hartson's work for elementary and secondary education clients has addressed the gamut of issues faced by school districts, including not only special education, but also other civil rights issues; employment issues, such as affirmative action, employment discrimination, and sexual harassment; federal contract and grant programs; First Amendment issues, such as aid to non-public schools, prayer in school, and freedom of speech; and various Washington-based activities, including representing school districts and their associations before Congress and federal agencies such as the Departments of Education and Justice, the Environmental Protection Agency, and the Federal Communications Commission. The firm has represented school districts in numerous special education due process hearings, as well as in appeals to the federal courts, and firm attorneys also have represented parents and students in similar proceedings against school districts. The firm regularly advises school districts regarding obligations under the Individuals with Disabilities Education Act ("IDEA"), 20 U.S.C. § 1400, *et seq.*, Section 504 of the Rehabilitation Act of 1973, 29 U.S.C. § 794, and the Americans with Disabilities Act, 42 U.S.C. § 12101, *et seq.*

[2] The federal Family Educational Rights and Privacy Act ("FERPA"), 20 U.S.C. § 1232g, also known as the "Buckley Amendment," does require school districts to provide a due process hearing of sorts when parents believe their children's educational records should be changed in some way and school officials disagree. Although FERPA itself does not provide federal funds to states or local school districts, the statute's enforcement mechanism provides for a cut-off of all other federal funding if FERPA's mandates (including provision of this hearing) are not met. This hearing, however, need not be "impartial" in the same sense as a special education due process hearing, in that (among many other things) a FERPA hearing may be conducted by an employee of the same school district where the child attends school. See generally 34 C.F.R. § 99.22(c).

[3] This first impartial due process hearing provision apparently was the product of an amendment offered by Senator Robert T. Stafford of Vermont and passed on the floor of the Senate, advancing procedural protections then under consideration as part of more comprehensive legislation (Senate Bill 6), which ultimately was enacted the following year as Public Law 94-142, the Education for All Handicapped Children Act (EAHCA). See 93 Cong. Rec. 15266-77 (1974).

[4] See 34 C.F.R. Parts 300 and 303.

[5] Upon an examination of the EHA's legislative history, the Supreme Court concluded (in the majority opinion authored by Justice Blackmun) that the absence of an attorneys' fee provision in the statute was no oversight:

> Congress did not explain the absence of a provision for a damages remedy and attorneys' fees in the EHA. Several references in the statute itself and in its legislative history, however, indicate that the omissions were in response to Congress' awareness of the financial burden already imposed on States by the responsibility of providing education for handicapped children. As noted above, one of the stated purposes of the statute was to relieve this financial burden. See 20 U.S.C. §§ 1400(b)(8) and (9). Discussions of the EHA by its proponents reflect Congress' intent to "make every resource, or as much as possible, available to the direct activities and the direct programs that are going to benefit the handicapped." 121 Cong. Rec. 19501 (1975) (remarks of Sen. Dole). See also Id., at 37025 (procedural safeguards designed to further the congressional goal of ensuring full educational opportunity without overburdening the local school districts and state educational agencies) (remarks of Rep. Perkins); S. Rep. No. 94-168, at 81 (minority views cognizant of financial burdens on localities). The Act appears to represent Congress' judgment that the best way to ensure a free appropriate public education for handicapped children is to clarify and make enforceable the rights of those children while at the same time endeavoring to relieve the financial burden imposed on the agencies responsible to guarantee those rights.

Smith v. Robinson, 468 U.S. at 1020-21.

[6] *Board of Education v. Rowley*, 458 U.S. 176, 205-06 (1982).

[7] See, e.g., *Tatro v. Texas*, 703 F.2d 823, 830 (5th Cir. 1983).

---

8 To protect privacy, we have altered names and some facts of a real case handled by Hogan & Hartson.

9 See note 6.

10 See, e.g., David M. Engel, "Law, Culture, and Children with Disabilities: Educational Rights and the Construction of Difference," 1991 *Duke L.J.* 166 (1991) (describing a study of the effectiveness of the IDEA in western New York).

11 See, e.g., James McLeskey, Daniel Heary and Michael I. Axelrod, "Inclusion of Students with Learning Disabilities: An Examination of Data from Reports to Congress," 66 *Exceptional Children* 55 (1999). The U.S. Department of Education presents annual Reports to Congress regarding implementation of the IDEA, which also include data on the identification and placement of students with disabilities.

12 See, e.g., S. Hasazi, et al., "A Qualitative Policy Study of the Least Restrictive Environment Provision of the Individuals with Disabilities Education Act," 60 *Exceptional Children* 491 (1994).

13 Project FORUM of the National Association of State Directors of Special Education (NASDSE) has published several papers funded by federal grants that summarize state-by-state data on the number of due process claims filed and how many hearings (first-tier and second-tier) were held. See NASDSE, "Due Process Hearings, 1999 Update" (Dec. 1999) (data for all states for 1996 through 1998); Eileen M. Ahearn, "Due Process Hearings: An Update" (NASDSE, Jan. 8, 1997) (data for 1992 through 1994); NASDSE, "Mediation and Due Process Procedures in Special Education: An Analysis of State Policies" (1994) (data for 1991 through 1993). This macro-level data showed a steady increase in the number of due process requests filed across the country (from 4,125 in 1991 to 9,827 in 1998), and an overall but less consistent increase in the number of hearings held (from 1,232 in 1991 to 3,315 in 1998). The studies cite an "acute need" for better and more detailed information on due process proceedings and costs. NASDSE also surveyed several states' use of mediation prior to the 1997 IDEA amendments encouraging use of mediation. See Gloria T. Symington, "Mediation as an Option in Special Education" (NASDSE, Jan. 13, 1995).

14 Cf. Joel F. Handler, *The Conditions of Discretion: Autonomy, Community, Bureaucracy* (1986), 69-72 (citing studies of due process hearings in the 1970s and 1980s). Some studies have examined win-loss records of parents vs. school districts and some characteristics of due process cases such as severity of disability, student gender, central issue in dispute, and occupation of the hearing officer. See, e.g., James R. Newcomer, Perry A. Zirkel and Ralph J. Tarola, "Characteristics and Outcomes of Special Education Hearing and Review Officer Cases," 123 *Educ. L.. Rep.* 449 (1998) (also citing additional earlier studies). However, these studies have not analyzed data addressing the principal questions raised in this paper regarding which claims end up in litigation, costs, and outcomes. Some studies do provide limited or anecdotal cost information. For example, one author reported that due process proceedings for a particular child in Pennsylvania consumed 19 sessions over two years, $27,000 for transcript fees and $20,000 for hearing officer costs, but other expenses (such as attorneys' fees for parents and district, expert witness fees, staff time, and more) were unavailable. This author also reported that the first-tier hearing stage in Pennsylvania averaged 110 days as of 1992, while second-tier reviews averaged 35 days. See Perry A. Zirkel, "Over-Due Process Revisions for the Individuals with Disabilities Education Act," 55 *Mont. L. Rev.* 403, 404-06 & n.12 (1994).

15 For example, in our experience, and perhaps not surprisingly, parents who file and aggressively press due process claims tend to be relatively affluent. One obvious reason for this is the relatively high cost of legal representation. As previously noted, since the web of IDEA regulations has become increasingly complex, the assistance of experienced counsel has become more important. This is true even in the early stages of a dispute, including IEP meetings and other contacts with the school district, which may be characterized by posturing and tactical gamesmanship. Although the IDEA fee-shifting provision gives lawyers some incentive to represent low-income parents, many plaintiff's lawyers seek a healthy proportion of paying clients to supplement the court-ordered fees they are able to collect when they "win" a case. We have observed that attorneys who litigate due process claims primarily against school districts with track records of litigating and declining to settle such claims are less willing to take on clients who cannot afford to pay their fees; plaintiff's lawyers in such districts cannot count on a steady flow of court-awarded fees in connection with settlements favorable to their clients. Conversely, we would expect that counsel practicing in areas where the school district has been more willing to settle claims would be able to rely more on winning court-ordered fees and thus might take on a greater proportion of low-income clients.

16 See H.R. Rep. No. 105-95, at 106 (1997).

17 See Zirkel, *Over-Due Process Revisions*, at 408.

18 See Md. Code Ann., Educ. § 8-413(a)(2).

19 See Zirkel, *Over-Due Process Revisions*, at 409-412.

Chapter 11

Navigating the Special Education Maze: Experiences of Four Families

Siobhan Gorman

Introduction

Austin and Christian are the far ends of the special education spectrum. Diagnosed with cerebral palsy when he was three months old, Austin immediately received therapy through both

> *The lens of special education magnifies some of the pre-existing problems in the general public education system.*

a state early intervention program and the additional services his parents sought on the side. Now in kindergarten, he attends a mainstream class with his own aide. Christian, whose parents immigrated to the United States from El Salvador and later divorced, has been tossed from Mom to Dad to foster care and reached seventh grade without having been taught to read. When his third grade teacher recommended him for a special education evaluation, the school placed Christian, who is fluent in English, in English as a Second Language classes and stonewalled further evaluation requests until legal action was threatened. After one year of regular tutoring, his self-esteem has improved, but it remains to be seen whether his reading skills have.

As with public education as a whole, families' experiences with special education can fall anywhere along the spectrum from Austin to Christian. The lens of special education, however, magnifies some of the pre-existing problems in the general public education system. The pressures placed on parents of children with special needs—from the logistical to the legal to the emotional—demand a higher level of sophistication and consumer awareness, which can widen the existing gaps in education quality and student achievement between rich and poor, or urban and non-urban. In a ground-level investigation of the quality of special education services, this chapter will look at the experiences of four families: (1) a wealthy family in suburban Massachusetts that has received high-quality services; (2) a middle-class family in rural North Carolina that resorted to litigation; (3) a lower-middle income foster family of a Hispanic child in Washington, D.C., who has significant reading delays; and (4) a lower-middle income black family in Colorado Springs with several children who have "social-emotional" disabilities.

The U.S. Department of education and various advocacy groups write frequently about an overrepresentation of poor and minority students in special education, but the limited statistics available send conflicting messages, and overrepresentation cannot be proven with demographic data alone. The Education Department found in the 1998-99 academic year that, although black students made up 15 percent of children in the public schools, they represented 20 percent of all children with disabilities. Hispanic students, who make up about 14 percent of all students and about 13 percent of special education students, appear to be proportionally represented.[1] But 1998 numbers taken from census data showed both black and Hispanic students representing about 15 percent of the special education population, which was actually 1 to 2 percent lower than their proportion of the overall student population that year.[2] New provisions in the federal Individuals with Disabilities Education Act (IDEA) may improve data collection in future years.

Although questions remain about the role of race and income in assigning children to special education, parents' stories highlight a disparity in the quality of services for poor and minority students in special education programs. All parents face challenges in helping a child with disabilities, and many say they have to push the system to get the services they feel their child needs. But those in the upper income and educational echelons tend to have greater success when navigating the ever-changing laws that govern the education of children with disabilities, as did Austin Lam's family in Wellesley, Massachusetts. And fighting for proper services took a heavy financial toll on the middle-class Eirschele family, but when battling their school system in rural North Carolina didn't work, the Eirscheles were able to stretch their income to send their son to a private school for children with learning disabilities. Children who grow up in low-income or under-educated families are more likely to fall through the cracks, as is evidenced by the experiences of the Trejo's foster son, Christian, in Washington, D.C. And some parents, like Alice Spencer of Colorado Springs, have found that, although their children need additional services, special education services—especially for poor and minority children—have become a catchall for children with problems.

> *Some parents have found that, although their children need additional services, special education services—especially for poor and minority children—have become a catchall for children with problems.*

Also contributing to a disparity in services is the relatively recent mass influx of children into the special education system. In the last decade, special education enrollment for school-age children increased by about 30 percent from 4,253,018 in the 1989-90 academic year to 5,541,166 in 1998-99.[3] Under pressure to expand special education services overall, school districts can lose track of an individual student if that student's parent is not vigilant. "The parents who get the most out of us are the ones who are persistent," says Larry Sargent, director for curriculum and instruction and former director of special education for Harrison School District No. 2 in Colorado Springs. But Sargent, who for the last 30 years has served on national special education committees, taught special education, and administered special education programs, says diplomacy is as important as persistence. "The schools often don't view the matters brought up by the parents as being as serious as the parents think they are," he says. "Parents who appear unreasonable can, like anybody would, be kind of disregarded by the school district; whereas a parent who is persistent and rational and polite, is going to get listened to."

Active Parenting in a Suburban System

Twenty kindergartners cluster at the front of Jim Razzano's classroom to form a pumpkin patch of students. The class sings a Halloween song about picking pumpkins, and Razzano "picks" a student-pumpkin by tapping him on the head. That student joins the parade of singing pumpkins in the classroom. When Austin Lam is picked, he beams, and with the help of an aide, he wheels around the room in the parade with his classmates. Unable to speak, he plays the refrain of the song on a tape recorder so that he can, in effect, sing along with the rest of the class by pressing the play button. "Pick a, pick a pumpkin from the patch...."

Austin's inclusion in regular classes is a priority for Austin's parents, Pam and James Lam. Austin, who has cerebral palsy, was scheduled to be fully included in the regular kindergarten class in the fall of 2000, but due to understaffing and start-up problems in Schofield Elementary's first program for children with multiple disabilities, he only made it to the regular kindergarten about three times a week during the first few months of kindergarten. The second quarter of school should be better, Pam says, now that the school is about to hire an aide just for Austin. "Things are falling into place," she says. Although the Lams' experiences with special education services have so far been positive, the school system's special education programs have experienced growing pains in recent years that Pam fears could reduce the quality of services Austin will receive in the future.

> **Most school districts across the country are facing special education staff recruitment challenges.**

Similar to the national trends, Wellesley Public Schools' special education population has increased by about one-third in the last five years. That expansion, combined with increased parental pressure to include severely disabled children in mainstream classes for longer stretches of the school day, have taxed this well-funded school district in the Boston suburbs, especially in terms of staffing. Scrambling to construct its new program—the first and only of its kind in the district—Schofield Elementary hired its new special education teacher, Susan Weiner, with two days to spare. There are four children in Austin's class—three who have cerebral palsy and one who is autistic—all of whom must be accompanied by an aide when in a mainstream classroom. Six-year-old Austin has anthetoid cerebral palsy as well as a hearing impairment and visual difficulties. Austin spends most of his day in a wheelchair and eats through a feeding tube. He needs help with most physical movement, but he can press buttons and activate a joystick.

Although Schofield immediately began searching for more aides, including one for Austin, the process was slow. "The school system was advertising," Weiner says. "But you know what? The help just isn't out there." Wellesley is not the only school system facing staff recruitment challenges; in fact, most school districts across the country are feeling a similar crunch, and Massachusetts recently began an innovative teacher recruitment plan aimed at alleviating the state's impending teacher shortage in such areas as math, science, and special education.

Special education became an explosive political issue in Massachusetts in 2000 when the state decided to lower the bar for required special education services. Massachusetts had held its special education programs to a higher standard than the one that the IDEA mandates by requiring schools to provide special education students with the "maximum feasible education." But as the state's enrollment in special education rose, political pressure mounted to change the laws to ensure that special education services were not being used by students who were perhaps academically behind but did not have an actual disability. In its 2001 budget, the Massachusetts legislature reverted to the federal requirement of providing a "free appropriate public education" (FAPE).

Though her tendency is not to be pushy, Pam is beginning to take pre-emptive actions to make sure Austin receives the most comprehensive services the district can provide. Noting the changes in Massachusetts law and the start-up problems her son's school experienced, Pam recently paid for a new evaluation for Austin by a highly regarded neuropsychologist in the area. "The reason I had the neuropsych exam is so I could use it for leverage to advocate for him in the schools," she explains. "This is a whole new program, and it's a lot of educating for me now and learning how to go about getting services for him in the Wellesley Public Schools." She said she did not want to have Austin evaluated by the school's psychologist because "I don't think she would know how to test him properly."

> *Special education became an explosive political issue in Massachusetts in 2000 when the state decided to lower the bar for required special education services.*

Austin Lam is one of a set of twins. Pam and James were living in Stamford, Connecticut, at the time the twins were born, and Pam had a normal pregnancy with close prenatal care. Ultrasound tests showed two normally developing fetuses. But when her twins were born on July 7, 1994, Austin looked very pale, and his twin brother Garrett was beet red. Tests showed that the two boys had twin-to-twin transfusion syndrome. After 11 days in the hospital on a blood-thinning routine, Garrett, who had received too much red blood in the womb, was ready to go home. But Austin, who had not received enough blood, developed an infection on Day Four and immediately went on a ventilator. He fought through the infection and left the hospital a month later after a blood transfusion, but Austin did not seem to be developing at the same rate as his brother. His joints were very stiff, and he cried constantly.

With Garrett's development as a baseline of sorts, Pam and James became increasingly worried about Austin's developmental delays. When Austin was four months old, they had him evaluated more thoroughly by a neurologist, who said Austin might have cerebral palsy—a catchall term for abnormal brain development. "It was very hard to accept at first after knowing that we had a normal pregnancy," Pam recalls.

Pam says she is fortunate to have had support from family, friends, and hired help since she gave birth to Austin. James's support is largely financial. He now runs his own New York City-based risk-management consulting business and makes a seven-figure income. He spends most weekdays in New York, where the Lams have an apartment, and flies home on the weekends. Pam has a full-time nanny to ease the stress of raising her three boys.

After Austin's preliminary diagnosis, Pam immediately began researching cerebral palsy to decide how best to proceed. Based on the test results, Austin qualified for special education, and a social worker at the hospital told Pam how to enroll Austin in early childhood special education services. During Austin's first year, a special educator came to the Lams' house once every week for an hour to work on basic cognitive development such as spatial relations. And twice a week for an hour, a physical therapist would come to the house to do stretching exercises with Austin. When Austin was one year old, Pam noticed that he still was not responding when she called his name, and she had his hearing tested. The tests showed that Austin could not hear high frequency sounds, and Austin's cognitive development speeded up once he got a hearing aid. He soon responded to his name and learned his family members' names.

When Austin was one-and-a-half years old, the Lams moved from Stamford to Wellesley, and they contacted the special education officials in Wellesley beforehand to ensure a smooth transition. Austin received similar services in Wellesley, and by age three, he was attending a preschool-like early intervention program once a week. At age four, Austin began a daily preschool program at the Concord Area Special Education (CASE) Preschool, a special education cooperative in Bedford for severely disabled children that is funded by 30 neighboring towns. Though Austin rode a bus for 17 miles to school each day, Pam chose the program because she liked both the teachers and the component of the program that integrated Austin into a regular preschool across the hallway for one to four hours each week. Integration was important to her because it was more similar to Austin's life at home with his brothers.

> **Austin's IEP set out clear short-term objectives aimed at finding the best ways for Austin to communicate.**

Pam had her first individualized education program (IEP) meeting in the fall of 1997, at which she met with Austin's teacher at CASE and other school officials to discuss what Austin's educational goals should be and how they planned to meet them. "I was a little nervous going in, but everybody tried to make it pleasant," she said. Pam left the meeting with an IEP that was the envy of several of her friends who also had disabled children. The plan set out clear short-term objectives aimed at finding the best ways for Austin to communicate. Those strategies were to be used to boost specific oral, auditory, motor, and cognitive skills. Most of these skills would be evaluated weekly or monthly. In addition to his three-and-a-half hours a day in the classroom, Austin would receive about 24 hours each week of additional speech and physical therapy.

Because Austin cannot speak, the school's top priority was to find the best way for him to communicate. Within his first year at CASE, Austin mastered "eye-gazing." Shown a few cards or objects representing different choices, Austin will direct his eyes toward his choice and occasionally will reach in that direction. By the time he was five years old, Austin could also use a "head mouse," a device attached to his head that allows him to move a cursor on a computer. Lessons targeted at sequencing or classifying different kinds of words were adapted to Austin's means of communication. Within a couple of years, he was also able to identify numbers. Pam was particularly pleased with his teachers, whom she says took time out to teach her how to reinforce at home what they were teaching Austin at school.

As he was finishing his third year there, Austin was outgrowing CASE. Because Pam and James wanted Austin to attend school in their community, Pam inquired about services for Austin in one of the Wellesley schools. She discovered that Schofield was starting up a program to serve children with multiple disabilities.

Although his IEP says Austin will be in the mainstream kindergarten at Schofield from 8:30 a.m. to 12 p.m. every day, for the first two months of school he averaged three days a week. Pam says Austin had some weeks in which he spent only one day in Razzano's class. One day when Austin was taking part in a dramatic play lesson, which is similar to dress-up, the other special education child in his class had a tantrum. Weiner, the special education teacher who was supporting both students in the mainstream classroom, had to take both children out of the class because there was no one who could attend to Austin. "He started to cry, and my heart just broke," Weiner recalls. Eventually, Austin was able to return to class with Weiner after the other child calmed down. Still, Pam worried that Austin not only was not getting enough time in the mainstream kindergarten classroom but also was lacking a regular schedule, which made it difficult for him to adjust to his new school. He was shuffled at irregular intervals from classes where he had a one-to-one teacher-to-student ratio to classes where he had a 1-to-20 teacher-student ratio.

> *Many of Austin's cognitive delays are a result of his inability to experience incidental learning.*

But Weiner and her staff have gone to great lengths to make Austin feel included. During the morning class routine, Razzano will review the day of the week and the weather outside. While Razzano writes the day of the week on the board, an aide will ask Austin which day of the week it is and show him a couple of cards that read different days so that Austin can eye-gaze to choose the right day. His regular kindergarten class has a music lesson twice each week, and his speech therapist will pre-record the songs for him so that he can "sing" with his classmates.

In the special education classroom, Weiner tries to reinforce the basics. For example, she read her class a Halloween book about Clifford the big red dog and then did reading comprehension exercises with Austin. She asked him whether Clifford was a fire engine or a police car for Halloween, and he directed his eyes toward the picture of the fire engine—the right answer. The head mouse, ordered long ago, recently arrived, and he should now be able to take part in more comprehensive lessons in simple math and reading comprehension with the aid of the computer.

In September 2000, Pam took Austin for a neuropsychological evaluation, which found that Austin is at the developmental level of a 4-year-old. The evaluator said his exact developmental stage is difficult to determine because Austin does not vocalize. Many of his cognitive delays, Pam says, are a result of his inability to experience incidental learning. Whereas his brothers can play in the backyard and learn by experience, Austin needs someone to take him outside and explain to him what he is observing. Pam says this is the main reason why he needs his own aide at school—to interpret the world for Austin.

Much to Pam's consternation, Austin did not have his own aide until the end of his first quarter of kindergarten. Although Pam says she wants to be understanding, as she continues to meet with school officials she sees more value in being the pushy parent. "I think they're very receptive in listening to my needs. But I think it's overwhelming, all the special-needs children they have in the town now. They're not as proactive as they could be," she says. "They're doing what they can do right now, and they have their budgets that they have to stick by. But I think it requires a lot more advocating on the parents' behalf, especially if you have a child that's multi-handicapped."

Pam has often supplemented Austin's education and therapies with new techniques she reads. When Austin was six months old, Pam learned about a treatment called conductive education that aims to build physical and mental independence skills, and she started taking him twice a week for treatments. Those sessions lasted about a year until the Lams moved to Massachusetts, and when Austin was four, Pam had a conductive education specialist live with them for a month to work with Austin. Although "it's not the miracle cure or anything," Pam says, it helped him gain more control over his hands. Two years ago, Pam also began using electrical stimulation therapy with Austin. She went to a private therapist for a few sessions to learn to use the electrical box that she now attaches to Austin's abdomen when he sleeps to increase blood flow to muscles that get little use when he is in his wheelchair. She said within six months, he was rolling over by himself, which in part could be due to his regular development. But she thinks the electrical therapy helped, too.

> **Whereas his brothers can play in the backyard and learn by experience, Austin needs someone to take him outside and explain to him what he is observing.**

Outside of school, Pam and James do their best to give Austin the same kinds of opportunities his brothers have. "As long as you keep networking and resourcing, there's so many things for kids to do," Pam explains. While his brothers spend hours at soccer and tae kwon do practice, or take piano and guitar lessons, Austin is enrolled in music therapy and therapeutic horseback riding. Austin and his 8-year-old brother Brandon are taking an enrichment course together—an archaeology class. And when the family goes on ski vacations, Austin rides in a sit-ski, which is one of his favorite activities because he reaches speeds he never experiences in a wheelchair.

One of the side benefits of having a brother with Austin's needs, Pam says, is that Brandon and Garrett have become very empathetic people at a young age. As the Lams were leaving a playground on the West Side of Central Park in New York on a recent afternoon, they passed a little boy who stopped when he saw Austin in his wheelchair with his feeding tube. "What's wrong with him? What's wrong with him? Why does he have that tube hanging out of him?" he asked. Garrett, a little defensive, took the question in stride. "Nothing's wrong with him. He has a medical feeding," he explained matter-of-factly. "He eats differently than we do."

But when it comes to school, Austin's special education teacher Susan Weiner says, Pam may discover in a few years that Austin is better served in a program exclusively for children with needs like Austin's. Although kindergarten children tend to be curious and open-minded, she noted that as they get older, children tend to choose friends who are more similar to them. And, as she has observed through 30 years of working with special-needs children, some children can get cliquey and even mean. "I think more kids with severe disabilities are being included [in mainstream classrooms]. That's the difference. I think there may be a point down the road where Austin's family might want to reevaluate and consider a type of program where the whole school is set up with communication devices. All the equipment would be in the rooms all the time," Weiner says. "He could be doing what everybody's doing. Everybody's communicating similarly."

Litigation: Winning the Battle, Losing the War

As Kathy Eirschele pulled into a motel parking lot just over the Tennessee border, her tears began to flow uncontrollably. It was the end of Day One of the drive back home from La Crosse, Wisconsin, where she had just moved her son, Nicholas, in with his grandparents. She had to drive alone because her husband, Chuck, could not afford to take time off from work, especially now that they were paying legal bills. But Kathy was convinced that they had made the right decision—one that would allow Nicholas to start the school year in what they hoped would be a safe and emotionally healthy environment.

> *After six years of trying to work with school officials to obtain the proper services for their severely dyslexic son, Nicholas, the Eirscheles felt they had no alternative but to sue the district.*

After six years of trying to work with school officials to obtain the proper services for their severely dyslexic son, Nicholas, the Eirscheles felt they had no alternative but to sue the Craven County Public School District, a rural district on the east coast of North Carolina. In the spring of 1995, Kathy and Chuck met with a well-respected lawyer and a veteran of special education law. The lawyer's $200 an hour advice: "If you have about $140,000 that you really don't know what to do with, you can pursue this. Otherwise, find a good school and put him there because if you get into the legal system, I'll tell you right now, it'll cost you probably somewhere in the neighborhood of $100,000 to get into the court system, and once we get in there, it'll be about another $40,000 before we're done."

Recounting that afternoon, Chuck says the advice dissuaded the Eirscheles for a few months, but when summer came, they couldn't bear to send Nicholas back to a school system they felt would continue to ignore his needs. They hoped that, by taking legal action, they could change the system to force the school district to serve all its special-needs children better. At the next meeting of a local learning disabilities group, Kathy told her story to Stacey Bawtinhimer, a local lawyer who knew special education law, and Bawtinhimer was willing to work for them as long as they kept up with her expenses. They decided to send Nicholas to live with his father's parents to ensure that his education would not be further disrupted by the lawsuit because they had already seen what they believed to be continued harassment of their family by school officials since they had begun to complain about Nicholas' experiences.

But two years later, when the judge ruled in their favor, all the Eirscheles had to show for their efforts was a $13,000 check. The Eirscheles' experiences reflect both the lack of satisfaction many parents of special-needs students derive from taking their school systems to court and the ways in which emotional judgments—on the parts of parents and school officials—can cloud the decisionmaking process and affect the implementation of IEPs.

Kathy first became concerned about Nicholas in 1987. At age four, he was not picking up early reading skills as quickly as their daughter, Sarah, had. After two years in preschool, he still could not remember his letters. When Kathy brought this issue up with his preschool teacher, Kathy was admonished for comparing her children. "I was a young mother, and they knew better than I did, so I just kind of said, well, they're right," said Kathy, who was 29 years old at the time. "So we put him in kindergarten, and he still struggled—same scenario. The teacher also said he's a very bright little boy, but she, too, couldn't explain why he couldn't learn these things."

After an initial protest, Kathy agreed to allow Nicholas to move on to first grade at Havelock Elementary School. But Kathy knew she was in for a difficult year after the first parent conference. She says Nicholas' teacher had only one positive comment—that he was "creative." The teacher often called Kathy to complain about Nicholas' inattentiveness in class. In December, Kathy discovered that in recent weeks Nicholas' desk had been moved out of one of the clusters of four, which were part of the setup of the classroom, to a back corner of the classroom. "Nick was always a very active, curious, inquisitive little boy, and throughout that first half of the year, he became more quiet, more withdrawn," Kathy says. He would often arrive home from school in tears and would complain that the other children were picking on him. And Nicholas was still making no progress in reading.

> The Eirscheles' experiences reflect both the lack of satisfaction many parents of special-needs students derive from taking their school systems to court and the ways in which emotional judgments can cloud the decisionmaking process and affect the implementation of IEPs.

In 1989, Kathy mentioned her frustrations with Nicholas' experiences in first grade to a friend, who asked Kathy if she had tested Nicholas for learning disabilities. Kathy had never heard about learning disabilities, but she wrote a letter to the school asking that Nicholas be tested. The May 1990 test results showed evidence of severe dyslexia. He was almost seven years old and had an IQ of 120. He was reading below a preschool level, but his listening comprehension was at a third-grade level. Angry that her concerns for the last two years had been dismissed, Kathy was relieved that she had discovered the source of the problem but worried about how she could help Nicholas. She said her concerns deepened when she saw what seemed to be a defensive response from Nicholas' teacher: Nicholas failed first grade.

Kathy and Chuck Eirschele went to their first IEP meeting at the end of the school year in May 1990. "They developed an IEP, and I remember at the time I was concerned because it was like a computer print-out, and it didn't look like it was individualized to Nick," she says. "I never really felt comfortable with it. But everybody kept telling us this is the way things are done, so I felt like they know more than I do. Again, I wish I would have had a little more self-confidence back then and trusted my gut feelings because in the end, my gut feelings were right."

Though the IEP slotted Nicholas in a generic "learning disabled" category, Kathy and Chuck signed off on the plan, which set out several objectives, including: "The student will continue to develop a familiarity with books and stories; the student will understand that written language conveys meaning; and the student will understand that own [sic] oral language can be written down and read." A month later, Kathy wrote one of the specialists who had evaluated Nicholas to express her concern that the IEP "seemed pretty generalized and not real [sic] measurable," and she asked for advice about how to proceed. Work with the school, was the specialist's response, says Kathy. Kathy then sought the advice of parent advocate groups, but she says that even parent advocates advised against seeking others to help her plead her case because it might make the school defensive and would work against the family's interests.

> Kathy says that even parent advocates advised against seeking others to help her plead her case because it might make the school defensive and would work against the family's interests.

Perhaps they were right, Kathy thought, as she saw Nicholas' spirits improve during his second year in first grade. His new teacher looked for creative ways to help. She gave him a word jar, which contained the words that Nicholas frequently forgot. As he was writing stories, Nicholas could dip into the jar to search for the word he was trying to recall. This teacher also had a teacher's aide, who was not designated specifically for Nicholas, but who spent a significant portion of time with him. "He was starting to make some progress. His self-esteem improved," Kathy recalls. "I think it was partly the relationship with the teacher in that classroom that made a difference."

Though unable to read, Nicholas moved along to second grade, but the school district was reconfigured, and Nicholas was assigned to Jesse Gerganus Elementary School. The new school was farther from home, and Nicholas was in a class of 30 students. Kathy made an appointment with his new second grade teacher two weeks in advance to discuss Nicholas' needs and had forwarded all the test results to her so that the teacher could review them before the meeting. But when Kathy arrived for her meeting, the teacher had not opened Nicholas' folder. Kathy says the teacher openly admitted to her that she could not take the extra time needed to work with Nicholas.

Told that her only other option for third grade was to put Nicholas in a segregated special education classroom at another school, Kathy placed Nicholas in a special education class at Arthur Edwards Elementary because she believed it would offer him the most specialized attention. Every morning Kathy put Nicholas on the school bus at 6:45. Nicholas would ride the bus to Gerganus, sit in the gym for a half hour until after classes started, and then take another bus to Edwards Elementary. Going home, the district pulled him out of class before school ended to transport him back to Gerganus Elementary, where he would sit in the gym for another half hour until he was put on the second shift of school buses.

Between Nicholas' third and fifth grade years, IEP meetings continued to fuel Kathy and Chuck's frustrations. They not only felt that the blueprints for Nicholas' education were insufficient, but also believed that the plans Nicholas had were not being implemented. Nicholas' IEPs called for him to have a computer keyboard to help him write, but Kathy says no one at his school would teach him to use it. The plan also called for Nicholas' textbooks to be transferred to audio tape so that he would not fall behind in his other subjects while he worked on improving his reading skills. But the Eirscheles say that the school often failed to follow through. Chuck complained of this stonewalling to the district superintendent. "Sometimes [district officials] said, 'we don't know which [textbooks] we're going to use.' Other times it was, 'well, we'll get back with you,' and they just never would," he says. "Of course, when you follow up they put you on hold and another day or another week passes, and our big concern was the time factor."

The Eirscheles would spend three or four hours each night doing homework with Nicholas, and they paid for special summer school classes after Nicholas' second and third grade years. Chuck rearranged his work schedule so he could take Nicholas to summer classes in Greenville, which was one-and-a-half hours from their home. He would work from 4 p.m. to 2 a.m., go home to sleep for a few hours, get up and drive Nicholas to Greenville, sleep for three hours in the car, drive Nicholas home, and go to work.

Though the Eirscheles still had complaints about the school's implementation of Nicholas' IEP, his fourth grade year was one of his best, Kathy says, because his special education teacher and his mainstream teacher, whom he saw for one period a day, were communicating well. His special education teacher went out of her way to help Nicholas. She even recorded an audio tape of one textbook for him when the school wouldn't. But when Nicholas had his year-end evaluation, his reading level was still below the first percentile. "Even though they were working together, something wasn't right, or we'd be narrowing that gap. We weren't qualified or smart enough to know what he needed," Kathy said. "I thought, why is he falling farther behind? Why is he continuing to lose ground? I guess we felt despair, just in despair because, like, what more can we do?"

> Said Kathy, "I thought, why is [Nicholas] falling farther behind? Why is he continuing to lose ground? I guess we felt despair, just in despair because, like, what more can we do?"

As Nicholas continued through fifth grade, the gap between his IQ and his reading level remained wide, and the Eirscheles consulted two independent evaluators who recommended that Nicholas receive intensive remedial reading help. But at the IEP meeting at the end of Nicholas' fifth grade year, the Eirscheles say the school refused to incorporate remedial reading into the plan, and the Eirscheles questioned whether the school could provide such services with its current staff because no teacher was trained in phonics reading instruction. "During that time, I really lost faith in the system," Chuck says, characterizing the school's attitude as one that just wanted to pass a child like Nicholas along until he was out of the school and became someone else's problem. "No matter what we did or where we went, there was always a hurdle. We did not want to, but we finally got to that point—and we didn't want to do it—where our only option was litigation."

The Eirscheles decided to send Nicholas to live with his grandparents in La Crosse because it seemed to them to be the safest and most affordable option. Kathy feared that Nicholas would face harassment at school. She says that once she began seeking legal counsel and advice from people outside the school system, Nicholas' teachers began "punishing" him for acting out by refusing to read his tests to him, even though that help was mandated in his IEP. But a school spokesperson denied the charges, saying, "The teachers made special efforts to work with [Kathy] and with Nick. There is reason to expect that especially during litigation they would be particularly careful to respond to Nick's needs."

In what Kathy sees as another attempt at harassment, the school also alleged that Kathy physically abused Nicholas. But when the department of social services investigated, they found no evidence of abuse. The charges were dropped.

Such practices, says lawyer Bawtinhimer, are common in rural North Carolina. "I'm seeing it more now in the more rural counties in North Carolina," she said. "What it does is instantly discredit a family."

But the effects were grave. The allegations prompted Kathy to attempt suicide. "I just couldn't cope anymore," she says. "I felt like I'd done the best I could, and I couldn't help my child. Maybe he'd be better off without me. Maybe my husband could do better." A district spokesperson pointed to the emotional fallout at the end of Nicholas' fifth grade year as one of the main forces preventing the Eirscheles and the school district from working out the dispute on their own. "I think a lot of this got derailed," the spokesperson said. "It was not about education; it was about Kathy feeling wrongly accused."

> *Once Kathy began seeking legal counsel and advice from people outside the school system, she says Nicholas' teachers began "punishing" him for acting out by refusing to read his tests to him, even though that help was mandated in his IEP.*

In La Crosse, Nicholas was assigned to a regular class in the morning, was pulled out for extra help with a special education teacher, and spent his afternoons at a reading clinic. The teachers at Longfellow Middle School communicated with each other, and the school provided him with the resources that the Eirscheles requested, such as after-school reading remediation. He began to make gains slowly and moved from a second grade to a third grade level in reading. "No, it was not exactly what he needed, but it was better than what he'd had in the past," Kathy said. "All in all, it was a good experience, and plus, he was real happy to be in with regular kids."

Nicholas came home to North Carolina after sixth grade while the lawyers were still investigating and deposing. Advised by Bawtinhimer to give Craven County Schools a second chance because it would strengthen their case, the Eirscheles placed Nicholas in seventh grade back in the Craven County school system. The school offered a detailed IEP that included nine weeks of in-class observation by a respected specialist who would then make further recommendations.

Ann Majestic, the lawyer representing Craven County Schools, said that because "no one seemed to really unlock what was going to help Nick," the child's lack of progress was not necessarily the school's fault, and it made the most sense to put him under observation for nine weeks to determine what additional measures should be taken.

But after three weeks, the Eirscheles pulled Nicholas out because they did not feel that Nicholas's teachers were properly trained, and the teachers in La Crosse had advised against his returning to Craven County. "I think it was an emotional decision on their part. I think it was an incorrect position," said Bawtinhimer, who said the Eirscheles did not give the school enough time to show whether or not it would improve its services for Nicholas. "That happens a lot."

After two years of litigation, the judge issued a ruling in August 1997. He awarded the Eirscheles $13,000 for the money they spent to send Nicholas to Wisconsin for sixth grade, and the school was directed to pay the family's legal fees. North Carolina's law places a 60-day statute of limitations on claims of negligence in special education, and the Eirscheles could only include costs that dated back 60 days from the time they filed suit. The judge ruled that the Eirscheles did not give the school district enough time to show they could rectify the situation when Nicholas was in seventh grade, and they therefore were not compensated for expenses during Nicholas's second year in Wisconsin. The judge ordered some changes to Nicholas's IEP for eighth grade, and the case was closed.

> The Eirscheles' case did set a precedent for granting payments to families who sent their special education child to another public school system.

Unwilling to endure further negotiations with Craven County Schools, they decided to make the financial sacrifice they had hoped to avoid and sent Nicholas to Trident Academy, a private school in Mount Pleasant, South Carolina, that specializes in children with learning disabilities. They felt that Trident was the school best equipped to get Nicholas up to speed so that by the time he graduated from high school he would be prepared to enter the workforce. The Eirscheles filed suit again for reimbursement of tuition at Trident, but the suit was thrown out early in the process for lack of evidence.

"The system is so resistant to helping out these children who need this type of help. I don't know why it is. For the amount of money the school system spends fighting this it seems more economically feasible to just provide the services," says Chuck. "I would think you would not have to go to the legal system to get a free education for your child in the United States of America. It's very, very disheartening. I would not recommend it to anyone."

The Eirscheles' case did set a precedent for granting payments to families who sent their special education child to another public school system. "They didn't appreciate the legal precedent they set because it was a hollow victory," Bawtinhimer said. "Like in any domestic case, nobody wins in these cases." Majestic, the school district's lawyer, agreed. "I think the process here of due process is long and costly and, in general, creates hard feelings," she said. "Nobody wins."

Nicholas, now 17 and a high school junior, has made significant progress in his four years at Trident. A recent assessment of his growth between the beginning of eighth grade and the end of tenth grade found that his vocabulary skills moved from a sixth-grade level to a post-high school level. For reading, he jumped from between a third- and fourth-grade level to an early tenth-grade level. In spelling, he went from just above a third-grade level to just above a sixth-grade level. Rebecca Felton, an adjunct professor at Simmons College in Boston who assessed Nicholas and who was a witness for the Eirscheles in their court case, said she would expect Nicholas to continue to have significant difficulty with spelling because that is the area affected most by his dyslexia. "My prediction would be that if Nick had not received direct intensive instruction, his reading and spelling skills would not have improved, certainly not to this dramatic degree," said Felton.

But paving the road to Trident has come at a high cost to the family. With a combined income of $100,000 a year, they have a second mortgage on their house and are about $40,000 in debt with no savings. During the litigation, Kathy became depressed again, was hospitalized, and was demoted at work for poor performance. Chuck is still working night shifts six and seven days a week because the money is better. Their daughter, Sarah, dropped out of the College of Charleston this year to attend the local community college because her family could not afford private tuition. She hopes to work and save up enough to pay the tuition herself next year. Prior to the litigation, the Eirscheles had about $40,000 in the bank.

> The school district's lawyer said, "I think the process here of due process is long and costly and, in general, creates hard feelings. Nobody wins."

"I'm just thankful we're able to do what we can," Kathy says with a sigh at the end of a three-hour interview. "But I wish the system would change because, you know what, even when you win, you don't win. What Nick needed was to learn how to read and write."

Filling in the Cracks in an Urban Education System

When they reached the reptile section at the National Zoo in Washington, D.C., Lita Trejo stopped and asked her new foster son, Christian, to read the plaque in front of one of the many lizards on display.

"I don't want to read," Christian told her.

Rather than inciting a fight, Lita slowly read the sign to him and followed each word with her finger. She stopped and encouraged him to take over. He got stuck on the first word: The.

"Th, th, th," he stuttered.

Realizing that 12-year-old Christian's unwillingness to read might be a symptom of a deeper problem, Lita read the rest of the sign to him and continued their tour of the zoo. Later that weekend, Lita found a seventh-grade-level book that had belonged to her grown son, sat down with Christian, and asked him to read it. He struggled and stumbled, and she then found a fifth-grade-level book, which still gave him considerable trouble. Lita rummaged through a storage closet and found "The Best Do-It-Yourself Book Ever," which was pegged at a first-grade level. Christian was able to read a few of the words, but even simple words like "barn," "cow," and "hat" were a challenge.

It was July 1999, and Christian would not start school again for two months. Lita and Christian read together every day for half an hour, and by the end of the month, they had finished the book and moved on to another. Concerned about Christian's inability to read when he would enter seventh grade at MacFarland Middle School, Lita contacted Christian's social worker, Berrie Lynn Tapia, and was told that a court-appointed lawyer, Myrna Fawcett, had been working to get Christian assigned to special education.

In fact, Fawcett had been actively pursuing the issue for the previous year-and-a-half with the District of Columbia Public Schools, but the district had failed repeatedly to deliver on its promises to evaluate Christian. When he began seventh grade in September, Christian, who speaks more English than Spanish, was placed in several English as a Second Language (ESL) classes in lieu of granting him a special education evaluation. "They were putting him in bilingual programs," Fawcett said. "These were not his issues. They were trying at least to do something to help him, but it wasn't really an appropriate placement for him." It wasn't until Fawcett threatened a court battle later that fall that the district granted Christian an evaluation, which landed him in special education.

Christian's experiences in the D.C. Public School system, Lita says, reflect an effort to use special education to make up for what schools had not provided Christian for seven years. "I'm not an expert on this, but I think he wasn't taught, and now that he's older, it's getting harder" to teach him to read, she says. "I told them that this is not that he has learning disabilities; it's that he's not been exposed to reading." His tutor, Leslie Charles, also sees special education as making up for lost education time for Christian. "I think it's more the home life he comes from that didn't allow him to be available for learning. And maybe some of the schools he went to, maybe the teachers just didn't have the gumption, the oomph to really dig in and work with him."

> **It wasn't until Fawcett threatened a court battle later that fall that the district granted Christian an evaluation, which landed him in special education.**

Now 13 years old, Christian, who was born in Washington, has been in and out of foster care since he was 5 years old. His parents immigrated together from El Salvador to the United States about 20 years ago but have since divorced. The youngest of 11 children, he left the foster care system to live with his father at age nine and then moved back in with his mother two years later when his father had a stroke. A judge placed Christian back in the foster care system a year later because Christian's mother, a housekeeper, was not home enough to keep track of her children. Christian was spending too much time on the streets with his older siblings who were involved in drugs. Christian's sister had been living with Lita and Freddie Trejo for two weeks, and Christian told Lita he wanted to live with her "because you eat together."

The quest for Christian's supplemental educational services had begun three years earlier. In May 1996, Christian's third-grade teacher referred him for a special education evaluation because he was reading at a kindergarten level, and his inability to read was inhibiting performance in other areas. The following month, Christian's mother signed a letter requesting an evaluation. "The school system did formally make the referral, and apparently nothing happened. The school didn't follow up," said Fawcett, who began representing Christian in 1998. Christian's reading skills showed little improvement in fourth grade, where he finished the year earning D's in language and spelling.

In February 1998, Fawcett filed a hearing request on behalf of Christian's father to press the district to evaluate Christian. She filed another in March. And in May, the school district agreed to a settlement in which the D.C. Public Schools acknowledged that it had failed to comply with providing Christian with a "free appropriate public education" as defined by the IDEA. The remedy was to conduct assessments by mid-June. Still, by the end of the summer, the district had not assessed Christian.

In November 1998, Fawcett commissioned private evaluations at the Hospital for Sick Children, which assigned him an IQ of 87. The speech and language tests found a "mild receptive language delay" that was "within normal limits" and recommended that Christian be re-evaluated in a year. But an evaluation of his reading and math skills found significant delays and said he "would benefit from special education." The reviewers recommended that Christian be placed in a class with a small student-teacher ratio, receive additional time to complete tests, and be given tests orally whenever possible. There was still no action from the D.C. Public Schools.

> *Fawcett wrote, "It has now been over two years since Christian was referred for testing, and he has yet to receive an evaluation or a placement, so DCPS is out of compliance...."*

Fawcett resumed the pursuit of services for Christian in January 1999 with a letter to the student hearing office at the D.C. Public Schools that detailed past attempts to obtain a formal evaluation for Christian. "It has now been over two years since Christian was referred for testing, and he has yet to receive an evaluation or a placement, so DCPS is out of compliance, and Christian has been denied FAPE (a free, appropriate public education)," she wrote. "Christian must receive complete evaluations and an eligibility meeting immediately. If he is found eligible for services, a notice of placement must be issued. Due to the failure to evaluate and comply with the settlement agreement in a timely fashion, and well over two years of waiting for placement, we are seeking for compensatory services."

She filed additional hearing requests in March and June 1999. In August, the school system again agreed to a settlement that promised to evaluate Christian for special education eligibility. But by October 1999, the district still had not evaluated Christian, and his skills remained low in all areas. His spring 1999 Stanford-9 standardized test scores placed him in the "below basic" achievement level in reading, vocabulary, math, and problem-solving. Below basic is defined "as little or no mastery of fundamental knowledge or skills."

Christian came to live with the Trejo family in June 1999. When Christian returned to MacFarland Middle School, Lita quickly discovered how Christian had reached seventh grade without learning to read. He would act out when called upon to read in class, and his teacher would send him out of the classroom instead of forcing him to read aloud. The school system continued to pass him along. Christian's first-quarter grades in seventh grade were mostly C's.

A class action lawsuit had been (and continues to be) pending in federal court since 1995 against the D.C. Public Schools for lack of compliance with its responsibility to provide a FAPE to several students who had been recommended for special education evaluations. In October, Fawcett included Christian in the class action suit. "Until I filed the court proceeding, they never sat down and looked at what he needed," Fawcett said. "In October, his case pushed forward rather quickly."

The federal judge granted Fawcett a mediator, and by November, Fawcett was granted an IEP meeting for Christian. The district's evaluation, which supplemented the private one from the previous year, placed Christian between a second- and third-grade level in reading comprehension; at nearly a second-grade level in spelling and vocabulary; at a third-grade level in writing; and at about a fourth-grade level in math.

Lita, several school officials, the evaluator, Fawcett and Tapia (Christian's social worker) met later that month to discuss Christian's IEP. Lita pushed for special education services in both English and math so that Christian could have tutoring in both. Initially promising to keep Christian in mainstream classes, the school cobbled together a new schedule including special education classes for English and math and ESL classes for science and social studies. Still bothered that Christian was continuing to be placed in ESL classes although language fluency was not a problem, Lita says that, given Christian's reading level, the ESL classes might be a better place for him than the regular classes. Upon hearing that he would be placed in special education, Christian burst into tears. "He kept saying, 'Oh, they're going to put me in the special ed because I'm stupid, because I'm crazy,'" Lita recalls.

> **A class action lawsuit had been pending in federal court since 1995 against the D.C. Public Schools for lack of compliance with its responsibility to provide a FAPE to several students.**

The IEP listed several "short-term objectives" within the categories of reading comprehension, writing, spelling and vocabulary, and math, but it did not set out a specific time frame for attainment of proficiency. Instead, the plan stated that his skills would be documented every nine weeks. "I felt that they wanted to just provide something for him but not base it on his needs. They wanted to say, 'okay, okay we'll give him this.' You know, like, 'shut your mouth, and we'll do this,'" Lita says. "They said that they did the evaluation, and he wasn't doing too bad. They even mentioned that his reading wasn't too bad. So I told them, 'What do you mean it isn't too bad? He's twelve. He's not six. He's not seven. He's reading at the level of first grade.'"

In December, Christian began his tutoring sessions with Leslie Charles, a speech and language pathologist with D.C. Public Schools. Though tests had shown Christian's problems to be in the areas of reading and math, not speech and language, Christian was referred to Charles for work with speech and language deficiencies. At their first meeting, she began assessing his skills: Could he categorize words, identifying, for example, those that described different kinds of foods? Could he sequence events? Could he match a picture with the situation described to him?

To Charles' surprise, he performed well on these diagnostic tests. "I didn't understand why [he was referred for speech] because his speech and language were just exceptional, and he's bilingual." But as they began reading and math exercises, Christian's deficiencies became clear. He had trouble sounding out words, and he did not know his times tables. She adapted her program to focus on reading and math skills. They began a reading program that took a more kinesthetic approach to reading, and Christian began learning tricks to help him memorize his times tables. They met for an hour three times each week, and each time an eager Christian would arrive with his backpack replete with pencils, notepaper, and photocopies of assignments when he had them—the school was not using textbooks. Almost immediately, Christian's attitude changed, and he ended his attempts to get sent to the principal's office every time he was asked to read aloud in class.

After his tutorial sessions with Charles, Lita read with him at home for another half-hour. At first, Christian would protest that Lita was asking too much of him, to which she responded, "It's never too much." But within a few months, Christian was voluntarily reading street signs to Lita when they rode in the car together. He talked about wanting to teach his mother to read, and he would often come home and tell Lita about what he had learned in class that day, especially in his science class. Lita tried to keep the momentum going by taking Christian on field trips that supplemented his school lessons. One night, they went to a local nature center to look at the moon.

> *Christian's IEP listed several "short-term objectives" within the categories of reading comprehension, writing, spelling and vocabulary, and math, but it did not set out a specific time frame for attainment of proficiency.*

In May 1999, Charles was reading the newspaper while she waited for Christian to arrive, and when Christian walked into the room, he told her, "Put the paper down, Ms. Charles. We have work to do." Throughout the second half of seventh grade, Charles says Christian became an increasingly eager worker, and she's been most impressed with Christian's recent focus on the future. He's showing a growing interest in college and jobs he might pursue afterwards. Right now, he wants to design cars. "If he has the backing, if he has people working with him, he's going to make it," Charles predicts.

At MacFarland, clerical errors and misinformed teachers are making things difficult for Christian. Christian's seventh-grade year should have ended far better than it began in terms of class performance. Christian regularly got A's and B's on homework assignments in his special education classes, but at the end of the school year, Christian was assigned C's in his special education math and reading classes. When Lita questioned these grades, she was told by both teachers that district policy states the maximum grade that can be given in a special education class is a C. Devonya Smith, a district spokeswoman, says that the district has no such policy, and that such a policy would be a violation of the rights of special education children.

Lita took this issue to Principal Antonia Peters, who, in a recent interview, struggled to explain why Christian had been assigned C's when he had been doing A and B work in class. Peters initially said that she did "not recall a conversation with [Lita] about Christian's grades" in June 2000, explaining that she was on leave from the school from December 1999 to April 2000. But in her next sentence, she began to recall the discussion. "I told [Lita] that the teachers were to give him the grades that he earned," Peters said. "The teacher that gave the final grade thought the highest grade she could give was a C." But when Lita asked for a copy of Christian's grades in fall 2000, the school took weeks to produce Christian's year-end grade report from seventh grade, and they were the same grades that Christian had been given in June. Only with further prodding did the school correct the grades two months later.

Although Christian is working hard and his grades seem to be improving in his special education classes, it's still not yet clear that his skills have. The most recent evaluation on record as of November 2000 (in a social work file that is missing many key pieces of information such as recent grade reports) was conducted in April 2000, and it found essentially no change in his grade-level abilities. Still, in her progress report, Charles wrote "Christian's reading comprehension level is very good." She says in her day-to-day work with Christian, he has mastered several lists of vocabulary words. Asked about Christian's grade-level skills, Charles said, "I don't know how much his reading level has gone up. I don't know how much his math level has gone up. All I know is he's trying hard, and he's doing well." The biggest change she has observed is in his attitude.

Although Lita believes Christian is benefiting from the tutoring he receives through special education, she says the main benefit is the remedial reading, which compensates not only for

> **Although Christian is working hard and his grades seem to be improving in his special education classes, it's still not yet clear that his skills have.**

what Christian has missed in past years but also for what he is not getting in class right now. In addition to the unresolved grade report issues, Lita complained of continuing difficulties in communicating with the school.

Lita visited MacFarland Middle School in September 2000 for parent-teacher conferences, and went to see the first teacher listed on the schedule the school gave her. It took 10 minutes for the teacher to admit that she did not know who Christian was; after a few more questions, Lita discovered that Christian was not in that class. Lita marched back to the office to track down Christian's English teacher and was told that Christian's teacher had not shown up. Neither had several other teachers. That evening, she met with only three of Christian's six teachers—the ones who had made the time to come.

This year, Christian is enrolled in no special education classes, though he still receives tutoring. He is instead enrolled in ESL versions of math, science and social studies. While Lita said it seems strange that ESL has again supplanted special education classes in Christian's schedule, her tendency has been to work with what she has rather than to fight the system. Regardless of her difficulties with the school, Lita said she is pleased that Christian has textbooks this year because it has given her more material with which to help Christian at home. She says Christian's homework assignment book, which she has to sign each night, usually reads "no homework," but Lita has taken to working with Christian through his textbooks chapter by chapter at home. Asked if she thinks Christian is learning anything in his classes at school, Lita said, "Not from the school, but at least [his classes] go in order with the book, and I can help him with the book."

Though impressed with what she sees as Christian's improvement in school, Charles acknowledges that Christian is receiving very little homework from his teachers at MacFarland. In addition to her own reading drills, Charles is reading the Harry Potter book series with

Christian as a substitute for the homework he is not receiving. "What [homework] he gets is not really challenging. I think that might be the school's fault. He's not in the top school in the city. He doesn't get enough. He's not challenged."

Compensating for Bad Parenting

When Alice Spencer asked her daughter, Kiyana, to come with her to her IEP meeting, Kiyana's immediate response was, "Am I in trouble?" Although Kiyana had been in special education classes since the age of nine, this was her first IEP meeting. Having moved up the special education learning curve over the past six years, Alice had made a practice of including her children who qualify for special education in such meetings. But Kiyana was new to the family. At age 13, she had just become Alice and David Spencer's eighth adopted child.

> *Christian's homework assignment book, which she has to sign each night, usually reads "no homework."*

Alice said that first meeting in fall 1998 at Watson Jr. High School in Colorado Springs set the tone for what life would be like in the Spencer household. "It was a forum for her to say whatever she needs to say, but here was a chance to say, 'guess what, everybody's talking, and they're talking about you,'" Alice explains. "And we can help you or we can hurt you, in some respect, with your grades, but it's going to be up to you."

To Kiyana, the forum resembled more of an inquisition, and she burst into tears more than once as the school officials and Alice fired questions large and small: "Why didn't you turn in your homework? What do you see as barriers to your learning? What is the matter in your history class; this is the only class you're failing?"

Kiyana first offered excuses and then gave in as her teachers and her mother traded stories about her. She had told one teacher that she had no notebook paper at home. She had told another that her mother was out of town and could not be contacted. After the meeting, Alice said, Kiyana knew that her mother was going to talk with her teachers and that there "was no way she could wiggle through that. She knew what the expectations were."

At that meeting, the expectations for Kiyana's behavior were made clear. The IEP, which Kiyana signed along with the others present at the meeting, stated that she would improve her grammar and spelling to 90 percent accuracy. She would have an assignment notebook, signed by her mother and her teachers every day, and would turn in her homework 90 percent of the time. She was assigned to lower-level math and English classes. If she did not turn in her homework, as she was known to do, the teacher was to call Alice immediately. If she began chattering during class, Mom would hear about that as well. If she didn't come to class on time, Alice would get a call. "That was waaaaaay out in left field for her," Alice recalls. "She didn't like it."

Though she is now balancing parenting with a full-time job, Alice has taken on her responsibility for reinforcing those expectations with a military-like zeal. When she came to Alice, Kiyana had been juggled around the foster care system for the past two years and had lived with an abusive father between the ages of nine and eleven. She had been living with her father because her mother, who was never legally married to her father, was abusing drugs and alcohol and couldn't raise her eight children. When she was placed in foster care, Kiyana was diagnosed with post-traumatic stress disorder that stemmed from abandonment by and abuse—physically and possibly sexually—from her parents. Such deep emotional wounds take years to heal. And though Kiyana has lived with the Spencers for the last two years, Alice says she is "a work in progress."

The Spencers, motivated by religious faith and earlier experiences as foster parents for black children from broken homes, now have 11 children—10 of them are adopted; 6 of the adopted children qualify for special education. Most of their children come from abusive or neglectful backgrounds, and many were born addicted to drugs or alcohol. Alice and her husband, David, collectively make about $50,000 a year. Alice is an adoptive parent advocate at Pike's Peak Mental Health, and David is a bus driver for the local bus system. They currently live in a middle-class neighborhood in southeast Colorado Springs, but until three years ago, the Spencers lived in a working-poor neighborhood, Pike's Peak Park.

> *In Kiyana's case, special education is largely being used to make up for the failings of her biological parents and the inability of public social services to subsequently guide her through school.*

In Kiyana's case, special education is largely being used to make up for the failings of her biological parents and the inability of public social services to subsequently guide her through school. Like several of Alice's adopted children, Kiyana's disabilities fall into the "social-emotional" category, which Alice says is more a product of dysfunctional parenting than a biological disability. Kiyana has shown at times that she can earn B's and C's in class, but her work is inconsistent. For Kiyana, special education has provided an educational safety net to catch her when she begins to fall academically, and sometimes the safety net breaks. "If there had been follow-through in the beginning, she would not be a special ed kid. I have no question in my mind," Alice says. The foster care system "was not designed to raise children, but this is where we are."

Kiyana's high school counselor, Jan Schuetz, agrees. "I think that's true about a lot of kids that end up with special services of some sort. We've known for a long time we are what we are by 5 years old," she said. "You're behind the rest of your life until something happens to catch you up. And for many of these kids, the best way to catch them up, educationally anyway, is through special education."

When she decided to adopt Kiyana, Alice visited Timberview Middle School, Kiyana's previous school, to speak with her teachers. She says the teachers told her that Kiyana was usually prepared for class, but her behavior would deteriorate when she socialized with troublemakers. As she left the school, Alice's verdict was that Kiyana's teachers never pushed her to meet their academic expectations because they were not sure how long a foster child would remain at the school. The teachers told Alice that Kiyana had been showing improvement. "Up to that point, a great job was [when] she brought her grade from an F to a D, and no one at home was reinforcing that that's not acceptable," Alice recalls. "I said, 'No, you're not. I need a C, B, or an A. I don't know what a D and an F is.'"

Jarred into good behavior for a few months after her first IEP meeting at Watson Jr. High, Kiyana brought her grades up to a C average. But as she worked through the second quarter of eighth grade, Kiyana began to wiggle out of the demands set in her IEP. A few months after the IEP meeting with Kiyana, Alice stopped by Watson to drop off some lunch money for one of her other children. On her way to the office, Alice passed Kiyana in the hallway and noticed that her daughter was wearing an outfit much tighter than the clothing she had worn out of the house that morning, and her hair was combed differently, too. Alice, who wasn't working at the time, stopped her daughter and said, "I think I'm going to hang with you today." They went from history to math to language arts together, and in every class Kiyana raised her hand and kept social chatter to a minimum. In the days after Alice's day-in-the-life experiment, Kiyana's teachers called Alice to say they had never seen Kiyana work so hard and participate so much in class. "She stayed on target with her work for awhile there," Alice says.

> *Like several of Alice's adopted children, Kiyana's disabilities fall into the "social-emotional" category.*

But Kiyana's problem has never been doing her assignments well sometimes; it has been doing all her work all the time. By the end of the second quarter, she was no longer bringing her homework assignment book home regularly and offered excuses, such as "I forgot it at school." Her grades fell to only a couple of C's with mostly D's and a few F's. Alice asked Kiyana's teachers to start writing short weekly progress reports so she could monitor her daughter more closely.

By the end of eighth grade, Alice had added more regular assignments to Kiyana's load. She would bring books home from the library once a month and ask Kiyana to read them and write a book report, and she asked Kiyana to write a few personal essays on such topics as "How do I feel about going to high school?" By the end of the eighth grade, Kiyana had shifted from turning in about half her homework assignments and bringing home mostly D and F grades to turning in about 80 percent of her homework and earning B's and C's.

Freshman year at Widefield High School started out well. Kiyana seemed to maintain the momentum from the end of her eighth grade year through the first semester of high school. Her IEP was similar to the previous year's, but she spent the first period of each day in the resource room with teachers who would check her homework assignment book and help her with unfinished homework. But in the second semester, boys entered the picture. Alice's rule was no dating until age 16, but Alice came upon pictures in Kiyana's room of her daughter wearing revealing blouses and short shorts, and she was with various boys. "A lot of it was her mentality from being in foster care," Alice explains. "In her mind, she was woman enough to do it. She could handle it. She wasn't going to get pregnant."

Throughout Kiyana's freshman year, Alice was called for teacher meetings more regularly. Kiyana's work would improve right after the meetings, but then she would slip back into the pattern of not turning in homework and making excuses. Alice would respond by restricting

Kiyana's freedom—for example, phone calls, social time. But despite Alice's and her teachers' efforts, Kiyana's grades slipped to a D average, and she finished freshman year with one C, three D's and three F's. Still, she had enough credits to become a sophomore.

Now with only one F on her report card for the first quarter of her sophomore year, counselor Schuetz says Kiyana has shown improvement. But even with weekly progress reports, Kiyana still tends not to turn in her homework. "Teachers now say to her, as well as to me, that she still isn't doing her best," Schuetz says. "That's when we bring it back on to her and say, 'Kiyana, what does this [behavior] mean?' Make her accountable—responsible for her own learning."

Alice's parent-intensive approach toward Kiyana's special education programs is, in a way, a culminating experience after attending countless IEP meetings over the last six years for her six children in special education. Asked how her approach to developing academic plans for her special education children has changed, Alice laughs, "I haven't stood on a desk for awhile." She says for a long time, her approach was "always angry," which she attributes in part to her own inflexibility and in part to what she perceived as economic, and possibly racial, biases from school officials.

> **Alice's parent-intensive approach toward Kiyana's special education programs is, in a way, a culminating experience after attending countless IEP meetings over the last six years for her six children in special education.**

Her first child who needed special education was Christopher, whom the Spencers adopted at six months old and is now nine years old. She said her initial instinct was to let the education experts—the school officials—make the judgments because they knew more than she did about teaching and learning. She can't say much beyond "I was there" when describing her first IEP meeting with Christopher in 1994 as they prepared for Head Start. Alice says there were a few early IEP meetings she did not attend at all because the school would mail her a notice of an upcoming meeting date and not follow up with phone calls. Sometimes she would not receive the notice in the mail, and the school would meet without her. After a few of these missed meetings, she began to make her voice known at the school. "I was ignorant," she says in retrospect. "That was my fault. I would sign off on stuff, and it was like, okay, the school knows what they're doing, and they'll do right by me and my child."

Alice says her initial encounters with school officials regarding special education for Christopher, who was born addicted to drugs and has cerebral palsy, were often judgmental of her as a parent and lacked respect. When she first enrolled Christopher in kindergarten at Centennial Elementary, she was called into school because Christopher was showing behavior problems and wasn't making academic progress. Alice explained that she was trying to work with Christopher on his behavior but that it was a challenge given his background. "I remember very clearly the principal saying to me, 'That's your problem. You chose to adopt him,' " Alice says. "I was so hurt, I couldn't say anything else....I felt this need to explain that I didn't do it to him. I didn't use drugs. It's not my fault that he's this way, and I'm really trying to work with you all and him and nobody's helping me."

Alice tried to find a voice. In 1995, she talked to other parents at Christopher's school and learned about the PEAK Parent Center, a local resource center for parents of children with special needs, where she took one of their parent-training classes. The classes taught her, among other things, that she should have received a parent handbook from her school. She began asking more questions, and she says she forced them to speak "in plain English."

But Alice's voice was too strong. She swung from following school officials to lecturing them. When called into school on a teacher's complaint that Christopher was sucking his fingers so much that they developed an odor and that other children and his teacher did not like him touching them, Alice stormed into Centennial Elementary and began shouting at his teacher: "Do you know anything about a kid born with drugs and alcohol [in his system]? I told you all what kind of kid he was and what his comforts are. You all are coming to me with things like this, and I don't care. Was it preventing him from learning? If I have to do everything for you, then you don't need your check. It's really that simple."

> **Alice still worries about how and why children are assigned to special education.**

By the following year, she had had one too many run-ins with Debbie Wynn, the new principal at Centennial Elementary. And Wynn took the time to calm Alice down and explain to her that, although some of her complaints might be valid, Alice was losing credibility with the school because she was being too confrontational, and that rarely was it the case that a given problem was entirely the school's fault. "I think she kind of laid the foundation for me to think differently and to feel differently," Alice says.

Wynn suggested to Alice that she join several district and school committees. Soon Alice joined the district's Special Education Accountability Committee. She also served on the District Accountability Committee and the Building Advisory Accountability Committees at two of her children's schools. Alice felt more comfortable with Centennial Elementary as she helped make decisions about textbooks, school-parent relations, and graduation requirements. "If there were problems, she was just comfortable calling me about it. We immediately established a good deal of rapport," says Larry Sargent, who was director of special education when Alice was in his school district. "Instead of being adversarial, we focused on problem-solving."

But Alice still worries about how and why children are assigned to special education. Although she believes that children with troubled upbringings like Kiyana are better served within the special education system than outside of it, she wonders why there appears to be a disproportionate number of black and Hispanic children in special education. She says part of what she sees as overrepresentation is the result of teaching techniques that assume all children learn the same way. "It may not be because they're dumb or don't catch on to what you have going on, but kids nowadays, I don't feel that you can teach them all the same way," she said, adding that Kiyana and many of her other children learn more by doing than by seeing or hearing.

Sargent, a former inner-city school principal, agrees. "She's got an issue there that has some validity to it," he says. "There is an issue about some differences in terms of behavioral styles of kids that could lead to some over-identification. The African-American kids tend to be more vocal....I think it's truly a cultural thing because I've had students from Africa who were different." Alice also described times in which she felt as if school officials were talking down to her either because she was in a lower socioeconomic group or because she was black. "You sit in an IEP, and they're saying, 'Well, do you have books at home that they can read?'" she recalls with an uneasy laugh. "Why are you asking a question like that?"

And Alice has fielded other questions: Are there books at home that are appropriate for them to read? "What kind of books do you think I got at home?" she remembers thinking. "You know, uh, *Playboy*? Gosh, we got a Bible even. We got that. They could probably pull out a few words there." She says she has not heard those kinds of comments in recent years. As she educated herself about the special education laws and services available, she earned the respect of school officials.

> **These four case studies highlight the influence of income; how schools are defining disabilities; and how parents' and schools' attitudes affect the process.**

But Alice is discovering that attentive parenting and IEPs cannot work miracles. A few weeks after Kiyana's freshman year ended, Alice learned that her daughter was six weeks pregnant, and the baby had been conceived at school.

This year, Kiyana's IEP remains the same, but both Alice and Kiyana's teachers are taking a tough-love approach. "I'm allowing her to meet her natural consequences. If she fails, she fails," Alice says. "At her age, no one should be saying to her you need to do your homework and turn it in; you need to slow down a little bit when you're writing; you need to become a better speller; you need to get to class on time."

Special Education: Stretched Too Thin?

Special education plays many different roles in children's lives. It tries to fill in where general classroom teachers cannot. It tries to fill in where Mom and Dad left off. It tries to fill in where the regular education system didn't. And the varying ways in which special education is employed in the lives of these four children raise questions for lawmakers about what the purpose of special education should be: Is it to compensate for a child's disability, for problems at home, or for failings elsewhere in the school system? Although it is dangerous to draw too many conclusions based on the experiences of a few families, these four case studies highlight several issues that deserve consideration: the influence of income; how schools are defining disabilities; and how parents' and schools' attitudes affect the process.

Income counts. As is the case in general public education, income correlates closely with student achievement and quality of services. The differences between Austin's and Christian's special education services illustrate the gap in services between the upper- and lower-income brackets. This difference also plays out along urban versus non-urban lines. Schools listen to parents who push, and children whose parents do not speak up—because they are working long hours, have language barriers, or have priorities other than education—can lose out.

Special education is defined so broadly that special education programs may not be the best way to serve some students. Austin Lam's needs are very different from Kiyana Spencer's. The federal laws originated with children like Austin in mind—children who have a strong capacity to learn but who need additional services to help them realize their potential. But the laws are also being stretched to serve children like Kiyana Spencer, whose problems stem from poor parenting, and the Trejo's foster son Christian, whose reading difficulties are probably a combination of educational neglect on the part of his parents and the school system. Based on their school performances in recent years, it is unclear that Kiyana's and Christian's needs are fully met through special education programs.

> *Future reforms might be well-served to allow schools the flexibility to better adapt programs to specific children's needs.*

Attitudes matter. Personalities were one of the main factors both parents and school officials cited as affecting services in these four case studies. Pam Lam's and Alice Spencer's prodding extracted additional services for their children while the Eirschele's crusade for improved services for their son dissolved into a highly personal legal battle with no winners. Schools should also consider the tone they set in the first IEP meetings. All parents interviewed for this chapter described their first encounters with special education as scary and uncertain.

Although one-size-fits-all approaches in education are often aimed at protecting those children who might fall through the cracks, these families' experiences suggest that sometimes such polices can have the opposite effect when they reach the implementation phase. It is not clear that the system is designed to fully serve the needs of two very different sets of children—those with physical and mental disabilities, and those with social-emotional problems and significant academic delays. Future reforms might be well-served to allow schools the flexibility to better adapt programs to specific children's needs. Still, recent trends in education reform that emphasize academic results may filter down to special education and highlight the kinds of children who are and are not being helped by the current laws. That could be good news for children like Kiyana and Christian.

---

[1] U.S. Department of Education, *Twenty-second Annual Report to Congress on the Implementation with Disabilities Education Act* (Washington, DC: U.S. Department of Education, 2000), II-26.

[2] U.S. Department of Education, Office of Special Education Programs, "Estimated Resident Population (Percent) for Children Ages 6-12 by Race/Ethnicity for the School Year 1998-1999," at <<http://www.ideadata.org/tables/ar_af8.htm>>.

[3] U.S. Department of Education, *Twenty-second Annual Report to Congress,* at II-19.

Chapter 12

Rethinking Learning Disabilities

G. Reid Lyon, Jack M. Fletcher, Sally E. Shaywitz, Bennett A. Shaywitz, Joseph K. Torgesen, Frank B. Wood, Ann Schulte, and Richard Olson

Introduction

This report is about learning disabilities (LD), the most frequently identified class of disabilities among students in public schools in the United States. Despite its apparently high—and rising—incidence, LD remains one of the least understood and most debated disabling conditions that affect school-aged children (and adults). Indeed, many disagree about the definition and classification of LD; the diagnostic criteria and assessment practices used in the identification process; the content, intensity, and duration of instructional practices employed; and the policies and legal requirements that drive the identification and education of those with LD.[1]

> Given what is now known about LD, it is irresponsible to continue current policies that dictate inadequate identification practices.

We take the position that many of these debates can be informed by converging scientific data. On the basis of this evidence, we contend that many of the persistent difficulties in developing valid classifications and operational definitions of LD are due to reliance on inaccurate assumptions about causes and characteristics of the disorders. Furthermore, we argue that sufficient data exist to guide the development and implementation of early identification and prevention programs for children at-risk for LD, particularly reading programs that can benefit many of these youngsters.

We contend that sound prevention programs can significantly reduce the number of older children who are identified as LD and who typically require intensive, long-term special education programs. Moreover, prevention programs will prove more effective than remedial programs. Finally, we contend that, given what is now known about LD, it is irresponsible to continue current policies that dictate inadequate identification practices. Instead, we must develop evidence-based alternatives, specific strategies to implement these alternatives, and a research and policy agenda to ensure that these changes are phased into practice as quickly as possible.

In this chapter, we offer alternatives to traditional identification, assessment, and educational strategies for children with LD, alternatives that close the gap between research and practice. We provide a description of the specific instructional needs of children whose low academic achievement can be strengthened by informed teaching.

The chapter is organized into three sections. In the first, we present the current federal definition of LD and trace the theoretical, clinical, and political bases for its construction.[2]

In the second section, we summarize a body of converging research on reading development, reading disabilities (RD), and reading instruction that underscores the importance of early identification and prevention intervention programs to reduce reading failure among many children at-risk for limited literacy development. Although RD represents only two (LD in basic reading skills; LD in reading comprehension) of the seven types of LD that can be identified according to federal law, our focus on RD is predicated on three facts. First, approximately 80 percent of children with LD have primary difficulties with reading.[3] Second, learning to read is essential for academic achievement and accomplishment in all subjects. Third, more is known about deficiencies in reading than about any other academic domain affected by LD, and much of what is known can effectively impact policy and instruction.[4]

> We estimate that the number of children who are typically identified as poor readers and served through either special education or compensatory education programs could be reduced by up to 70 percent through early identification and prevention programs.

We have chosen to combine the following within the RD designation: (1) those children who meet criteria for LD and typically receive services through special education; and (2) those who read below the 25th percentile but do not qualify for the diagnosis of LD and often receive services through compensatory education. Our decision to combine the two groups is predicated on data indicating little difference between them in the proximal causes of their reading difficulties. We estimate that the number of children who are typically identified as poor readers and served through either special education or compensatory education programs (as well as children with significant reading difficulties who are not formally identified and served) could be reduced by up to 70 percent through early identification and prevention programs.

In the third section, we examine a number of issues that should be considered when addressing the educational needs of children at risk for learning failure and children identified as LD at later ages. Under current policies and practices, the number of older children identified as LD continues to increase without concomitant improvements in their learning abilities. We explain why this is the case and provide alternatives for meeting the educational needs of these students.

Finally, we are mindful of the complexity of translating research findings into policy and practice. Policy can have unintended outcomes. Evidence-based alternatives can have few benefits or even harmful effects if implementation strategies are not informed by a clear understanding of specific needs for capacity building at the teacher, school, and system levels. In response, we outline a series of short- and long-range initiatives designed to optimize instruction for all students.

Definitions of Learning Disabilities

What is a Learning Disability?

The term *learning disability* (LD) is traditionally synonymous with the concept of *unexpected underachievement*—specifically, students who do not listen, speak, read, write, or develop mathematics skills commensurate with their potential, even though there has been adequate opportunity to learn. Historically, unexpected underachievement has been attributed to intrinsic neurobiological factors that indicate that students with LD will require specialized instruction to achieve at expected levels based upon some index of aptitude, usually an IQ test score.[5]

The concept of unexpected underachievement has been reported in medical and psychological literature since the mid-19th century under the rubrics of dyslexia, word blindness, dysgraphia, dyscalculia, and other terms.[6] However, it has only been since 1962, when Samuel Kirk, a psychologist at the University of Illinois, coined the term *learning disabilities*, that the concept of unexpected underachievement attained formal recognition in the education community. Kirk used the term to refer to a variety of syndromes affecting language, learning, and communication; like his more medically oriented predecessors, he felt that LD reflected unanticipated learning problems in a seemingly capable child. Writing in 1962, Kirk defined LD as "a retardation, disorder, or delayed development in one or more of the processes of speech, language, reading, spelling, writing, or arithmetic resulting from a possible cerebral dysfunction and not from mental retardation, sensory deprivation, or cultural or instructional factors."[7] Speaking at a 1963 conference, Kirk further noted that LD represented a discrepancy between a child's achievement and his or her apparent capacity to learn. As in the current federal definition, Kirk recognized that LD represented an amalgam of disabilities, all grouped under a single label. He did not feel that the term was synonymous with RD.[8] However, RD was the most frequently identified type of LD in Kirk's day, as today.

> **The term learning disability gained rapid acceptance in the 1960s and 1970s because it addressed a critical need of concerned parents and professionals.**

The term *learning disability* gained rapid acceptance in the 1960s and 1970s because it addressed a critical need of concerned parents and professionals. The concepts represented by LD also made educational sense.[9] Previously, children whose failure to learn could not be explained by mental retardation, visual impairments, hearing impairments, or emotional disturbance were disenfranchised from special education. Their learning characteristics simply did not correspond to existing categories of special education. Thus, the needs of these children were not being met by the educational system; it was through parental and professional advocacy efforts that special education services were ultimately made available for them through the 1969 Learning Disabilities Act.[10] The same legislative language later appeared in the Education for All Handicapped Children Act of 1975 (EAHCA), now the Individuals with Disabilities Education Act (IDEA).[11]

The concept of *learning disabilities* and the need for different specialized educational services also made intuitive sense to parents, teachers, and policymakers. The term did not stigmatize children. Specifically, the learning difficulties displayed by youngsters with LD were not due to mental retardation, poor parenting, or psychopathology. The term likewise reflected optimism. Students with LD had not yet reached their potential: Their difficulties in learning to read, write, and/or calculate occurred despite adequate intelligence, sensory integrity, healthy emotional development, and cultural and environmental advantage. Education programs were needed that recognized differences among children with LD, those who learned "normally," and those who manifested physical, sensory, and intellectual handicaps that affected academic achievement.

This view of educational need continues to maintain considerable currency. Since the mid-1970s, when the EAHCA first required an accounting of the number of children with LD identified and served in public schools, the number of children served has increased from 1.8 percent of school-aged students (1976-1977) to almost 5.2 percent in 1997-1998. Moreover, in 1976-1977, students with LD comprised 22 percent of school-aged students in special education programs; in 1997-1998, the percentage came closer to 52 percent. In just the past 10 years, the number of students ages 6-21 identified as LD under the IDEA has increased 38 percent, with the largest increase (44 percent) among students between 12 and 17 years of age. These increases are not limited to public schools. The number of students identified with LD that attend private schools and post-secondary institutions has increased by similar proportions in the same time period.[12]

> *In just the past 10 years, the number of students ages 6-21 identified as LD under the IDEA has increased 38 percent.*

Few would disagree that 5 percent or more of our school-age population experience difficulties with language and other skills that would be disruptive to academic achievement, or that the factors that led to the concept of LD have lost their salience. The concept of LD is valid, and there are many children and adults whose difficulties in learning are indeed the result of genuine learning disabilities. The issues we raise involve whether classifications used for LD identify *all* children who would benefit from special education services and/or specialized instruction. Similarly, we ask whether younger children who have severe (difficult to remediate) forms of LD are being adequately served given identification rates that point toward disproportionate representation of older children within this category.

What underlies this disproportionate increase in the prevalence of children with LD, particularly in the 12-17 age range? Is it because of improvements in diagnostic and identification practices, or are other factors at work? Is the definition of LD that guides assessment and diagnostic practices too general and ambiguous to ensure accurate identification of younger students? Are the constructs and principles inherent in the definition of LD even valid? Are diagnostic practices biased against the identification of younger, poor, or ethnically different children with LD? Are some students identified as LD actually underachieving in school because of poor teaching and inadequate services? Or has the education profession failed to tolerate individual differences in learning and to properly train regular teachers and special educators to address these differences? Is teacher preparation an issue in the emergence of a child as LD?

Such questions must be answered honestly for the sake of our nation's children. We believe some of the answers can be found through close examination of the features that comprise the

> ## Table 1. Federal definition of learning disabilities
>
> The term "specific learning disability" means a disorder in one or more of the basic psychological processes involved in understanding or in using language, spoken or written, which may manifest itself in an imperfect ability to listen, speak, read, write, spell, or to do mathematical calculations. The term includes such conditions as perceptual handicaps, brain injury, minimal brain dysfunction, dyslexia, and developmental aphasia. The term does not include children who have learning disabilities which are primarily the result of visual, hearing, or motor handicaps, or mental retardation, or emotional disturbance, or of environmental, cultural, or economic disadvantage.
>
> (a) A team may determine that a child has a specific learning disability if:
>
> (1) The child does not achieve commensurate with his or her age and ability levels in one or more of the areas listed in paragraph (a) (2) of this section, when provided with learning experiences appropriate for the child's age and ability levels; and
>
> (2) The team finds that a child has a severe discrepancy between achievement and intellectual ability in one or more of the following areas: (i) Oral expression; (ii) Listening comprehension; (iii) Written expression; (iv) Basic reading skill; (v) Reading comprehension; (vi) Mathematics calculation; or (vii) Mathematics reasoning.
>
> *Sources:* Assistance to States for the Education of Children with Disabilities Program and Preschool Grants for Children with Disabilities Final Rule, 34 C.F.R. pts. 300, 301 (1992); see also note 2.

current definition(s) of LD, as well as those that preceded it. We also propose that the disproportionate increase in the numbers of older children identified as LD during the late elementary to middle school years is, in part, attributable to the following: (1) the limited effectiveness of remediation after age nine; (2) measurement practices that are biased against the identification of children before age nine; and (3) socio-educational factors operating within the public school enterprise. Within this context, we have organized the rest of this section to address the scientific integrity of major themes that guide identification and instructional practices in the field of LD. We conclude it with an examination of the function of the current LD category within the larger educational enterprise and the effects of this function on education policies and practices, particularly those involving the definition of LD. It is important to point out that many of the concerns we address in this chapter (for example, the overuse and over-interpretation of discrepancy data, as well as the misinterpretation of disclaimers in the exclusion language of the IDEA) frequently reflect misinterpretation of the actual regulatory language in the IDEA by schools determining eligibility for special education. Nevertheless, these concerns are frequently cited and are predicated on less than optimal translation of the federal law into identification practices at the school level.

The Critical Conceptual Elements Within Definitions of LD

The federal definition of LD (see Table 1) has four conceptual elements that are common across a number of definitions of LD.[13] These elements are (1) the heterogeneity of LD; (2) its intrinsic/neurobiological nature; (3) a significant discrepancy between learning potential (typically assessed by measures of intelligence) and academic performance (typically assessed by measures of reading, writing, mathematics, and oral language skills); and (4) the exclusion of cultural, educational, environmental, and economic factors, or other disabilities (mental retardation, visual or hearing impairments, emotional disturbance) as causes of LD. Despite the ubiquity of these elements in LD definitions, their validity is rarely examined.

The Heterogeneity Element

As defined in federal legislation, LD is not a single disability but a general category of special education composed of disabilities in any one or a combination of seven skill domains: (1) listening; (2) speaking; (3) basic reading (decoding and word recognition); (4) reading comprehension; (5) arithmetic calculation; (6) mathematics reasoning; and (7) written expression. Disabilities in these areas frequently occur together and can also be accompanied by emotional, social, and behavioral disorders, including disorders of attention. However, these companion conditions cannot be the *primary* cause of the LD.

> **LD is not a single disability but a general category of special education composed of disabilities in any one or a combination of seven skill domains.**

Although the inclusion of these seven areas of disability in current definitions ensures that an expansive diagnostic net can be cast around a wide range of learning difficulties, heterogeneity within and across each academic domain renders diagnostic precision impossible. There are, by and large, different forms of LD. Their characteristics and learning needs vary. Reading and mathematics disorders, for example, vary along multiple dimensions. There is little evidence that the precise causes of different forms of LD are the same, so treating them as seven separate, heterogeneous disorders makes sense. However, we presently have one definition for all of these forms of LD. In the future, separate evidence-based definitions for each of these disabilities should be developed to enhance the assessment and instruction of children with different forms of LD.[14]

The Intrinsic/Neurobiological Element

The field of LD was founded on the assumption that neurobiological factors are the basis of these disabilities. In the main, neurobiological dysfunction was inferred from what was then known about the linguistic, cognitive, academic, and behavioral characteristics of adults with documented brain injury, as well as the observation that reading problems ran in families. As the field progressed, definitions of LD continued to attribute disabilities in learning to intrinsic (neurobiological) rather than extrinsic (for example, environmental or instructional) causes, even though there was initially no objective way to assess the presence of putative brain dysfunction.[15]

Neurobiological factors have been most closely studied in the area of reading. A considerable body of evidence indicates that poor readers exhibit disruption primarily, but not exclusively, in the neural circuitry of the left hemisphere serving language. Both a range of neurobiological investigations using postmortem brain specimens and, more recently, quantitative assessment of brain anatomy using magnetic resonance imaging (MRI) suggest that there are subtle *structural* differences in several brain regions between RD and nonimpaired readers. Converging evidence from neuroimaging modalities that measure brain *function* (for instance, a functional MRI) indicates a pattern of brain organization in RD that is different from nonimpaired readers. Specifically, these studies show reductions in brain activity while performing reading tasks usually, but not always, in the left hemisphere.[16]

Of particular interest from the studies of brain function is the possibility that the resultant neural circuitry reflects not only the individual's biological makeup, but also environmental influences. Central among these influences is how reading instruction impacts brain circuitry. The findings suggest that neural systems develop and are deployed for specific cognitive functions through the interaction of the brain and the environment (including instruction).

This "interaction" perspective is supported by genetic studies of individuals with RD. It has long been known that reading problems recur across family generations, with a risk in the offspring of a parent with RD eight times higher than the general population. Studies with identical and fraternal twins have shown that a significant portion of this familial risk is due to genetic factors. Yet such factors account for only about half of the variability in reading skill development; environmental factors account for the other half and therefore have a significant influence on reading outcomes. Thus, what may be inherited is a susceptibility for RD that may manifest itself given specific interactions, or lack thereof, with the environment. For example, parents who read poorly may be less likely to read to their children. The quality of reading instruction provided in the school may be most critical for children when there is a both a genetic risk for poor reading and a family situation giving rise to limited instructional interactions in the home.[17]

> **No definitional element of LD has generated as much controversy as the use of IQ-achievement discrepancy in the identification of students with LD.**

The Discrepancy Element

No definitional element has generated as much controversy as the use of IQ-achievement discrepancy in the identification of students with LD.[18] When resources (funding) are limited, a valid classification must give rise to operational criteria that can guide the reliable identification of individual cases. Indeed, the adoption of the concept of an IQ-achievement discrepancy as only one, but clearly the primary, operational criterion commenced in 1977, shortly after passage of the EAHCA, to "objectively and accurately" distinguish the child with LD from children with other academic deficiencies.[19]

When the EAHCA was enacted in 1975, states reported that the definition of LD provided insufficient criteria for identifying eligible children. In response, the Office of Education developed more explicit criteria for eligibility and published guidelines for identification which included a severe discrepancy between achievement and intellectual ability (see Table 1). These criteria maintained the heterogeneity and exclusionary elements of the 1969 definition, but added the IQ-discrepancy component as an additional criterion. Inherent in this criterion is an implicit classification of low-achieving students into those who are LD (those with unexpected underachievement) and those who simply underachieve (those with expected underachievement).

The idea of using an IQ-achievement discrepancy metric as one way to "objectively determine" the presence or absence of LD was probably reasonable at the time. Long before "severe discrepancy" became synonymous with LD, practitioners had been intrigued by the seemingly paradoxical inability of some children of average and superior intelligence to master academic concepts. Following repeated reports of this phenomenon in the literature, clinicians and researchers saw value in distinguishing between a subset of low achievers who displayed pervasive limitations in cognitive ability (for example, students with mild mental deficiency) and a subgroup of children with academic deficits displayed against a background of normal intelligence.[20]

The notion of using an IQ-achievement discrepancy as a marker for unexpected underachievement was also consistent with the still-prevailing, albeit inaccurate, view that IQ scores were robust predictors of an individual child's ability to learn. Given this view, children who displayed a gap or discrepancy between their measured IQ and their achievement in oral language, reading, writing, and/or math were viewed as not achieving at levels commensurate with their potential. Thus, despite admonitions by R. L. Thorndike and others throughout the 20th century that IQ scores reflect primarily a gross estimate of *current* general cognitive functioning and should not be used as a measure of *learning potential*,[21] the idea of an IQ-achievement discrepancy as a meaningful diagnostic marker for LD was accepted in policy and practice in 1977 and has been in general use ever since.

> *The IQ-achievement discrepancy, when employed as the primary criterion for the identification of LD, may well harm more children than it helps.*

There are many problems with the concept of an IQ-achievement discrepancy. It not only embodies sometimes naive and erroneous assumptions about the adequacy of an IQ score as an index of learning potential, but the actual comparison of academic achievement scores with IQ scores to derive a discrepancy value is fraught with psychometric, statistical, and conceptual problems that render many comparisons useless.[22] Of even greater significance, the IQ-achievement discrepancy, when employed "inappropriately" as the primary criterion for the identification of LD, may well harm more children than it helps. Not only do discrepancy formulas differ from state to state, making it possible for a student to lose special education services following a family move, but also reliance on a measurable discrepancy between IQ and achievement makes early identification of LD difficult. An overreliance on discrepancy means that children must fail or fall below a predicted level of performance before they are eligible for special education services. Because achievement failure sufficient to produce a discrepancy from IQ cannot be reliably measured until a child reaches approximately nine years of age, the use of IQ-discrepancy constitutes a "wait-to-fail" model.[23] Thus, the student has suffered the academic and emotional strains of failure for two to three years before potentially effective instruction can be brought to bear. This order of events has devastating, lifelong consequences. In the area of RD, epidemiological data show clearly that the majority of children who are poor readers at age nine or older continue to have reading difficulties into adulthood.[24]

Another potentially serious flaw in the use of an IQ-achievement discrepancy metric concerns the unsystematic and frequently inequitable provision of educational services and accommodations based on the presence or absence of a discrepancy. Because there is no strong evidence that the IQ-achievement discrepancy criterion either (1) describes an intrinsic reading-related processing difference within low achieving readers (nondiscrepant versus discrepant), or (2) provides a differential prediction of response to intervention or educational outcomes, the use of such discrepancy requirements to deny specialized services and/or accommodations to nondiscrepant poor readers is arbitrary and problematic.[25]

In the area of RD, the issue is further complicated when some individuals score in the average range on word reading tasks but exhibit significant difficulties when reading connected text. Here, their reading comprehension is impaired primarily because they read slowly. These individuals are disabled in reading and clearly require specialized instruction and accommodations. They do not receive such instruction and accommodations because reading fluency is rarely assessed in current identification procedures. If a slow-reading student scores significantly above the average range on a measure of intelligence, services may be afforded on the basis of the discrepancy between the average untimed word reading score and the above-average IQ score. However, slow-reading students who score within the average range on both the untimed reading measures and the IQ test will typically be denied services because there is no discrepancy—even though they also have a disability that requires specialized services and/or accommodations. The bottom line is that the IQ-achievement discrepancy formulation provides access to services for only some individuals and sometimes denies services without appropriately measuring the fundamental problem.

> *No child is born a reader; all children in literate societies have to be taught to read.*

In sum, the use of an IQ-achievement discrepancy to identify children with LD appears to move many students further away from the education they need. Because the discrepancy hinges on the IQ level of students rather than on their specific academic needs, the emphasis is on eligibility rather than instruction. This situation reflects the orientation of special education in public schools toward compliance with federal regulations rather than positive educational outcomes. Such an emphasis is unfortunate since we have little evidence that the special education remediation services provided to children with LD help them catch up to their peers in academic skills. This issue is addressed below.

The Exclusion Element

Most definitions of LD have an exclusion clause, stating that LD is not the primary result of other conditions that can impede learning. These other conditions include mental retardation; emotional disturbance; visual or hearing impairments; inadequate instructional opportunities; and cultural, social, or economic conditions. Given the primacy of the exclusion element within definitions of LD (in combination with the discrepancy element), many children identified as LD have been diagnosed on the basis of what they are not, rather than what they are.[26] This is unfortunate for three major reasons. First, identifying children with LD on the basis of exclusions downplays the development of clear inclusionary criteria. Second, an exclusionary definition is a negative definition that adds little conceptual clarity and clearly constrains understanding LD to its fullest extent. As Michael Rutter has argued,[27] this approach to definition suggests that if all known causes of the disorder can be excluded, the unknown (in the form of LD) can now be invoked. Third, and most important, many of the conditions excluded as potential influences on LD are themselves factors in impeding the development of cognitive and linguistic skills that lead to the academic deficits frequently observed in RD children.

One exclusion criterion for LD that is especially difficult to reconcile is the student's instructional history. All definitions of LD exclude children from consideration if their learning problems are primarily a product of inadequate instruction. Of all the different assumptions in the concept of LD, this one is the least examined yet perhaps the most important. Some would interpret this exclusion feature to indicate that children who profit from instruction do not have a biologically based LD, yet functional imaging studies suggest that in the area of reading this is not so. Instruction may be necessary to establish the neural networks that support reading. No child is born a reader; all children in literate societies have to be taught to read. The ability to read and write is explicitly built upon our natural capacities for developing oral language.[28]

> *From its inception as a category, LD has served as a sociological sponge that attempts to wipe up general education's spills and cleanse its ills.*

Similarly, most definitions exclude children from the LD category whose learning difficulties may be primarily related to environmental, cultural, or economic disadvantage. Yet these very conditions place some children at significant risk for weaker neural development and secondary learning difficulties. Given the emphasis within current definitions of LD on the causal role of the central nervous system in academic skills disorders, it seems unwise to reject the possibility that the environment (including social and cultural factors) can affect brain development and function, and thus affect learning. Poor socio-economic conditions are related to a number of factors—including malnutrition, limited pre- and post-natal care, exposure to teratogens and substance abuse—all of which can place children at risk for neurological dysfunction, leading to cognitive, linguistic, and academic deficits.[29]

In sum, the brain and the environment operate in reciprocal fashion, pushing or limiting development according to the frequency, timing, and quality of the interactions. To exclude children from specialized services because of instructional, environmental, social, and cultural factors ignores the importance of these factors in shaping the central nervous system and the child's cognitive and linguistic repertoire. Many lives can be improved significantly by identifying those children most susceptible to possible cognitive and academic difficulties. These children need the best instruction at the earliest possible time. To do this will require reconsideration of current definitions of LD. Unfortunately, this is easier said than done because of the sociological role that LD has come to play within the larger educational enterprise.

LD's Sociological Function

Discussions of LD frequently become mired in attempts to explain frequent inconsistencies in definitions, identification practices, and instructional needs of children with the disorder. Some critics of the LD diagnostic concept argue that the category is a "catch-all" for low-achieving students who don't fit anywhere else within the special education system. However, these arguments fail to address the real reasons the category has expanded exponentially in the last three decades. To paraphrase Gerald Senf's analysis,[30] from its inception as a category, LD has served as a sociological sponge that attempts to wipe up general education's spills and cleanse its ills. Today's classrooms are heterogeneous and teachers are expected to address a wide range of individual differences in cognitive, academic, and behavioral development. Unfortunately, many regular classroom teachers have not been trained to accommodate different students' learning needs, and they understandably seek assistance that typically takes the responsibility of educating the child away from the classroom teacher.[31]

There is no doubt that, because of limitations in training, many general education and special education teachers are not prepared to address and respond to these individual differences in an informed manner. For example, a large number of teachers report that their training programs did not adequately prepare them to impart effective reading instruction, particularly to children with limited oral language and literacy experiences or to children with the most severe forms of reading disabilities.[32] This is a significant concern, given that many children at risk for reading failure come from disadvantaged backgrounds, where early childhood education and preschool experiences are less available. Many of these children fail to read because they did not receive effective instruction in the early grades. Some may then, in later grades, require special education services to make up for this early failure in reading instruction.

Senf's metaphor is particularly apt as one observes the "sponge" expand or contract when standards for academic accountability stiffen, demographics of school communities change, administrative concerns increase because LD students are being over- or under-identified, or parental pressures are brought to bear on behalf of their struggling children. In general, the LD sponge has expanded since the advent of the EAHCA because it has been able to absorb a diversity of educational, behavioral, and socioemotional problems irrespective of their causes, their responses to good teaching, or their prognosis.

> **Children who get off to a poor start in reading rarely catch up. We wait—they fail. But it does not have to be this way.**

The effects of these practices on our scientific understanding of LD have been devastating and insidious. It is important to understand that, for the most part, knowledge about LD has been obtained by studying heterogeneous samples of children identified by their schools as LD without attention to how or why the diagnosis was applied. The differences observed within and across samples have been so extensive that the research data are often difficult to interpret.

Where Do We Go From Here?

The current federal definition of LD is conceptually weak. The inclusionary criteria (such as the IQ-achievement discrepancy criterion) and most exclusionary criteria do not appear to be valid markers for LD. The primary use of the IQ-achievement discrepancy criterion comprises a "wait to fail" model: many children cannot be reliably identified as LD and begin to receive specialized services until approximately third grade because of the psychometric limitations inherent in the use of discrepancy formulas. All of this reflects the emphasis within special education on compliance as opposed to results. In the next section, we show that the results of remedial services for children with LD in reading are poor.

We contend, therefore, that it is not in the best interest of children to continue to use present policies and practices as the primary means to provide appropriate instruction to children with LD, particularly students with reading difficulties. A strong statement? Yes, but it is one that is based on research indicating that, without early intervention, the poor first-grade reader almost invariably becomes a poor middle school reader, high school reader, and adult reader. In short, children who get off to a poor start in reading rarely catch up. We wait—they fail. But it does not have to be this way. It is a tragedy that both general and special education practices and policies continue unchanged even as extensive converging evidence makes clear that one major solution to the problem of school failure in general, and reading failure in particular, is early identification and prevention.

Figure 1. Growth in Reading Skills

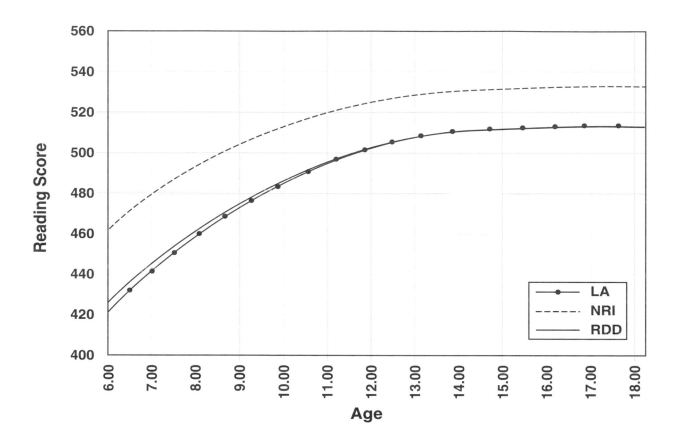

Figure 1. Growth in reading skills by children in the Connecticut Longitudinal Study from the Woodcock-Johnson Psycho-Educational Test Battery from 6-18 years of age (Grades 1-12) by children identified at 8 years of age (Grade 3) as not reading impaired (NRI) or reading disabled according to a discrepancy between IQ and reading achievement (RDD) or low reading achievement with no discrepancy (LA). The figure shows that growth in the two groups with reading disability is similar (the growth curves are indistinguishable); neither catches up to the NRI group; and the differences between the NRI group and the two groups with reading disability are apparent well before Grade 3.

An Evidence-Based Argument for Early Identification, Prevention, and Early Intervention

Good readers understand how print represents the sounds of speech, can apply phonemic and phonics skills in a rapid and fluent manner, and possess sufficient vocabularies and other language abilities to actively connect what they are reading to their background knowledge and experiences. Conversely, children who are most likely to have reading difficulties enter kindergarten lacking sufficient phonological processing skills and fail to develop adequate word reading ability. This bottleneck in word reading skills limits their ability to learn how to read text in a fluent fashion. Their text reading is typically slow and laborious, which impedes their comprehension of what is read. Among these children, the effort exerted in reading is frequently not rewarded by enjoyment and learning. Frustration on the part of the child and a decrease in reading behavior are often observed. Limited reading practice and experience result in weak vocabulary development and difficulties in learning other academic subjects. And the cycle goes on.[33]

> **Special education professionals and programs should become a source for preventative interventions.**

Given that the underlying causes of most early reading difficulties are similar for children regardless of whether they are currently served in special or compensatory education programs, we argue that the most valid and efficient way to deliver this early intervention in reading is through regular education. This approach allows limited funds to be targeted at intervention rather than expensive eligibility determination practices. Initially, however, the specialized instructional approaches that will be necessary for some children are typically not within the purview of general education teachers. Thus, special education professionals and programs should become a source for preventative interventions. Regardless of the approach to classification, we contend that it is critical to provide this instruction as early as possible in a child's school career to avoid the reading failure that will otherwise occur. That is the major message of this chapter.

As mentioned before, children identified as RD after Grade 2 rarely catch up to their peers. Thus, the long-term development of reading skills appears to be set early and is difficult to alter. Figure 1 shows the development of reading skills of children in the Connecticut Longitudinal Study, which followed them from kindergarten through Grade 12.[34]

Three groups are depicted, including children who are not reading impaired (NRI) as well as groups defined in Grade 3 as RD using either IQ-discrepancy (RDD group) or low-achievement (LA group) definitions. Thus, one group of children would qualify for special education as LD under federal guidelines (RDD), while the other group (LA) would not qualify despite the fact that Figure 1 shows the RDD and LA groups are comparably impaired in reading ability. The overall pattern depicts large differences in the development of the NRI and two RD groups. However, the two RD groups are almost indistinguishable and neither catches up to the NRI group despite the fact that schools identified at least half the children as eligible for special education services. Particularly sobering is the finding that over 70 percent of the group identified as RD in Grade 3 was still identified as RD in Grade 12. Regardless of how they are defined, reading disabilities are often chronic, lifelong incapacities that lead to problems in a variety of social and vocational areas in adolescence and adulthood.

By measuring reading skills longitudinally from kindergarten, the Connecticut Longitudinal Study also shows that children are behind in reading long before Grade 3. Other studies support the view that many children are behind in reading early in their development and that they can be reliably identified well before Grade 2. For example, in a study conducted by Connie Juel and her colleagues at the University of Texas, it was found that word recognition skills at the end of first grade were strongly related to reading proficiency at the end of Grade 4.[35] Indeed, almost 9 of 10 children who were deficient in word recognition skills in first grade were poor readers in fourth grade. Similarly, 8 of 10 children with severe word reading problems at the end of the first grade performed below the average range at the beginning of the third grade. Joseph Torgesen and his associates at Florida State University showed that these

> *The importance of early intervention is clearly apparent from studies of typical special education remediation services for reading and math skill development.*

patterns could be detected as early as kindergarten and persisted through Grade 5.[36] This research has been the basis for early reading assessments in Texas and Virginia.

These and other longitudinal studies indicate that early reading difficulties portend later reading difficulties. Further, these studies tell us that children do not typically "catch up" on their own. Unless addressed with well-designed instruction, struggling readers stay that way. Historically, schools have opted to address these persistent reading difficulties through the provision of remedial and special education services typically beginning in second grade and beyond. Yet the majority of children provided such services fail to become skilled readers. We will now examine specific attempts to improve reading skills, first through remedial efforts, then through preventative efforts.

Remediation

The importance of early intervention is clearly apparent from studies of typical special education remediation services for reading and math skill development. Perhaps most revealing is an analysis of a large data set by Eric Hanushek and colleagues. They found that placement in special education was associated with a gain of 0.04 standard deviations in reading and 0.11 in math. Unfortunately, these gains are so small that children are not closing the gap between their academic performance and the performance of their higher achieving classmates. Thus, many of these children remain for lengthy periods of time in special education programs that were ostensibly meant to close the academic gaps.[37]

Remediation models for older children have been ineffective for several reasons, but two stand out. First, the standard instruction provided through remediation is frequently too little, too general, and too unsystematic. Second, even if the instruction were of high quality, it may be too late given that many children are already far behind and less motivated to learn to read following a year or more of reading failure.

Regarding the first reason, Sharon Vaughn and her colleagues studied children with RD who were served for an entire year in public elementary school special education resource rooms.[38]

The researchers found that their instruction was characterized primarily by whole group reading instruction to large groups of children (5-19) who also varied widely in grade level (3-5 grades). Despite this variation, little individualized or differentiated instruction occurred. Although a follow-up study two years later showed that more of the teachers were utilizing materials that supported differentiated instruction, none of these studies found evidence that children made significant gains in reading. Several earlier studies also failed to find evidence supporting significant gains in reading skills through specialized reading instruction programs.[39]

These observations do not represent new findings. Special education classes often reflect what happens in general education classes; over the past two decades, there has been a gradual movement away from small-group, differentiated instruction and towards the inclusion of special education students in general education classes, as well as a gradual trend towards more undifferentiated whole group instruction, even in pull-out classrooms. Moreover, other studies show that placement in special education commonly results in *less* reading instruction for students with RD because it takes the place of language arts instruction in the general education classroom. In addition, despite the fact that most students with LD require direct and intensive instruction in reading, even special education teachers spend little time directly teaching reading skills, and remedial students spend very little of their time reading in these "specialized" programs.[40] In short, the remediation services for elementary grade children in today's special education classrooms are not particularly effective.

These and similar findings which demonstrate a lack of efficacy for conventional "pull-out" special education instructional-remediation models served as a major impetus for the "inclusion movement" in special and general education that currently guides instructional practices in many states. Unfortunately, several studies have documented that inclusion practices are especially ineffective for older poor readers. For example, in one study, 80 percent of the poorest readers made no measurable gain over the school year.[41] What is clear is that neither traditional "pull-out" programs nor inclusion practices have been effective in helping poor readers in Grades 2 and beyond develop the critical literacy skills they need.

> **Several studies have documented that inclusion practices are especially ineffective for older poor readers.**

It is possible that the lack of progress in reading made by these relatively "older" students can be attributed to insufficient teacher preparation, large class sizes, and the lack of specialized reading instruction. Yet even where teachers received professional development and support, the amount of progress made by the end of the year did not close the reading gap.[42] Because the purpose of reading remediation is to close the achievement gap, these findings, like those obtained by Hanushek and associates, were not very positive.

Even with as few as eight children in a group, teachers find it difficult to impart the necessary individualized instruction with appropriate intensity. Many programs have been developed that provide individualized tutoring. Unfortunately, such programs have been infrequently evaluated, particularly for older poor readers. They have also been difficult to introduce into public schools given their cost, the need for specialized professional development, and the sheer number of children who need to be served. However, there is little evidence that 1:1 (one teacher to one student) instruction is

Figure 2. Growth in Total Reading Skill Before, During, and Following Intensive Intervention

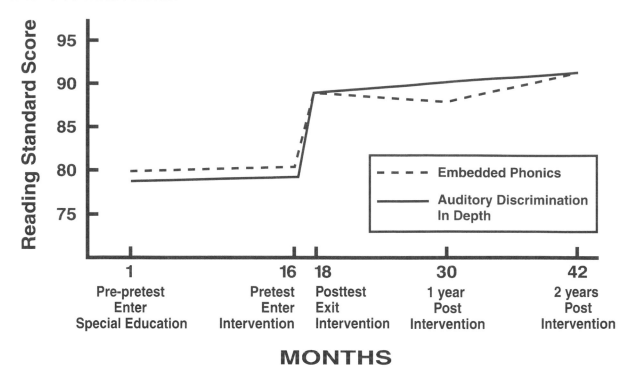

Months	1	16	18	30	42
	Pre-pretest	Pretest	Posttest	1 year	2 years
	Enter	Enter	Exit	Post	Post
	Special Education	Intervention	Intervention	Intervention	Intervention

MONTHS

Figure 2. Changes in broad reading skills on the Woodcock-Johnson Psycho-Educational Test Battery by disabled readers in Grades 3-5 during 16 months of placement in special education prior to intensive reading remediation (pre-pretest to pretest), a 2 month intervention with random assignment to the Auditory Discrimination in Depth (ADD) or Embedded Phonics (EP) programs (pretest to posttest), and one- and two-year follow-up assessments after completion of the intervention. The figure shows little change in reading skills prior to the two-month intervention remediation, significant improvement from (on average) below the 10th percentile (standard score of 80) to the average range (25th percentile; standard score of 90). There were no differences in the efficacy of the two programs, and children maintained the gains after the two month intervention at one and two year follow-ups.

necessary. Groupings of 3:1 up to 5:1 have been found effective, and sometimes more effective than a 1:1 teacher/student ratio if the children are similar in their reading levels.[43]

With regard to older poor readers, unfortunately, even the best studies using highly intensive remediation approaches have improved only a subset of critical reading skills. For example, Torgesen and his group conducted a series of well-designed reading remediation trials with severely disabled readers in grades 3-5.[44] The students were randomly assigned to one of two remediation approaches. One intervention was the Lindamood Auditory Discrimination in Depth (ADD) program; the other was labeled "Embedded Phonics" (EP). Both programs provided explicit instruction in phonics but varied in the amount of phonics instruction and the amount of practice in reading and writing connected text. Students received 67.5 hours of individualized instruction in one of these two programs over an eight-week period.

Figure 2 describes the growth in broad reading ability (a combination of word reading accuracy and reading comprehension) by the children during their 16 months of special education prior to the research intervention (pre-pretest to pretest, with pre-pretest based on the school's assessment). It also shows the growth they made during the eight weeks of intervention (pretest to posttest) and in the two years following the interventions. The children showed little change in the 16 months preceding the interventions, major improvements from pretest to posttest, and maintenance of the gains for two years after the intervention.

Although these results show that appropriate and intensive interventions can help older children substantially improve their reading accuracy and comprehension, almost all the children in the study remained very slow readers. Their scores on standardized measures of reading fluency remained below the 5th percentile two years after the intervention. In attempting to account for these mixed findings, Torgesen's group theorized that a major factor in the development of fluency is the number of words to which a child is exposed through frequent reading practice. Children with word recognition difficulties avoid reading, so these children build up enormous deficits during the time they remain poor readers in elementary school. Thus, it is extremely difficult for them to "catch up" to their peers in total amount of reading practice time, particularly because their normally reading peers are continuing their high rates of reading practice.

> *Although time and expense should not dictate how we address the educational needs of children, the reality is that few school systems presently have access to the necessary resources.*

Although the children remained slow readers, Torgesen and colleagues' study is noteworthy because the gains in reading accuracy and comprehension were maintained after the intervention was terminated. The study is also significant because it shows that more intensive instruction than is typically provided in special education classrooms can have a very significant effect on some reading skills of children with severe reading disabilities in a relatively short period of time. Keep in mind that during the 16 months prior to the intervention, the children made almost no progress toward closing the gap in word reading and comprehension skills. After the intervention, however, many of the children maintained some reading skills within the average range. Moreover, despite the reading fluency weaknesses, 40 percent were returned from special education to regular education classes, which greatly exceeds the 5 percent figure commonly cited for leaving special education. These remediated students returned from a program that lasted 8 weeks but was very intense, and they occurred under two different types of intervention.

It is likely that understanding of how to improve all reading skills among older disabled readers will increase in the next few years. But we must expect that the reading programs and strategies found to be effective through this research will continue to require low teacher-student ratios, highly trained personnel, and a level of instructional intensity and duration that is time-consuming and expensive. Although time and expense should not dictate how we address the educational needs of children, the reality is that few school systems presently have access to the necessary resources. In reading, this is partly because of the sheer number of older children with RD who require services. The number of students identified as LD and provided special education services increases with age for two major reasons. First, as pointed out previously, many children identified at approximately nine to ten years of age are not effectively remediated and therefore continue to receive services. Second, a large number of children are identified as LD during middle and high school primarily because their reading difficulties preclude learning in content areas.

Prevention

Because most reading remediation efforts have not been effective, a number of recent studies have looked at prevention and early intervention approaches that have the potential to reduce the number of children who eventually qualify for special education or compensatory education programs. In reading, prevention research efforts have been especially promising. Both the consensus report of the National Research Panel (NRP)[45] and the evidence-based report of the National Reading Council (NRC)[46] concluded that reading problems for many children could be prevented.

> *There is substantial evidence that early identification and intervention in kindergarten and Grade 1 may substantially reduce the number of children that might otherwise be eligible for special services.*

The NRC report suggested that in kindergarten, for example, children could be identified as "at-risk" for word reading difficulties on the basis of their performance on tasks that assess phonemic awareness and naming abilities. The types of measures that are most predictive of later reading ability involve the child's knowledge of letter sounds, the ability to blend sounds into words (done orally), and, at the end of kindergarten, the ability to name letters rapidly. By first grade, the child's ability to read appropriately leveled words is the best predictor of later reading success.

The beneficial effects of early identification and intervention are apparent in many studies. The NRP identified a large body of research showing that explicit teaching of the relation of print and sounds through phonological awareness training and phonics was especially effective in kindergarten and Grade 1, with the instructional effects diminishing in subsequent grades when word recognition skills had been developed to a level that adequately supported reading of connected text.

There is substantial evidence that early identification and intervention in kindergarten and Grade 1 may substantially reduce the number of children that might otherwise be eligible for special services. Torgesen recently summarized five such studies, all of which resulted in a reduction in the number of potentially eligible children.[47] In all these studies, children were identified as at-risk for RD in kindergarten or Grade 1 based on assessment results that identified the children in the bottom 12-18 percent (depending on the study) of the school population in either reading skills (Grade 1) or phonological processing (kindergarten). After intervention, the reading performance of the primary intervention groups in each of the five studies was well within the average range. But not all programs work with all children. Across the five studies, 8-30 percent of the children completed the intervention with reading scores below the average range. On the other hand, these children fell in the bottom 12-18 percent of all kindergarten/Grade 1 students in reading skills, and the response rate for the interventions suggests that if they were available to all children at-risk for reading difficulties, less than 6 percent of the population would be eligible for services later in school. Simply stated, when an intervention is used with the bottom 18 percent of the student population and works with 70 percent of them, the number of at-risk children requiring services is reduced from 18 percent to 5.4 percent.[48] Across the five studies, the expected incidence of RD was reduced from 12-18 percent to 1.4-5.4 percent.

The five studies varied in how children were identified as "at-risk," the types of early interventions employed, and the student-teacher ratios. All studies followed children for 2-5 years and all showed that the gains were maintained. Moreover, in contrast to the remedial studies described above, improvement in both accuracy and fluency of word recognition skills was apparent, with gains also present in comprehension skills.[49]

> *The goal of remedial reading instruction should be to improve reading skills as quickly as possible so the student can "read to learn" in critical content areas.*

None of the intervention programs were equally effective for all of the children studied. There may be individual characteristics of children that predispose them to more or less success with a particular program. Research examining this possibility is underway, but it's already clear that we need to move away from a "one-size-fits-all" mentality and apply continuous assessment approaches that evaluate how well an instructional program is working with particular youngsters. The growth of reading skills can be constantly measured over time in the classroom, and these "curriculum-based" approaches can identify children who are not responding optimally to a particular instructional strategy. This information can then give the teacher an objective basis for modifying instruction to address a particular student's needs.[50]

The prevention and early intervention research has its critics. Some argue that early identification is fraught with errors leading to misidentification and may incorrectly label a student as at-risk for academic failure.[51] We respond by suggesting that a label is not necessary for implementation of prevention programs and the costs of delaying intervention are too great to wait. Indeed, we hope that, at some point, all kindergarten and elementary grade teachers will have had sufficient training to provide instruction that incorporates prevention into the normal course of their teaching. Even with this enhanced capacity, however, some children will need more instructional intensity than they can obtain in a typical classroom.

Other critics identify studies that show greater gains in word recognition than comprehension, and suggest that many early intervention studies show diminished gains in the later grades.[52] We respond by pointing out that the so-called "fourth-grade" slump does not mean that children begin to decline in the reading abilities gained; rather, they simply begin to show a reduction in the rate of growth. The key is to continue reading instruction throughout elementary school with a focus on continually integrating word-reading skills, fluency instruction, and reading comprehension skills in the later grades. Learning to read words is necessary but not the only condition for literacy proficiency.

Not all children will benefit from early intervention. Nevertheless, as stated in the above discussion of prevention studies, children whose word recognition skills were not brought into the average range did improve to some degree in the five studies. These children may require different interventions over time and/or more intensive programs to foster compensatory learning strategies while continuing to work on basic academic skills deficits. The goal of remedial reading instruction should be to improve reading skills as quickly as possible so the student can "read to learn" in critical content areas. To accomplish this, students, particularly at older age ranges, require highly intensive and systematic instruction provided in settings characterized by low teacher-student ratios. This can only be done when the potential number of children with reading difficulties has been reduced to manageable levels through early intervention.

> **Even the best evidence-based recommendations will not be utilized and sustained in practice unless careful thought is given to identifying the conditions that will increase the probability of their successful implementation.**

How Policies and Practices Must Change

We have endeavored to illustrate the following: (1) the origins of the concept of LD; (2) old and sometimes incorrect assumptions about LD that have been maintained in public policy; (3) the specific scientific and educational problems with current definitions of LD; (4) the limited effectiveness of current reading remediation approaches; and (5) the potential value of early identification and intervention approaches in reducing reading failure. We conclude that significant improvements in education policies and practices related to the definition of LD, changes in teacher preparation, and development and implementation of early intervention and remediation programs must occur if the educational needs of children are to be met. However, we realize that even the best evidence-based recommendations will not be utilized and sustained in practice unless careful thought is given to identifying the conditions that will increase the probability of their successful implementation.

These conditions include our ability to (1) ensure that all recommendations have been sufficiently tested to acknowledge clearly their strengths and weaknesses and evaluate their specific impact on the children and adults to be served; (2) anticipate the effects of changes in policies and practices on federal, state, and school communities and address them effectively; (3) take into account barriers to change in public school policy and practice; and (4) articulate specific areas where capacity must be developed to ensure successful implementation. We recognize that our recommendations will require time and resources to determine whether these essential conditions can be met. Hasty implementation of these recommendations without full knowledge of the challenges that confront such significant change could put students in jeopardy. *Thus, we recommend that the relevant government agencies undertake a consensus development initiative through which the federal definition of LD and attendant eligibility and intervention issues raised in this chapter are evaluated in an attempt to align policy with research.*

With this as background, we now summarize our major recommendations for improvements in the definition of LD, teacher preparation, and the development and implementation of early intervention and remediation programs. We conclude by articulating what we consider to be the significant factors that must be addressed if productive implementation of these recommendations is to occur.

Recommendations for Improvement in the Definition(s) of LD

First, replace the current generic exclusionary definition of LD with evidence-based definitions that specify precise characteristics necessary to identify children with LD in reading, mathematics, written expression, and oral language. This type of effort has already been accomplished in the area of reading disabilities, giving rise to greater precision in describing children under study and in providing appropriate instructional services. Until such definitions are developed for all types of LD, reliable assessment and appropriate instruction of children with LD will continue to be compromised.

> **There is a pressing need for early, intensive, empirically based interventions to be made easily available to children through general education.**

Second, jettison the IQ-achievement criterion as a primary marker for LD. Assessment and identification strategies that replace the use of IQ-achievement test comparisons are clearly possible. In most cases, student underachievement can be predicted on the basis of performance on tasks assessing skills directly related to the academic domain in question. Further, underachievement can be documented by direct comparisons of students' age and grade with their academic functioning in oral language, reading, mathematics, and written language.

Third, stop excluding children because of inadequate instruction, cultural and social factors, and emotional disturbance. These exclusions may be policy-driven, designed to avoid commingling of funds for compensatory and special education, but we should not allow our conceptualizations of LD to be driven by policy issues. In the case of inadequate instruction and cultural/social factors, we have argued that it is just these factors that may lead to inadequacies in neural and cognitive development that place children at significant risk for LD. Thus, decisions to maintain distinctions between compensatory and special education services should not drive our conception of LD. Instruction is the key for all children who are not achieving according to expectations.

Fourth, include consideration of a student's response to well-designed and well-implemented early intervention as well as remediation programs as part of the identification of LD. Recall Senf's sponge metaphor. There is a pressing need for early, intensive, empirically based interventions to be made easily available to children through general education. There are too many "spills" in the current system. The complex identification criteria and expensive due process procedures of special education should be reserved for children who have not responded to the powerful shorter-term interventions that are presently available. No doubt, children who do not benefit from these interventions will require even more intensive remediation programs as well as educational accommodations as they proceed through school.

These four recommendations are offered with two caveats. First, the assessment practices and criteria that we have proposed should not lead to the identification of LD without input from teachers, parents, and others responsible for the child's education. Typically a multidisciplinary school-support team undertakes this function. Such teams should have sway over decisions based solely on test scores, as provided in the IDEA.

Second, our recommendations can be expected to change who is identified as LD. The exclusionary and IQ-achievement elements of the LD definition have served as artificial "caps" on LD prevalence, while the lack of robust interventions for academically unsuccessful students in general and compensatory education has inflated LD identification rates. A key to more effective responses to learning difficulties in general education and lowered LD prevalence will be policies that do not simply change the criteria for identifying LD, but that truly improve the capacity of teachers and schools to implement sound early interventions with the necessary fidelity. Years of disappointing outcomes in special and compensatory education have taught us that mandated instructional/intervention programs (usually watered-down to allow rapid dissemination and a quick fix), ultimately cost more than a reasoned, systematic approach that uses science as a base. Such an approach assures that the policy and implementation issues inherent in broadening from practice to large scale are anticipated and addressed.[53]

> *Teachers must be provided the critical academic content, pedagogical principles, and knowledge of learner characteristics that they need in order to impart systematic and informed instruction to their students.*

Recommendations for Improving Teacher Education

We have noted problems with teacher education as well as the need to incorporate the notion of adequate instruction into definitions of LD. The often-heard statement that many children identified as LD are actually "teaching-disabled" is unfortunately accurate in many cases. Our research has taught us that almost all children can learn to read if taught by appropriate methods, but clearly many students are not receiving appropriate instruction for their reading needs. Is this the teacher's fault? We don't think so. In our experience, people become teachers in order to help make significant positive changes in student's lives and teaching children to read is certainly one of those goals. Teachers, however, like the rest of us, frequently teach what they have been taught. Much evidence shows that teachers are not trained to address individual learning differences in general and specifically are not prepared to teach reading to students who arrive in their classrooms from highly diverse backgrounds and a range of initial abilities. Nor are teachers trained to study and apply research. Once in the classroom, no matter how much teachers want to "keep up" with the most recent research, they are not encouraged to do so.[54]

We doubt that the colleges of education will change their current preparation practices in the near future. What is clear is that teachers must be provided the critical academic content, pedagogical principles, and knowledge of learner characteristics that they need in order to impart systematic and informed instruction to their students. Some states (such as Texas) and communities (for example, the Houston Independent School District) have considered alternatives to traditional teacher preparation to ensure that teachers can close the gap between research and practice. These initiatives should be carefully evaluated to determine whether such large-scale efforts are effective.

Recommendations for the Development of Prevention and Early Intervention Programs

The technology for implementing early identification and intervention programs is undergoing rapid development. Many states, notably Texas and Virginia, have developed reading assessments for K-2 children that are teacher-administered. Although the purpose of these instruments is to guide instruction, they also serve to signal further evaluation for LD by identifying at-risk children. Through the Reading Excellence Act, some states are developing intensive programs for children who are at-risk for reading difficulties because they are socially disadvantaged. These programs are required to use scientifically based research and to focus on accelerated reading instruction in kindergarten and the early grades. Such strategies may prevent reading failure in many children. The key is to enhance classroom instruction accompanied by targeted intervention programs for children who require more help.

> *An important lesson can be drawn from compensatory education, where entry criteria are relatively simple and much more funding is targeted for intervention programs.*

A major problem with such efforts is that special educators who typically provide instruction to children with LD have not been integrated into the early identification and prevention initiatives and have not had a role in efforts to design and implement early intervention programs. It is important that both regular and special education embrace these efforts and view prevention as part of their mission. The IDEA today allows states to identify 6- to 9-year-old children as eligible for special education services based on a designation of "developmental delay," which means the child is not making progress. Although developmental delay is a fairly meaningless term, especially given the evidence that reading problems become persistent deficits early in schooling, the idea that special education funds can be used for early identification and prevention is critical. Unfortunately, the most recent report to Congress (for 1997-1998) on implementation of the 1997 revision of the IDEA—which permitted use of "developmental delay"—indicated that only eight states actually utilized this eligibility category. Children served under "developmental delay" represented only 1.32 percent of children with disabilities in the 6- to 9-year-old age group.[55]

Although special educators may not be directly involved in the provision of classroom instruction for at-risk children, they should have a clear role in activities related to prevention. This includes early identification and the implementation of specialized interventions within the classroom and elsewhere. Such specialized services and programs should not be oriented toward a determination of eligibility as is presently the case. An important lesson can be drawn from compensatory education, where entry criteria are relatively simple and much more of the funding is targeted for intervention programs rather than administrative issues relevant to eligibility determination.

What is a Disability?

The emphasis on prevention begs the question of what constitutes the disability in LD. If the role of inadequate instruction is taken seriously, and more aggressive attempts are made to teach all children to read, the meaning of disability could change in the future. In this scenario, the actual diagnosis of LD could be reserved for children whose reading or other academic problems are severe and intractable (that is, for children who do not adequately respond to a variety of intervention approaches). With documented lack of adequate response, eligibility should be more streamlined and less adversarial than is presently the case with LD.[56]

> *There are few areas where the relationship of science and policy are more loosely linked than LD.*

In particular, we do not know if there are characteristics of the environment, the brain, or heredity that make it difficult to teach all children to learn to read, write, and/or develop mathematics competencies. Yet a child who has difficulty learning to read early and whose reading skills never develop to a level commensurate with stronger reading peers will most likely show improved reading levels after aggressive attempts to provide sound early intervention. Such a child may also need extensive modifications of his or her educational environment, more extensive compensatory techniques, and other changes in curriculum such as those made for youngsters with more obvious disabilities.

This is by no means an attempt to "write off" children who do not respond to aggressive instruction, but it is recognition of the role of instruction in the definition of LD. Thus, it may be reasonable to reserve the term "learning disabled" for individuals who clearly do not respond to intensive intervention and who may need more significant modifications of their educational environment in order to maximize their learning experiences in school. It would be important to identify these children and look more closely at both neurobiological and environmental factors that characterize them. With the opportunity to conduct research on children who clearly do not respond to even the best of current interventions, we may be able to understand the causes of this intractability and develop interventions that may further reduce the prevalence of LD in the future. Regardless, such efforts should be tied into preventative approaches through an attempt to implement what is essentially a public health model and reduce the overall prevalence of LD. Under no circumstances should inadequate instruction be used as an excuse for denying access to special education services. Poor instruction *causes* LD and should not be exclusionary.

Science and Policy

There are few areas where the relationship of science and policy are more loosely linked than LD. This is unfortunate. In too many instances, policy-related issues have driven the scientific agenda relevant to LD. This situation should be reversed; research should drive policy on LD. But the production of clear, convergent findings is only the first step. Effecting meaningful change in the lives of children and teachers requires that we not only have sound scientific findings, but also that we understand how to formulate policies based on these findings to produce changes we desire at the individual child level. It is unlikely the formulators of the EAHCA envisioned that the majority of those served by their legislation would be children in a relatively new disability category. Similarly, although changes needed in the LD identification criteria and intervention practices seem obvious based on the research presented here, we must expect unintended consequences to follow from any changes. Considering that enhancing local capacity is key to any change efforts, the fundamental changes we desire in educational practice will require time and resources to implement.

It is time to more tightly link policy, research, and practice in LD. Programs that are implemented on the basis of policy should be continuously evaluated for their efficacy. Similarly, instructional interventions for children with LD should carry with them the expectation that they will be based on research and evaluated in a serious way. Decisionmaking in education, whether it involves policy or practice, should be guided by research. Society should have the same expectations for education policy and practice that it has for medicine. We do not believe that the criteria used to evaluate evidence are meaningfully different, nor that decisions on how much research is necessary to implement a particular policy or practice are particularly different in education, medicine, or related areas.

Such a radical restructuring of education policy and practice can only be successfully accomplished if we acknowledge the complexity of the task before us. We have a model of successful inquiry into the nature of reading disorders that can be applied to other learning disorders. We now need to use what we know about LD and about education change to construct and evaluate models for successful change in educational policy and practice for children with learning difficulties. It is time to apply the same care and precision used in conducting the original research to the task of effecting serious policy change based on that research. The real tragedy is that conceptualizations of LD have not changed over 30 years despite the completion of significant research in the past 15 years. What we know from research now needs to be implemented. Children deserve no less.

---

[1] See B.K. Keogh, "A Shared Attribute Model of Learning Disabilities," in *Research in Learning Disabilities: Issues and Future Directions*, eds. S. Vaughn and C. Bos (Boston, MA: Little, Brown and Co., 1987), 3-18; and L.C. Moats and G.R. Lyon, "Learning Disabilities in the United States: Advocacy, Science, and the Future of the Field," *Journal of Learning Disabilities* 26 (1993): 282-294.

[2] See Cecil Mercer, et al., "Learning Disabilities Definitions and Criteria Used by State Education Departments," *Learning Disabilities Quarterly* 19 (1996): 217-232; "Definition and Criteria for Defining Students as Learning Disabled," 42 Fed. Reg. 65,083 (1977); and "Assistance to States for the Education of Children with Disabilities Program and Preschool Grants for Children with Disabilities Final Rule," 34 C.R.F. 300 and 301 (1992).

[3] See J. Lerner, "Educational Intervention in Learning Disabilities," *Journal of the American Academy of Child and Adolescent Psychiatry* 28 (1989): 326-331.

[4] See M. Kamil, et al., *Handbook of Reading Research: Volume III* (Mahwah, NJ: Erlbaum, 2000); National Institute of Child Health and Human Development, *The Report of the National Reading Panel: An Evidence-Based Assessment of the Scientific Research Literature on Reading and Its Implications for Reading Instruction* (Bethesda, MD: National Institutes of Child Health and Human Development, 2000); and C. Snow, et al., *Preventing Reading Difficulties in Young Children* (Washington, DC: National Academy Press, 1998).

[5] See K. Kavale and S. Forness, *The Nature of Learning Disabilities* (Hillsdale, NJ: Erlbaum, 1995); and J.L. Wiederholt, "Historical Perspectives on the Education of the Learning Disabled," in *The Second Review of Special Education*, eds. L. Mann and D. Sabatino, (Austin, TX: PRO-ED, 1974), 103-152.

[6] See J. Doris, "Defining Learning Disabilities: A History of the Search for Consensus," in *Better Understanding Learning Disabilities: New Views from Research and Their Implications for Educational and Public Policies*, eds. G.R. Lyon, et al. (Baltimore, MD: Paul H. Brookes, 1993), 97-115.

[7] S. Kirk, *Educating Exceptional Children* (Boston, MA: Houghton Mifflin, 1962), 263.

[8] See S. Kirk, "Behavioral Diagnosis and Remediation of Learning Disabilities," in *Proceedings of the Conference on Exploration into the Problems of the Perceptually Handicapped Child* (Evanston, IL: Fund for the Perceptually Handicapped Child, Inc., 1963), 1-7.

[9] See N. Zigmond, "Learning Disabilities from an Educational Perspective," in *Better Understanding Learning Disabilities: New Views from Research and Their Implications for Education and Public Policies,* eds. G.R. Lyon, et al. (Baltimore, MD: Paul H. Brookes, 1993), 251-272.

[10] Education of the Handicapped Act, Title VI, Pub. L. No. 91-230 (1969-1970).

[11] Individuals with Disabilities Education Act Amendments of 1991, Pub. L. No. 102-119, 20 U.S.C. § 1401 et seq.

[12] See Office of Special Education Programs, *Implementation of IDEA.*

[13] See Individuals with Disabilities Education Act, Pub. L. No. 102-119. Other definitions and their historical origins are discussed in G.R. Lyon, "Learning Disabilities," *The Future of Children* 6 (1996): 54-76.

[14] See G.R. Lyon, "Toward a Definition of Dyslexia," *Annals of Dyslexia* 45 (1995): 3-30; and K. Stanovich, "The Construct Validity of Discrepancy Definitions of Reading Disability," in *Better Understanding Learning Disabilities: New Views from Research and Their Implications for Education and Public Policies,* eds. G.R. Lyon, et al. (Baltimore, MD: Paul H. Brookes, 1993), 273-295.

[15] See K. Kavale and S. Forness, *The Science of Learning Disabilities* (San Diego, CA: College Hill Press, 1985).

[16] Literature on post-mortem and structural imaging studies was reviewed in P. Filipek, "Structural Variations in Measures in the Developmental Disorders," in *Developmental Neuroimaging: Mapping the Development of Brain and Behavior,* eds. R. Thatcher, G. Lyon, J. Rumsey, and N. Krasnegor (San Diego, CA: Academic Press, 1996), 169-186. Functional imaging studies involve several modalities, such as positron emission tomography, functional magnetic resonance imaging, and magnetoencephalography. See S.E. Shaywitz, K.R. Pugh, A.R. Jenner, R.K. Fulbright, J.M. Fletcher, J.C. Gore, and B.A. Shaywitz, "The Neurobiology of Reading and Reading Disability (Dyslexia)," in *Handbook of Reading Research, Volume IIi,* .eds. M.L. Kamil, P.B. Mosenthal, P.D. Pearson, and R. Barr (Mahwah, NJ: Lawrence Erlbaum, 2000), 229-249.

[17] See Richard K. Olson, "Genes, Environment, and Reading Disabilities," in *Perspectives on Learning Disabilities,* eds. R.J. Sternberg and L. Spear-Swerling (Oxford: Westview Press, 1999), 3-22; and B. Pennington, "Dyslexia as a Neurodevelopmental Disorder," in *Neurodevelopmental Disorders,* ed. H. Tager-Flusberg (Cambridge, MA: MIT Press, 1999), 307-330.

[18] Detailed reviews of the issues with discrepancy models can be found in J.M. Fletcher, D.J. Francis, S.E. Shaywitz, G.R. Lyon, B.R. Foorman, K.K. Stuebing, and B.A. Shaywitz, "Intelligent Testing and the Discrepancy Model for Children with Learning Disabilities," *Learning Disabilities Research & Practice* 13 (1998): 186-203; and L.S. Siegel, "Learning Disabilities: The Roads We Have Traveled and the Path to the Future," in *Perspectives on Learning Disabilities,* eds. R.J. Sternberg and L. Spear-Swerling (Oxford: Westview Press, 1999), 159-175.

[19] These recommendations can be found in Assistance to States for Education for Handicapped Children: Procedures for Evaluating Specific Learning Disabilities, 42 Fed. Reg. G1082-G1085 (1977).

[20] The 20th century reflects a period of extensive discussion of how to define different groups of low achievers that culminated in the concept of LD. This history is discussed by J.L. Doris, "Defining Learning Disabilities: A History of the Search for Consensus," in *Better Understanding Learning Disabilities,* eds. G.R. Lyon, D.B. Gray, J.F. Kavanaugh, and N.A. Krasnegor (Baltimore, MD: Paul H. Brookes, 1993), 97-116; see also M. Rutter, "Syndromes Attributed to Minimal Brain Dysfunction in Childhood," *American Journal of Psychiatry* 139 (1982): 21-33.

[21] See R.L. Thorndike, *The Concepts of Over and Under Achievement* (New York: Columbia University Bureau of Publications, 1963).

[22] The statistical problems with the use of IQ-discrepancy scores have been widely documented. See C.R. Reynolds, "Critical Measurement Issues in Learning Disabilities," *Journal of Special Education* 18 (1974): 451-476.

[23] Longitudinal research has shown that IQ-discrepancy scores are not reliable in Grade 1, but are reliable in Grade 3 (and most likely in Grade 2, which was not included in the following study). See S.E. Shaywitz, M.D. Escobar, B.A. Shaywitz, J.M. Fletcher, and R. Makuch, "Distribution and Temporal Stability of Dyslexia in an Epidemiological Sample of 414 Children Followed Longitudinally," *New England Journal of Medicine* 326 (1992): 145-150.

[24] See S.E. Shaywitz, J.M. Fletcher, J.M. Holahan, A.E. Schneider, K.E. Marchione, K.K. Stuebing, D.J. Francis, and B.A. Shaywitz, "Persistence of Dyslexia: The Connecticut Longitudinal Study at Adolescence," *Pediatrics* 104

(1999): 1351-1359.

[25] See J.K. Torgesen, R.K. Wagner, C.A. Rashotte, E. Rose, P. Lindamood, J. Conway, and C. Garvan, "Preventing Reading Failure in Young Children with Phonological Processing Disabilities: Group and Individual Responses to Instruction," *Journal of Educational Psychology* 91 (1999): 579-594; and F.R. Vellutino, D.M. Scanlon, and G.R. Lyon, "Differentiating Between Difficult-to-Remediate and Readily Remediated Poor Readers: More Evidence Against the IQ-Achievement Discrepancy Definition for Reading Disability," *Journal of Learning Disabilities* 33 (2000): 223-238.

[26] See A.D. Ross, *Psychological Aspects of Learning Disabilities and Reading Disorders* (New York: McGraw-Hill, 1976).

[27] See M. Rutter, "Prevalence and Types of Dyslexia," in *Dyslexia: An Appraisal of Current Knowledge*, eds. A.L. Benton and D. Pearl (New York: Oxford University Press, 1978), 3-28.

[28] See P.B. Gough and M.L. Hillinger, "Learning to Read: An Unnatural Act," *Bulletin of the Orton Society* 30 (1980): 179-196; and A.M. Liberman, "How Theories of Speech Effect Research in Reading and Writing," in *Foundations of Reading Acquisition and Dyslexia: Implications for Early Intervention*, ed. B. Blachman (Mahwah, NJ: Lawrence, 1997).

[29] For an excellent discussion of the relationship between environmental, cultural, and economic factors; the presence of teratogens; neural development; and learning, see D.P. Hallahan, J.M. Kauffman, and J.W. Lloyd, *Introduction to Learning Disabilities* (Boston, MA: Allyn and Bacon, 1996).

[30] See G. Senf, "LD Research in Sociological and Scientific Perspective," in *Psychological and Educational Perspectives on Learning Disabilities*, eds. J. Torgesen and B. Wong (Orlando, FL: Academic Press, 1986), 27-53.

[31] See American Federation of Teachers, *Teaching Reading Is Rocket Science: What Expert Teachers of Reading Should Know and Be Able to Do* (Washington, DC: American Federation of Teachers, 1999).

[32] See G.R. Lyon, M. Vaasen, and F. Toomey, "Teachers' Perceptions of their Undergraduate and Graduate Training," *Teacher Education and Special Education* 12 (1989): 164-169; and L.C. Moats, "The Missing Foundation in Teacher Preparation," *American Educator* 19 (1995): 43-51.

[33] See J.M. Fletcher, and G.R. Lyon, "Reading: A Research-Based Approach," in *What's Gone Wrong in America's Classrooms*, ed. W. M. Evers (Stanford, CA: Hoover Institution Press, 1998), 49-90; and S. Shaywitz, "Dyslexia," *Scientific American* 275 (1996): 98-104.

[34] See S.E. Shaywitz, J.M. Fletcher, J.M. Holahan, A.E. Schneider, K.E. Marchione, K.K. Stuebing, D.J. Francis, and B.A. Shaywitz, "Persistence of Dyslexia: The Connecticut Longitudinal Study at Adolescence," *Pediatrics* 104 (1999): 1351-1359.

[35] See C. Juel, "Learning to Read and Write: A Longitudinal Study of 54 Children from First through Fourth Grades," *Journal of Educational Psychology* 80 (1988): 437-447.

[36] See J.K. Torgesen, "The Prevention and Remediation of Reading Disabilities: Evaluating What We Know from Research," *Journal of Academic Language Therapy* 1 (1997): 11-47.

[37] See E.A. Hanushek, J.F. Kain, and S.G. Riukin, "Does Special Education Raise Academic Achievement for Students with Disabilities?" (National Bureau of Economic Research working paper no. 6469, 1998).

[38] See S.W. Moody, S.R. Vaughn, M.T. Hughes, and M. Fischer, "Reading Instruction in the Resource Room: Set Up for Failure," *Exceptional Children* 16 (2000): 305-316; J.S. Schumm, S.W. Moody, and S.R. Vaughn, "Grouping for Reading Instruction: Does One Size Fit All?" *Journal of Learning Disabilities* 5 (2000): 477-488; and S.R. Vaughn, S.W. Moody, and J.S. Shuman, "Broken Promises: Reading Instruction in the Resource Room," *Exceptional Children* 64 (1998): 211-225.

[39] See R.L. Allington and A. McGill-Franzen, "School Response to Reading Failure: Instruction for Chapter One and Special Education Students Grades Two, Four, and Eight," *Elementary School Journal* 89 (1989): 529-542; M.C. Haynes and J.R. Jenkins, "Reading Instruction in Special Education Resource Rooms," *American Educational Research Journal* 23 (1986): 161-190; and A. McGill-Franzen, "Compensatory and Special Education: Is There Accountability for Learning and Belief in Children's Potential?" in *Getting Reading Right from the Start: Effective Early Literacy Interventions*, eds. E.H. Hiebert and B.M. Taylor (Boston, MA: Allyn and Bacon, 1994), 13-35.

[40] See R.L. Allington, H. Stuetzel, M.C. Shake, and L. Lamarch, "What is Remedial Reading? A Descriptive Study," *Reading Research and Instruction* 26 (1986): 15-30; and G. Leinhardt, C. Weidman, and K. Hammond, "Introduction and Integration of Classroom Routines by Expert Teachers," *Curriculum Inquiry* 17 (1987): 135-176.

[41] See J.K. Klingner, S.R. Vaughn, J.S. Schumm, M. Hughes, and B. Elbaum, "Outcomes for Students with and

Without Learning Disabilities in Inclusive Classrooms," *Learning Disabilities Research & Practice* 13 (1997): 153-161. These results are consistent with other studies. See, for example, N. Zigmond and J.M. Baker, "Concluding Comments: Current and Future Practices in Inclusive Schooling," *The Journal of Special Education* 29 (1995): 245-250.

[42] See B. R. Foorman, D.J. Francis, T. Beeler, D. Winikates, and J.M. Fletcher, "Early Interventions for Children with Reading Problems: Study Designs and Preliminary Findings," *Learning Disabilities* 8 (1997): 63-71.

[43] See B.E. Elbaum, S. Vaughn, M.T. Hughes, and S.W. Moody, "How Effective are One-to-One Tutoring Programs in Reading for Elementary Students At-Risk for Reading Failure? A Meta-Analysis," *Journal of Educational Psychology* (in press).

[44] See J.K. Torgesen, A.W. Alexander, R.K. Wagner, C.A. Rashotte, K. Voeller, T. Conway, and E. Rose, "Intensive Remedial Instruction for Children with Severe Reading Disabilities: Immediate and Long-Term Outcomes from Two Instructional Approaches," *Journal of Learning Disabilities* 34 (2001): 33-58.

[45] See National Institute of Child Health and Human Development, *The Report of the National Reading Panel: An Evidence-Based Assessment of the Scientific Research Literature on Reading and Its Implications for Reading Instruction* (Bethesda, MD: National Institute of Child Health and Human Development, 2000).

[46] C. Snow, et al., *Preventing Reading Difficulties in Young Children* (Washington, DC: National Academy Press, 1999).

[47] See J.K. Torgesen, "Individual Responses in Response to Early Interventions in Reading: The Lingering Problem of Treatment Resisters," *Learning Disabilities Research & Practice* 15 (2000): 55-64. The five studies are as follows: R.H. Felton, "Effects of Instruction on the Decoding Skills of Children with Phonological-Processing Problems," *Journal of Learning Disabilities* 26 (1993): 583-589; B.R. Foorman, D.J. Francis, J.M. Fletcher, C. Schatschneider, and P. Mehta, "The Role of Instruction in Learning to Read: Preventing Reading Failure in At-Risk-Children," *Journal of Educational Psychology* 90 (1998): 37-55; J.K. Torgesen, R.K. Wagner, C.A. Rashotte, and J. Herron, "The Effectiveness of Teacher Supported Computer Assisted Instruction in Preventing Reading Problems in Young Children: A Comparison of Two Methods" (unpublished manuscript, Florida State University, Tallahassee, FL); and J.K. Torgesen, R.K. Wagner, C.A. Rashotte, E. Rose, P. Lindamood, and C. Galvan, "Preventing Reading Failure in Young Children with Phonological Processing Disabilities: Group and Individual Responses to Instruction," *Journal of Educational Psychology* 91 (1999): 1-15; and F.R. Vellutino, D.M. Scanlon, E. Sipay, S. Small, A. Pratt, R. Chen, and M. Denckla, "Cognitive Profiles of Difficult-to-Remediate and Readily Remediated Poor Readers: Early Intervention as a Vehicle for Distinguishing Between Cognitive and Experiential Deficits as Basic Causes of Specific Reading Disabilities", *Journal of Educational Psychology* 88 (1996): 601-638.

[48] The reduction in eligible children is calculated by multiplying the criterion for designating a child at-risk by the number of children who would continue to need services. In Foorman, et al., "The Role of Instruction in Learning to Read," this is .18 times .30 equals .054.

[49] See J.K. Torgesen, C.A. Rashotte, and A.W. Alexander, "Principles of Fluency Instruction in Reading: Relationships with Established Empirical Outcomes," in *Time, Fluency, and Dyslexia*, ed. M. Wolf (Parkton, MD: York Press, in press).

[50] See L. Fuchs and D. Fuchs, "Treatment Validity: A Simplifying Concept for Reconceptualizing the Identification of Learning Disabilities," *Learning Disabilities Research and Practice* 4 (1998): 204-219.

[51] This issue has been discussed since the advent of the idea of early identification. See P. Satz, H.G. Taylor, J. Friel, and J.M. Fletcher, "Some Developmental and Predictive Precursors of Reading Disabilities: A Six Year Follow-up," in *Dyslexia: An Appraisal of Current Knowledge*, eds. A.L. Benton and D. Pearl (New York: Oxford Press, 1978), 313-348; A.A. Silver, "Prevention," ibid. at 349-377; and J.J. Jansky, "A critical review of 'Some Developmental and Predictive Precursors of Reading Disabilities,'" ibid. at 377-395. A more contemporary discussion is in D. Speece and L.P. Case, "Classification in Context: An Alternative Approach to Identifying Early Reading Difficulty" (unpublished manuscript).

[52] See M. Pressley and R. Allington, "What Should Reading Instructional Research Be the Research Of?" *Issues in Education* 5 (1999): 1-35. See the responses in the same issue by B.R. Foorman, J.M. Fletcher, and D.J. Francis, "Beginning Reading is Strategic and By Design Multi-Level"; G.R. Lyon, "In Celebration of Science in the Study of Reading Development, Reading Difficulties, and Reading Instruction: The NICHD Perspective"; J.K. Torgesen, "Placing NICHD-Supported Research on Reading With the Proper Context"; and F.R. Vellutino and D.M. Scanlon, "Focus, Funding, Phonics—What's the Point?"

[53] See M. Fullan and M. Miles, "Getting Reform Right: What Works and What Doesn't," *Phi Delta Kappan* 74 (1992): 745-752; B. Rowan and L.F. Guthrie, "The Quality of Chapter 1 Instruction: Results From a Study of Twenty-four Schools," in *Effective Programs for Students at Risk*, eds. Robert E. Slavin, N. L. Karweit, and N.A.

Madden (Boston, MA: Allyn and Bacon, 1989), 195-219; and R. Weatherly and M. Lipsky, "Street-level Bureaucrats and Institutional Innovation: Implementing Special Education Reform," *Harvard Educational Review* 47 (1977): 171-197.

[54] See S.L. Hall and L.C. Moats, *Straight Talk About Reading* (Chicago, IL: Contemporary Books, 1999).

[55] See U.S. Department of Education, *Twenty-first Annual Report to Congress on the Implementation of the Individuals with Disabilities Education Act* (Washington DC: U.S. Department of Education, 1999).

[56] These issues are extensively discussed by V.W. Berninger and R.D. Abbott, "Redefining Learning Disabilities: Moving Beyond Aptitude Achievement Discrepancies to Failure to Respond to Validated Treatment Protocols," in *Frames of Reference for the Assessment of Learning Disabilities*, ed. G.R. Lyon (Baltimore, MD: Paul H. Brookes, 1994), 143-162; and F.R. Vellutino, D.M. Scanlon, and E.R. Sipay, "Towards Distinguishing Between Cognitive and Experimental Deficits as Primary Sources of Difficulty in Learning to Read: The Importance of Early Intervention in Diagnosis Specific Reading Disability," in *Foundations of Reading Acquisition and Dyslexia*, ed. B. Blachman (Mahwah NJ: Erlbaum, 1997), 347-380.

Chapter 13

The Little-Known Case of America's Largest School Choice Program

Daniel McGroarty

Imagine an education program not dictated by a rigid, one-size-fits-all course of study, but individually tailored to each child's needs.

Imagine public education not constrained by cost factors, but based on the legally binding promise of a "free appropriate public education."

> **What would the American education system look like if all students were considered "special," and therefore worthy of the broad array of choices now accessible only in the company of significant physical, emotional, or mental disability?**

Imagine a *public* system that provides *private* school placement when public schools can't meet students' needs.

Far from being a flight of pedagogical fantasy, such a system does in fact exist today—for the subgroup of students categorized as having disabilities.

The purpose of this chapter is to examine special education not as a *sui generis* program, but as a variation on the school choice theme. Given that most parents of special-needs children see their youngsters' life options constrained by their physical, mental, and emotional challenges, it is ironic that special education should constitute the one branch of American public education that gives parents more choices and control, more involvement and influence than any other. That irony is compounded by the public education establishment's ready acceptance of significant choice elements in the context of special education that are anathema when applied to education more generally.

What would the American education system look like if all students were considered "special," and therefore worthy of the broad array of choices now accessible only in the company of significant physical, emotional, or mental disability?

Special Education as School Choice

Do parents of special-needs children really have a greater degree of latitude in choosing educational options?

The answer is a "qualified yes," says Sherry Kolbe, executive director of the National Association of Private Schools for Exceptional Children (NAPSEC),[1] depending to a large degree on the parent and his or her pushiness. Parental involvement in developing a special-needs child's individualized education program (IEP) is required by law, giving parents significant input in shaping both their child's educational program and the setting in which that education will take place. (For a District of Columbia parent's perspective, see Box 1.) Says Kolbe, whose

---

Box 1. A Parent's Perspective (Mother, Washington, D.C.)

What does the private placement process look like from a parent's perspective? One Washington, D.C., mother whose daughter has Down Syndrome offers this account:

"We found ourselves dependent on the public system, which my husband and I never intended to be. But then you learn by talking to other parents how to make the system work. You register your child—we did that for [our daughter] when she turned three." On the advice of other parents with special-needs children, the mother also "hired a lawyer the minute my daughter turned three."

"Then the public system assesses your child—it's a battery of physical therapists, social workers, psychologists, the whole panoply." The District then proposes a placement based on that assessment. In this child's case, a District public elementary school with a special education program comprising approximately three percent of the overall student body. The parents, leery of an inclusionary placement, decided to contest the District's proposal.

"The problem," recalls the mother, "is that with [the public school placements], so many kids with disparate needs have to be grouped together. I've talked to other parents. Inclusion sounds good, but then you find your child's just put over in the corner of the classroom." The family retained an educational consultant expert in the District's special-needs process and formally requested an administrative hearing to contest the placement proposal.

"We prepared a full IEP. We spent about $15,000 [in legal and consulting fees] to get ready for the hearing," the mother relates. The day before the hearing was to be held, "we were on a conference call going over what would happen at the hearing, and [the public school representative] made a settlement offer." The child would be placed in a private day school in the suburban Washington area, with the costs paid by the District.

"It's hard to take a vulnerable child into a bureaucracy for assessment," observes the mother. "The whole thing is so regulated by law, it's adversarial to begin with—a really charged situation. But the irony is that the [District's] system is so bad, their placement options are so limited when you're trying to fit a child into a broken system, that you can put together pieces of the program best for your child, and they fund it."

---

organization assists special-needs families seeking private placements: "The process is quite specific. Parents are required to be there every step of the way. There are requirements that notice be given in the parents' native language, that the meetings be set at a time convenient for them—and even that the parents have the right to request meetings to review their child's situation whenever they want, as often as they want," not just annually as the law mandates.

Nor are the options for special-needs students limited to traditional private and public schools. The growing charter school movement has spawned a significant effort to serve special-needs students; although the U.S. Department of Education's Office of Special Education Programs keeps no official statistics on the number of charter schools specializing in special education, one OSEP official acknowledged that a significant number of charter schools do so, perhaps as many as 20 percent, or approximately 350 schools nationwide.[2]

> *Education writer Jonathan Fox reports that public school districts are paying private school tuition for approximately 2 percent of the nation's 5.6 million special-needs students, or about 126,000 children, "at an estimated cost of $2 billion to taxpayers."*

How fully parents of special-needs students exercise their educational options is another matter. Kolbe recounts a recent call from a District of Columbia mother requesting help finding a school for her mentally disabled son. When Kolbe inquired as to whether the boy had been assessed by D.C. school authorities and what public placement they had recommended, the mother said her son had been ill and missed the first day of school. "She said they'd told her, 'you missed the assessments—come back next year, and we'll test him then,'" Kolbe says incredulously. "I said, 'Wait a minute. You've got to go back in and push to have your child evaluated *now.*'"

Other parents do push, securing special consideration—at times under threat of litigation. Nowhere is the range of possibilities more evident than in the practice of securing private school placement at public expense. Although extended to an extremely small percentage of the special-needs population, the very possibility of private placement creates a precedent for other parents.

To see how much power this puts into parents' hands, consider the case of an engineer from India who researched the best schools for autistic children over the Internet and located one such private school in New Jersey. He proceeded to apply for and win a job at the New Jersey-based Bell Labs, obtained an H1-B skilled-laborer visa, moved his family more than 8,000 miles, and enrolled his son in that school.[3]

If in-state choices are inadequate or inappropriate, parents can press for out-of-state private residential placements, paid for by public funds. NAPSEC's Kolbe tells the story of one California child, deaf and with multiple disabilities, whose family moved 13 times in an effort to find the public school district that would optimize their educational options. "They'd move," recounts Kolbe, "enroll their child in the public schools, and when it became clear the [public] in-school programs weren't helping their child, they'd push for alternate arrangements. If the school wasn't willing to talk about a private placement, they'd move again and start the whole process over." In the end, the family found a California public school district that would approve a private school placement. "That's where they've lived ever since," concludes Kolbe.[4]

How widespread is private placement nationally? According to the U.S. Department of

Education,[5] 1,387 private schools—or about 5 percent of the private school universe—specialize in serving special-needs students. Of course, not all special-needs students attend private schools, nor do all of those who attend private schools do so at public expense. Using both federal data and industry estimates, education writer Jonathan Fox reports that public school districts are paying private school tuition for approximately 2 percent of the nation's 5.6 million special-needs students, or about 126,000 children, "at an estimated cost of $2 billion to taxpayers." Nearly half of those students receive private placement at full public expense, while the others receive partial public support. With private placement ranging from paying tuition at day schools to meeting all costs at residential facilities for more severely challenged students, costs routinely range from $20,000 to $60,000 per child per year.[6]

> *NAPSEC executive director Sherry Kolbe notes, "We get calls every day from parents who say, 'We've taken out a second mortgage, we'll pay what it costs—we're just tired of fighting the [public] system.'"*

Not that private placements for special-needs students are in any way automatic, says NAPSEC's Kolbe. "I've had [public school] special education teachers tell me, 'We're not allowed to tell parents private placement is an option.' And even when public school administrators do [talk about private placement], they make it sound unattractive—like it's segregating special-needs students to take them out [of public schools]." Kolbe notes the hypocrisy in the public school position: "They like to say that 'only the public schools have to educate all kids.' But meanwhile, in the Chicago public schools, under a no-exceptions 'zero tolerance' policy, they've suspended and expelled 44,000 kids—in just one year."

Kolbe continues: "In terms of policy, public schools are the placement of preference for special-needs kids. We get calls every day from parents who say, 'We've taken out a second mortgage, we'll pay what it costs—we're just tired of fighting the [public] system.'"

Not all states take a hostile stance toward private placement. As an exception, Kolbe cites Maryland: "It's a great system there. They see the value of private placement—that [public and private systems] can work hand-in-hand to do what's best for each child." Kolbe does, however, see in other states rising evidence of resistance to the high cost of private placement: "Dollars aren't supposed to enter into it, but they do." As proof, she cites a recently revised New York State budget mechanism that, although purporting to be "placement neutral," puts in place dollar incentives to encourage school districts to place fewer special-needs students in private schools.[7] Says Kolbe: "The public schools are pressured not to pay for [private placements]. In Massachusetts, for instance, 600 special-needs students are served out of state. The public system doesn't like to lose that money, so they're looking for ways to bring those kids back into the public system. But even if all those kids were brought back [to public schools], they have no idea whether they could be educated—and what it would cost." Indeed, as Jonathan Fox observes, "The truth is that little research has been done on special education outcomes or the average state spending per disability in private schools."[8] Public education officials may decry the sums involved, but it is entirely possible that, for certain types of disabilities, private school out-placement may be the most efficient option.

The possibility of private placement serves to highlight equity issues because the high cost of special education forces public systems to make hard choices in allocating education dollars. Witness an experimental early-intervention autism program in Fairfax County, Virginia, that offers intensive home treatment to preschool children at an annual cost of about $30,000 per child versus $8,203 for the average Fairfax student.[9] Observing that open-ended special-needs funding saps dollars from general education students does nothing to settle the question as to where limited dollars should be directed. Says one Virginia parent of a special-needs child: "It isn't a fair argument to say your child needs a computer in his classroom when my child is facing institutionalization."

As parents and educators grapple to set the boundaries of special-needs policy, they do so with the heavy involvement of a third party—the courts. As former Reason Foundation researcher Janet Beales notes, the Individuals with Disabilities Education Act (IDEA) "mandates that every child with a disability be provided with a free and appropriate public education—regardless of cost. Because the term 'free appropriate public education' (or FAPE) has never been well-defined, parents and educators often disagree over how a child is to be educated, which can lead to intense litigation." Indeed, the 13 IDEA disability categories may be established by law,[10] along with a general state responsibility for providing a continuum of services across the disability spectrum, but how states meet this requirement—in particular, whether and how often they provide private school placement—varies widely from state to state and even district to district. Add to that the fact that services are being provided to students whose conditions range from mild learning disabilities and behavior problems, where differences in diagnoses are possible, to more severe and self-evident physical and mental conditions including severe emotional disturbance, blindness, deafness, and retardation, and it is easy to see how the lack of uniformity amounts to an invitation to litigation.

> *Special education costs run rampant: Although approximately 11 percent of D.C. students are categorized as special-needs, the program consumed nearly 30 percent of all school funds in 1999.*

A Tale of Two Systems

Because the degree of choice extended to special-needs students depends in large part on parents' pushiness, it should come as no surprise that, in many school districts, there is not one special education system, but two, separate and unequal. This dual system, depending on the degree of parents' savvy and persistence, unlawfully deprives some special-needs students of essential services promised by federal law while providing others with premium private education at public expense.

To see how these two systems coexist, witness the District of Columbia. With the start of each new school year, readers of *The Washington Post* encounter "exposés" about special-needs students stranded at home, missing school because their bus never arrives. Admittedly, Washington, D.C., presents an extreme case: So chaotic is the District's special education office that school officials admit they don't even have a solid count of the number of special-needs students in the system[11]—to say nothing of the quality of education services they receive.

Indeed, in addition to the system's approximately 8,000 special-needs students, as recently as early 1999, 5,000 more languished on waiting lists at various stages in the assessment process, a violation of federal law. Costs run rampant: Although approximately 11 percent of D.C. students are categorized as special-needs, the program consumed nearly 30 percent of all school funds—$170 million out of $575 million—in 1999.[12]

Contrast the unfortunate experience of those 5,000 wait-listed children with the 1,500 disabled D.C. students enrolled in private schools, at an annual public cost in 1999 of $44 million, or nearly $30,000 per student. By 2000, then-D.C. School Superintendent Arlene Ackerman was asking for $100 million for transportation and private school tuition payments for this special-needs cohort.[13] In a system where the superintendent acknowledged that special education was in such chaos that it could take five years to fix, the head of one District special education advocacy group asked: "And we wonder why so many parents fight to send their children to private schools."[14]

From a public policy perspective, the Washington, D.C., experience presents an unattractive picture: activist, often affluent parents aggressively "gaming" the system to obtain special options paid for by the public—in some instances with the public school system even reimbursing them for hiring private lawyers to sue the public schools—while poor, predominantly minority parents find their special-needs children treated like "non-persons" by the same school system.[15]

> *Is it possible to remedy the inequities of the de facto "choice" system that exists in special education at present, not by eliminating the degree of parental choice that exists for some families, but by extending greater choice to all parents of special-needs students?*

Such is the state of special education as a genre of school choice in America.

From Rhetoric to Reality

Is it possible to remedy the inequities of the *de facto* "choice" system that exists in special education at present, not by eliminating the degree of parental choice that exists for some families, but by extending greater choice to all parents of special-needs students?

For opponents of private school choice, the idea that vouchers might benefit special-needs students is dismissed out of hand. Indeed, private schools' alleged refusal to educate special-needs students is often advanced as a potent argument against vouchers. Says Sandra Feldman, president of the American Federation of Teachers: "Private schools are not required to accept special education students." Or as a prominent Milwaukee anti-school choice activist asserts, "Kids with learning disabilities...kids who have behavioral problems, kids who have been involved in the juvenile criminal justice system: Those kids get left behind [by school vouchers] because...a lot of private schools...don't have to take them, so that leaves it for public education to deal with those children."[16]

Are such charges true? Do private schools shun special-needs students, as critics contend? Or could more widespread private school choice expand educational options for special-needs children?

With private school tuition averaging $3,116 per year[17] and true per-pupil costs averaging perhaps a thousand dollars more,[18] serving special-needs students constitutes a formidable financial challenge. Educating special-needs students even on the mild end of the disability spectrum is costly. As Janet Beales noted in her study of the Los Angeles school system's special education expenditures, "Taking total costs into account, the average cost of educating a student with a disability in the Los Angeles Unified School District was approximately $11,500 during 1991-92. For non-disabled students, spending averaged $4,000 per pupil."[19] Advocates of public education aggressively argue the need for additional funds for educating their own special-needs students—even as they adamantly oppose providing private schools supplemental vouchers to do the very same thing.

The implications for school choice programs are obvious. As Polly Williams, the African-American legislator who was the driving force behind passage of Milwaukee's seminal Parental Choice Program in 1990, told this author years ago, "We can't expect...private schools to do with $2,500 what the public schools do with $15,000. I call it MPS [Milwaukee Public Schools] math: They want to give choice schools all of the regulations and one-sixth of the money."[20]

Milwaukee Parental Choice Program

First Year in Operation: 1990-91
Eligibility:
- 175% of federal poverty level
- Resident of Milwaukee
- Students selected by lottery, if more applicants than seats available

Value of voucher:
- $5,300 in 2000-2001
- No adjustment for special-needs students

Current participation:
- 9,638 students at 105 schools in 2000-2001
- Program capped at 15 percent of Milwaukee's public school enrollment, or approximately 15,000 students

Williams' logic was that the city's private schools were willing to educate special-needs students if the state would give them "cost-plus vouchers," adjusted to meet the higher cost of educating such youngsters—which, of course, enemies of the Milwaukee voucher program would never permit.

Because Wisconsin's Parental Choice law makes no distinctive provisions for special-needs students, no one knows precisely how many choice children would warrant special-needs classification, save for those enrolled at specialized facilities such as Milwaukee's Lutheran Special School. Interviews with administrators at Milwaukee choice schools suggest, however, that the voucher program attracts disabled students at a rate similar to their percentage in the Milwaukee Public Schools, or approximately 12 to 15

percent. (See Box 2 for a parent's perspective on the Milwaukee Parental Choice Program.) With the Parental Choice Program serving over 9,600 students citywide, it is likely that the number of special-needs children receiving vouchers exceeds 1,200.

One would not know this from the media, however, nor from the rhetoric of program

Box 2. A Parent's Perspective (Single Mother, Milwaukee)

This woman has three children, all of school age, the oldest of whom has attention deficit disorder (ADD) as well as a history of physical ailments that have necessitated periodic hospital or home stays, placing further strains on the boy's educational progress. She has enrolled her son in both public and private schools at various times. She now enrolls him in a private school via the Milwaukee voucher program. This mother views the evaluation process leading to an IEP in negative terms, and has resisted repeated public school recommendations to have her son formally evaluated.

"I didn't want the label on him. I don't want it following him through school, so every time there's any problem, they go to the file and say, 'Well, you see?' But they [administrators at the public school her son attended as a 5th grader] just kept pushing me, so finally I saw the school psychologist, and she asked to see my son. So I asked [my son], would he see her, and he said, 'Sure, Mom. What do they think is wrong with me?' It hurt me to hear that. So when the psychologist said her recommendation was to have him tested, we were right back where I started.

"Everyone kept saying, 'We can give him better service if he's tested,' but they could never spell out just what that would mean. I asked them, but after a while I just started to think what the labeling would do was get the school more money.

"It wasn't that I didn't want my son to see someone who could help. In fact, there was a point when I was married and I had health insurance covering psychological visits, and I had my son evaluated privately. He saw three different doctors at that time, and one of them wrote up a letter about the best ways to teach my son, by visual learning and not just lectures or reading textbooks—that kind of thing. It wasn't an IEP, but I showed it to each teacher at the beginning of the year because I thought it could be a help.

"At [his private school], he's not labeled, and he's making dramatic improvement. The way he talks about school, you can tell he thinks he can learn. And his behavior at school is so much better—the teachers are pleased, and he's happy that they're happy.

"I've had my son in public schools and private schools at different times, whichever I thought would be best. But where he is now is the first school that's really figured out how to teach [my son], not just how to label him."

opponents. Because choice schools do not typically have the resources to test and classify disabled youngsters—and since the state statute establishing the program is silent on the subject of special-needs students—opponents of Milwaukee's voucher program continue to claim that special-needs students are not served, even as a steady flow of IEP students moves out of the city's public schools and into private schools of choice.

What these observations suggest is that we know too little today about how special education works in the school choice setting—and what little we think we know may well be wrong. What follows are snapshots from each of the three publicly financed school choice programs that have been enacted by state legislatures—the Milwaukee, Cleveland, and Florida programs.[21] Together, they help round out the picture of how school choice serves special-needs students in

America today.

Milwaukee

How do Milwaukee's choice schools cope with the challenge of special-needs students? At Marva Collins Prep, a K-6 school on Milwaukee's Near North Side now in its fifth year of operation, the school policy is not to "label" students. As Principal Robert Rauh explains, the non-labeling approach owes in equal parts to the school's philosophy and to the design of the admissions mechanism of the Milwaukee Parental Choice Program. "First of all, Marva Collins' philosophy is that 'all children can learn,'" says Rauh. "So there's a general attitude that, given our philosophy, there's no reason to label our students. But second, the way [the Milwaukee Parental Choice Program] is structured, it's a blind admissions policy," Rauh continues. "If we agree to put our school into the choice program, it's the parents who choose us. And since we don't pick our students, putting labels on them wouldn't get us any additional funds"—in contrast to the extra monies allotted for special-needs children in public schools. For the 1999-2000 school year, each choice student enrolling at Marva Collins Prep brought a voucher worth $5,300, whether disabled or not.

> *For the 1999-2000 school year, each choice student enrolling at Marva Collins Prep brought a voucher worth $5,300, whether disabled or not.*

When choice students arrive at Marva Collins, however, Rauh finds that as many as 12 to 15 percent of them would in fact warrant designation as special-need students, "whether it would be various learning disabilities or ADD."[22] Rauh hastens to add that categorizing students matters little compared with assessing their individual educational needs: "We work to where the student is, and bring them forward."

At present, Marva Collins enrolls four students with more severe special needs, three of whom attend the school via Milwaukee's voucher program. One child experienced brain trauma at birth, says Rauh. "He'd been in a special education program as a K-4 student in MPS [Milwaukee Public Schools]. He came to our school, and we had him repeat K-4 again. We ended up hiring a part-time teacher's assistant basically dedicated to him." The boy's family happens to be just above the income limit that would qualify them for a voucher [the limit is an income no higher than 175 percent of the cutoff for the federal free- or reduced-price lunch program], "so we're not getting anything through the Parental Choice Program for him," says Rauh. Indeed, the child's parents are paying approximately $2,000 a year tuition for their son: "It's all they can afford—really more than what they can afford," says Rauh.

Another boy at Marva Collins, also a transfer student from MPS, had been in a prolonged coma several years earlier. Rauh reports that the boy's parents are considering transferring the child to the Lutheran Special School, established for the sole purpose of educating special-needs children. "We have another girl who's been with us from K-5, who is mentally retarded, and another girl—again another MPS transfer—with serious emotional disabilities." Regardless of the additional costs of educating these children, each child carries a voucher worth the same $5,300 as every other student in Milwaukee's Parental Choice Program.

I asked Rauh why parents of such children would choose Marva Collins over public schools that offer special-needs programs. "Our classrooms are smaller, they're very structured," he responds. "I guess parents come in and see the way we work, and decide we're right for their child—whether or not we officially serve special-needs kids."

When asked how the school affords even part-time special staff, Rauh answers readily: "We just take a hit on it. It's costing us about $10,000 for special assistance for just the four students I mentioned." Rauh relates that there used to be a Head Start program housed in the same building as his school. "Their speech pathologist used to keep working with her [Head Start] kids, even after they came to [Marva Collins]. But that's gone now. So far, [incurring the added expense] hasn't been a huge problem because there hasn't been huge demand."

Aware of how tenuous such a position may be as policy, Rauh continues: "There was a time when we looked at converting to charter status," a move that would have entitled the school to $6,494 per pupil, rather than the $5,300 provided by the Milwaukee Parental Choice Program, "but we dropped the idea. Special money always comes with strings attached," concludes Rauh.

Three miles west of Marva Collins, Lutheran Special School serves 32 special-needs students in Grades 1 through 8, 13 of whom attend via the Milwaukee Parental Choice Program. Principal Judy Schultz describes her students as "on the mild end of the special-needs spectrum: cognitively disabled, ED [emotionally disabled] kids, LD [learning disabled], ADD [attention deficit disorder] and ADHD [attention deficit hyperactivity disorder], gray-area kids [a Milwaukee Public School designation]—plus several students with cerebral palsy. We're not set up to serve students with severe physical disabilities."[23] Supported by the Lutheran Church Missouri Synod, Lutheran Special School opened its doors in 1958. It has participated in the choice program for the past three years, since the Wisconsin Supreme Court upheld the constitutionality of the expansion of the program to religious schools.

> *Judy Schultz, principal of Lutheran Special School, notes one irony, given critics' charge that Milwaukee choice schools cherry-pick the best students: "Under the random assignment rules of [the choice] program, we don't get the students' records to look at before they select us.*

"Our tuition is $2,900 a year for members of the Lutheran Church Missouri Synod," Schultz explains, "and $3,500 otherwise. We have a handful of kids whose families actually pay full tuition." Schultz adds that she regularly "writes off" about 20 percent of tuition due the school: "We call it tuition assistance, but it's really just what the families can't pay." Lutheran Special School's full cost of education is about $8,400 per student, says Schultz, with the difference being supplied by charitable giving from individuals and institutions. The 13 choice students bring vouchers in the amount of $5,300 apiece, which—though equal to just 60 percent of the true per-pupil cost of public education—has been a stabilizing factor in the school's finances.

Lutheran Special School first opened one-fifth of its full-enrollment slots to choice students in 1998; it now allots one-fourth. "We wanted to see how it worked," relates Schultz. "It's helped us financially. There really hasn't been a downside. We've enrolled more African-American students through the choice program," Schultz continues, noting the program's positive impact on the school's diversity. "Now our student population is about 50-50, half white kids and half African-American, plus two Asian-American students."

Schultz notes one irony, given critics' charge that choice schools cherry-pick the best students: "Under the random assignment rules of [the choice] program, we don't get the students' records to look at before they select us. So sometimes we get general education kids—kids who don't really need the kind of education we provide."

In addition to the students who attend Lutheran Special School, Schultz deploys two school psychologists, one full- and one part-time, to 60 other Lutheran schools across southern Wisconsin, including four Lutheran grade schools in Milwaukee that participate in the Parental Choice Program. "The need [for special education services] is huge. The four Milwaukee schools have a total student population of about 400," says Schultz, "and of that, about one-third of those students see our consultants for special-needs services." With no supplemental assistance from the Parental Choice Program for this outreach program, Lutheran Special Schools absorbs its cost.

Cleveland Scholarship and Tutoring Program

First Year in Operation: 1996-97

Eligibility:
- Priority given to students from families with income below 200 percent of the federal poverty level
- Grades K-7 eligible in 2000-2001; program expands one grade per year
- Resident of the Cleveland Municipal School system
- Students selected by lottery if more applicants than scholarships available

Value of voucher:
- Maximum of $2,250 for 2000-2001 year
- Parents responsible for 10 percent of tuition
- Value of voucher for special-needs students is open-ended; must reflect the instruction, related services, and transportation costs of educating such students

Current participation:
- 3,688 students at 50 schools in 2000-01

Cleveland

As in Milwaukee, anecdotal evidence from Cleveland indicates that special-needs students on the milder end of the disability spectrum routinely utilize vouchers to obtain private school placement. Indeed, according to one source closely involved with the Cleveland Scholarship Program, although the public school system remains officially opposed to the program, vouchers have proven a welcome safety valve for public schools anxious to off-load difficult children: "I know in the case of one [public] school, when some of the students used vouchers to enroll at [a nearby private school], their old teachers threw a going-away party."[24]

Other participants suggest, however, that the voucher program works both ways: At one Cleveland choice school, an administrator's off-the-record observation is that some of the "learning disabled" students coming to his school via vouchers proved, upon additional testing, not to be special-needs students at all, raising the possibility that a certain amount of budget-driven over-classification may be occurring in the Cleveland Public Schools. "It's like there's a bounty on these kids; in the public system, special needs bring special funding," says the private school administrator.

"The sending [public] school wouldn't forward student files," says the administrator, "so we had kids coming in in September, and from the point of view of the teacher and the student, it was a fresh start. Then in April, when the school year was almost over, the file would arrive, and we'd see these kids labeled as special needs. We'd look at their test scores and the progress they'd made since they started with us, and say, 'No way.'

"We had one boy, 10 years old, come in labeled 'special needs.' His file was full of evaluations and reports, but when we sat him down with our counselors, we found despite all those reports that no one had ever really talked to the child. His mom worked two jobs, one in the morning and one at night, and here this 10-year-old-boy was going home from school, picking up his younger siblings, making them dinner, bathing them, and getting them to bed. Then he was up in the morning to get them fed and dressed so they could be picked up for preschool. By the time he came to school, he wasn't ready to learn, he was exhausted. He just wanted people to leave him alone. We got his mother some help, and he just blossomed. Thing was, in public school he would have been labeled special needs all the way through.

> *By statute, Cleveland special-needs students who qualify for the choice program are entitled to a voucher that, in the open-ended wording of the law, "take[s] into account the instruction, related services, and transportation costs of educating such students."*

"The way I saw it, the public schools thought they were penalizing us, sending us these kids. On our end, it was lemons to lemonade."[25]

Although Cleveland may have such experiences in common with Milwaukee, one sharp difference remains: By statute, Cleveland special-needs students who qualify for the choice program are entitled not to the ordinary $2,250 voucher, but to a voucher that, in the open-ended wording of the law, "take[s] into account the instruction, related services, and transportation costs of educating such students."[26]

To date, only one Cleveland private school enrolls students under this provision: The Hanna Perkins School, an institution dating back to the early 1960s, whose mission is to educate "children with developmental difficulties, emotionally based," explains executive director Joan Horwitz.[27]

At Hanna Perkins, individually tailored education is the norm, and each student's family works with a therapist to strengthen the connection between school and home environments. Hanna Perkins charges $9,000 annual tuition, an amount Horwitz says does not reflect the true cost of educating each child, which runs over $12,000 per student. "We're fortunate to have an endowment, as well as funding from the United Way," she notes.

Located near the campus of Case Western Reserve University and the renowned Cleveland Clinic, but also just blocks away from Cleveland's impoverished Hough Avenue neighborhood, Hanna Perkins' 40-student population is remarkably diverse: "We've got families from Bangladesh, Pakistan, and China," says Horwitz. "We've got white kids, Hispanic kids, and African-American kids, from all different income levels, too. Some pay full tuition [$9,000 per year], while others are 'dollar-a-day' families,"[28] making the minimum "co-pay" required by the Cleveland Scholarship Program ($250 per year).

Hanna Perkins runs three programs: One for toddlers, a half-day preschool, and a kindergarten program. Only the kindergartners, Horwitz explains, are eligible to participate in the Cleveland Scholarship program. Four of the school's 12 kindergartners attend via the voucher program, which pays Hanna Perkins $9,000 per student, four times the value of an ordinary voucher.[29] "It's been a good experience," says Horwitz of Hanna Perkins' participation in the program. "It's giving children a chance to come [to Hanna Perkins] that they would never have had before," she continues. "It's been a positive experience for both our students and our school."

Florida Opportunity Scholarships for Students with Disabilities

First Year in Operation: 2000-2001

Eligibility:
- Student must demonstrate failure to improve in prior public school

Value of voucher:
- Equal to pupil's public school funding
- Range is from $6,000 to more than $20,000 per student, depending on severity of disability

Current participation:
- 1,100 students statewide in 2000-2001
- 105 private schools in 36 school districts

Horwitz can only speculate about what will happen when her kindergartners graduate to first grade and leave Hanna Perkins behind. Will they enroll in another private school under the Cleveland Scholarship Program's special-needs provision? Thus far, the only voucher student who has left Hanna Perkins enrolled in a Catholic special education school that does not participate in the Cleveland Scholarship Program. "The program's been good for us," says Horwitz. "We'll just have to wait and see if other schools come in."[30]

Florida

Florida won national attention in 1999 for establishing the first statewide voucher program—albeit limited to students attending failing public schools. Less well-known but equally important is the step Florida took in the 2000 legislative session to extend school choice to the state's vast special-needs population.

The brainchild of then-state senator, now Senate president John McKay, Florida's special-needs voucher is an example of the way politics can make use of paradox, turning legal setback to legislative gain. McKay drove the expansion through a legal loophole left by state Circuit Court Judge L. Ralph Smith, who, at the urging of the American Federation of Teachers, the National Education Association, the ACLU, and People for the American Way, struck down the voucher component of Governor Jeb Bush's Florida A+ plan on March 14, 2000. (In October 2000, a state appeals court reversed that ruling.)

A supporter of Bush's omnibus education plan and particularly its "Opportunity Scholarship" component, McKay had been following the court case closely. With a special-needs child of his own, McKay was well aware that Florida paid private schools to educate a small number of disabled students who could not be accommodated in public schools. When the state's attorneys argued that invalidating the voucher component of the A+ program would strike at public assistance to Florida's special-needs students in private school placements, McKay took note. When Judge Smith struck down the governor's voucher program but left standing the state's private outplacement of special-needs students—on grounds that special education students differ because they have needs that cannot be met by public schools—McKay took action.

As he describes it, Senator McKay interpreted Judge Smith's constitutional carve-out for special-needs students as an invitation. "I grew up in a small country town," deadpans the canny McKay, "so I won't say the light went on immediately, but in my layman's terms, I saw an opening."[31] With Florida's abbreviated legislative session fast approaching, McKay prepared a bill to "voucherize" funding for all special-needs students across the state who weren't succeeding in public school. His vehicle: a simple amendment to a little-noticed section of the Governor's A+ plan that had been spared by Judge Smith.

> *Florida won national attention in 1999 for establishing the first statewide voucher program. Less well-known but equally important is that the Florida legislature extended school choice to the state's special-needs population in 2000.*

"When [Governor Bush] proposed his A+ Plan, I told him I'd be there, provided he put in a pilot program for special-needs children," explains McKay.[32] Bush did, establishing a one-city experiment that McKay designated for Sarasota. While national public attention in August 1999 focused on the 52 children using vouchers to leave two failed public schools in Pensacola, little notice attended the two Sarasota special-needs children who used McKay's Scholarships for Students with Disabilities to enroll at the private school of their choice. As a pilot project, the legislation identified the special-needs voucher as specific to Sarasota; McKay's amendment in the wake of Judge Smith's ruling simply deleted the Sarasota reference. The result: Special-needs scholarships would henceforth be available to any student across the state.

With Florida's legislative session racing to a close, McKay pursued a stealth strategy: "I didn't even call a press conference about [the amendment]," he says. Yet traditional voucher opponents saw huge implications in the small change. "We're adamantly opposed to it," said Wayne Blanton, executive director of the Florida School Boards Association. "We're opposed to vouchers, and that's a backdoor approach to vouchers."[33] When McKay offered his amendment on the Florida Senate floor, however, opposition was muted. "Nobody wanted to attack head-on," recalls McKay. "Every objection was put forward as a kind of question about the program. So when the person was done, I just said, 'Thank you for your concern about Florida's special-needs children.' I did that a few times, and folks got the message as to how it would look if they opposed [McKay's plan]." Having deflated the opposition, McKay's plan passed without incident. Special-needs students would be eligible to request vouchers for the 2000-2001 school year.

McKay's program differs in significant respects from the "failed schools first" approach favored by Governor Jeb Bush. In contrast to the Opportunity Scholarship program—under which vouchers are available only to students attending public schools that receive two "F's" for student achievement in any four-year period[34]—special-needs students are eligible for vouchers if they demonstrate failure to improve at their public school, regardless of whether their school has received a poor grade from the state. Pat Heffernan, executive director of Floridians for School Choice, a Miami-based advocacy group supporting vouchers, lauds McKay's approach for focusing on individual student performance rather than school-wide achievement: "The [special-needs] scholarships are available not based on how public schools are doing, but based on how students are doing, so that's closer to the original vision."

> *For the 2000-2001 school year, 105 private schools in 36 of Florida's 67 school districts indicated they would accept students enrolling with special-needs scholarships.*

According to the statute, special-needs scholarships are available, so long as:

- the student has an active IEP or family support plan;

- the student's academic progress in at least two areas has not met expected performance levels for the previous year as determined by the student's IEP—or, absent specific performance levels identified in the IEP, the student performed below grade level on state or local assessments and the parent believes that the student is not progressing adequately towards his/her IEP goals; and

- the scholarship is requested prior to the time at which the number of valid requests exceeds the districts' cap for the year in which the scholarship will be awarded.[35]

For the 2000-2001 school year, 105 private schools in 36 of Florida's 67 school districts[36] indicated they would accept students enrolling with special-needs scholarships.[37]

"The way the program is designed, students are supposed to carry over [to the private school] the funds allotted to their education in public school," says Heffernan. "Not a penny more, not a penny less."[38] As a result, the value of Florida's special-needs vouchers dwarfs even the most ambitious proposals advanced in other states. Private schools will receive between $6,000 and $20,000 per child, depending on the severity of a child's disability, but they must accept all applicants if they sign up to participate in the program.

In August 2000, with the new school year just weeks away, Florida's new special-needs voucher program was essentially still a secret, hampered by a low-key effort to notify eligible parents. As one Florida news account put it: "The quiet start of the new 'Scholarship Program for Students with Disabilities' has provided a curious contrast to Florida's first voucher program for students from failing schools."[39] Another newspaper observed, "In Miami-Dade County, where 39,000 children are eligible, just 51 parents had picked up applications for the state program. In Broward, where there are 28,000 such children, only 35 parents have made telephone inquiries."[40] Once a long-awaited letter from the state commissioner of education was sent to parents of disabled children statewide and the program's initial enrollment deadline was waived, the number of special-needs students receiving scholarships grew to 1,100 by mid-October.[41]

Florida's barely-known special-needs voucher program started its first year with twenty times as many students as the state's much-watched Opportunity Scholarship Program, an initial enrollment that makes it the third largest publicly funded voucher experiment in the nation. With 350,000 Florida children categorized as "special-needs" students, Senator McKay's deletion of a few statutory words has the potential to create the country's largest private school choice program. Indeed, McKay predicts that the next phase will see the creation of new special-needs schools and expansion of existing schools to accommodate more students. "It's a simple case of supply and demand. That's what I see the next few years out."

> *School choice may well be a way to serve special-needs students in keeping with the expansive ideal that originally animated the IDEA.*

Yet what moves McKay is the need to level the playing field for parents of disabled children. "I'd filed bills [for special-needs vouchers] before," says the Senator, referring to efforts he'd made in the early 1990s. "I talked with the state education commissioner," recalls McKay. "I told him, 'Look at what happens when parents come in with a lawyer who can quote the case law. The state ends up paying for private placement.' We were doing a great job of empowering the powerful. My question was: What about the rest of parents?

"This program is for them," says McKay.

Conclusions and Recommendations

Clearly, choice can be a valuable tool in serving the educational needs of disabled children. Today, however, disabled students are caught up in a separate and unequal system, one that "empower(s) the powerful," as Senator McKay puts it, while treating other special-needs students as second-class citizens. As we've seen, choice in special education can be highly dependent on whether a special-needs child has parents with sufficient energy, interest, ability, and often income to press for the student's full range of rights.

As in all considerations of public policy, our assessment of special-needs programs should be guided by considerations of both *efficacy* and *equity*: What works—and for whom? For policymakers troubled by the separate and unequal aspects of special education today, existing school choice programs—Cleveland, with its special-needs provision, and particularly Florida, with its ambitious effort to "voucherize" special education—point to a possible remedy. School choice might well be a way to serve special-needs students in keeping with the expansive ideal that originally animated the IDEA.

Looking beyond special education to education reform in general, those who believe that individualized education and parental choice are positive values for special-needs students might well ask themselves: What would be wrong with extending more individualization and choice to all children?

[1] Sherry Kolbe, executive director, National Association of Private School for Exceptional Children, telephone interview with author, 1 August 2000.

[2] Troy Justison, Office of Special Education Programs, U.S. Department of Education, telephone interview with author, 11 January 2001.

[3] See Iver Peterson, "High Rewards and High Costs as States Draw Autistic Pupils," *New York Times*, 6 May 2000, sec. A, p. 1.

[4] Kolbe, telephone interview with author, 8 September 2000.

[5] National Center for Education Statistics, data from "Private School Universe Survey, 1997-98," provided by Vance Grant, U.S. Department of Education, 10 January 2001.

[6] Jonathan Fox, "Sending Public School Students to Private Schools," *Policy Review* no. 93 (1999). Cost range confirmed by NAPSEC's Kolbe.

[7] Kolbe, telephone interview with author, 1 August 2000.

[8] Fox, "Sending Public School Students to Private Schools." On the difficulties in measuring inputs and their impact, Janet Beales cites special education finance scholar Thomas Parrish:

> Of the 24 states responding to a recent survey administered by the national Center for Special Education Finance (CSEF), exactly one-half reported that they did not know the statewide cost of their special education programs. In addition, while national special education data were reported for the 1982-83 through 1987-88 school years, the federal government no longer requests these data from the states. While three different studies measuring the cost of special education to the nation have been conducted since the inception of the IDEA, the last of these was completed in 1988 and reported data from the 1985-86 school year. Thus, as there is no current information on the national expenditure for special education, the CSEF estimate of over $32 billion, presented at the beginning of this paper, is based on 10-year-old estimates.

Janet Beales, "Meeting the Challenge: How the Private Sector Serves Difficult-to-Educate Students," Reason Public Policy Institute Policy Study No. 212, August 1996.

[9] See Victoria Benning, "Fairfax Autism Program Ignites Battle Over Access," *Washington Post*, 30 June 2000, sec. A, p. 1.

[10] According to Section 602(3) of the amended Individuals with Disabilities Education Act (1997), disabilities are defined as follows:

(3) CHILD WITH A DISABILITY—

(A) IN GENERAL—The term 'child with a disability' means a child—

(i) with mental retardation, hearing impairments (including deafness), speech or language impairments, visual impairments (including blindness), serious emotional disturbance (hereinafter referred to as 'emotional disturbance'), orthopedic impairments, autism, traumatic brain injury, other health impairments, or specific learning disabilities; and

(ii) who, by reason thereof, needs special education and related services.

(B) CHILD AGED 3 THROUGH 9—The term 'child with a disability' for a child aged 3 through 9 may, at the discretion of the State and the local educational agency, include a child—

(i) experiencing developmental delays, as defined by the State and as measured by appropriate diagnostic instruments and procedures, in one or more of the following areas: physical development, cognitive development, communication development, social or emotional development, or adaptive development; and

(ii) who, by reason thereof, needs special education and related services.

[11] See Valerie Strauss, "Special-Ed Woes Persist in the District," *Washington Post*, 15 March 1999, sec. B, no. 1.

[12] See ibid.

[13] See Debbi Wilgoren, "School Money Plan Pleases No One," *Washington Post*, 20 January 2000, sec. B, no. 7.

[14] Strauss, "Special-Ed Woes Persist in the District."

[15] Two years ago, Congress attached to the D.C. appropriations legislation a provision that limits attorney fees for special education cases to $50 an hour, capped at $1,300 per student. Done to prevent the payment of open-ended legal costs to parents suing the public system for preferred placement, the measure has had the paradoxical impact of discouraging D.C. attorneys from taking special-needs cases brought to them by poorer parents, whose inability to pay made the prospect of public reimbursement the only payment option.

[16] Tammy Johnson of Wisconsin Citizen Action, as quoted with Sandra Feldman in Howard L. Fuller's "The Saturation Campaign of Lies and Distortions About Educational Vouchers," Marquette University/Institute for the Transformation of Learning, March 2000. Fuller's study is a devastating compendium of what he terms "a conscious effort to contaminate public debate" on the part of voucher opponents.

[17] This figure is for 1993-94, the last year for which U.S. Department of Education data are available. It should be noted that the range of private school spending is notoriously wide, with Lutheran day schools averaging as little as $2,200 and boarding school tuition at the other end of the spectrum at $19,200. Vance Grant, U.S. Department of Education, interview with author, 11 January 2001.

[18] Although the U.S. Department of Education does not track private school per-pupil costs, the Department's Vance Grant estimates private school per-pupil costs averaged $4,085 in 1997-98. Ibid.

[19] See Beales, "Meeting the Challenge."

[20] Daniel McGroarty, *Break These Chains: The Battle for School Choice* (Rocklin, CA: Prima Publishing, 1996): 88.

[21] Milwaukee's Parental Choice Program dates to 1990-1991, while the Cleveland program began in 1996-1997 and Florida's statewide voucher program started with students from two schools in Pensacola in 1999-2000.

[22] Robert Rauh, principal, Marva Collins Prep, interview with the author, 10 August 2000.

[23] Judy Schultz, principal, Lutheran Special School, telephone interview with the author, 20 September 2000.

[24] Confidential telephone interview with author, 20 July 2000.

[25] Confidential interview with the author, 26 September 2000.

[26] Section (2) of the statute establishing the Cleveland Scholarship and Tuition Program states: "The state superintendent shall provide for an increase in the basic scholarship amount in the case of any student who is a mainstreamed handicapped student and shall further increase such amount in the case of any separately educated handicapped child. Such increases shall take into account the instruction, related services, and transportation costs of educating such students."

[27] Joan Horwitz, executive director, Hanna Perkins School, telephone interview with the author, 11 August 2000.

[28] Horwitz, telephone interview with the author, 14 September 2000.

[29] J.C. Benton of the Ohio Department of Education, whose division oversees the Cleveland Scholarship program, confirms that, at present, the four students at Hanna Perkins are the only students being served under the special-needs provision of the Cleveland voucher statute. Telephone interview with the author, 26 September 2000.

[30] Horwitz, telephone interview with the author, 17 January 2001.

[31] John McKay, president, Florida State Senate, telephone interview with the author, 18 September 2000.

[32] Ibid.

[33] Shelby Oppel, "Vouchers Proposed for Disabled Students," *St. Petersburg Times*, 3 May 2000, sec. B, p. 5.

[34] In the 1999-2000 school year, two public schools in Pensacola received F's, making their students eligible for vouchers. Fifty-two students used those vouchers to attend the private school of their choice. In the summer of 2000, none of the state's 60-plus "1-F" schools received a second consecutive F, leaving the Pensacola students the only children eligible for Opportunity Scholarships.

[35] See the following Florida Department of Education site: <<www.opportunityschools.org/osas/spswd/law.pdf>>.

[36] As of October 18, 2000. For a current tally of schools and districts participating, visit the following Florida Department of Education site: <<www.opportunityschools.org>>.

[37] See Stephen Hegarty, "Disabled Step Up Use of Vouchers," *St. Petersburg Times*, 11 September 2000, sec. B, p. 1. Florida's transition to a full "special-needs voucher" program will be phased in as follows: For its first year, the program is limited to 5 percent of students with disabilities in each school district; with 350,000 students statewide classified as special-needs, this means a program cap of 17,500 vouchers. In the second year, the percentage rises to 10 percent, and then to 20 percent in the third year. After that, the limits come off, and the program opens to all of Florida's special-needs students.

[38] Heffernan underscores the provisional nature of the program in its first year and expects both guidelines from Florida's Department of Education and further legislative action in 2001 to clarify gray areas. For instance, although private special-needs schools cannot charge parents fees in excess of the voucher, it is uncertain as to whether they can accept benefits available to parents of special-needs students, such as medical insurance that may cover certain services. Telephone interview with the author, 12 September 2000.

[39] Hegarty, "Disabled step up use of vouchers."

[40] Analisa Nazareno, "Voucher plan has few takers," *Miami Herald*, 2 August 2000, sec. B, p. 1.

[41] Data provided by Diane McCain of the Florida Department of Education, 18 October 2000.

Chapter 14

Effectiveness and Accountability (Part 2): Alternatives to the Compliance Model

Bryan C. Hassel and Patrick J. Wolf*

Introduction

As we described in Chapter 3, effectiveness and accountability policy and practice in special education have traditionally been shaped by a "compliance model" that defines effectiveness largely in terms of following certain processes and ensures accountability through the documentation of procedural compliance. Although the Individuals with Disabilities Education Act amendments passed in 1997 (IDEA 97) were billed as the start of a new regime of results-based accountability, we have seen that they did not replace the traditional compliance-based model. Instead, the 1997 amendments merely grafted performance measurement onto the pre-existing compliance approach. In addition, IDEA 97 allowed critical exceptions and exemptions, which have enabled a number of state and local education agencies to postpone if not entirely avoid the day in which documented changes in educational achievement drive effectiveness and accountability in special education. Moreover, both the accountability system designed by the Department of Education in the wake of IDEA 97 and its operation "in the trenches" preserved much of the process-focus and procedural-documentation components of the familiar compliance model described in Chapter 3.

> If the effectiveness standards and accountability mechanisms of IDEA 97, did not accomplish the "regime-shift" that its backers claim, what alternatives might be available to promote outcome-based measures of achievement and real accountability for performance?

If the effectiveness standards and accountability mechanisms of IDEA 97 did not accomplish the "regime shift" that its backers claim, what alternatives might be available to promote outcome-based measures of achievement and real accountability for performance? In this chapter, we address that question in two stages:

---

* The authors would like to acknowledge the insightful comments of Chester E. Finn, Jr.; Charles R. Hokanson, Jr.; and participants in the November 2000 "Rethinking Special Education for a New Century" conference. Wendy Wendt provided valuable research assistance. All viewpoints and errors are those of the authors.

First, we examine promising alternatives to the compliance model that have arisen outside of special education, indeed outside of education altogether, as policymakers in other domains have prompted shifts from a compliance-based to a results-based approach. These developments in other fields may provide inspiration and lessons for special education policy.

Second, we develop a broad framework for the application of these approaches within special education. The framework we propose makes student learning results the central driving force of special education policy, not an overlay on a pre-existing compliance system. Though certain procedural requirements remain in force, they do so to make it possible for results-based accountability to fulfill its potential.

> *The framework we propose makes student learning results the central driving force of special education policy, not an overlay on a pre-existing compliance system.*

Alternatives to the Compliance Model

Special education is not the only domain in which policymakers have sought to achieve a worthy goal by setting hard-and-fast procedural rules and then creating an enforcement apparatus to ensure that regulated parties meet their responsibilities. When environmental degradation began to concern us decades ago, Congress and state legislatures responded with an array of detailed prescriptions for how industry and citizens should reduce the amount of pollution and waste they produced, and empowered the Environmental Protection Agency and parallel state and local offices to enforce these rules.[1] Problems with safety and health in the workplace prompted the creation of a similar apparatus, embodied in the Occupational Safety and Health Administration and its state counterparts.[2] Within government, the prevalence of political patronage and other questionable practices in hiring and procurement led policymakers to create the civil service and detailed procurement regulations to ensure that government managers gave out jobs, promotions, and contracts according to merit-based criteria.[3]

These approaches have successfully eliminated some of the troubling behaviors that they targeted. The release of dangerous pollutants into the atmosphere has been greatly reduced. The incidence of certain workplace injuries has dropped dramatically. Handing out jobs and contracts to political cronies has become less common in government. As has happened in special education, however, observers of these other domains have become critical of their nearly exclusive reliance on the enforcement approach to achieving desired policy objectives. Here are some of the major criticisms, many of them summarized by Harvard public-management professor Malcolm Sparrow[4]:

- **The inflexibility of regulations impedes effective practice.** Because regulations are designed as "one-size-fits-all" interventions, they often block local actors from doing what's best in a given situation. They also may fail to adjust over time to changes in best practice or in the nature of the problem to be solved. And to the extent that regulations prescribe in detail how a problem should be handled, they do not provide incentives for regulated parties to work out better ways of achieving the same results.

- **The attention of regulators is distributed irrationally**. Because the enforcement approach directs regulators to enforce rules rather than solve problems, regulatory attention does not necessarily focus on the most pressing or highest-impact activities. Analyses of the regulation of risk have shown that regulatory action often focuses massive resources on activities with little payoff.[5] For example, if environmental regulations require officials to concentrate on reducing particular toxins, they may thereby ignore other threats to health that are more severe. Some policy scholars have argued that, in the extreme, the "capture" of a regulatory agency by its regulatory target leads the agency to partner with the people it is supposed to oversee and deliberately shine its regulatory light only in the places where mischief is not occurring.[6]

- **The sheer volume and complexity of regulation diminish its effectiveness.** As requirements increase, it becomes less likely that regulated parties can keep up with their obligations, even if they would like to comply. It also becomes less likely that regulators can effectively monitor compliance and apply sanctions.[7]

- **The costs of regulation outweigh the benefits.** According to one estimate, the cost of complying with federal regulations reaches nearly $700 billion per year.[8] Concerns about cost, of course, lead to constant calls by business organizations and scholars to reduce the regulatory burden on their industries.[9]

- **Regulation of process ignores results.** A focus on procedural rules induces regulated parties to focus on checking off procedural elements rather than ensuring that they are achieving the results the regulation intends to produce.

> *Regulators elicit compliance not just through detailed command-and-control regulation, but also by deploying a broad range of tools to achieve the intended results.*

In response to these criticisms, policymakers and regulators have begun to experiment with a wider range of tools. Though they are diverse, one central concept ties them together—*a focus on results*. In each instance described below, policymakers or agency officials sought to replace a system that focused purely on regulatory compliance with one that *concentrates the efforts of regulated parties on achieving superior outcomes*. The following subsections describe some of these alternative approaches, provide examples of their use, and discuss their potential and limitations. Note that these approaches are not mutually exclusive; indeed, as the next section will argue, joining them into coherent policies is the principal challenge policymakers and regulators face in special education and elsewhere. The approaches are presented under three headings, which represent increasingly radical departures from the compliance model.

Smart Regulation

"Smart regulation" shares a great deal with the compliance model.[10] Basic norms of behavior remain in place, regulators can still check to see whether regulated parties are following them, and regulators can still impose sanctions when parties fail to comply. But regulators elicit compliance not just through detailed command-and-control regulation; instead, they deploy a broader range of tools to achieve the intended results. This section discusses four such tools: forging voluntary agreements (with technical assistance); using information to spur good behavior; addressing underlying causes of noncompliance; and replacing procedural controls with after-the-fact checks.[11]

Voluntary agreements. Perhaps the best way to understand the idea of voluntary agreements is to look at examples of how they have worked in practice. One illustration is the Occupational Safety and Health Administration's Maine 200 program, launched in 1993. OSHA offered Maine's 200 employers holding the worst records of on-the-job injuries a choice: either develop a company-designed comprehensive health-and-safety program with employee involvement, or undergo a traditional OSHA inspection. Companies that opted for the voluntary plan would also receive extensive technical assistance from OSHA in identifying and remedying workplace hazards. The program immediately motivated a profound shift in responsibility for identifying and abating workplace hazards. Within its first year, companies themselves had cited nearly three times as many hazards (95,800) as OSHA had managed to identify in the eight previous years (36,780). In addition, worker compensation claims in Maine dropped by 35 percent during the first two program years.[12]

> *These examples of voluntary agreements share an important element: They focus on results. The regulators asked: What are we trying to accomplish, and are there better ways to reach those goals?*

Though OSHA's Maine 200 program is one of the better-known examples of voluntary agreements (it won a Ford Foundation/Kennedy School of Government Innovations Award), it is by no means the only one. During the Clinton administration, the Environmental Protection Agency was the site of numerous similar initiatives. In Project XL, for example, regulators gained the authority to offer flexibility to companies in exchange for agreements to produce superior environmental results. This initiative responded to bizarre situations like one involving Amoco, which was required by EPA regulations to spend $31 million to recover a small amount of benzene when an alternate approach (which ran against regulations) would have allowed the company to recover five times as much benzene for only $6 million.[13] Numerous other federal, state, and local agencies have adopted similar approaches. These examples share an important element: They focus on results. Regulators stepped back from their standard operating procedures and asked: What are we trying to accomplish, and are there better ways to reach those goals? They then worked with the regulated parties to produce better outcomes, even if it meant scrapping some conventional compliance requirements.

Using information. A twist on voluntary agreements involves the use of information-based strategies to achieve compliance.[14] Under this approach, regulators require regulated parties to disclose certain facts about their operations to the media and the wider public. Because most companies do not want to be embarrassed publicly, disclosure may induce compliance where traditional enforcement mechanisms have failed. For example, the Toxics Release Inventory (TRI) requires more than 20,000 facilities to provide information to the Environmental Protection Agency about their release and transfer of toxic chemicals. The EPA then publishes the information. Though analysts stress that it is difficult to attribute reductions solely to TRI, the numbers are impressive: Between 1988 (when the program began) and 1997, "total releases of toxic chemicals tracked by TRI declined 49 percent nationwide."[15] The Consumer Product Safety Commission traditionally has also used an information-based strategy in an attempt to shame the manufacturers of dangerous products as well as reward companies that go out of their way to produce safer toys and household goods.

Addressing root causes. In another form of smart regulation, agencies sometimes try to induce compliance by addressing the underlying causes of failure to adhere to rules. A good example is the Immigration and Naturalization Service's Operation Jobs, which sought to break a cycle of repeated enforcement of laws prohibiting the employment of undocumented immigrants in Dallas, Texas. Traditionally, the INS's unannounced visits to companies and subsequent arrests of illegal workers would produce a surge of job openings that all-too-often were immediately filled by a new group of illegal hires. As a result, traditional enforcement had no lasting effect. Under the new program, The INS helped to match these jobs with legal replacements by partnering with public and nonprofit organizations that worked with women transitioning off welfare, unemployed youth, documented immigrants, and other people seeking work. The effect was immediate. Within the first two weeks of the program, Operation Jobs produced 1,400 job placement referrals, and, by the end of the year, 2,500 employable adults and youth had gone to work.

> *Because smart regulation leaves in place some of the basic regulatory apparatus, it appears to retain a check against flagrant violations by regulated parties.*

Moving to after-the-fact audits. Often a particular regulation is not objectionable in itself, but the detailed procedural requirements imposed to ensure that regulated parties comply with it are onerous and counterproductive. Consider procurement. Many of the basic concepts of government procurement policy are essentially sound. For example, government buyers should not use the government's checkbook to make personal purchases, or enter into contracts with companies solely because their owners have strong political or family connections to agency officials. Few people would say such restrictions should vanish entirely, but the way government agencies have gone about ensuring compliance with them has been, in the eyes of some observers, excessively procedural, requiring government buyers to go through numerous hoops and fill out reams of paperwork to make even the smallest purchases. Over the last decade, reformers have tried to do away with such procedural hurdles while maintaining essential safeguards. One wide-ranging reform allowed buyers to use credit cards to make purchases up to a certain amount, bypassing the usual submit-and-wait requisition process. In the Agriculture Department, according to one analysis, "costs per transaction have dropped from $77 per paper purchase order to $17 per electronic transaction, a decrease of almost 80 percent. The agency stands to save $29.5 million annually as a result of its award-winning program."[16] To prevent abuse, an automated monitoring system triggers alerts if users appear to be logging personal expenses with their cards or making multiple purchases from the same vendor within a day. And an *ex post* review of one out of every 100 transactions creates a strong deterrent against fraud at a much lower cost than *ex ante* reviews of all transactions.

Post-audits, by definition, catch problems only after the proverbial cow has escaped from the barn. Fines and other *ex post* sanctions can punish offenders, and thereby possibly deter others from leaving the barn door open. Yet such punishments often cannot undo the damage that has occurred. When the consequences of noncompliance are truly dire, post-audits are an inappropriate accountability mechanism. One way to address this problem is by offering flexibility not across the board, but to those agents that have proven through past performance that they are good stewards of resources or policy.

Benefits and Drawbacks of Smart Regulation

These examples illustrate the central features of smart regulation. First, the *underlying norms or principles* often do not change. Second, the ultimate *threat of sanctions* still looms in the background for regulated parties. Indeed, it sometimes looms larger than before, as in the case of the threatened OSHA inspections in the Maine 200 program. Third, the approaches provide some flexibility to regulated parties about *how to comply*. They do not dictate in great detail the precise actions that parties must take, just the basic principles they must uphold. Fourth, the strategies often use decidedly *non-regulatory* tactics to induce performance, such as technical assistance, publicity, or efforts to address underlying causes of problems. Finally, and perhaps most importantly, smart regulation *focuses relentlessly on results*. The purpose of each change is to achieve a better outcome, whether that is reduced pollution, decreased hiring of illegal immigrants, or other policy goals.

> **When regulations appear ineffective, stifling, inflexible, or too costly to continue, the search is on for forms of accountability that can replace the focus on compliance.**

Smart regulation is appealing for a number of reasons. Because it leaves in place some of the basic regulatory apparatus, it appears to retain a check against flagrant violations by regulated parties, assuming that the existing regulatory regime is appropriately designed and well targeted. If negotiations, technical assistance, or other approaches fail to produce results, the agency can still throw the book at an uncooperative organization. This ultimate threat of sanctions provides the motivation for regulated parties to come to the negotiating table or accept technical assistance in the first place. At the same time, though, the flexibility built into these approaches arguably leads to better outcomes, or equal outcomes at lower cost. In the case of Maine 200, though OSHA retained final say, negotiated plans were likely to be more sensible and better tailored to companies' circumstances than plans handed down by OSHA would have been. In the credit card procurement initiative, illicit contracting is still policed, but honest government buyers are spared the hassles of command-and-control procurement systems.

Smart regulation has drawbacks, too. Critics of regulation assail it for not going far enough, leaving in place a regulatory apparatus that needs to be dismantled altogether. Proponents of regulation attack it for allowing regulated parties to skirt important constraints, negotiating their way out of obligations. They also worry that these new approaches will lead to non-uniformity in the implementation of regulations, with some offenders getting a pass while others comply. Many regulatory regimes were put in place precisely to ensure that everyone is treated alike, and proponents of that approach resist any changes that might lead to differential treatment.

The approach may also create an ambiguous situation for both regulated parties and regulators, leaving it unclear what kinds of behaviors and activities are permissible under the new regime. In the OSHA case, for example, what happens if a worker in a company with an OSHA-approved plan finds a specific safety violation? Can OSHA inspect the plant and levy any justified sanctions? If so, what has the company really gained by going through the negotiating process? If not, how can workers at the plant gain protection from unsafe conditions? Can regulators negotiate away elements of law, or are there some constraints that must remain in place? This kind of ambiguity apparently led to an internal slogan at EPA for Project XL: "If it ain't illegal, it ain't XL."[17] More seriously, it has often made it difficult for companies and regulators to come to final agreements. Despite the appeal of Project XL, only a small number of agreements have been negotiated under it.[18] As a result of these ambiguities, attempts to implement negotiated arrangements have frequently resulted in litigation.[19]

Because of these problems, some regulatory reformers have looked beyond smart regulation to more radical approaches in which existing rules and restrictions are actually scrapped and replaced with other means of producing desired results. The next two sections describe a pair of such approaches.

Incentives for Performance

Though some enthusiasts of deregulation call for an end to regulation altogether, most recognize that simply throwing rules on the trash heap will not suffice. As inane as many specific regulations may be, broad regulatory structures (such as environmental protection and workplace safety) often have valuable social purposes that policymakers and regulators remain eager to advance. Accordingly, when regulations appear ineffective, stifling, inflexible, or too costly to continue, the search is on for forms of accountability that can replace the focus on compliance. Chief among these is accountability for "results," "performance," or "outcomes." Accountability for results starts from the reasonable premise that results are what matter most. The aim of public policy, this reasoning goes, should be to produce the intended outcomes, not to prescribe the means of getting there. Policymakers (and their delegates in public agencies) should set goals for performance, and then create a system of incentives to induce relevant parties to achieve those goals, by whatever means make sense.

> *Policymakers should set goals for performance, and then create a system of incentives to induce relevant parties to achieve those goals, by whatever means make sense.*

Of course it is not necessary to look outside the domain of education to find examples of performance-based reform. Almost every state has instituted standards for student learning, required schools to administer tests to determine whether pupils are meeting those standards, and attached at least some consequences to how schools, school districts, and/or students perform on these tests. Even within special education, the 1997 IDEA amendments sought to place more emphasis on the setting and achieving of learning goals by disabled students. However, in many of these educational settings (including special education, as discussed in Chapter 3), performance accountability has been primarily an *overlay* on the existing compliance-oriented system, rather than a replacement for it. Though standards-and-accountability reforms often carry with them a great deal of rhetoric about giving districts and schools more authority in exchange for their enhanced accountability, the vast majority of public schools have little control over their budgets, personnel, use of time, or even their instructional programs. Charter schools and some unique public schools are exceptions, but they represent a small fraction of all public schools. The 1997 IDEA amendments pressed for more performance accountability, but also left compliance in place as the essential core of special education policy.

> An important subset of performance accountability seeks to encourage a particular kind of outcome: prevention of problems before they develop.

Success stories. Consequently, it is helpful to look outside of education for some examples of regulatory reform in which moves toward performance-based accountability were actually moves away from compliance-based approaches. Perhaps the best example was Great Britain's "Next Steps" initiative, launched in 1988. Over the course of several years, most of the country's government agencies negotiated performance agreements (known as "framework documents") with the ministers or departments overseeing them. These documents specified results the agency would achieve over a three-year period and the flexibility and autonomy it would achieve in return. They also set forth consequences that would attach to performance and nonperformance. The chief executive of each agency would be required to reapply for his or her job every three years, and the agency's performance over that time would play a central role in the decision about rehiring.

As the approach—which resembles American charter schools—spread across the government, success stories spread as well. Though many of these successes involved cost savings, the arguably more important outcome was improvements in the quality of services provided. The Vehicle Inspectorate—newly judged by measures such as waiting times and customer satisfaction—immediately opened its offices on Saturdays and Sundays, making it much easier for people with Monday-to-Friday jobs to have their cars inspected. The Employment Service began publishing comparative data about local offices. Offices responded by cutting waiting times, increasing the accuracy of unemployment-check payments, and reducing costs. Most significantly, the service as a whole increased job placements 40 percent with no new resources.[20]

An important subset of performance accountability approaches seeks to encourage a particular kind of outcome: *prevention of problems before they develop.* By providing incentives for public agencies or private actors to take preventive steps, overseers have managed to reduce the incidence of problems and the costs of dealing with them. Often, the mechanism used to encourage prevention is a set of fiscal incentives that, in effect, provide bonuses for agents that do a good job with prevention. For example, Scottsdale, Arizona (like many other municipalities), provides a lump-sum budget to an employee-owned company that operates its fire department. The company may keep any surplus left after a year of firefighting. As a consequence, the incentives are strong for the company to focus on preventing fires altogether. The company works closely with developers of new homes and commercial establishments to help them construct fire-safe structures. The company also led the charge to pass a local ordinance requiring sprinkler systems in new buildings. The results: between 1986 and 1991, as the value of property in the city rose 86 percent, fire losses *dropped* by 15%.[21]

In another example, the state of Oregon provides $48,000 to counties for each bed in juvenile detention centers that is *not* used. Consequently, Deschutes County established a community-based alternative to state incarceration for non-violent juvenile offenders that focuses on early intervention, prevention, and creative reinvestment of public money. The results are telling: Between 1997 and 2000, Deschutes County saw its average incarceration rates drop from 23 to 5 youths (the lowest in the country), while earning $630,000 in unused-bed resources to support prevention efforts.[22]

Benefits and Challenges to Incentives for Performance

These examples demonstrate the basic principles of the performance-based approach. Overseers *set goals or standards* for regulated parties to meet. To the extent practicable, these goals and standards concern ultimate destinations (*outcomes*) rather than procedural steps along the way (*inputs*). Overseers establish *measures* that will allow everyone to assess the extent to which regulated parties are meeting goals and standards. They give regulated parties the flexibility to pursue these goals as they see fit, retaining only the most basic rules to guard against gross malfeasance. And they impose *consequences* based on how well the regulated parties achieve their objectives—often both positive consequences for success and negative consequences for failure.[23] In the case of Britain's Next Steps program, these features are recorded in framework documents that govern each agency's conduct. In cases of the prevention-based approaches, standards, measures, and consequences are more indirect. Scottsdale's fire department, for example, is not given an annual goal for fire losses. Instead, the built-in fiscal incentives encourage the fire department to establish its own ambitious standards and measure its results; the consequences come out in the bottom line.

> *Rather than prescribe a single way to achieve goals, the performance-based approach gives regulated parties incentives and flexibility to figure out new and better (or less expensive) ways of producing outcomes.*

The performance-based approach boasts many appealing features. It focuses the attention of both regulators and regulated parties on what matters most: the outcomes of their actions, at least as they are defined by the goals and standards. Rather than prescribe a single way to achieve goals, it gives regulated parties incentives and flexibility to figure out new and better (or less expensive) ways of producing outcomes. This flexibility allows parties to adapt to local circumstances and invent "better mousetraps" over time. The goal, of course, is simply to "catch mice."

The performance-based approach faces challenges as well. For some opponents of regulation, it still does not go far enough. Bureaucrats are still put in charge of setting standards and goals which may be unreasonable, inflexible, or ill-suited to local circumstances or changes over time in the regulated activities.[24] Even proponents note technical challenges in creating incentives for performance. First, it is often difficult to set goals and standards that strike the right balance between being ambitious and being attainable, especially when attempting to do so for an entire state or nation. Second, it is often challenging to find instruments that truly measure the outcomes that policymakers most want. Without credible measures, it is hard to generate support for the consequences that attach to inadequate performance.[25] Third, because performance-measurement systems tend to rely on aggregate measures (in order to be manageable and "objective"), they can ignore problematic situations within the broader system. For example, suppose a firm achieves exemplary workplace safety results on a company-wide basis but has one plant where safety is abysmal. Is there any protection for workers at that plant in a system with no rules for specific workplaces, just overall goals? In principle, it is possible to design a system of goals and measures that attends to the problem of the smallest units, but in practice doing so can magnify the difficulties of goal-setting and data-gathering. A fourth and related problem arises when policymakers care not just about ultimate outcomes, but also about how regulated parties pursue these goals. In such cases, an outcomes-based regime does not guarantee all the desired results. For example, regulation in air safety is very compliance-oriented, requiring airlines to employ particular equipment and follow specified procedures. A results-based alternative—allowing airlines to do as they please so long as they kept the number of air deaths per year below an acceptable number—would not be appropriate. Passengers want assurance that airlines are making an effort to ensure that *every airplane* is safe for *every flight*, and that *every pilot and crewmember* is well-trained.

> *Market-based reforms seek to hold regulated parties accountable via a market-like mechanism rather through a set of goals, measures, and consequences.*

Customer Choice

Another technique that policymakers have utilized to move away from enforcement-based systems is the use of market mechanisms. Like performance management, market-based approaches eliminate many of the constraints that formerly governed the behavior of regulated parties. But instead of replacing them with goals, measures, and consequences imposed by public entities, market-based reforms seek to hold regulated parties accountable via a market-like mechanism. Markets, of course, are not a recent invention of regulatory theorists. The idea that market mechanisms can maximize *public* benefit through an "invisible hand" goes back to Adam Smith and, in less sophisticated forms, even further.

Market-based approaches come in different shapes depending upon the particular regulatory problem being addressed. This section discusses one important variant: customer choice.[26] The basic idea is to empower a set of customers to make decisions about the providers from which they will buy the service (or whether they will buy it at all). Often, the immediate customers are the ultimate beneficiaries of the service—such as families of school-aged children, recipients of public assistance seeking job training, or government employees who need to purchase supplies or equipment. Other times, the customer acts on behalf of the ultimate beneficiaries—such as a city agency purchasing garbage-removal services or water. Instead of dictating in detail how providers will carry out the activity, overseers leave those decisions to providers on the theory that those who perform poorly will simply "go out of business."

A good example comes from America's experience with public housing. For many years, the primary way in which the government helped the poor afford shelter was by constructing public housing "projects" and subsidizing the rent of low-income residents (usually by charging them a percentage of their income). Because this housing was often the only realistic alternative for its residents, public housing did not really have "customers"; its residents were not likely to go elsewhere if they were unhappy with their dwellings. To maintain quality, therefore, overseers of public housing had to employ a compliance model, specifying in detail how units would be constructed and maintained. This approach, however, could not overcome the tendencies toward decline and chaos that infected these complexes. No handbook of regulations on safety or building upkeep could stem the tide of vandalism and neglect. The compliance model did not cause this decline, but it was woefully inadequate as a solution.

By contrast, the federal Section 8 program pursued a similar goal but used customer choice rather than compliance to achieve quality and satisfaction. Under Section 8, low-income families receive subsidies that they can put toward the housing of their choice. If unhappy with the housing they have selected, they can search for alternatives. Landlords have new incentives to provide quality housing that is affordable to Section 8 recipients because their ability to pay is enhanced by the subsidy. To be sure, Section 8 is not a perfect system. The supply of affordable housing is limited, and many landlords resist Section 8 tenants. Compared with traditional public housing, however, most would judge Section 8 a success, providing homes for millions of people in places they want to live outside the confines of public housing projects.

> *The main appeal of empowering customers lies in the fact that customers with a choice of providers are more apt to receive services that meet their needs and suit their preferences.*

By way of further example, many government agencies across the world have been transformed into "enterprise" functions, living or dying based on their ability to convince other agencies to deliver their services. If the central supply depot cannot produce the right supplies in a timely and cost-effective manner, managers may shop at Office Depot or other vendors instead. If the human resources department cannot stir up good pools of candidates for job openings, managers can place their own classifieds or hire headhunting firms. If the sanitation department cannot deliver better service and/or lower costs than alternate providers, the city can contract with the private firms for this service.[27] In all these examples, providers face strong incentives to provide excellent service. They are not told what to do but are induced to figure out the "best" approaches by their need to attract and retain customers.

Benefits and Drawbacks of Customer Choice

The advantages and drawbacks of this approach have been voluminously discussed in general and more specifically in reference to K-12 education, where reforms that give families more choice over the schools their children attend are both popular and controversial. The main appeal of empowering customers lies in the fact that customers with a choice of providers are more apt to receive services that meet their needs and suit their preferences. Moreover, providers that must attract customers in order to survive and prosper are likely to be better motivated to improve the quality of services. Finally, to the extent that providers are paid on a per-customer basis for their services, they also face strong incentives to reduce the costs of delivering those services. The drawbacks of customer choice as an accountability mechanism include (1) the potential disconnect between what individual customers want and "the public interest"; (2) the fact that customers in some markets may not possess sufficient information to make sensible choices; and (3) the related fact that the customers who are least informed or motivated to seek out quality services may be those in greatest need. Like performance management, choice-based approaches might result in aggregate improvements in service but leave significant sub-groups with the same or inferior levels of service.

> *One theme that runs through the various approaches discussed in this chapter is the importance of high-quality information about the regulated activity.*

Tying it Together: Transparency and Problem-Based Thinking

In other regulatory domains, recent decades have witnessed much experimentation with alternatives to traditional command-and-control structures, adding many tools to regulators' toolboxes. But simply having the tools has not by itself revolutionized regulatory domains. Harvard professor Malcolm Sparrow has noted: "Regulators face no shortage of strategies, methods, programs, and ideas. Rather they face the lack of a structure for managing them all."[28] This section outlines two important ideas that contribute to such a structure, with examples of how these ideas have been put to work. We then explore how these ideas might apply to special education.

The Importance of Information and Transparency

One theme that runs through the various approaches discussed above is the importance of high-quality information about the regulated activity. The need for information is perhaps most obvious in the case of performance-management approaches, which rely centrally on measuring the progress of regulated parties toward pre-defined goals. But information is also critical in the other approaches. Under smart regulation, regulators need ways of knowing whether their creative approaches are indeed yielding better results. Regulators in a variety of fields have developed elaborate systems of random sampling to keep tabs on critical outcomes as new approaches go into effect.[29] And in some smart-regulation approaches, information plays an even more direct role as regulators seek to use publicity about compliance and/or outcomes to motivate regulated parties to comply. In customer-based market approaches, consumers need good information about services and performance in order to make intelligent choices among providers.

Too often, regulatory bodies lack the systems and expertise to acquire and use information in these ways. Many problems can contribute to this. First, good measures of newly important behavior or outcomes may not exist at the outset. Regulators may be faced with the task of developing such indicators from scratch, which is time-consuming and may require technical expertise not present in the agency. Second, information-gathering systems currently in place may not meet new information needs. In agencies that have traditionally relied on command-and-control regulation, information flows have been developed that mesh with those approaches. Agencies keep track of whether forms have been filed, deadlines met, counts taken, inspections conducted, dollars spent within the appropriate line items, and so on. Shifting to systems that focus on other tasks or measurements involves changing long-standing routines, which takes time and sometimes training. Third, although the technology available to regulatory agencies for information collection and analysis has improved dramatically in recent years, many agencies still lag behind. Finally, in agencies that have not heretofore relied heavily on data analysis, staff may lack technical skills required to make the best use of incoming information.

> *One of the greatest barriers to change in regulatory practice is fear on the part of policymakers, regulators, and interest groups that it will be difficult to tell whether new strategies are working.*

As severe as these problems may be, solving them is generally worth the investment. One of the greatest barriers to change in regulatory practice is fear on the part of policymakers, regulators, and interest groups that it will be difficult to tell whether new strategies are working. Consider the case of Maine 200, which provides incentives for companies to comply voluntarily with regulations. Suppose that, after a few years of this approach, the agency's traditional measures showed a significant trend—the number of enforcement actions against companies was down. But did workplace safety actually improve? Sparrow writes, "In the absence of such measures, the ambiguity persists: maybe compliance improved. Or maybe the department got distracted or captured. No one can tell which, so observers remain free to choose whichever explanation suits their purpose."[30] In the case of OSHA in Maine, the agency did develop alternative measures, tracking the number of workers' compensation claims filed by employees. Because these dropped dramatically, the agency had some confidence that its tactics were actually improving worker safety, not just letting companies off the hook. Without such indicators, however, it would have been difficult for the agency to muster political support to change its approach in this way.

Problem-Based Thinking

Another theme in the discussion of these new regulatory tools is that each seems well-suited for some situations but not others. Part of the criticism of the command-and-control approach is that it has been applied indiscriminately to a wide range of regulatory problems regardless of whether it was the most effective strategy for solving a problem. As appealing as these alternate approaches may be, it would be incorrect to assume that any of them can solve every problem faced by policymakers and regulators.

Instead, the most sophisticated thinking about regulatory strategy proposes a "problem-based approach" whereby policymakers or regulators identify concrete problems that need to be addressed if outcome goals are to be achieved.[31] For each, they assemble a set of tools that seem likely to solve that particular problem. Rather than choose a specific tool (such as customer choice) in advance and go looking for ways to use it, the results-based approach suggests applying a great deal of energy to *defining problems and then selecting appropriate tools* to address them. Within any broad regulatory domain such as the environment or special education, there will be many different problems, each demanding its own tailored set of solutions. The aim of regulatory policy should be to create a system in which these problems are identified and then addressed using an array of tools.

Two implications of the problem-based approach are worth noting. First, it magnifies the informational needs sketched above. Understanding what the problems are, the contexts in which they arise, and the likely effectiveness of different tools requires large amounts of information. Assessing whether coordinated strategies are working also requires good measures of the incidence of the problem that is being addressed.

Second, an agency adopting the problem-based approach uses different tools in different situations. Though this point may seem obvious, it runs counter to traditional regulatory thinking, which tends to value consistency and uniformity. An agency taking a problem-based approach may end up applying different strategies to different problems under its purview, different regions of its jurisdiction, and different categories of regulated parties, even to specific regulated parties. Within the context of problem-solving, these variations are not capricious or arbitrary; instead, they are what Sparrow calls "rational inconsistencies," justified by the fact that they make it possible to solve problems that would go unsolved if the agency were required to apply a uniform approach across its entire domain.[32]

> *We believe three principles should guide any redesign of special education policy: (1) an obsession with results; (2) a big toolbox; and (3) residual rules that buttress the results obsession.*

Implications for Special Education

Based on these experiences in other domains, this section sets forth principles for a reworked special education accountability system and then outlines how such a system might work.

Principles for Redesign

Here are three principles that we believe should guide any redesign of special education policy:

- **An obsession with results.** First and foremost, every element of the system should focus on student learning. This obsession must begin at the federal level, with the way Congress frames the federal mandate and the way Washington structures its funding and oversight of states. Through those mechanisms it must create the same obsession in state education agencies, so that they in turn structure their funding and oversight of school districts, charter schools, and other entities with student-learning results in mind. Prodded by those systems to focus intently on learning outcomes, districts must structure their relationships with schools and other providers to produce results. Ultimately, the people on the front lines, those who work directly with children, must share this obsession.

- **A big toolbox.** Within that results-driven framework, people involved at all levels should have access to a wide range of tools for achieving the desired outcomes. Taking a page from "problem-based thinking" in other regulatory domains, policymakers and officials at each level must give those at lower levels the authority to reach into a big toolbox and select the tools most likely to solve problems, including but not limited to the strategies discussed earlier in this chapter: customer choice; incentives for performance; and "smart regulation" approaches such as technical assistance, information, and addressing root causes of shortcomings. Many different problems get in the way of effectively educating disabled students, and they arise at different stages of the educational process. They have different underlying causes. They vary by place and disability. Rather than replacing the one-size-fits-all compliance model with another monolithic approach, a new system should provide the incentives and flexibility to enable problems to be solved.

- **Residual rules that buttress the results obsession.** To the extent that some compliance obligations remain in place, they should be limited to those that enable the results-obsessed system to function properly. As we discuss below, certain aspects of the compliance model probably need to stay. However, in contrast to the current approach, which makes compliance paramount, we propose limiting compliance obligations to a minimal list that supports the overall results-orientation of the system by ensuring that goals are set for student learning, results are measured, and a safety net remains in place for students who still are not learning despite the system's intense new incentives for performance.

Using New Tools Within Special Education

This section frames a new approach to special education policy, drawing on lessons from other regulatory fields. We aim merely to set out a conceptual framework here with the understanding that it would require a great deal of elaboration and detail beyond the scope of this chapter to implement such a framework.

Intense incentives for performance. The main substitute for the old compliance model is a system of performance incentives to (1) maximize the degree to which students with identified special needs achieve (effective intervention); (2) maximize the chances that students with remediable special needs go "off the special education rolls" (effective remediation); and (3) minimize the incidence of preventable special needs in the first place (effective prevention). Like any good performance-management system, the approach we propose involves clear goals for performance, careful measurement of results, and the application of consequences based on those results. We do not address the difficult issue of how to measure results in this chapter and instead concentrate on the critical issues of goal-setting and consequences.

> *We propose limiting compliance obligations to a minimal list that supports the overall results-orientation of the system by ensuring that goals are set for student learning, results are measured, and a safety net remains in place.*

Goal-setting up and down the system. We propose a system of goal-setting that is *nested, negotiated,* and *diverse*. Just as the current compliance system is "nested" (with federal constraints binding states, whose constraints bind local education agencies (LEAs), whose constraints bind schools, teachers, and contractors), so too must a system of goal-setting have this nested quality. As a nation we must have goals for states, which must have goals for LEAs, which must have goals for schools and contractors, which in turn have goals for individual students. It's possible to imagine two extreme ways to arrive at such a nested system: a top-down approach, in which the federal government dictates goals for states, which dictate goals for LEAs, and so on; or a bottom-up approach, in which schools (or other providers) set goals for students, which are rolled up into LEA-wide goals, which are in turn rolled up into statewide goals, which are finally rolled up into national goals. Each has its drawbacks. A purely top-down system would lack responsiveness to local needs and would have difficulty taking into account divergent starting points. It would run counter to the "problem-based" approach advocated in this chapter which calls for tailored responses to different problems. At the same time, a strictly bottom-up system would tend to generate mediocre, easy-to-reach goals and would foster unacceptable inconsistencies in the learning achieved by disabled students between one school or district and others.[33]

Our proposal represents a middle path in which entities at each level negotiate performance agreements with the next level up, each spelling out the performance targets the entity is expected to reach.

Our proposal represents a middle path in which entities at each level *negotiate* performance agreements with the next level up. These agreements would spell out in yearly or multi-year fashion the performance targets the entity is expected to reach. Because the higher-level entity has the final say, it can bring a degree of uniformity and ambition to the lower-level party's goals sufficient to allow the higher-level entity to meet targets agreed to with *its* controlling authority. But because agreements would be forged independently, they would have the capacity to reflect the particular situation of the entity in question. An LEA or state with one set of daunting challenges and a particular starting point might have a different set of goals for the year than does a neighboring LEA or state. A school facility operating an all-day pullout program for students with certain acute needs would have completely different goals from a "regular" school whose student body includes a small number of learning-disabled children.

As implied by the previous paragraph, these negotiated agreements would contain diverse types of goals. For example, a high school's agreement might contain goals regarding outcomes as varied as exceptional students' mastery of state standards (and their progress over time toward such mastery), scores on standardized tests (and changes over time in individuals' scores), achievement of more student-specific learning goals measured in other ways, graduation rates, and post-school outcomes such as employment. If the school housed unique populations or had distinct historical problems, its agreement might address those issues with goals unlike those of other high schools in an LEA. An LEA's agreement with the state might contain similar measures, aggregated across all its high schools, plus analogous goals at the middle and elementary levels. Like the high school example, if the LEA faced singular challenges (such as especially low performance of special-needs children of a particular race), its agreement might contain goals relevant to those issues.

At the bedrock of the goal-setting system are the goals set for individual students. In contrast to the current system, which mandates individual goals but does not make attainment its central focus, goals for individual students should become the guiding force for all activities within special education so that the attainment of goals by individual students would be the foundation for schools' achievement of *their* goals, which would in turn be the foundation for LEAs' attainment of *their* goals, and so on.

Consequences for performance. Though arguably the process of goal-setting and measuring would induce some improvements in performance, a full system of performance incentives needs consequences tied to progress toward goals. In particular, we must consider sanctions which might be applied to entities that fall short of their goals. Most obvious is withholding funds. Because special education is expensive and because most entities receive special education funds from the next level up the chain, this threat is likely to be potent. However, it is a blunt instrument that tends to involve all-or-nothing decisions, when in fact the performance picture for an LEA or state is likely to be mixed as it achieves goals in some areas but not others. Withholding funds also has perverse effects, penalizing students for the errors of educators (though these side effects can be mitigated by withholding administrative rather than program funds).

> *Census-based (rather than need-based) funding can create strong financial incentives to prevent and remediate without the threat of losing funds.*

Furthermore, high-stakes organizational punishments such as funding reductions for sub-par performance can create strong incentives to employ "creative" strategies for measuring and reporting results, a phenomenon that is often referred to as "gaming the numbers." Consequently, although withholding funds may be a viable *ultimate* sanction for agencies to wield, a fine-tuned system of performance incentives should offer more options. Here are some examples:

- **Limited census-based funding.** To encourage entities to achieve certain kinds of goals—notably those having to do with preventing specific learning disabilities from developing altogether or eliminating learning disabilities that can be remedied over time—census-based (rather than need-based) funding can create strong financial incentives to prevent and remediate without the threat of losing funds.[34] In a fiscal system that provides more resources as more students are identified with special needs, states, LEAs, and schools have no financial incentive to engage in preventive or remedial activities. If the system provides parts of special education funding on a "census" basis—a certain amount per pupil, counting *all* the entity's students—entities acquire incentives to prevent and remediate learning disabilities. To account for differences in the incidence of these preventable and remediable learning disabilities, some kind of modified census system that adjusts for school-to-school or district-to-district differences would likely make sense. But the basic notion of providing built-in, self-enforcing incentives for achieving desirable outcomes is sound. Note, however, that this strategy works best for a limited class of disabilities. Pure census-based funding would create incentives for LEAs to find ways to exclude children with expensive disabilities altogether. LEAs that happened to have high proportions of children with expensive disabilities would face significant cost pressures. To avoid this, a fiscal system that blends census-based funding with funding linked to the actual presence of students with certain types of disabilities makes the most sense. Census funding works best for broader geographic entities, such as states and large districts, which are more likely to possess an average incidence of a given disability.

It is less appropriate for smaller LEAs and particular schools, which might by chance enroll disproportionately large numbers of such children.

- **Rewards for exceptional performance.** Another fiscal approach is to provide bonuses for exemplary performance. Bonuses can function at all levels of the system—federal bonuses to states, state bonuses to LEAs, LEA bonuses to schools, and LEA or school bonuses for teachers or other providers.

- **Market testing.** In many cases, it may be possible to create performance incentives by putting providers of special education to a market test, requiring them to compete with other potential providers for the "business" of a school or LEA. "Providers" could be organizations that deliver special education services, or they could be individual teachers. Either way, the idea is to make continued contracts or employment contingent on performance. In essence, this approach pushes the notion of performance agreements another notch down the chain, closer to the actual instructional process. Market testing is more acceptable than simply withholding funds because it does not penalize students for the poor performance of providers, except as they suffer from disruptions caused by changes in providers. This practice is already in use for providers of highly specialized placements and services, such as private facilities that offer residential treatment and services.

> *Giving individual families the opportunity to choose providers—with funding following children to the new provider—creates a more targeted form of performance accountability.*

- **Offer family choice.** In contrast to the bluntness of a threat to withhold funds from an LEA, school, or provider, giving individual families the opportunity to choose providers—with funding following children to the new provider—creates a more targeted form of performance accountability. This approach would work better in some situations than others. Choice is less promising, for example, where the supply of providers is thin; more promising where many providers are eager to compete for students. This latter variable is not, of course, fixed, and policymakers eager to use this approach to promote accountability would do well to consider ways of stimulating the supply of effective providers of needed services. Such supply stimulation would be more likely if the funding that followed the child increased with the severity of the disability in question. (As described in Chapter 13, Florida recently instituted a program whereby families of special-needs students who do not meet the goals of their individualized education programs (IEPs) may select other providers, taking their special education funding with them.)[35]

- **Remove flexibility.** Another potential sanction is a return to command-and-control-style oversight. An entity that fails to meet performance targets could be placed on probation in which it must adhere to stricter procedural controls until its record improves. Note that such a removal of flexibility need not be an all-or-nothing move by an overseer; it could be applied to certain aspects of the process and not others (based on where the weaknesses lie), to certain kinds of disabilities, and so forth.

- **Using information-based approaches.** Finally, policymakers should not underestimate the power of transparency as a performance incentive. If schools, LEAs, states and federal officials know that the extent to which they are (or are not) achieving their goals with special-need students is going to be widely disseminated to parents, policymakers, the media, and the wider public, they are likely to focus more energy on achieving those goals.

With an array of possible accountability tools, an important question becomes how policymakers can blend them into a coherent system of consequences. What we propose here, once again, is a *nested* approach in which each level of the system takes two actions with regard to entities at the next level "down":

> **Why does the framework retain some elements of compliance and omit others? Our problem-solving orientation recognizes that there are some problems that are more successfully addressed with compliance approaches than others.**

First, each level of the system sets consequences for the entities below it. Each level makes clear what consequences will result from different levels of performance, utilizing tools such as those noted above.

Second, each level empowers the entities below to use the full range of consequences in their own oversight of succeeding levels. The word "empowers" is key; in the envisioned system, Washington would neither require states to mete out any particular consequences for LEAs nor require LEAs to deal with their schools and providers in any particular fashion; nor would it forbid any such actions. Rather, federal policy would make clear that these entities may use the full range of consequences in their efforts to induce performance from those they oversee. By the same token, state policy would make clear that LEAs are free to use the full arsenal in their oversight of schools and providers.

It is worth noting that, although different tools are easier to use at different levels, there is no reason to restrict their use to one level or another. For example, market testing is most obvious as a strategy for an LEA or charter school. It becomes more difficult to devise a market-testing approach that a state could use in its oversight of LEAs, and more difficult still to devise a federal market test for states. But state agencies facing strong pressures from the federal government to produce results would have an incentive to investigate such an option. For certain specialized services, for example, it might be possible for a state to contract directly with another provider rather than route funding to a low-performing LEA. What is important is that states be empowered to pursue such options as they see fit and that they face strong incentives to pursue strategies that are likely to yield results.

Residual base of essential compliance obligations. In addition to the basic obligation to educate all children, including those with disabilities, we suggest four fundamental processes that local education agencies (and states) should be responsible for carrying out. First, LEAs should continue to be required to identify potential special-needs children and assess those special needs. Second, for each child so identified and assessed, LEAs should be required to establish year-by-year goals for the student's learning—again reinforcing the fundamental results orientation of special education policy. Third, LEAs should be required to assess students' progress on these goals and report the results to parents, schools, the state, and the public.

Finally, LEAs should be required to involve and inform parents and guardians throughout this process. States should monitor LEAs' compliance with these obligations and disseminate their own reports on compliance and progress toward meeting goals.

Readers will likely note that this list retains a significant degree of procedural compliance but omits several significant aspects of the current regime. Omissions include the requirement that each student have an IEP, specific requirements about the nature of IEPs (such as the mandate that students be placed in the "least restrictive environment"), limitations on the type of personnel that can work with special-needs children, and stipulations about the membership of committees that oversee the residual procedural requirements (beyond the required involvement of parents).

> *In cases where IEPs, "least restrictive environments," specially certified personnel, and highly choreographed committees produce the best outcomes for students, schools will likely use them even when not required to do so.*

Why does the framework retain some elements of compliance and omit others? The answer lies in the problem-solving orientation laid out above; there are some problems that are more successfully addressed with compliance approaches than others. The problems singled out for continuing compliance regulation share two important characteristics:

First, addressing them is essential to the results-oriented approach of the proposed system. Without knowing which children have disabilities—and the nature of those disabilities—it is impossible to set goals and measure performance for their learning. As we discussed in Chapter 3, without having a clear set of goals for each student and measuring progress toward them, it is impossible to judge the progress of students, schools, LEAs, states, or the nation as a whole. Without widely reporting the results of those measurements, it is impossible for LEAs, states, the federal government, and families to exercise the strategies envisioned here. If families are not in the loop, the system loses (potentially) the most effective and self-managing accountability mechanism of all—the needs and priorities of the ultimate "client."

Second, they require a basic "safety net" to help ensure that no child falls through the cracks. One potential pitfall of an approach that relies heavily on performance measurement is that it tends to focus on aggregate results. Under such an approach, it is possible for a system (like an LEA) to meet all of its performance goals even as a subset of students fails to learn. To the extent that such failure is due to lack of effort by—or incompetence among—school officials, a safety net can be helpful. Part of that net can be built into a performance-based system through the use of customer choice which—unlike other possible consequences—focuses not on aggregate numbers but on the performance of individual students and the satisfaction of their families. The compliance requirements outlined here enhance that safety net, helping to assure that individual students are not ignored by the system.

Omitted steps—such as the required IEP, rules prescribing the nature of education programs for disabled students, restrictions on personnel, and stipulations about committee makeup—all lack one or both of these characteristics. Although it is plausible that these omitted steps can contribute to good outcomes for special-needs children, there is no reason to think they are *essential*. Indeed, current experience makes clear that even with all these trappings, many disabled students receive a poor education. Well-structured performance incentives and family choice can produce better overall results than these procedural requirements. In cases where IEPs, "least restrictive environments," specially certified personnel, and highly choreographed committees produce the best outcomes for students, schools will likely use them even when not required to do so.

> *A perfect system of measurement is a chimera, but policymakers can move toward a results-based system even though measurement systems are imperfect.*

Enabling "smart regulation." Within the limited scope of residual compliance obligations, states and LEAs would be free to use "smart regulation" to increase the level of compliance, reduce its burden, or, most importantly, enhance the results achieved. Because the essence of smart regulation is the use of creative strategies to induce desired behavior in particular situations, it is impossible to lay out in the abstract all forms that smart regulation might take in special education. But it is possible to offer some illustrations:

- **Addressing underlying causes.** A state finds that an LEA chronically fails to meet its compliance goals regarding identification and assessment of certain kinds of disabilities. State officials realize that this LEA is plagued by turnover of personnel needed to assess these conditions. Conversations with other districts that have similar compliance issues reveal that they face similar problems. The state responds by working with select LEAs to (1) create a training institute to boost the supply of needed experts, or (2) use Internet and satellite technology to give LEAs access to a statewide pool of specialists.

- **Negotiated solutions with technical assistance.** Much like OSHA's Maine 200 program, the state identifies the LEAs with the most severe compliance difficulties. It asks them to develop acceptable plans for boosting their compliance and outcomes or face a thorough inspection of their operations.

Though these two examples illustrate smart regulation, the idea is not to mandate such tactics from Washington but to encourage federal, state, and local officials to use such approaches as they pursue their goals within the broader context of the performance incentives they face. In order to meet their performance targets, agencies would utilize Professor Sparrow's problem-solving methodology on a regular basis—identifying problems, devising approaches using diverse tools, monitoring results, and moving onto the next problem.

Challenges

The framework outlined above is not without transition problems. Here are several:

Measurement. Most of the proposed strategies require significant specification and measurement of outcomes. Although special education has moved in this direction in recent years, problems still bedevil efforts to assess how students, schools, LEAs, states, and the nation as a whole are performing; and the IDEA's 1997 amendments did not adequately solve these problems. Because special-needs students are, by definition, more severely challenged than regular students in their quest for educational achievement, we particularly urge that any performance measurement system (1) either eschew special testing accommodations or use the same accommodations consistently for a given student, and (2) focus on gains in test scores rather than whether a given pupil reaches a fixed achievement level. A perfect system of measurement is a chimera, but policymakers can move toward a results-based system even though measurement systems are imperfect. In any case, a major investment of state, federal, and local resources in improved goal-setting and measurement systems is a must for the success of this proposal, and for most other worthwhile reforms of special education.

Personnel. One challenge faced universally by regulatory agencies that have reinvented their oversight systems is the fact that today's personnel are not necessarily equipped for their new tasks.[36] Under the proposal outlined here, special education agencies would shift much of their resources to tasks like defining outcomes, devising measurement systems, negotiating performance agreements with entities under their jurisdictions, monitoring outcomes, and creating innovative problem-solving strategies that utilize tools beyond the enforcement of rules. Though special education agencies do some of

> *A perfect system of measurement is a chimera, but policymakers can move toward a results-based system even though measurement systems are imperfect.*

these things now, as mentioned in Chapter 3, significant retooling, in the form of professional development and new hiring, would likely be needed.

The civil rights question. Current special education regulation rests upon a civil rights foundation. Students are entitled to due process and certain kinds of treatment, and they may pursue litigation if they believe their rights have been violated. This proposed set of reforms retains some aspects of due process, requiring that LEAs identify and assess children for special needs, set goals for their performance, monitor and report progress, and involve and inform families. But other aspects of current due process would vanish, to be replaced by strong performance incentives. Unfortunately, as in any system (including the current compliance-based one), some students could slip through the cracks in a performance-oriented system. An LEA, for example, could meet or exceed all of its goals for the year, even as some individual students within the system are poorly served. Could those youngsters sue the LEA for neglecting their specific needs, even as the LEA met its general performance goals? If so, would the threat of litigation induce the special education system to cling to today's compliance approach as a defense mechanism? In line with the new focus on results suggested above, could the civil rights of students with disabilities be redefined from a "right to be served" to a "right to be educated"? We pose these as questions to be addressed among the many challenges that any significant reform of an entrenched system invariably faces.

Conclusion

This outline of a new policy framework does not explore all the ramifications or supply all the details that would need to be worked through. What is most important is the set of underlying principles—the obsession with learning results; the provision of a wide range of tools to participants in the system; and the limited, residual base of compliance requirements. Where we have suggested details, we remain open to alternative approaches as long as they live up to these principles. In fact, we believe that "openness to alternatives" may be what is needed most in special education, where it is common for any criticism of the status quo to be taken as an attack on disabled children. Unless people involved in this policy area are willing to weigh proposals for change, it is difficult to imagine that progress will be made. We hope the ideas set forth here will generate that kind of open discussion.

> *The accountability system governing special education is beginning to evolve away from a "one-size-fits-all" compliance system; we think policymakers should accelerate this evolutionary process.*

Though it centers on results, the system of accountability and effectiveness oversight that we advocate relies upon a mix of performance incentives, professional judgment, and limited rule-based compliance. As such, it is a hybrid of the three "pure" types of accountability systems of hierarchy, markets, and clans discussed in Chapter 3. Each of those regimes has strengths and weaknesses that make it a particularly good or bad fit for various aspects of special education. Today's system is itself a hybrid: it remains heavily influenced by the hierarchical compliance model, yet at times places its trust in "clan-like" organizations of professionals even as market-inspired "results-based" performance systems and requirements have begun to be incorporated into it. The accountability system governing special education is beginning to evolve away from a "one-size-fits-all" compliance system; we think policymakers should accelerate this evolutionary process.

One-size-fits-all systems are common in part because they are easy. Unified systems of rules and procedures are relatively easy to justify, design, document, and communicate to interested parties. They also feature less ambiguity than the alternative system we propose here. In the context of special education, our proposal would require that we rely heavily upon the informed judgments of professionals in the special education field. We expect that, with the sort of performance incentives we envision, the vast majority of those judgments will prove to be sound ones that redound to the benefit of children with special needs. Still, any accountability system that admits to ambiguity and relies upon professional judgment will produce the occasional mistake. If such mistakes become scandals, then the entire accountability system will be vulnerable to attack and modification. All regulatory systems, even those that fit the compliance model, are susceptible to mistakes and subsequent backlashes. However, it is more difficult to defend results-based systems with claims that personnel were "simply following the rules" or that the agency involved was in "full compliance" with existing standards. Thus, we might expect the alternative system for special education accountability and oversight that we present here to prove not only difficult to obtain, but also even more difficult to sustain. Still, we think the ineffectiveness of the current compliance model of oversight does a great disservice to many of our country's most vulnerable children. We think there is a better way.

1 See, for example, Mark K. Landy, Mark J. Roberts, and Stephen R. Thomas, *The Environmental Protection Agency: Asking the Wrong Questions* (Oxford: Oxford University Press, 1990); National Academy of Public Administration, *Resolving the Paradox of Environmental Protection: An Agenda for Congress, EPA, and the States* (Washington, DC: National Academy of Public Administration, 1997); and National Academy of Public Administration, *Setting Priorities, Getting Results: A New Direction for the Environmental Protection Agency* (Washington, DC: National Academy of Public Administration, 1995).

2 See Susannah Zak Figura, "The New OSHA," *Government Executive,* May 1997 (available at <<http://www.govexec.com/features/0597s4.htm>>); and Sidney A. Shapiro and Randy S. Rabinowitz, "Punishment Versus Cooperation in Regulatory Enforcement: A Case Study of OSHA," *Administrative Law Review* 49, no. 4 (1997).

3 See Steven Kelman, *Procurement and Public Management: The Fear of Discretion and the Quality of Government Performance* (Washington, DC: American Enterprise Institute, 1990); and Jack H. Knott and Gary J. Miller, *Reforming Bureaucracy: The Politics of Institutional Choice* (Englewood Cliffs, NJ: Prentice-Hall, 1987).

4 See Malcolm K. Sparrow, *The Regulatory Craft: Controlling Risks, Solving Problems, and Managing Compliance* (Washington, DC: The Brookings Institution, 2000), 22. Numerous critiques and discussions of regulatory problems exist, including Eugene Bardach and Robert A. Kagan, *Going by the Book: The Problem of Regulatory Unreasonableness* (Philadelphia: Temple University Press, 1982); Eugene Bardach and Robert A. Kagan, eds., *Social Regulation: Strategies for Reform* (San Francisco: Institute for Contemporary Studies, 1982); Robert W. Crandall, et al., *An Agenda for Federal Regulatory Reform* (Washington, D.C.: American Enterprise Institute, 1997); Robert W. Hahn and Robert E. Litan, *Improving Regulatory Accountability* (Washington, DC: American Enterprise Institute and Brookings Institution, 1997); and Phillip K. Howard, *The Death of Common Sense: How Law is Suffocating America* (New York: Random House, 1994).

5 See, for example, Stephen G. Breyer, *Breaking the Vicious Cycle: Toward Effective Risk Regulation* (Cambridge, MA: Harvard University Press, 1993).

6 See, for example, Marver Bernstein, *Regulating Business by Independent Commission* (Princeton: Princeton University Press, 1955).

7 See Organization for Economic Cooperation and Development, *OECD Report on Regulatory Reform: Synthesis* (Paris: Organization for Economic Cooperation and Development, 1997); and Organization for Economic Cooperation and Development, *Recommendation of the Council of the OECD on Improving the Quality of Government Regulation* (London: OECD Public Management Service, 1995).

8 Thomas Hopkins, *Regulatory Costs in Profile* (St. Louis: Washington University Center for the Study of American Business, 1996), 5.

9 See Committee for Economic Development, *Modernizing Government Regulation: The Need for Action* (New York: Committee for Economic Development, 1998); Crandall et al., *An Agenda for Federal Regulatory Reform*; John D. Graham, "Legislative Approaches to Achieving More Protection Against Risk at Less Cost," *University of Chicago Legal Forum* 13 (1997): 13-58; Robert W. Hahn, "Achieving Real Regulatory Reform," *University of Chicago Legal Forum* 13 (1997): 143-158; and Hahn and Litan, *Improving Regulatory Accountability*.

10 See Archon Fung, "Smart Regulation: How Government is Marshalling Firms and Citizens to Protect the Environment," *Taubman Center (Harvard University) Annual Report* (2000), 2-3.

11 See Ian Ayres and John Braithwaite, "Designing Responsive Regulatory Institutions," *The Responsive Community* 2, no. 3 (1992); Ian Ayres and John Braithwaite, *Responsive Regulation: Transcending the Deregulation Debate* (Oxford: Oxford University Press, 1992); Mary Graham, "Putting Disclosure to the Test," *Taubman Center (Harvard University) Annual Report* (2000), 6-7; Neal Shover, Donald A. Clelland, and John Lynxwiler, *Enforcement or Negotiation: Constructing a Regulatory Bureaucracy* (Albany: State University of New York Press, 1986).

12 See Sparrow, *The Regulatory Craft*, 86-87.

13 Ibid., 22; see also Elizabeth Glass Geltman and Andrew E. Skroback, "Reinventing the EPA to Conform with the New American Environmentality," *Columbia Journal of Environmental Law* 23, no. 1 (1998): 1-56.

14 See Graham, "Putting Disclosure to the Test."

15 Archon Fung, "Reinventing Environmental Regulation from the Grassroots Up: Explaining and Expanding the Success of the Toxics Release Inventory," *Environmental Management* 25, no. 2, (2000): 115-127.

[16] Allan V. Burman, "Federal Marketplace," *Government Executive*, April 1999 (available at <<http://govexec.com/procure/articles/0499mark.htm>>).

[17] Sparrow, *The Regulatory Craft*, 23.

[18] See ibid.

[19] See Cary Coglianese, "Assessing Consensus: The Promise and Performance of Negotiated Rulemaking," *Duke Law Journal* 46, no.6 (1997): 10.

[20] See David Osborne and Peter Plastrik, *Banishing Bureaucracy: The Five Strategies for Reinventing Government* (New York: Penguin Group, 1997), 23-30.

[21] See David Osborne and Ted Gaebler, *Reinventing Government* (Reading, MA: Addison-Wesley, 1992), 223-26.

[22] See Program on Innovations in American Government, *2000 Finalists*, available from <<http://www.innovations.harvard.edu/Finalists/2000/index.html>>.

[23] Refer to Figure 1 in Chapter 3 for the essential elements of a results-measurement accountability system.

[24] For example, in their work on improving the performance of government organizations, Osborne and Plastrik list performance management as the least desirable of several approaches to imposing "consequences" for performance, favoring instead (where practical) the more market-oriented approaches discussed in the next section. See Osborne and Plastrik, *Banishing Bureaucracy*.)

[25] For a probing discussion of these issues in the education setting, see Richard Rothstein, "Toward a Composite Index of School Performance," *Elementary School Journal* 5 (2000): 411-417.

[26] This section focuses only on customer choice because of its relevance to special education, in which there are readily definable "customers." Another significant variant is "tradable permits," of which the most prominent examples have emerged in the environmental field. Regulators have set overall targets for the amount of certain pollutants that they are willing to tolerate, issued permits to potential polluters allowing (in the aggregate) the targeted level of emission, and created marketplaces in which permit-holders can buy and sell the right to emit different amounts of pollutants. See Allen V. Kneese and Charles L. Schultze, *Pollution, Prices, and Public Policy* (Washington, DC: The Brookings Institution, 1975); Richard Kosobud and Jennifer Zimmerman, eds., *Market-Based Approaches to Environmental Policy* (New York: Van Nostrand Reinhold, 1997); and Thomas Schelling, *Incentives for Environmental Protection* (Cambridge, MA: MIT Press, 1983).

[27] For examples, see Michael Barzelay and Babak Armanjani, *Breaking through Bureaucracy: A New Vision for Managing in Government* (Berkeley: University of California Press, 1992); and Osborne and Plastrik, *Banishing Bureaucracy*.

[28] Sparrow, *The Regulatory Craft*, 43.

[29] See ibid., 255-278.

[30] Ibid., 113.

[31] See, for example, Herman Goldstein, *Problem-Oriented Policing* (New York: McGraw-Hill, 1990); and Sparrow, *The Regulatory Craft*.

[32] See Sparrow, *The Regulatory Craft*, 251-252.

[33] The argument for goals set at higher levels parallels arguments within regular education for having statewide rather than local standards for student learning.

[34] See Richard Rothstein, "Rethinking Special Education Without Losing Ground," *New York Times*, 5 July 2000, sec. B, p. 12. For more on preventable and remedial disabilities and their policy implications, see Chapters 2 and 12 in this volume.

[35] See Chapter 13 in this volume.

[36] See Sparrow, *The Regulatory Craft*, especially 155-170, 224-237, and 255-278.

Conclusions and Principles for Reform

Chester E. Finn, Jr., Andrew J. Rotherham, and Charles R. Hokanson, Jr.

Our purpose in organizing and publishing this volume has been to identify problems that have crept into special education over the years, analyze their causes, and suggest a range of possible solutions. Above all, our goal is to stimulate thinking about how best to educate disabled youngsters in today's America, open some sealed assumptions to the fresh breeze of ideas, invite rigorous thinking in lieu of defensive posturing, and begin to point the way toward a different future. The fourteen essays that precede this one are our main contribution to that important conversation. Our intention in these concluding pages is not to summarize them or to propose solutions for every problem, but to underscore the challenges that strike the editors as most vexing and to outline some principles that might guide their solution. With this in mind, the next stage of our joint special education efforts is likely to include a detailed blueprint for IDEA reform, to be released when the start of the 2002 reauthorization process is closer at hand.

> **The past 25 years' record of accomplishment is at best half the story of the IDEA in particular and special education in general, for this program that has done so much is also sorely troubled.**

Before reviewing problems that have crept into the special education program, we want to hail its accomplishments. Millions of children with handicaps, disabilities and special needs have received—and are receiving—a better education thanks to the IDEA. Millions of parents have found in it a source of hope and possibility for their daughters and sons, as well as an avenue for their own direct involvement in key education decisions affecting their disabled children. Tens of thousands of teachers have devoted themselves, heart and soul, to the schooling of these youngsters. Thanks to the IDEA, Section 504, and the state and local special education programs that complement and reinforce them, today many disabled children in America have the opportunity to obtain a high-quality educational experience tailored to their needs and circumstances, the priorities of their parents, and the judgments of their teachers. No other country tries harder to do right by its disabled citizens and its girls and boys with special educational needs.

And yet this record of accomplishment is at best half the story of the IDEA in particular and special education in general, for this program that has done so much is also sorely troubled. America's program for youngsters with disabilities has itself developed infirmities, handicaps, and special needs of its own. Twenty-five years after President Ford signed the Education for All

Handicapped Children Act, we are not educating many disabled children to a satisfactory level of skills and knowledge. Too often we are frustrating their parents, distracting their teachers, hobbling their schools, and making it harder to keep order in their classrooms, all this despite the best of intentions and the most earnest of efforts by families, educators, and policymakers. We are sawing down forests to create paperwork that sometimes seems to have become the program's raison d'être; filling courtrooms with angry litigants and costly litigators; snarling state and local education reform efforts; legitimizing double standards and new forms of segregation; and hitting taxpayers with ever-larger bills for a lengthening list of services provided to a burgeoning population of children, many of whom might not have even become candidates for special education had they been given a first-class regular education.

Putting it bluntly, special education is broken for too many children. Think of it as "a program at risk." As the new administration and Congress prepare for the IDEA's reauthorization, it is vital to recognize this. Our conclusion has nothing to do with political party or ideology. It arises from an intense concern for the well-being of children and families, the quality of education, and the effectiveness of these government programs.

> **The choice confronting today's policymakers is not whether to keep the program as it is or return to the unacceptable pre-IDEA status quo. Rather, the challenge is to modernize the program, building on what we've learned about both special education and education in general.**

Perhaps it goes without saying that special education is but one domain of American K-12 education in need of fundamental reform. Indeed, the shortcomings and rigidities of regular education—the subject of many earnest reform efforts in recent decades, especially since 1983's *A Nation At Risk*[1] report—exacerbate the troubles of special education. If, for example, we did a better job of individualizing the educational experience of every child within a standards-and-results-based framework, the special education program would also work better. If we did a better job of preventing and forestalling education problems rather than relying on compensatory and remedial activities, disabled children would benefit enormously. If we routinely gave parents more education choices. If we had a fair and efficient system for apportioning education resources. And so forth. The fact that such problems remain largely unsolved complicates the job of reforming special education. But it does not justify our failure to undertake that job.

We have been in Washington long enough to know that any long-established program becomes encrusted with strongly held assumptions, interlocking interests, acquired habits, ingrained procedures, and plenty of suspicion toward anyone who suggests that change is needed. Nowhere in our experience is this truer than in special education.

We therefore invite readers to remind themselves that what matters is what is good for children. The fact that something has been done in a certain way for a quarter-century does not mean that it works well for the girls and boys in whose name it is done. Few would argue that the way America treated its disabled youngsters for the 25 years *before* 1975 should have continued. So a huge and necessary change was made. We submit that it's time for another one. Fortunately, the choice confronting today's policymakers is not whether to keep the program as it is or return to the unacceptable pre-IDEA status quo. Rather, the challenge is to modernize the program, building on what we've learned about both special education and education in general.

25 Years Later: What We've Learned

The original problems to be solved by special education were that many handicapped children were denied access to public education, were segregated in warehouse-style schools, or had access only to classrooms that took no account of their distinctive needs.

This was wrong. It was un-American. It was bad education. And it was bad for children. Because it appeared that states and communities could not be trusted to do right by their disabled youngsters, the federal government stepped in, much as it had done earlier for black children. The education of disabled girls and boys thereupon became a civil right, enshrined both in the new federal special education programs that took shape after 1975 and in a series of court rulings and anti-discrimination statutes, especially Section 504 of the Rehabilitation Act.

> *Special education still operates strictly according to the procedures manual, while being vague about its standards and surprisingly relaxed about results. It's ironic that a law intended to put special-needs students into the least restrictive environment often ends up putting their schools into the most restrictive environment.*

A quarter-century later, we are pleased to report, the original problem is largely solved. Disabled youngsters have access to public education, indeed to a more individualized and generously funded form of public education than their non-disabled age mates, and to a system that gives their parents greater say over their education than the families of other children.

We laud this success. It is a huge, albeit overdue, accomplishment for human decency and fairness. Nothing in this volume is intended to detract from it or to take credit away from those who made it possible.

But how well is it really working? What exactly have these youngsters been given access to? Is the edifice of programs, services, procedures, and rights erected in the 1970s succeeding for disabled children today? And has it kept pace with important changes in the larger world of American education?

We think not. Over the past 25 years, K-12 education in the United States has undergone a profound paradigm shift, from access-and-services to results-and-accountability. During the most recent decade, this change has been especially dramatic. Special education simply hasn't kept up. It's still an access-and-services program enveloped by a civil rights orientation. It still has more to do with combating discrimination than teaching children what they need to learn. It's not really a quality-and-performance-enhancing education program. Despite the efforts of many people of goodwill, and notwithstanding numerous fine-tunings of the law, it still has little to do with the standards-based reforms that are today's engines of education change.

Surprisingly, special education hasn't even kept up with changes elsewhere in the civil rights movement. When it comes to race and education, for example, the country has been moving, if slowly and painfully, from a preoccupation with barriers, access, and nominal integration to an obsession with strengthening academic results and narrowing the learning gap. Most parents of African-American and Hispanic children today are less interested in the skin color of the youngster in the next seat than in the school's success at imparting important skills and knowledge to their own sons and daughters. Government programs for poor and minority youngsters are gradually catching up to that important shift in priorities. But no such shift has occurred in special education. Some assert that the 1997 IDEA amendments brought about such a refocusing, but they are mostly wrong. The intent was there, but in the end Congress simply added a layer of standards-related rules without fundamentally changing the existing regulation-and-compliance structure.

> *We recognize that money must be part of any thoroughgoing reform of special education; the federal government has a legitimate obligation here. But adding dollars to the current program will not reform it.*

Special education is also out of sync with profound organizational changes taking place elsewhere in K-12 education and in the larger world outside. Most successful modern organizations operate by being clear about their goals and demanding about results, but loose—and decentralized—about the means to those ends. Special education, however, still operates strictly according to the procedures manual, while being vague about its standards and surprisingly relaxed about results. So long as the forms are properly filled in and all the boxes checked, nobody seems too concerned about how much and how well disabled children learn or how effectively their schools operate. It's ironic that a law intended to put special-needs students into the least restrictive environment often ends up putting their schools into the most restrictive environment.

Hence, it's not really surprising that many children in special education aren't learning enough. Academic progress is scant. Too few disabled youngsters graduate from high school—and, for many that do, the diploma is more a mark of persistence than a certificate of attainment. Special education, moreover, has become a one-way street. It's relatively easy to send children down this street, but they rarely return.

The most striking thing about special education is that, even as many people endorse the program's intentions and salute its accomplishments, few are happy with how it actually works. Most of its constituents acknowledge substantial problems (though not necessarily the same ones). Overall, we repeat, America's special education program has urgent special needs of its own. It is, in many ways, broken.

Some people insist otherwise. They contend that special education is soundly conceived and properly structured but inadequately funded. Their solution is for Washington to spend more money on existing programs. We recognize that money must be part of any thoroughgoing reform of special education; the federal government has a legitimate obligation here. But merely adding dollars to the current program will not reform it. Even bringing the federal appropriation up to the long-promised 40 percent of additional costs would not address the underlying problems. Indeed, an infusion of dollars might even make people more complacent about this troubled program, notwithstanding the less-than-satisfactory effects that it has on many children. In any case, a larger appropriation is at best a temporary palliative. It will not long quell the complaints (from states, districts, and schools) that result from the "unfunded mandate" nature of today's program, its ever-escalating costs, and its ever-growing student rolls.

Eight Policy Failures in Need of Attention

Preventable and remediable conditions grow into intractable problems. Particularly in the burgeoning category of "learning disabilities" (LDs), which now accounts for half of all special education cases, we are persuaded by the evidence reported in Chapter 12 and elsewhere that millions of youngsters probably would not need to be in special education at all if they were properly taught to read at an early age. Yet, despite vigorous efforts by some in the special education and disability communities, prevention and early intervention remain low priorities in a program that continues to focus on the identification and remediation of learning problems after they have grown severe.

> **Today, special education attempts to serve an ever-growing population of youngsters with an ever-lengthening list of problems and difficulties. Special education now has far too many categories and is too vague about which children need this assistance.**

Special education suffers from what the Pentagon calls "mission creep." That phrase describes a carefully targeted undertaking that keeps on expanding until its goals become unattainable, its operation impossibly complex and costly, and its purpose clouded. Special education began as a program for children with clearly identified physical and mental handicaps. Today, however, it attempts to serve an ever-growing population of youngsters with an ever-lengthening list of problems and difficulties, some of them ambiguous in origin, subjective in identification, and uncertain as to solution. Special education now has far too many categories—particularly in the "LD" area—and is too vague about which children need this assistance. (For evidence on this point, see especially Chapters 2, 4, and 9.)

Our one-size-fits-all approach has created a legal and policy straitjacket. One of the lessons of the last century, finally recognized in most realms of American education outside special education, is that there is no such thing as "one best system" for all students. Children are too different in their needs and interests; communities in their priorities and values; families in their enthusiasms and attitudes; and educators in their passions and talents. We celebrate diversity throughout our education system—except in special education. Here we insist on following the same rules and procedures whether a child is multiply handicapped or has a mild reading disability. This creates a system that is full of adversarial procedures, rife with litigation, unresponsive to innovation, discouraging to diversity, and hostile to creativity. (For further discussion, see especially Chapters 7, 10, 11, and 14).

The IDEA creates perverse incentives for educators and schools. Particularly as other programs such as Title I evolve into schoolwide "improvement" efforts, many teachers and principals find that special education is their only source of help for individual children who need extra attention and the only remedy for classrooms plagued by disruptive youngsters. (See Chapter 7.) We do *not* contend that school districts have fiscal incentives to place more children in special education (see Chapter 9); the cost to the district almost invariably exceeds the added state and federal dollars that accompany those youngsters. We do believe, however, that at the classroom and building levels there are rational incentives to move certain kids into special education even when this may not be the best way to solve the perceived problem.

Parents have perverse incentives, too. Because of the program's legalistic orientation, some parents (often egged on by eager attorneys) opt for the adversarial procedures of due process hearings and litigation rather than conferring with their child's teachers and school administrators. Because of the unique "accommodations" that special education status confers on students, some families now agitate to have their own children diagnosed as disabled in order to gain extra time on college entrance tests and the like. How sad, it seems to us, that a parent's ardor to have a child admitted to a competitive university would lead his or her to seek this costly remedy, which can bring with it a permanent label and even a lifetime of double standards. (See Chapters 2, 10, and 11.)

> *Different rules for disabled children foster a "separate but unequal" education system. It strikes us as ironic or worse that laws meant to break down barriers and open doors now serve to promote separatism and inequality.*

As the largest unfunded federal mandate in K-12 education, special education distorts the priorities and fractures the programmatic coherence of schools and school systems. At both local and state levels, it also causes budgetary havoc. Making a school function as an effective organization is difficult enough, yet both research and experience make clear that this is vital for successful teaching and learning to occur. It becomes doubly difficult, however, when different rules and procedures exist for some of the children within that school. As for budget, it's well-known that federal (and sometime state) law requires a school system to set aside sufficient funds for special education before it can pay for any of its other programs, services, or activities. As special education costs reach 25-30 percent of total budgets of many districts—and as much as 40 percent in some—this can drastically distort the school system's education priorities and interfere with its capacity to accomplish other important objectives. Moreover, in small and rural communities, the stress that high-need students can place on schools and district budgets creates painful tensions within the community. (See Chapters 7 and 9.)

Different rules for disabled children foster a "separate but unequal" education system. It strikes us as ironic or worse that laws meant to break down barriers and open doors now serve to promote separatism and inequality. As examples, consider the controversial double standard that has emerged for student discipline, and the dual approach that has arisen in the area of achievement testing. (See Chapter 8.)

Special education collides with standards-based reform, exempting many students (and the educators and schools that serve them) from meeting state or district academic standards, even as such standards are being strengthened for the "regular" education system. Special education has at best a troubled relationship with assessment arrangements that states and districts are putting into place for their "regular" schools and pupils. And the incentives and sanctions that apply in special education differ greatly from those that represent "accountability" in regular education. Perhaps this was inevitable, considering the IDEA's focus on compliance rather than achievement, on inputs instead of results, and process in lieu of cognitive skills and knowledge. Obviously, the standards that states have developed over the last ten years are not appropriate for every disabled youngster. But the inevitable effects thus far have been to frustrate important education reforms that would benefit all children, and to deepen the distinctions between disabled children and their classmates. (See Chapter 3.)

> *To keep pace with promising education changes at the local, state, and national level, it is essential to redefine the IDEA from a compliance-oriented program to one focused on results and performance.*

Principles for Reform

To reform the IDEA in ways that address the issues raised in the preceding paragraphs and the earlier essays in this volume, we urge policymakers to consider six principles. Together, we believe, they build on special education's successes of the past quarter-century and would make the program work better for more children. These principles should guide federal policymakers during the next IDEA reauthorization cycle, and should also inform state and local discussions of program implementation.

1. *Make the IDEA standards- and performance-based wherever possible*, using Section 504 as the civil rights underpinning of special education but viewing the IDEA as a bona fide education program that is judged by its results.

2. *Streamline the number of special education categories into a very few broad groupings,* distinguished by whether the basic conditions they address are primarily in need of prevention or intervention, remediation or accommodation, or some combination thereof.

3. *Focus on prevention and early intervention wherever possible,* using research-based practices.

4. *Encourage flexibility, innovation, and choices,* allowing schools to work with students and parents to customize services and placements to meet varying needs, and foster the integration of special education into the school's larger mission and program, while giving parents sound options for their children's education.

5. *Provide adequate funding to ensure the program's success,* assigning to Washington full responsibility for funding the education of the country's growing population of severely disabled students.

6. *End double standards wherever possible.*

We now amplify these principles.

Make the IDEA Standards- and Performance-based

To keep pace with promising education changes at the local, state, and national level, it is essential to redefine the IDEA from a compliance-oriented program to one focused on results and performance.

Section 504 of the Rehabilitation Act of 1973 should be viewed as the guarantor of disabled youngsters' civil rights. It states that, "No otherwise qualified individual with a disability in the United States, as defined in section 706(8) of this title, shall, solely by reason of her or his handicap, be excluded from participation in, be denied the benefits of, or be subject to discrimination under any program or activity receiving Federal financial assistance."[2]

> *Rather than today's "one-size-fits-all" IDEA mandates and procedures, policymakers should consider creating two or possibly three categories of students within the special-needs population.*

In fact, it is Section 504, not the IDEA, which lays out the states' primary obligation in this area. The procedural requirements of the IDEA apply only if a state accepts funding under the statute. The Section 504 requirements apply regardless. These requirements, however, are fairly vague and do not themselves provide states with a suitable framework for special education results.

Fortunately, the progress that many states and localities have made in standards-based reform also provides some direction for special education. Although it is neither fair nor pedagogically sound to hold all disabled students to the same standards that are expected of general education students, for many special education students these standards can offer suitable goals and expectations.

We believe that standards-based reform, coupled with the civil rights protections of Section 504, offers policymakers an avenue to rethink the IDEA as a service- and performance-based program for students with exceptional needs rather than a compliance-based program. Using standards as the education polestar and Section 504 as the "safety net" to guard against discrimination, states and localities could be given greater flexibility so long as they and their students attain concrete goals. In this volume, Chapter 14 examines alternatives to the compliance approach and offers insights into the potential benefits (and challenges) of such an approach.

Streamline the Number of Special Education Categories

Rather than today's "one-size-fits-all" IDEA mandates and procedures, policymakers should consider creating two or possibly three categories of students within the special-needs population. Chapter 2 suggests one approach to this that we think has considerable merit. Like the ESEA reauthorization proposals recently advanced by President Bush and the New Democrats in Congress, present categories within the IDEA should be blended around their core purposes rather than ever more numerous sub-groups. Essentially, students eligible for the IDEA should be clustered by broad areas of need rather than specific disabilities. Obviously, this doesn't mean that individual children with special needs do not require individualized attention and customized education strategies; that remains absolutely essential. However, attempting through the IDEA to prescribe these strategies, or to identify the full range of student circumstances that exist in the real world, is a Sisyphean task that substitutes the judgments of bureaucrats and rule-makers for those of educators and parents.

Broad areas of need, however, can readily be outlined. Some youngsters require accommodations while others need mainly corrective assistance. For example, with regard to vision- and hearing-impaired students, the goal of the IDEA (and the obligation under Section 504) should be to ensure that accommodations are in place so these youngsters can take full advantage of the education program. However, for many children with learning disabilities, particularly reading problems, the goals of special education should be preventive and corrective. For those with serious mental retardation, goals should include maximum attainment in the domains of cognition, self-reliance and socialization.

Focus on Prevention and Early Intervention

Chapter 12 presents a compelling case for early identification, prevention, and intervention in what will otherwise emerge as learning disabilities. (This should, of course, be rooted in effective and research-based reading instruction.) Similarly, Chapter 4 raises important questions about the civil rights paradigm as it applies to students with reading problems. We believe that a focus on reading for young children is one of the most cost-effective and important reforms that policymakers can undertake, one that would have singular benefit for youngsters otherwise apt to be headed toward special education classrooms.

> *More choices should be given to parents of severely disabled students without having to go through elaborate, contentious, and costly legal proceedings (that often work better for affluent families than poor ones).*

Encourage Flexibility, Innovation, and Choices

During the November 2000 conference at which the various chapters in this volume were first presented, both the presentations and ensuing dialogue underscored the reality that, at the school and classroom levels, students are often assigned to special education in order to secure additional needed services for them. This, rather than district-level activity, is probably the primary reason for higher costs resulting from over identification. The motivation is unimpeachable: to help students in need. Yet the result is that special education programs end up playing catch-up for poor or indifferent instruction.

Wherever possible, therefore, policymakers should grant to schools flexibility to design education programs that meet the needs of children they serve within a results-based framework. Essential to this end is a healthy market of education choices for parents. To encourage this, funding should be allocated to ensure that public charter schools receive their full "share" of special education resources for children they serve. (At the same time, public charter schools must stay true to their birthright as public schools and not shun more costly or difficult-to-educate students.)

We also believe that more choices should be given to parents of severely disabled students without having to go through elaborate, contentious, and costly legal proceedings (that often work better for affluent families than poor ones). For students with severe needs, we believe, policymakers should explore ways to create a federally funded weighted "entitlement" that parents can use at the school of their choice.

Essentially, such a system would place accountability for the quality of services in the hands of parents rather than in a procedure-bound system of regulation and litigation.

Public schools have a legal obligation to be a provider of special education services for severely disabled students, too, and in most cases they will be the provider of "first resort" for parents with options. But they must not be the only alternative. We urge policymakers to consider replacing the current "due process" system for severely disabled students with a system that empowers parents to select what they believe is the best provider of the special services their children need, while preserving public responsibility to ensure that all students receive a free appropriate public education.

> *Exactly what gives students with specific learning problems an entitlement to greater education resources than their peers who simply are slow learners and/or struggling for other reasons? This difficult question needs a full airing.*

Provide Adequate Funding

If it is to succeed, the IDEA must be funded so that it *can* succeed. Nationwide, 43 percent of education spending comes from localities. The result is a tremendous disparity in the ability of school districts to accommodate high-need students. In addition to the structural and programmatic reforms considered in this volume, therefore, adequate funding must be provided for special education services and prevention and intervention activities. Policymakers should seek to ensure not only that funding mechanisms are identification-neutral but also that schools and school systems have the resources to meet demands placed on them by Section 504 and the IDEA.

It is worth considering the establishment of a special fund (at a national or regional level) to provide additional financial assistance as needed for the education of "high cost-low incidence" students. (Former Vice President Al Gore proposed such a fund during the 2000 campaign.) In addition, clear lines of responsibility and access with regard to Medicaid must be established. For students with severe medical needs, schools and school districts must be able to access resources to provide the requisite medical services. Furthermore, there must be accountability for this spending to ensure it subsidizes student services, not administration, and there must be clear guidelines so that those running schools are not subject to the whims of distant Medicaid bureaucrats.

End Double Standards

We urge an easing of today's double standards with regard to special education. The much-discussed discipline issue is the most contentious of these situations but not the only one. Disagreement continues about the extent to which the IDEA's procedural requirements prevent school administrators from disciplining disruptive special education students. We believe this issue warrants further study and discussion, as does the issue of student discipline in general. A worthy solution may incorporate aspects of the IDEA into general education while also changing today's separate disciplinary track for disabled youngsters. Such a compromise would not only give school administrators greater latitude to remove disruptive students and place them in alternative settings but also require school districts to continue serving *all* students until they reach the age of majority. Ideally, such an arrangement would encourage administrators to weigh options other than suspension and expulsion for difficult students while strengthening their ability to ensure an orderly learning environment for all youngsters.

Learning disabilities pose issues of their own. Chapter 4 is instructive because it asks a fundamental question that is frequently answered with more shrillness than empirical evidence:

> *As the education landscape changes with regard to choice, policymakers must keep abreast of new ways to ensure that disabled children also benefit to the maximum degree from this important strand of reform.*

Exactly what gives students with specific learning problems an entitlement to greater education resources than their peers who simply are slow learners and/or struggling for other reasons? As policymakers struggle to correct the chronic dysfunction plaguing many of the nation's largest school districts serving high concentrations of poor and minority students, this difficult question needs a full airing.

With regard to teacher training, it is clear that many general-education teachers do not feel themselves well-equipped to deal with special education issues, no doubt in part because they learned little about these matters during their training. Nor are there enough interactions between special education teachers and their colleagues in general education. This "silo" effect results from the long-standing disconnect between special education and general education. This is an issue that must be addressed if special education students are to be genuinely incorporated into the education programs of their schools. It must be addressed in schools of education and in the schools themselves. So, too, must the preparation of special education teachers. Deficiencies in this area were noted at the November conference and are frequently cited in the special education literature.

Future Challenges

The principles enumerated above point toward significant changes that policymakers can consider and act on during the upcoming reauthorization of the IDEA, in deliberations about state special education laws, and in state and local decisions about program implementation. Over the longer term, however, there are additional important policy issues that need to be pondered.

A number of federal education programs are linked to some of the problems that the IDEA addresses. Title I and Head Start are the most notable examples because they focus on reading and are targeted toward disadvantaged populations. It is likely that the current Elementary and Secondary Education Act (ESEA) reauthorization cycle will result in greater flexibility for states and districts to use federal funds to address diverse educational needs and circumstances. Policymakers should study these changes carefully to find ways in which more flexibility and integration can be achieved between the IDEA and these programs. As the IDEA moves toward a results-based orientation, this added flexibility is a natural corollary.

Such integration would also help address the "isolation" of special education. In several of the preceding chapters, and at the November conference, analysts and stakeholders expressed concern that the IDEA is often seen as an entity unto itself rather than in the context of overall school reform. Further integrating it with other federal reform efforts for needy children is one way to address this issue.

Effective education requires a degree of customization and individual attention too often lacking in general education and, ironically, frequently in special education as well. Several conference participants expressed concern that individualized education plans are frequently not truly individualized and instead are more focused on legal protection and regulatory procedure. Policymakers must endeavor to ensure that *all* students receive individualized attention suited to their specific learning needs.

> *We urge policymakers to question the status quo, explore ways to improve education for youngsters, and not shy from taking on the tough task of improving efforts to ensure that all our children are afforded the education they deserve.*

Edison Schools founder Chris Whittle notes that, although Federal Express can locate one of its packages anywhere in the world at any specific moment, many schools can't identify the progress a particular student is making over the course of a year. He's right, of course, and the result is that too many students, particularly poor and minority youngsters, fall through the education cracks.

In the 1920s, Helen Parkhurst developed what became known as the Dalton Plan, individualized contracts that teachers negotiated with students to determine the goals that they would meet. The intention was that such contracts would replace the traditional approach to schooling in favor of a more flexible one. The hazard here is obvious and shared with other "progressive" reforms of the time: without some sort of external standards or benchmarks, it becomes difficult to ensure rigor in individual contracts. In addition, such individualization is time-consuming for teachers. In fact, by 1949 researchers could find only one school still using the Dalton model. Yet when coupled with today's movement toward clear common standards, tests, and accountability systems, Parkhurst's plan might well provide a model for customization within that broader common framework. Policymakers should seek to ensure individualized attention for all students, particularly poor, disabled, and immigrant youngsters, so that differences in learning styles and needs are accommodated within the context of rigorous and common academic standards.[3]

It is also clear that the movement for greater parental choice is changing education policy and practice around the country. At this writing, 36 states and the District of Columbia have laws supporting public charter schools, and there are now more than 2,000 such schools in operation enrolling more than half a million youngsters. In addition, two cities (Milwaukee and

Cleveland) and one state (Florida) have publicly funded school voucher programs. Although there is disagreement about these and other choice strategies, just about everyone recognizes that choice is increasing today and will increase further tomorrow. The principles for reform set forth above incorporate a great deal of parental empowerment. Coupled with public accountability for results, increasing parental authority and responsibility is a key strategy to drive better results for children and schools. As the education landscape changes with regard to choice, policymakers must keep abreast of new ways to ensure that disabled children also benefit to the maximum degree from this important strand of reform.

Special education has accomplished a great deal for American children in the past and can accomplish more in the future. But this will require an openness to criticism and fresh ideas, a willingness to entertain reforms, and a capacity to change. We urge policymakers to question the status quo, explore ways to improve education for youngsters, and not shy from taking on the tough task of improving efforts to ensure that all our children are afforded the education they deserve.

---

[1] National Commission on Excellence in Education, *A Nation at Risk: The Imperative for Educational Reform* (Washington, D.C.: U.S. Department of Education, 1983).

[2] 29 U.S.C. § 794(a).

[3] See David Tyack and Larry Cuban, *Tinkering Toward Utopia: A Century of Public School Reform* (Cambridge, MA: Harvard University Press, 1995), 94-96.

Contributors

Rose Marie L. Audette, Esq.

Associate • Hogan and Hartson L.L.P.

Rose Audette is an attorney specializing in education law and litigation. She has represented public school districts in federal and state cases involving school desegregation, affirmative action, diversity, gender discrimination, and special education. She has represented a variety of other business and individual clients in civil cases involving employment discrimination claims, business disputes, and family law issues.

Ms. Audette received her J.D. from Georgetown University Law Center. She was an editor of the *Georgetown Law Journal* and a member of the Order of the Coif. Ms. Audette graduated with *magna cum laude* and Phi Beta Kappa honors from Georgetown University. Prior to attending law school, Ms. Audette was an editor and writer for non-profit publications. She is a member of the bars of the District of Columbia, Maryland, and several federal courts.

Sheldon Berman, Ed.D.

Superintendent • Hudson Public Schools

Dr. Berman is the Superintendent of the Hudson Public Schools. He serves on the Executive Committee of the Massachusetts Association of School Superintendents and is the author of the MASS report, "Education Reform at Risk"; the co-chair of MASS's Special Education Task Force; and the co-author of the MASS 1997 report, "The Impact of Special Education on Education Reform." He is the author of *Children's Social Consciousness*, an editor for *Promising Practices in Teaching Social Responsibility*, and the author of numerous articles on education.

Frederick J. Brigham, Ph.D.

Assistant Professor • University of Virginia

Dr. Brigham teaches in the University of Virginia's special education program. Prior to entering higher education, he was a specialist in charge of adaptive technology for individuals with disabilities at one of the largest special education cooperatives in North Dakota. His emphasis is in secondary education and the use of technology for instruction in content areas.

Dr. Brigham is currently involved in maintaining the University of Virginia's office of special education, and he is one of the departmental representatives on the Curry School Educational Technology Committee. He is currently developing student leadership and self-advocacy materials via a grant from the Virginia Board for People with Disabilities.

Robert Cullen

Freelance writer and editor

Robert Cullen's writings on foreign affairs, the environment, travel, and golf have appeared in *The Atlantic Monthly, The New Yorker, National Geographic,* and *Golf Digest*, among other publications. He is also the author of ten books, most recently *Heirs of Fire* and *Dispatch from a Cold Country*.

Previously, Mr. Cullen served as general editor of *Newsweek International* and as a diplomatic correspondent for *Newsweek*, during which time he covered the Reagan-Gorbachev summits and the INF and START negotiations.

Mr. Cullen received his B.A. in international relations from the University of Virginia and was a Professional Journalism Fellow at Stanford University.

Perry P. Davis, Ed.D.

Superintendent • Dover-Sherborn Public Schools

Dr. Davis is the Superintendent of the Dover-Sherborn Public Schools. Prior to becoming superintendent, he was a special education teacher and director of special education. He is a former president of the Massachusetts Association of School Superintendents, the co-chair of MASS's Special Education Task Force, and the co-author of the MASS 1997 report, "The Impact of Special Education on Education Reform."

Alexander E. Dreier, Esq.

Associate • Hogan and Hartson L.L.P.

Mr. Dreier is an attorney specializing in education law. He works with both higher education institutions and their associations and with public school districts. Mr. Dreier has represented higher education associations in the U.S. Supreme Court and other federal courts in litigation concerning affirmative action and diversity. He also has represented clients in litigation involving special education, school funding, and employment discrimination, and has counseled higher education clients with respect to a wide variety of issues, such as conflicts of interest, student privacy, tenure rights, and institutional governance.

Mr. Dreier graduated with *magna cum laude* and Phi Beta Kappa honors from Harvard University in 1988. A Rhodes Scholar, he received an M.A. in philosophy and politics from Oxford University in 1990 and attended Yale Law School, receiving his J.D. in 1995. Before joining Hogan & Hartson, he held the positions of Adjunct Professor of Law at the University of Oklahoma College of Law and law clerk to the Honorable Robert H. Henry on the U.S. Court of Appeals for the Tenth Circuit.

Mr. Dreier is co-author of articles published annually in *West's Education Law Reporter* on the impact on public schools of recent Supreme Court decisions, and of briefs published in the *Journal of College and University Law*. He is a member of the bars of the District of Columbia, Maryland, and several federal courts.

Anna Bray Duff

Freelance writer

Anna Bray Duff is a freelance writer living in Menlo Park, California. For five years, Ms. Duff worked as a reporter covering public-policy issues for *Investor's Business Daily*. She graduated from Princeton University in 1992 with an A.B. in history, and she was a Rotary Foundation Graduate Scholar at the University of Lyon, France.

Chester E. Finn, Jr., Ed.D.

President • Thomas B. Fordham Foundation

Chester E. Finn, Jr., scholar, educator, and public servant, has devoted most of his career to improving education in the United States. As the John M. Olin Fellow at the Manhattan Institute for Policy Research and President and Trustee of the Thomas B. Fordham Foundation, his primary focus is the reform of primary and secondary schooling.

In addition to his work with the Foundation and the Manhattan Institute, Dr. Finn is a Distinguished Visiting Fellow at Stanford's Hoover Institution and an Adjunct Fellow at the Hudson Institute, where he was a senior fellow from 1995 through 1998. From 1992 through 1994, he served as founding partner and senior scholar with the Edison Project.

His commitment to education is multifaceted. Dr. Finn has been Professor of Education and Public Policy at Vanderbilt University since 1981 (he is currently on leave). From 1985 to 1988 he served as Assistant Secretary for the Office of Educational Research and Improvement at the U.S. Department of Education and Counselor to the U.S. Secretary of Education.

For nearly 20 years Dr. Finn has immersed himself in education policy issues and has often been in the forefront of the national debate about school reform. His participation in seminars, conferences, and hearings has taken him to colleges, education and civic groups, and government organizations throughout the United States, and he has been a visiting lecturer in more than a dozen countries.

Author of 13 books, Dr. Finn's most recent, released in March 2000 by Princeton University Press, is *Charter Schools in Action: Renewing Public Education*, co-authored with Bruno V. Manno and Gregg Vanourek. In 1999, with William J. Bennett and John Cribb, he published *The Educated Child: A Parent's Guide from Pre-School Through Eighth Grade* (The Free Press).

As well, he is the author of over 300 articles. A native of Ohio, he holds an undergraduate degree in U.S. history, a master's degree in social studies teaching, and a doctorate in education policy and administration from Harvard University.

Jack M. Fletcher, Ph.D.

Professor, Department of Pediatrics • Associate Director, Center for Academic and Reading Skills • University of Texas-Houston Health Science Center

For the past 20 years, Dr. Fletcher, a child neuropsychologist, has completed research on many aspects of the development of reading, language, and other cognitive skills in children. He has worked extensively on issues related to learning and attention problems, including definition and classification, neurobiological correlates, and most recently, intervention. He collaborates on several grants on reading and attention funded by the National Institute of Child Health and Human Development (NICHD), as well as a grant funded by the National Science Foundation, Department of Education, and NICHD under the Interagency Educational Research Initiative. Dr. Fletcher is also Principal Investigator or Co-Principal Investigator on NIH-funded research projects involving children with brain injuries, including a program project on spina bifida and other projects involving children with traumatic brain injury.

Dr. Fletcher served on and chaired the NICHD Mental Retardation/Developmental Disabilities study section and is a former member of the NICHD Maternal and Child Health study section. He chaired a committee on children with persistent reading disability for the Houston Independent School District (HISD) and served on a task force on reading for HISD that produced a report widely cited within the state of Texas as a model for enhancing reading instruction in elementary school children. Dr. Fletcher has received several service awards from local school districts and previously directed the School Problems Clinic at the University of Texas-Houston.

Siobhan Gorman

Reporter • National Journal

Ms. Gorman covers education and agriculture for *National Journal*. She has written on such education topics as presidential politics, federal policy, state trends, local innovations, bilingual education, and affirmative action. On the agriculture front, she has covered such issues as civil rights, federal farm policy, biotechnology, and anti-trust. During the 2000 presidential campaign season, she provided political commentary for MSNBC.com. A reporter with *National Journal* since April 1998, she has also edited the magazine's "People" column, which covers the occupational comings and goings of Washington players. Prior to joining *National Journal,* Ms. Gorman was with *The Washington Post*'s "Bob Levey's Washington," where she wrote feature columns and did research for the daily column. She graduated from Dartmouth College in 1997 with a B.A. in government.

Christopher Wade Hammons, Ph.D.

Assistant Professor of Political Science • Houston Baptist University

Dr. Hammons joined the faculty of Houston Baptist University in 1998 and offers courses in American political thought, democratic theory, and quantitative methods. His academic research, in which he evaluates the long-term repercussions of national versus local control of social institutions and, specifically, education, has been published in *American Political Science Review.*

Dr. Hammons earned a B.A. in government from the University of Texas, Austin, and he received both his M.A. and Ph.D. in political science from the University of Houston.

Bryan C. Hassel, Ph.D.

Director • Public Impact

Dr. Hassel directs Public Impact, an education policy consulting firm. He conducts research and consults nationally on charter schools and the comprehensive reform of existing public schools. He is the author of *The Charter School Challenge: Avoiding the Pitfalls, Fulfilling the Promise*, published by the Brookings Institution Press in 1999. Dr. Hassel received his doctorate in public policy from Harvard University and his masters in politics from Oxford University, which he attended as a Rhodes Scholar.

Frederick M. Hess, Ph.D.

Assistant Professor • University of Virginia

Dr. Rick Hess has been an assistant professor of education and government at the University of Virginia since 1997. He has also taught public high school social studies in Baton Rouge, Louisiana.

Dr. Hess has authored *Spinning Wheels: The Politics of Urban School Reform* (Brookings Institution Press 1999) and *Bringing the Social Sciences Alive* (Allyn & Bacon 1999) and has co-edited *School Choice in the Real World: Lessons from Arizona Charter Schools* (Westview Press 1999). He has contributed articles to various scholarly journals. He has received research grants or fellowships from organizations including the National Science Foundation, Mellon Foundation, Ford Foundation, Bodman Foundation, Bradley Foundation, Olin Foundation, Spencer Foundation, WKBJ Foundation, and the National Academy of Education. Other roles include serving as a consultant to the National School Board Association, as a research associate in the Harvard University Program on Education Policy and Governance, and on the board of advisors for the *FamilyPC* Teacher's Technology Foundation.

Dr. Hess earned his Ph.D. from the Harvard University Department of Government and his M.Ed. in teaching and curriculum from the Harvard University Graduate School of Education. He earned his B.A. in politics, *summa cum laude*, from Brandeis University.

Charles R. Hokanson, Jr.

Finance Director and Research Fellow • Thomas B. Fordham Foundation

Charles R. Hokanson, Jr. is Finance Director and Research Fellow at the Thomas B. Fordham Foundation and a Research Fellow at the Manhattan Institute for Policy Research.

Prior to joining the Foundation's staff, Mr. Hokanson worked as an associate in the regulatory practice group of Steptoe & Johnson L.L.P., a Washington, D.C., law firm. Mr. Hokanson has also served as a research assistant at the American Federation of Teachers Educational Issues Department, where he focused on state systemic education reforms and educational standards and assessments abroad, and as a Fellow at both the California Department of Education and the California Senate Judiciary Committee.

Mr. Hokanson earned a J.D. from Harvard Law School and a master in public policy (M.P.P.) degree from the John F. Kennedy School of Government at Harvard University and served as Editor-in-Chief of the *Harvard Journal of Law & Public Policy*, the nation's largest-circulated student-edited law review. He holds a B.A. in history and American studies, with distinction and Phi Beta Kappa honors, and an M.A. in history, both from Stanford University.

Mr. Hokanson's writings have recently appeared in *The Wall Street Journal, The Washington Times,* and *World & I* magazine. He is a member of the religious liberties practice group of the Federalist Society for Law and Public Policy Studies and serves on the Board of Visitors of the Ave Maria School of Law.

Wade F. Horn, Ph.D.

Assistant Secretary Designee • U.S. Department of Health and Human Services

Currently awaiting confirmation as an Assistant Secretary at the U.S. Department of Health and Human Services, Dr. Horn is President of the National Fatherhood Initiative (NFI), whose mission is to improve the well-being of children by increasing the number of children growing up with involved, committed, and responsible fathers. From 1989-1993, Dr. Horn was the Commissioner for Children, Youth and Families and Chief of the Children's Bureau within the United States Department of Health and Human Services. Dr. Horn also served as a Presidential appointee to the National Commission on Children from 1990-1993, a member of the National Commission on Childhood Disability from 1994-1995, and a member of the U.S. Advisory Board on Welfare Indicators from 1996-1997. Prior to these appointments, Dr. Horn was the Director of Outpatient Psychological Services at the Children's Hospital National Medical Center in Washington, D.C., and an Associate Professor of Psychiatry and Behavioral Sciences at George Washington University.

Dr. Horn is the author of numerous articles in both the popular and scholarly press relevant to children and family policy issues, including a weekly newspaper column entitled "Fatherly Advice," and is the co-author of several books. Dr. Horn is frequently featured on television and radio as a child development expert and commentator.

Dr. Horn received his Ph.D. in clinical child psychology from Southern Illinois University in 1981.

Mark G. Kelman

William Nelson Cromwell Professor and Academic Associate Dean Stanford Law School

Mark Kelman is the William Nelson Cromwell Professor of Law and Academic Associate Dean at Stanford Law School. Mr. Kelman began his career as the Director of Criminal Justice Projects at the Fund for the City of New York. In 1977 he joined the Stanford University faculty. The principal subjects of his writings and teachings are in the areas of criminal law, antidiscrimination, income distribution theory, and special education.

His writings have been published in *Journal of Legal Studies, Harvard Law Review, Stanford Law Review,* and *Southern California Law Review.* He is the co-author of *Jumping the Queue: An Empirical and Ethical Inquiry into the Legal Treatment of Students with Learning Disabilities* (Harvard University Press, 1997).

Mr. Kelman received his A.B. and J.D. from Harvard University.

Maya Kobersy, Esq.

Associate • Hogan and Hartson L.L.P.

Ms. Kobersy joined the law firm of Hogan and Hartson in Washington, D.C., in 1999 after earning a J.D. from Harvard University. From 1997-1999, Ms. Kobersy served as the Executive Editor of the *Harvard Law Review* (vols. 111 and 112). She previously worked as a summer associate in the law firms of Hogan and Hartson and Kaye Scholer. Ms. Kobersy received her B.A. in history and French, with high distinction, from the University of Michigan.

Ann Koufman-Frederick, Ph.D.

Director of Technology Initiatives • Massachusetts Association of School Superintendents

Dr. Koufman-Frederick is the Director of Technology Initiatives at the Massachusetts Association of School Superintendents. Previously she was an instructional technology specialist with the Brookline (MA) Public Schools and a school psychologist for children with learning disabilities.

Matthew Ladner, Ph.D.

Director of Communications and Policy • Children First America

Prior to recently joining the staff of Children First America, Dr. Ladner served as Senior Education Policy

Analyst in the Texas Office of the Comptroller, where he conducted performance audits of school districts as a member of the Texas School Performance Review and provided policy analysis as a member of the E-Texas Education Team. Since 1997, Dr. Ladner has provided public policy research, statistical analysis, and expert testimony as a principal for Capital Research and Consulting.

In addition, Dr. Ladner has been a professor of government at Austin Community College since 1996, where he teaches courses in American politics and Texas government. He received a M.A. and a Ph.D. in political science from the University of Houston, and he earned a B.A. from the University of Texas at Austin.

Kevin Lanigan, Esq.

Partner • Hogan and Hartson L.L.P.

Mr. Lanigan's practice focuses on litigation in the field of education. After working for a year as an Assistant State Attorney General in Arizona, he joined the firm as an associate in 1983. He was appointed Executive Director of the Arizona Center for Law in the Public Interest in 1988, serving there until rejoining the firm in 1990. He was elected to the partnership in 1992.

Mr. Lanigan's education practice has included representation of urban school districts in desegregation litigation in remedy design, implementation, and funding. He also has represented districts pursuing reform, including litigation, of state school finance provisions for elementary and secondary education, including special education and related services. He has represented individuals and school districts on a variety of other issues arising under the Individuals with Disabilities Education Act.

Mr. Lanigan received his B.A., with distinction, from the University of Kansas in 1979 and his J.D. from the University of Virginia School of Law in 1982. He is a member of the D.C., Maryland, and Arizona Bars and is admitted to practice before various federal courts.

G. Reid Lyon, Ph.D.

Chief of Child Development and Behavior • National Institute of Child Health and Human Development • National Institutes of Health

Dr. Lyon is a research psychologist and the Chief of the Child Development and Behavior Branch within the National Institute of Child Health and Human Development (NICHD) at the National Institutes of Health (NIH). He is responsible for the direction, development and management of research programs in developmental psychology, cognitive neuroscience, reading, and learning disorders. Before joining the NIH on a full-time basis in 1991, Dr. Lyon served on the faculties of Northwestern University (Communication Science and Disorders/Neuroscience, 1980-1983) and the University of Vermont (Neurology, 1983-1991). He was a member of the Maternal and Child Health Scientific Peer Review Group at NICHD/NIH from 1987 to 1991. Dr. Lyon's research program was supported, in part, by the NIH, the National Science Foundation, and the U.S. Department of Education.

Dr. Lyon received his Ph.D. from the University of New Mexico with a dual concentration in psychology and developmental disabilities. He completed a fellowship in developmental neuroscience at the University of New Mexico Medical Center. He has taught children with learning disabilities, served as a third-grade classroom teacher, and worked as a school psychologist for 12 years in the public schools.

Dr. Lyon has authored, co-authored, and edited over 90 journal articles, books, and book chapters addressing learning differences and disabilities in children. He is currently responsible for translating NIH scientific discoveries relevant to the health and education of children to the White House, the United States Congress, and other governmental agencies.

Daniel McGroarty

Senior Director • White House Writers Group

Mr. McGroarty is Senior Director with the White House Writers Group, a public policy communications consulting firm based in Washington, D.C., and Bradley Fellow with the Heritage Foundation. He is author of *Trinnietta Gets a Chance: Six Families and Their School Choice Experience* (2001, Heritage Foundation Press), as well as *Break These Chains: The Battle for School Choice* (Prima Publishing), selected in 1996 as one of 25 titles on politics recognized by the National Press Club.

During the first Bush Administration, Mr. McGroarty served as Special Assistant to the President for Communications and Deputy Director of White House Speechwriting. Prior to serving the President, he held the position of Senior Speechwriter to Secretary of Defense Frank C. Carlucci, III and Speechwriter to Secretary of Defense Caspar W. Weinberger.

Richard Olson, Ph.D.

Professor, Department of Psychology • University of Colorado

Tyce Palmaffy

Articles Editor • Education Matters

Tyce Palmaffy is the Articles Editor at *Education Matters*, a new journal of research and opinion jointly sponsored by the Hoover Institution, the Thomas B. Fordham Foundation, Harvard University, and the Manhattan Institute for Policy Research. The first issue appeared in January 2001. He was formerly a reporter for *New Republic, Policy Review,* and *Investor's Business Daily*. His survey of the federal Title 1 program appeared in *New Directions: Federal Education Policy in the Twenty-first Century* (Thomas B. Fordham Foundation, 1999.)

Andrew Rotherham

Director, 21st Century Schools Project • Progressive Policy Institute

Andrew Rotherham is the Director of the 21st Century Schools Project for the Progressive Policy Institute (PPI), where he writes and speaks frequently about educational issues.

While on a leave of absence from PPI, Mr. Rotherham served at the White House as Special Assistant to the President for Domestic Policy. Mr. Rotherham advised President Clinton on educational issues, including re-authorization of the Elementary and Secondary Education Act (ESEA), charter schools and public school choice, improving educational options for disadvantaged students, and increasing accountability in federal policy. Mr. Rotherham also coordinated education policy activities at the White House and led the White House Domestic Policy Council education team.

Previously, Mr. Rotherham was the Legislative Specialist and Policy Analyst for the American Association of

School Administrators (AASA), a professional association representing more than 14,000 public school superintendents. At AASA, Mr. Rotherham analyzed and wrote for publication on policy issues including school finance, the federal budget, appropriations, school infrastructure, and electric utility deregulation. He also coordinated AASA's grassroots and Capitol Hill advocacy efforts in these areas.

Mr. Rotherham earned a bachelor's degree from the Virginia Polytechnic Institute and State University (Virginia Tech), double majoring in history and political science. He also holds a master's degree in education from the University of Virginia.

Ann Schulte, Ph.D.
Department of Psychology • North Carolina State University

Bennett A. Shaywitz, M.D.
Department of Pediatrics and the Center for Learning and Attention Yale University School of Medicine

Sally E. Shaywitz, M.D.
Department of Pediatrics and the Center for Learning and Attention Yale University School of Medicine

Joseph K. Torgesen
Department of Psychiatry • Florida State University

Doug Tynan, Ph.D.
Director, ADHD Program • E.I. duPont Children's Hospital, Wilmington, DE

Dr. Tynan, a 1974 graduate of Boston University, was one of the first full-time special education teachers in the Boston area in the mid-1970s at the Language and Cognitive Development Center. He attended the University of Connecticut, where he received a master's degree in child development, and Binghamton University, where he earned a Ph.D. in clinical psychology. He interned at the University of Florida and then served on the faculty at Michigan State University. Dr. Tynan spent 11 years working at the Children's National Medical Center, where he founded the Psychosocial Program in Diabetes Clinic, served as the director of the Psychology Internship, and set up the Psychosocial Program for children with ADHD and their parents.

Dr. Tynan's major areas of research and clinical interest have been the reciprocal effects of family and child in chronic medical and behavioral disorders and the development of effective psychotherapy to help in those disorders. He serves on the Board of the American Board of Clinical Health Psychology, reviews articles for several psychological journals, and has served as a consultant for early intervention programs. After serving as a clinical psychologist at the Penn State Geisinger Medical Center in Danville, Pennsylvania. He recently became Director of the ADHD Program at the E.I. duPont Children's Hospital in Wilmington, Delaware.

David Urion, M.D.

Director, Learning Disabilities/Behavioral Neurology Program
Children's Hospital, Boston

Dr. Urion is a clinical child neurologist and the Director of the Learning Disabilities/Behavioral Neurology Program at Children's Hospital in Boston. He has faculty appointments at Harvard Medical School's Department of Neurology and the Harvard Graduate School of Education.

Madeleine Will

Vice President of Strategic Planning and Advocacy • Community Options, Inc.

Ms. Will is Vice President of Strategic Planning and Advocacy at Community Options, Inc., a Princeton-based nonprofit agency providing employment services and appropriate housing for people with disabilities. She formerly served as Assistant Secretary for the Office of Special Education and Rehabilitation Services in the U.S. Department of Education.

Patrick Wolf, Ph.D.

Assistant Professor • Georgetown Public Policy Institute

Dr. Wolf joined the Georgetown Public Policy Institute in 1998 after four years on the faculty at Columbia University's School of International and Public Affairs. He serves as co-director of the Public Management and Nonprofit Studies Track. He has served as a Guest Scholar at the Brookings Institution and is a Faculty Associate of the Program on Education Policy and Governance at Harvard University. His primary research interests are in the fields of public management and education policy.

Currently, he is writing a book about the systematic factors that affect the ability of U.S. federal agencies to "reinvent" themselves and perform effectively. A 1997 journal article based on his research was given the "Best Article Award" of the Academy of Management, Public and Nonprofit Management Division.

Dr. Wolf also is the Director of Field Research for an evaluation of the Washington Scholarship Fund, a private charity that provides school vouchers to poor families in D.C., permitting them to attend the private school of their choice.

Dr. Wolf received his Ph.D. in government from Harvard in 1995. He completed his undergraduate degree in 1987, *summa cum laude*, at the University of St. Thomas in St. Paul, Minnesota, where he double-majored in political science and philosophy.

Frank B. Wood, Ph.D.

Section of Neuropsychology and Program in Neuroscience
Wake Forest University School of Medicine

Conference Participants and Attendees

"Rethinking Special Education for a New Century"
November 13-14, 2000 • Washington Hilton Embassy Row • Washington, D.C.

Eileen Ahearn	Project Director, Educational Outcomes	NASDSE	Alexandria, VA
Kelly Amis	Program Director	Thomas B. Fordham Foundation	Washington, DC
Rick Apling	Specialist in Social Legislation	Congressional Research Service	Washington, DC
Rose Marie Audette	Associate	Hogan & Hartson, LLP	Washington, DC
Susan Axelrod	Executive Director of Early Childhood Services	Elwyn Incorporated	Philadelphia, PA
Schuyler Baab	Vice President of Government Relations	Intellectual Development Systems	Washington, DC
Patte Barth	Senior Associate	Education Trust	Washington, DC
Andrea Becker	Legislative Counsel	Office of Senator Frist	Washington, DC
Sheldon Berman	Superintendent	Hudson Public Schools	Hudson, MA
Leslie Blakey	Senior Associate	Blakey & Associates	Washington, DC
Marion Blakey	Principal	Blakey & Associates	Washington, DC
Frederick Brigham	Assistant Professor	University of Virginia	Charlottesville, VA
Megan Burns	21st Century Schools Project	Progressive Policy Institute	Washington, DC
Paula Butterfield	Chief Academic Officer	Pittsburgh Public Schools	Pittsburgh, PA
Carol Cichowski	Division Director; Budget Director	U.S. Department of Education	Washington, DC
Candace Cortiella	Consultant	National Center for Learning Disabilities	Burke, VA
Robert Cullen	Freelance Writer	—	Chevy Chase, MD

Perry Davis	Superintendent	Dover-Sherborn Public Schools	Dover, MA
Vicki Devins	Associate, Educational Issues Department	American Federation of Teachers	Washington, DC
Suzanne Donovan	Deputy Director for Education	National Academy of Scientists	Washington, DC
Denis Doyle	CAO	Schoolnet	Chevy Chase, MD
Anna Duff	Freelance Writer	—	Menlo Park, CA
Joan Ehrlich	Teacher for the Deaf and Hard of Hearing	Fairfax Public Schools	Dunn Loring, VA
Megan Farnsworth	Bradley Fellow of Education Affairs	Heritage Foundation	Washington, DC
Chester Finn, Jr.	President	Thomas B. Fordham Foundation	Washington, DC
Jack Fletcher	Professor, Department of Pediatrics	University of Texas-Houston	Houston, TX
Michelle Galley	Writer	*Education Week*	Bethesda, MD
Jen Garrett	Research Assistant for Domestic Policy Studies	Heritage Foundation	Washington, DC
Benny Goodman	Superintendent	Fort Smith Public Schools	Fort Smith, AR
Siobhan Gorman	Reporter	*National Journal*	Washington, DC
Ted Gotsch	Reporter	*Education Daily*	Alexandria, VA
Joan Grady	Education Consultant	—	Highlands Ranch, CO
David Gray	Counsel	U.S. Senate Governmental Affairs Subcommittee	Washington, DC
William Grobe	President-Elect	NASSP	Reston, VA
Charlene Haar	President	Education Policy Institute	Washington, DC
Janet Hamel	Special Ed Parent and Doctoral Student	—	Vienna, VA
Jane Hannaway	Director, Education Policy Center	Urban Institute	Washington, DC

Michael Hardman	Associate Dean for Research	University of Utah	Salt Lake City, UT
Bryan Hassel	Director	Public Impact	Charlotte, NC
Frederick Hess	Assistant Professor	University of Virginia	Charlottesville, VA
Judith Heumann	Assistant Secretary of Education	U.S. Department of Education	Washington, DC
Charles Hokanson	Finance Director and Research Fellow	Thomas B. Fordham Foundation	Washington, DC
Wade Horn	President	National Fatherhood Initiative	Gaithersburg, MD
Bruce Hunter	Director of Public Policy	American Association of School Administrators	Arlington, VA
Leslie Jackson	Federal Affairs Staff Member	American Occupational Therapy Association	Bethesda, MD
Stephanie Jackson	Senior Research Associate	American Institutes of Research	Washington, DC
Nancy Lee Jones	Legislative Attorney	Congressional Research Service	Washington, DC
Laura Kaloi	Director of Public Policy	National Center for Learning Disabilities	Washington, DC
Marci Kanstoroom	Research Director	Thomas B. Fordham Foundation	Washington, DC
Mark Kelman	Professor	Stanford Law School	Stanford, CA
Eugenia Kemble	Executive Director	Albert Shanker Institute	Washington, DC
Anne Kim	Social Policy Analyst	Progressive Policy Institute	Washington, DC
Jim Kitterman	Vice President	Intellectual Development Systems	Annapolis, MD
Vic Klatt	Vice President	Van Scoyec and Associates	Washington, DC
Dick Komer	Senior Litigator	Institute for Justice	Washington, DC
Anne Kornblet	Acting Executive Director	Learning Disability Association of America	Saint Louis, MO

Matthew Ladner	Senior Education Policy Analyst	Texas Comptroller of Public Accounts	Austin, TX
Diane Lenz	Fellow	Office of Senator Jeffords	Washington, DC
Lu Leon	Writer and Editor	Blakey & Associates	Washington, DC
Sally Lovejoy	Education Policy Coordinator	House Committee on Education and the Workforce	Washington, DC
Tom Loveless	Director, Brown Center	Brookings Institution	Washington, DC
Bonnie Lundy	Director, Philadelphia Pre-School Early Intervention	Elwyn Incorporated	Philadelphia, PA
G. Reid Lyon	Chief of Child Development and Behavior	National Institute of Child Health and Human Development	Bethesda, MD
Gina Mahoney	Senior Policy Advisor	Office of Representative Dooley	Washington, DC
Pamela Mahoney	Special Education Teacher	—	Alexandria, VA
Justine Maloney	Washington Representative	Learning Disability Association of America	Arlington, VA
Bruno V. Manno	Senior Program Associate	Annie E. Casey Foundation	Baltimore, MD
Richard Manzier	Assistant Executive Director	Council for Exceptional Children	Reston, VA
Paul Marchand	Chairman	Consortium for Citizens with Disabilities	Washington, DC
Will Marshall	President	Progressive Policy Institute	Washington, DC
Maureen Marshall	Education Legislative Assistant	Office of Senator Collins	Washington, DC
Chris Martes	Executive Director	Massachusetts Association of School Superintendents	Boston, MA
John McDonnell	Professor	University of Utah	Salt Lake City, UT
Hal McGrady	Executive Director	Division for Learning Disabilities	Arlington, VA
Daniel McGroarty	Senior Director	White House Writers Group	Chevy Chase, MD

Denzel McGuire	Professional Staff Member	Office of Senator Judd Gregg	Washington, DC
Jeff Meador	Legislative Assistant	Office of Representative Stenholm	Washington, DC
Larry Miller	Superintendent	Millville Public Schools	Millville, NJ
Louisa Moats	Director of Public Policy	NICHD Early Intervention Project	Fairlee, VT
Leah Morfin	21st Century Schools Project	Progressive Policy Institute	Washington, DC
Eric Morse	Assistant Director	Domestic Policy Council	Washington, DC
Tyce Palmaffy	Articles Editor	*Education Matters*	New Haven, CT
Louann Bierlein Palmer	Professor	Western Michigan University	Kalamazoo, MI
Nick Penning	Senior Policy Analyst	American Association of School Administrators	Arlington, VA
Mary Podmostko	Project Director, 21st Century Project	Institute of Education Leadership	Washington, DC
Nina Shokraii Rees	Senior Education Policy Analyst	Heritage Foundation	Washington, DC
Sallie Rhodes	Disability Policy Director	Office of Senator Jeffords	Washington, DC
Patti Richards	Chairman, Advocacy & Public Affairs Committee; Member, Executive Committee	Learning Disability Association of America	Alexandria, VA
Michael (Chad) Rodi	Research Analyst	American Institutes of Research	Washington, DC
Andrew Rotherham	Director, 21st Century Schools Project	Progressive Policy Institute	Washington, DC
David Rowe	Program Examiner	Office of Management and Budget	Washington, DC
Joetta Sack	Reporter	*Education Week*	Bethesda, MD
Katherine Schantz	Head of School	Delaware Valley Friends School	Paoli, PA

Kirk Schroder	President	Virginia State Board of Education	Richmond, VA
Kelly Scott	Executive Assistant	Thomas B. Fordham Foundation	Washington, DC
Sally Shake	President and CEO	Education Legislative Services	Washington, DC
Russell Skiba	Professor	Indiana University	Bloomington, IN
Nelson Smith	Executive Director	DC Public Charter School Board	Washington, DC
Michele Stockwell	Legislative Assistant	Office of Senator Lieberman	Washington, DC
Tracy Straub	Legislative Assistant	Office of the State of Oregon	Washington, DC
Bob Sweet	Majority Staff Member	House Committee on Education and the Workforce	Washington, DC
James Traub	Writer	*New York Times Magazine*	New York, NY
David Urion	Director, Learning Disabilities/Behavior Neurology Program	Children's Hospital	Boston, MA
Dustin Valerias	Education Policy Analyst	Education Leadership Council	Washington, DC
Jeff Viehl	Federal Liaison	Office of the State of Indiana	Washington, DC
Donna Waghorn	Assistant Director	Academy for Education Development	Washington, DC
Richard Wenning	President	Choice Strategies Group	Washington, DC
Christie Wolfe	Professional Staff Member	House Committee on Education and the Workforce	Washington, DC
Patrick Wolf	Assistant Professor	Georgetown Public Policy Institute	Washington, DC